Methodism and the
Shaping of American Culture

Methodism and the Shaping of American Culture

Edited by
Nathan O. Hatch
and
John H. Wigger

KINGSWOOD BOOKS
An Imprint of Abingdon Press
Nashville, Tennessee

METHODISM AND THE SHAPING OF AMERICAN CULTURE

Copyright © 2001 by Abingdon Press

This book is printed on recycled, acid-free paper.

Library of Congress Cataloging-in-Publication Data

Methodism and the shaping of American culture / edited by Nathan O. Hatch and John H.
Wigger.
    p. cm.
Based on a conference held in Oct. 1994 at Asbury Theological Seminary, Wilmore, Ky.
Includes bibliographical references.
ISBN 0-687-04854-0 (pbk. : alk. paper)
    1. Methodist Church—United States—History. I. Hatch, Nathan O. II. Wigger, John H., 1959-

BX8233 .M48 2001
287'.673'09034—dc21

                                                                                        2001029317

All scripture quotations are from the King James Version of the Bible.

01 02 03 04 05 06 07 08 09 10 —10 9 8 7 6 5 4 3 2 1

MANUFACTURED IN THE UNITED STATES OF AMERICA

To Grant Wacker,

friend, colleague, and

exemplar of Methodist

warmth and wisdom

Acknowledgments

The essays in this book were presented in earlier versions at the conference "Methodism and the Shaping of American Culture" held in October 1994 at Asbury Theological Seminary, Wilmore, Kentucky. We are grateful to those who presented papers and to those who offered comments on them, both formally and informally. We would also like to thank the Pew Charitable Trusts for generously providing the funding to make the conference possible. Nathan Hatch's chapter, "The Puzzle of American Methodism," first appeared in *Church History* 63, no. 2 (June 1994), and Richard Carwardine's chapter, "Methodists, Politics, and the Coming of the American Civil War," first appeared in *Church History* 69, no. 3 (September 2000). Both are reprinted here by permission.

Contents

Introduction

Nathan O. Hatch and John H. Wigger

This book is about the meteoric rise in the number of Methodists in America between the American Revolution and the Civil War, and the ways in which Methodism came to reflect and to influence the character of American life. As the second great English religious movement transported to America, Methodism rivals Puritanism in its force and intensity, its ability to mobilize followers, to generate new modes of communication and organization, and to instill habits of industry, sobriety, and mutual accountability. Both of these movements of popular mobilization, so profoundly linked with politics, society, and the economy, had profound cultural consequences. During the first half of the nineteenth century, the Methodists became the largest religious body in the United States and the most extensive national organization other than the Federal government.

Yet few historians have given Methodism a central place in the shaping of American culture.[1] Part of the rationale for this book is to

---

1. Some excellent books have appeared in the last few years placing Methodism in the larger context of antebellum history. These include: Christine Leigh Heyrman, *Southern Cross: The Beginnings of the Bible Belt* (Chapel Hill: University of North Carolina Press, 1997); Cynthia Lynn Lyerly, *Methodism and the Southern Mind 1770–1810* (New York: Oxford University Press, 1998); Christopher Owen, *The Sacred Flame of Love: Methodism and Society in Nineteenth-Century Georgia* (Athens: University of Georgia Press, 1998); Lester Ruth, *A Little Heaven Below: Worship at Early Methodist Quarterly Meetings* (Nashville: Abingdon Press, 2000); and Dee E. Andrews, *The Methodists and Revolutionary America, 1760–1800: The Shaping of an Evangelical Culture* (Princeton, N.J.: Princeton University Press, 2000). Recent books dealing with early American Methodism by the authors of this volume include: Catherine Brekus, *Strangers and Pilgrims: Female Preaching in America, 1740–1845* (Chapel Hill: University of North Carolina Press, 1998); Richard Carwardine, *Evangelicals and Politics in Antebellum America* (New Haven: Yale University Press, 1993; Knoxville: University of Tennessee Press, 1997); Nathan O. Hatch, *The Democratization of American Christianity* (New Haven: Yale University Press, 1989); Kathryn Long, *The Revival of 1857–58: Interpreting an American Religious Awakening* (New York: Oxford University Press, 1998); Russell Richey, *Early American Methodism* (Bloomington: Indiana University Press, 1991); William Sutton, *Journeymen for Jesus: Evangelical Artisans Confront Capitalism in Jacksonian Baltimore* (University Park: Pennsylvania State University Press, 1998); and John Wigger, *Taking Heaven by Storm: Methodism and the Rise of Popular Christianity in America* (New York: Oxford University Press, 1998; Urbana: University of Illinois Press, 2001).

explain why scholars have been so uninterested in exploring the cultural implications of American Methodism. More positively, the book presents a series of suggestive studies by leading historians at work on these themes. The book is timely because so much excellent work is currently being done that addresses religious history as the study of popular movements rather than as a branch of intellectual history—a context that brings American Methodism sharply into focus. These essays are a superb introduction to the dynamics of Methodist growth and to the relationship of the movement to broader questions about the rise in America of capitalism, mass democratic politics, bitter sectionalism, and the Christianizing of popular culture.

The fourscore years between the era of the American Revolution and that of the Civil War represent a decisive moment of change in American history in at least four related ways. First, a sudden bursting forth of entrepreneurial energy, what scholars call the market revolution, transformed the United States into a liberal, competitive, market-driven society—instead of a hierarchical society like Britain or a republican society envisioned by the Founding Fathers. A small-scale eighteenth-century world characterized by individual artisans and farmers, patriarchy and inheritance, became transformed into a society characterized by commercial advancement, individual pursuit of self-interest, and legitimation of competing factions.[2]

Second, in these same years citizens of the United States also embraced mass democratic politics: overt political campaigning, aspiring professional politicians, universal male suffrage, and the domination of government by political parties. In his book *The Radicalism of the American Revolution*, Gordon S. Wood recounts the pervasive pessimism that descended upon those Founding Fathers who lived into the early decades of the nineteenth century. A sense of unease and bewilderment courses through their later writings. Benjamin Rush looked back with despair upon his efforts in the Revolution, claiming to feel "like a stranger" in his native land. He decided to burn all his notes for a once-planned memoir of the Revolution. "We are indeed," he said in 1812, "a bebanked, bewhiskied, and a bedollared nation." The dejected John Adams asked in 1813, "When? Where? and How? is the present Chaos to be arranged into Order?" Thomas Jefferson distrusted the new demo-

---

2. Gordon S. Wood, *The Radicalism of the American Revolution* (New York: Alfred A. Knopf, 1992), 232; and Charles Sellers, *The Market Revolution: Jacksonian America 1815–1846* (New York: Oxford University Press, 1991).

cratic world he saw emerging in America. The classical republic of the founders' dreams had been transformed by what one of them called "the fiery furnace of democracy." Their own fate now depended upon the opinions and votes of small-souled and largely unreflective ordinary people.[3]

The early American republic also became a crucible of intense sectionalism. In a nation premised on liberty, time alone would not heal the unresolved dilemma of slavery, particularly after cotton became the mainstay of the southern economy. As early as 1820 the issue of slavery, unsettling Jefferson as a "firebell in the night," turned the national asset of cheap arable land for a swelling population into a recurring nightmare: would new territories and states be slave or free? Americans also witnessed the explosion of mass printing, in which the Methodists played a leading role, and many hoped that shared opinions would bind together isolated and diverse communities. In reality, the mass distribution of books, magazines, journals, and newspapers intensified sectional mistrust by airing in every hamlet the most intransigent opinions, abolitionist and fire-eater alike.

The early American republic also witnessed a fourth transition. It became a period of great religious ferment and originality. The wave of popular religious movements that broke upon America in the generation after independence decisively changed the center of gravity of American religion, worked powerfully to Christianize popular culture, splintered American Christianity beyond recognition, divorced religious leadership from social position, and above all, proclaimed the moral responsibility of everyone to think and act for themselves. In this ferment, often referred to as the Second Great Awakening, Christendom witnessed a period of religious upheaval comparable to nothing since the Reformation—and an upsurge of private initiative that was totally unprecedented.[4]

The mainspring of the Second Great Awakening was that religion in America became dominated by the interests and aspirations of ordinary people. In the generation after the Revolution, American Christianity became a mass enterprise—and not as a predictable outgrowth of religious conditions in the British colonies. The eighteen hundred Christian ministers serving in 1775 swelled to nearly forty thousand by 1845. While the American population expanded tenfold, the number of preachers per capita more than tripled; the colonial

3. Wood, *Radicalism of the American Revolution*, 365-69.
4. Jon Butler, *Awash in a Sea of Faith: Christianizing the American People* (Cambridge, Mass.: Harvard University Press, 1990), and Hatch, *The Democratization of American Christianity*.

legacy of one minister per fifteen hundred people become one per five hundred. This dramatic mobilization indicates a profound religious upsurge—religious organizations taking on market form—and resulted in a vastly altered religious landscape. Religious activists pitched their messages to the unschooled and unsophisticated. Their movements offered the humble a marvelous sense of individual potential and of collective aspiration.

Each of these four transitions—economic, political, sectional, and religious—is intertwined with the explosive growth of the Methodist movement, a surprising development in a republic that shunned state-sponsored religion. Perhaps one of the reasons that American Methodism has been so underappreciated has been the focus of scholars on urban centers. It is curious that so many social historians have focused their attention on the urban working class at a time when America was so profoundly rural. Between 1800 and 1820 the percentage of the American labor force in agriculture had increased from 75 to 80 percent—in sharp contrast with England where only about one-third of its workers engaged in agriculture. In 1830 only 9 percent of Americans lived in cities with populations over twenty-five hundred. In contrast, well over a third of the English population was urban, with 20 percent in cities larger than twenty thousand. The Methodists, under Bishop Francis Asbury, crafted an organization ideally suited to pursue an expanding agrarian and rural society. While Methodism retained a stronghold in the seaports of the middle states, Asbury hammered its organization into one that had a distinct rural orientation adept at expanding into thinly populated areas. "We must draw resources from the centre to the circumference," Asbury wrote in 1797.[5]

When the first Methodist conference in America met in 1773 those present could count only ten preachers and 1,160 members. The movement had only begun to take hold when all of Wesley's missionaries, save Francis Asbury, returned to England, leaving the

---

5. *JLFA* 3:332. For examples of the focus on cities and industrial workers, see Alan Dawley, *Class and Community: The Industrial Revolution in Lynn* (Cambridge, Mass.: Harvard University Press, 1976); Paul G. Faler, *Mechanics and Manufacturers in the Early Industrial Revolution: Lynn, Massachusetts 1780–1860* (Albany: State University of New York Press, 1981); Charles G. Steffen, *The Mechanics of Baltimore: Workers and Politics in the Age of the Revolution, 1763–1812* (Urbana: University of Illinois Press, 1984); and Sean Wilentz, *Chants Democratic: New York City and the Rise of the American Working Class, 1788–1850* (New York: Oxford University Press, 1984). Wilentz is perceptive and judicious in treating the role of popular religion in New York City, particularly the role of Methodism; but it is only incidental to the purposes of his work. A good example of what might be called the "new rural history" is Steven Hahn and Jonathan Prude, eds., *The Countryside in the Age of Capitalist Transformation: Essays in the Social History of Rural America* (Chapel Hill: University of North Carolina Press, 1985).

Methodist faithful to struggle with the stigma of Toryism throughout the war. Under Asbury's tireless direction the Methodists proclaimed a message that spoke to the hopes and fears of tens of thousands of Americans from the eastern seaports to the west, across the Mississippi River. Methodists were particularly adept at recognizing the needs of people whose lives were in transition—the case for many in the fluid years of the early national period—and the validity of the religious expression of people otherwise held on the margins of society, including women and African Americans. Methodist theology emphasized God's free grace and the responsibility of each person to embrace that grace, a message that fit well in the cultural context of postrevolutionary America. Led by preachers who had never seen the inside of a college, but who were committed to sacrifice and travel and to an often genuine devotion to God and neighbor, the Methodists organized local class meetings, or small groups, and preaching circuits at a rate that alarmed more respectable denominations. Early Methodism offered converts salvation in an emotionally charged and satisfying manner. It also demanded that the liminal energy of conversion be channeled into disciplined lives, offering new believers a place within a well-ordered community. By adhering to the church's rules, early Methodists carved out both a religious and a social identity for themselves. When Asbury died in 1816 the Methodists could claim over two thousand preachers and two hundred thousand members, more than forty-two thousand of whom were African Americans. By 1840 the Methodist Episcopal Church alone could count more than thirty-six hundred preachers and nearly one million members. By 1876 all branches of Methodism in the United States could boast more than fifty-three thousand itinerant and local preachers, more than 2.9 million members, and more than 2.2 million children enrolled in Sunday schools.[6]

These figures are even more impressive when one considers the movement's wider influence. Many more Americans attended Methodist gatherings, especially in the movement's early phase, than actually joined the church. In 1805 Asbury estimated that membership stood at one hundred thousand, but that up to one million people "regularly attend our ministry." Although Asbury clearly overestimated the

6. *Minutes MEC* (1840), 5, 268-87. Roger Finke and Rodney Stark, *The Churching of America, 1776–1990: Winners and Losers in Our Religious Economy* (New Brunswick, N.J.: Rutgers University Press, 1992), 55; C. C. Goss, *Statistical History of the First Century of American Methodism: With a Summary of the Origin and Present Operations of Other Denominations* (New York: Carlton & Porter, 1866), 85; Matthew Simpson, *Cyclopedia of Methodism* (Philadelphia: Louis H. Everts, 1881), 841, 880.

number of Methodist adherents on this occasion, he was correct that the movement's influence extended far beyond its membership. Methodism's style and tone worked their way deep into the fabric of American life, influencing nearly all other mass religious movements that would follow it, and many facets of American life not directly connected to the church as well. Under Methodism's influence, American evangelicalism became far more enthusiastic, egalitarian, entrepreneurial, and lay oriented—characteristics that continue to shape and define American popular religion today. Richard Carwardine has argued convincingly that the internal stresses of Methodism, the largest religious force in the nation at midcentury, profoundly influenced the course of the Union in the years before the Civil War.[7]

Although early Methodism was a complex phenomenon and incapable of reduction to any single economic or political orientation, the movement eroded patterns of deference to established authority and tradition, and dignified the convictions of ordinary people on important matters—whether religious, political, or economic. It elicited choice and participation by people long ignored, and bound them together in disciplined and supportive groups. Methodist culture also instilled habits of industry, sobriety, and mutual accountability. This kind of popular mobilization did not immediately transform yeoman-artisans who distrusted market society into individualists and petty entrepreneurs; but it did call them emphatically into a new life, an orientation whose latent capacity for affecting economic and political behavior awaits exploration. Religious leaders from the rank and file were phenomenally successful in reaching out to marginal people, in promoting self-education and sheltering participants from the indoctrination of elite orthodoxies, in binding people together in supportive community, and in identifying the aspirations of common people with the will of God. It is not surprising that Methodist artisans in Philadelphia in the 1830s were more successful than their non-Methodist peers, more likely to end up master craftsmen and small retailers.[8]

But as Methodism grew it was transformed by its own success in deep and enduring ways. For American Methodism, numerical growth and economic advancement were inextricably linked. Both were swift because of the way Methodists so readily adapted to American culture. In the early nineteenth century Methodists began using their newfound wealth and social status to construct increas-

---

7. *JLFA* 3:310; Carwardine, *Evangelicals and Politics in Antebellum America*.

8. Bruce Laurie, *Working People of Philadelphia, 1800–1850* (Philadelphia: Temple University Press, 1980), 46-48.

ingly ostentatious churches, open colleges and universities, and expand their role in the popular press. They also became a political force to be reckoned with in Delaware, Ohio, Indiana, and a number of other states. But many discerned a darker side to Methodism's rising social status. So common were complaints about Methodism's lost zeal by the mid–nineteenth century that dissidents became known by the widely recognized label of "croakers." The croakers lamented the decline of the itinerancy and the class meetings, and the church's general loss of communal discipline and spiritual enthusiasm in preaching and worship. But for most Methodists there seemed no turning back. By the Civil War the Methodist Episcopal Church had come to increasingly represent the nation's stable middle class.[9]

The purpose of the present book is to collect the best contemporary scholarship on the relationship of Methodism and American culture. The first two essays (by Nathan Hatch and David Hempton, respectively) address broad questions about how the study of Methodism has been shaped both in America and in Great Britain. In "The Puzzle of American Methodism" Nathan Hatch attempts to explain why and for what reasons the Methodists in America have shown so little attraction for historians—unlike Great Britain where a wide range of scholars, including Elie Halévy, E. P. Thompson, and Eric Hobsbawm, have viewed Methodism as central to understanding Britain in the age of democratic revolutions. The essay argues that the Methodists have escaped the attention of traditional religious historians who linked their work closely to the history of ideas, of recent students of popular religion who find the Methodists insiders rather than outsiders, and of the new social and labor historians who are preoccupied with the formation of social classes and the assumption that religion is generally a conservative and repressive force.[10]

---

9. Wigger, *Taking Heaven by Storm*, 173-95.

10. On the work of E. P. Thompson, see David Hempton, *Methodism and Politics in British Society, 1750–1850* (Stanford: Stanford University Press, 1984), 75-76. Initial standard works in this regard include Elie Halévy, *England in 1815*, trans. E. I. Watkin and D. A. Baker (First published in French in 1913; reprint, New York: Barnes & Noble, 1949); E. P. Thompson, *The Making of the English Working Class* (New York: Pantheon Books, 1964); and Eric J. Hobsbawm, *Labouring Men: Studies in the History of Labour* (London: Weindenfeld & Nicolson, 1968). Specific studies of British Methodism include Bernard Semmel, *The Methodist Revolution* (New York: Basic Books, 1973); James Obelkevich, *Religion and Rural Society: South Lindsey 1825–1875* (Oxford: Clarendon Press, 1976); Deborah M. Valenze, *Prophetic Sons and Daughters: Female Preaching and Popular Religion in Industrial England* (Princeton, N.J.: Princeton University Press, 1985); Alan D. Gilbert, *Religion and Society in Industrial England: Church, Chapel and Social Change, 1740–1914* (London: Longman, 1976); David Hempton and Myrtle Hill, *Evangelical Protestantism in Ulster Society 1740–1890* (London: Routledge, 1992); David Hempton, *Religion of the People: Methodism and Popular Religion c. 1750–1900* (London: Routledge, 1996); and David Hempton, *Religion and Political Culture in Britain and Ireland: From the Glorious Revolution to the Decline of Empire* (Cambridge: Cambridge University Press, 1996).

David Hempton offers a stunning interpretive backdrop for the study of American Methodism: a broadly comparative view of the expansion of Methodism in the era of democratic revolution. Hempton frames his essay with questions posed by E. P. Thompson and offers an insightful critique of the merits and liabilities of Thompson's influential interpretation. Hempton is excellent in portraying the "interior dialectic" of Methodist experience, its combination of spiritual freedom and order. He focuses on the variety and adaptability within the Methodist movement, its rich mosaic of political allegiances, and its appeal to sections of populations whose interests were sometimes antithetical to one another. Hempton concludes that some kinds of societies were more receptive to Methodist experience than others. It was a religion that chipped away at conventional boundaries of clericalism, gender, age, and education, and thus found its most conducive environments in interstitial and marginal areas where traditional hierarchical structures were either absent or perceived to be antithetical to new interests—from the Kingswood collieries to the American frontier.

The next three essays (by John Wigger, Catherine Brekus, and Will Gravely, respectively) demonstrate the profoundly altered relationship of class and religion that emerged in the new American republic. According to John Wigger, Methodist itinerants were predominantly artisans: carpenters, blacksmiths, hatters, tanners, farmers, and the like. Educationally and socially they were cut from the same fabric as the people who came to hear them. The only real distinction between a Methodist preacher and the bulk of his audience was which side of the pulpit each was on. Methodist leaders did not have to *learn* to speak the language of the people. Spiritually, their similar conversions, disciplined practice of piety, and enthusiasm all worked to draw them closer to the people and to one another. The early itinerants represented a different kind of clergy than had ever been seen before in America.

Catherine Brekus explores the familial and pragmatic style of early Methodists that allowed, and even invited, far greater participation by women—as class leaders, as exhorters, and even as preachers. Several factors worked together to open early Methodism to the possibility of public ministry by women, including shortages of qualified preachers; the belief that God could speak directly to any believer regardless of their sex, race, or social background; and a theology that stressed the spiritual equality of all believers. More than any other

18

large-scale religious movement of the time, early Methodists allowed women to speak in their meetings, but not without limits. By the 1830s and 1840s Methodists had largely turned their backs on female preachers and exhorters in search of middle-class respectability.

In similar fashion, Will Gravely explores how readily African Americans turned to Methodism, partly because of Methodist opposition to slavery and partly because the Methodists enfolded them in meaningful communities, inviting them to share their distinct gifts in word and song. African American Methodists embraced class meetings, love feasts, and other uniquely Methodist institutions, eventually forming their own congregations and recognizing their own leaders. African American Methodists comprised about 20 percent of the total membership in the Methodist Episcopal Church in the late eighteenth and early nineteenth centuries, making the church an essentially biracial institution. Surprisingly, most of these black Methodists did not live in cities.

Two essays (by Russell Richey and Richard Shiels, respectively) explore issues of regionalism in the development of early American Methodism. Russell Richey argues that the movement was profoundly influenced by its close association with the Chesapeake region. Eighteenth-century Methodism was not so much divided north and south as it was centered in the Chesapeake. There, Methodists learned to deal with questions of race, gender, ethnicity, and social hierarchy in ways that would influence the development of the movement for decades to come. In a similar vein, Richard Shiels argues that Methodism was far more influential in the early-nineteenth-century history of New England religion than has generally been recognized. The story of the Second Great Awakening in New England is usually told as the resuscitation of Congregationalism. But Shiels points out that by the time the Second Great Awakening had passed, Methodist churches were nearly as prominent as Congregational churches in New England. Moreover, the Congregationalist revival of the early nineteenth century owed much to copying practices and even doctrines from the Methodists. In the end, Methodists were also deeply changed by this encounter, which had a lasting impact on both churches.

William Sutton explores a residual theme in Methodist annals: how religious convictions inspired some to oppose the emerging capitalism of early America. The initial phase of industrialization in the United Sates, in urban centers like New York, Philadelphia, and

Baltimore, shattered the personalized work relations based on mutual obligation, and threatened the prerogatives and standard of living of many artisans. Coming to the defense of laboring people, Methodist firebrands like John Hawkins, William Stilwell, and John Hersey developed scripturally grounded and thoroughgoing critiques of capitalist practices. These critiques sustained the long-standing Wesleyan identification with common people and precautions against spiritual as well as social pretensions of wealth. They also emphasized a practical respectability that celebrated the tenets of traditional economic morality and the virtues of industry, mutuality, and self-discipline—even as much of Methodism evolved toward bourgeois refinement.

Kathryn Long, by contrast, uses a case study of the influential Methodist teacher Phoebe Palmer to chart the evolution of mainstream Methodism toward "consecrated respectability." Long notes that many Methodists like Palmer sought to create their own distinctive synthesis, balancing the religious zeal of the denomination's early years with the propriety and decorum of mainstream respectability. Palmer's teaching on holiness and the consecrated life offered a way to do just that. From her spacious home in New York, solidly a part of upper-middle-class gentility, Palmer called people to higher spiritual attainment. Her path of holiness rejected both the identification of piety with beauty and taste—a danger she perceived in Harriet Beecher Stowe—and the severe call to identify holiness with a church of poor and plain people, the position of the Free Methodists.

Richard Carwardine charts a similar trajectory of Methodist involvement in the political arena. Francis Asbury shunned temporal power and looked askance at Methodist involvement in the rough-and-tumble of politics. By the time of the Civil War, Methodists not only held their share of high political office but represented an important electoral presence north and south. Carwardine notes the irony that the Methodists actually came to develop a "Reformed" view of politics, viewing the state as a moral being and political action as a way to introduce God's kingdom.

Carwardine also argues convincingly that Methodism, the largest religious force in the nation at midcentury, profoundly influenced the course of the Union as it tumbled toward the carnage of the Civil War. In the first place, the popular enthusiasm for politics, he suggests, could not have occurred without the thorough integration of evangelicals like the Methodists into the new political order. Methodism provided a model for the language as well as the form of democratic politics. Second, the moralistic politics that flourished in evangelical environments, with conflicts seen as the cause of God against evil, allowed little scope for compromise, complexity, or consensus. Third, the sectional fracturing of the Methodist Episcopal Church itself in 1844 led Methodists in each section to develop increasingly hostile mutual perceptions, with profound consequences for politics. Carwardine concludes that the poison of sectionalism seeped along ecclesiastical channels, too.

These ten essays combined give us a rich picture of American Methodism, and a strong sense of the unique perspective it provides for understanding American religion as a whole. Puritanism left a legacy of intellectual sophistication and social vision that has long captivated scholars and inspired religious leaders. But the power of the Puritan vision comes largely from its suggestion of what might have been, from its promise of transcending ourselves and escaping the unpleasant realities of modern life. The story of Methodism tells us much more about American religion as it actually unfolded, not always great or sophisticated or awe inspiring, but pervasive and deeply connected to the development of American religious life and culture.

CHAPTER 1

The Puzzle of American Methodism

Nathan O. Hatch

Picture, if you will, the rich landscape of American religious history that has taken shape over the last half century. At least three features of this terrain stand out, the first being a richly textured panorama before us, a recognizable field of study that has come into existence in a relatively short span of time. This field has been shaped by a variety of forces, among them the vast expansion of religion departments since 1960; the recovery of the role of religion in the broader disciplines of history, literature, sociology, and political science; and the stubborn persistence of religion in modern American life, which scholars struggle to explain.

A second feature of this terrain worth noting is the coherence of the background, the distinct set of towering peaks that frame the discussion on religion in America. The recovery of American religious history, announced by Henry May in 1964, was the signal achievement of a generation that began in the 1930s and 1940s.[1] Its pioneers were scholars such as Perry Miller, Samuel Eliot Morison, and Ralph Barton Perry, and its builders were luminaries such as Alan Heimert, Edmund Morgan, William McLoughlin, Sydney Ahlstrom, Timothy Smith, and May himself—all trained at Harvard. In the middle

---

1. Henry F. May, "The Recovery of American Religious History," *American Historical Review* 70 (1964): 79-92.

decades of this century this momentum shifted to New Haven where a compelling vision of American religious history proceeded from the lectures and writings of a constellation of Yale professors: H. Richard Niebuhr, Edmund Morgan, Sydney Ahlstrom, and John Smith and a host of students who, under their tutelage, explored the significance of American religion and, in particular, the tenacity of the Puritan vision.[2] The University of Chicago also played a signal role in this resurgence through the work of scholars such as William Warren Sweet, Sidney Mead, Robert Handy, Winthrop Hudson, Jerald Brauer, and Martin E. Marty.[3]

For all their differences, these historians shared a common outlook: most linked the study of religion tightly to intellectual history, and most shared a basic story line of American religious development following a Puritan-turned-mainline-Protestant form of Christianity—in Winthrop Hudson's phrase, "the great tradition of the American churches."[4] Most of these historians were also consensualists, believing in a common American character, and most held a positive, affirmative reading of the overall achievement of American culture and its religion. Until the mid-1960s, it is safe to say, the canon of American religious history was surprisingly uniform and coherent. Its primary institutional base remained divinity schools at elite universities, its institutional focus the intellectual history of American mainline Protestants.[5]

Since the 1960s a clash of convictions about the meaning of America has undermined this coherent and affirmative reading of the American religious experience. Instead of studying insiders, we have turned to studying outsiders, subcultures, and the vast population of women, Native Americans, and African Americans that the consensus school overlooked or subordinated to the main story of American religion. Fresh studies have poured forth on Pentecostalism, Holiness groups, and Fundamentalism; on Mormonism and Adventists and Shakers; on occultists and spiritualists; on Native American religion

---

2. The epitome of this tradition is Sydney E. Ahlstrom's brilliant synthesis, *A Religious History of the American People* (New Haven: Yale University Press, 1972).

3. See Sidney E. Mead, *The Lively Experiment: The Shaping of Christianity in America* (New York: Harper & Bros., 1963) and Martin E. Marty, *Righteous Empire: The Protestant Experience in America* (New York: Dial Press, 1970).

4. Winthrop S. Hudson, *The Great Tradition of the American Churches* (New York: Harper & Row, 1953).

5. James D. Bratt, "A New Narrative for American Religious History?" *Fides et Historia* 23 (1991): 19-30; and Harry S. Stout and Richard Taylor, "Studies of Religion in American Society: The State of the Art," in *New Directions in American Religious History*, ed. Harry Stout and Darryl Hart (New York: Oxford University Press, 1997), 15-47.

and nature religion; and on Roman Catholics of every ethnic stripe. This pluralistic enterprise has worked to redeem those on the margins and has shattered the dominant canon for American religious history. Laurence Moore, for example, has identified religious outsiders as the central theme of American religion, and Jon Butler has woven magic and folk supernaturalism into the tapestry of American faith.[6] In explaining the essence of American religion, literary critic Harold Bloom assigns the role of protagonist to Mormons, Seventh Day Adventists, Jehovah's Witnesses, Pentecostals, and Southern Baptists. With equally iconoclastic intent, sociologists Roger Finke and Rodney Stark have isolated the central theme of American religion as upstart growth and mainline decline.[7] This scholarly ferment has been a creative, invigorating process, and it is far from complete.

The Scholarly Neglect of American Methodism

Amid all of this study of insiders and outsiders, of religion elite and popular, one glaring omission becomes apparent. It is the lack of attention given to American Methodism. More accurately, what I find surprising is the lack of interest in studying American Methodists, both among religious historians and the broader historical community. Put simply, neither Ahlstrom's and Niebuhr's generation nor the more recent revisionists have questions for which Methodist sources seem to provide clues or answers. For Perry Miller, the Methodists represented the banal residue in America of what had been the noble and intellectually rich tradition of Puritanism and Edwardsian Calvinism. For Laurence Moore or Harold Bloom, the Methodists are an essential part of the mainstream and are far too bland to merit inclusion among real outsiders.

The result is that most American historians predictably treat Methodism blandly and uninspiringly as a component of the Western phase of the Second Great Awakening. The subject never quite comes into focus and the Methodists, as historical actors, appear either as mere imitators or as faceless representatives of surging revivalism. In

---

6. R. Laurence Moore, *Religious Outsiders and the Making of Americans* (New York: Oxford University Press, 1986); Jon Butler, *Awash in a Sea of Faith: Christianizing the American People* (Cambridge, Mass.: Harvard University Press, 1990).

7. Harold Bloom, *The American Religion: The Emergence of the Post-Christian Nation* (New York: Simon & Schuster, 1992); Roger Finke and Rodney Stark, *The Churching of America, 1776–1990* (New Brunswick, N.J.: Rutgers University Press, 1992).

teaching a course covering the period from the Revolution to the Civil War, one would have trouble thinking of a single imaginative treatment that could be assigned, save Donald Mathews's book, *Methodism and Slavery*, or Timothy Smith's *Revivalism and Social Reform*.[8] There are few arresting biographies, compelling local studies, or renditions of Methodist ideology; no study of Methodists and the revolution in print communications; no overall treatments of the development of Methodism as an organization or of its spirituality and its music. Unlike their British cousins, American Methodists have no Elie Halévy, E. P. Thompson, or E. J. Hobsbawm.[9]

The most basic features of the Methodist terrain remain unknown and unexplored, and there has been no graduate center that has taken up the challenge of using Methodist sources to shed light on broad historical questions. There continues to be a wealth of Methodist church history and some of it—the work of Russell Richey and Gregory Schneider, for instance—has begun to engage the larger historical profession.[10] Yet our understanding of the growth of Methodism remains fragmentary, cutting short discussions of the relationship of Methodism to the shaping of American culture.

American Methodism is a historical gold mine that awaits serious quarrying. Quite simply, Methodism remains the most powerful religious movement in American history, its growth a central feature in the emergence of the United States as a republic. Historians have ceased being surprised at how unpredictable American Methodism's growth was. The fault is not in the sources, nor in the number of indicators pointing to their importance. The fault lies within our own historical conventions, the basic framework or set of assumptions that have governed the way scholars have approached American religious history.

The theme of this essay is the puzzle of American Methodism— why and for what reasons the meteoric rise of Methodism in America

8. Donald G. Mathews, *Slavery and Methodism: A Chapter in American Morality: 1780–1845* (Princeton, N.J.: Princeton University Press, 1965); Timothy L. Smith, *Revivalism and Social Reform: American Protestantism on the Eve of the Civil War* (New York: Harper & Row, 1957).

9. Elie Halévy, *England in 1815*, translated by E. I. Watkin and D. A. Barker (New York, Barnes & Noble, 1949), first published in French in 1913; E. P. Thompson, *The Making of the English Working Class* (New York: Vintage, 1963); Eric J. Hobsbawm, *Labouring Men: Studies in the History of Labour* (London: Weindenfeld & Nicolson, 1968).

10. Russell E. Richey, *Early American Methodism* (Bloomington: Indiana University Press, 1991); Russell E. Richey, Kenneth E. Rowe, and Jean Miller Schmidt, *Perspectives on American Methodism: Interpretive Essays* (Nashville: Kingswood Books, 1993); and A. Gregory Schneider, *The Way of the Cross Leads Home: The Domestication of American Methodism* (Bloomington: Indiana University Press, 1993).

has so little attraction for scholars. After exploring the significance of Methodism's explosive growth between the Revolution and the Civil War, the article will suggest why historians have been largely inoculated from interest in the subject. It will also argue that Methodism, far more than Puritanism, offers insight into the distinct character of religious life in the United States.

The Vitality and Prominence of Methodism in Antebellum American Religion

The explosive growth of the Methodist Episcopal Church was the most surprising development in a republic that turned its back on state-sponsored religion. The American followers of John Wesley, who could boast no more than four ministers and three hundred laypeople in 1771, were threatened with extinction during the Revolution. All their leaders, save Francis Asbury, returned to England, leaving the Methodist faithful to struggle with the stigma of disloyalty throughout the war.

Under the tireless direction of Asbury, the Methodists advanced from Canada to Georgia emphasizing three themes that Americans found captivating: God's free grace, the liberty of people to accept or reject that grace, and the power and validity of popular religious expression—even among servants, women, and African Americans. Led by unlearned preachers committed to sacrifice and to travel, the Methodists organized local classes, or cells, and preaching circuits at a rate that alarmed more respectable denominations. When Asbury died in 1816, he could claim over two thousand preachers and two hundred thousand Methodist members.[11]

Between 1776 and 1850 the Methodists in America achieved a virtual miracle of growth, rising from less than 3 percent of all church members in 1776 to more than 34 percent by 1850, making them far and away the largest religious body in the nation and the most extensive national institution other than the Federal government. Methodist growth terrified other more established denominations. By the middle of the nineteenth century, Methodists boasted four thousand itinerants, almost eight thousand local preachers, and over a million members. It was nearly one-half larger than any other

---

11. *Minutes MEC* (1840), 282-87.

Protestant body and could muster more than ten times the preaching force of the Congregationalists, who in 1776 had double the number of clergy of any other church. By 1850, in a nation where only 25 to 30 percent of the people claimed any religious affiliation, almost one in fifteen Americans belonged to a Methodist church (1.5 million out of 23 million).[12] In a state like Indiana, Methodists outnumbered Presbyterians four to one by midcentury, and leaders like Matthew Simpson were well aware of Methodist political clout.[13]

The Methodists enjoyed great strategic advantage in the free-religious economy of a westward-moving nation that was increasingly suspicious of the pretensions of educated professionals—lawyers, physicians, and clergymen. The Methodists could function anywhere. Boasting almost no college-educated clergy among their thousands of circuit riders and local preachers before 1840, the Methodists exploded in the American backcountry from Maine and the hill country of Vermont to Tennessee and Kentucky, Ohio and Indiana. Most Congregational ministers, educated at Yale, Harvard, and Dartmouth, chose to remain and serve congregations in "civilized" areas. While Methodism retained a stronghold in the seaports of the middle states, Asbury hammered its organization into one that had a distinct rural orientation, adept at expanding into thinly populated areas. "We must draw resources from the centre to the circumference," Asbury wrote in 1797.[14]

Methodism in America transcended class barriers and empowered common people to make religion their own. Unlike Calvinism, which emphasized human corruption, divine initiative, and the authority of educated clergymen and inherited ecclesiastical structures, the Methodists proclaimed the breathtaking message of individual freedom, autonomy, responsibility, and achievement. More African Americans became Christians in ten years of Methodist preaching than in a century of Anglican influence. Methodism did not suppress the impulses of popular religion, dreams and visions, ecstasy, unrestrained emotional release, preaching by blacks, by women, by any-

12. Roger Finke and Rodney Stark, "How the Upstart Sects Won America: 1776–1850," *Journal for the Scientific Study of Religion* 28 (1989): 27-44. By this time the influence of once dominant churches had declined precipitously: Congregationalists from 20.4 percent to 4 percent of adherents, Episcopalians from 15.7 percent to 3.5 percent, and Presbyterians from 19 percent to 11.6 percent. See also Robert Emerson Coleman, "Factors in the Expansion of the Methodist Episcopal Church from 1784 to 1812" (University of Iowa Ph.D. thesis, 1954), 363-99.

13. Richard J. Carwardine, *Evangelicals and Politics in Antebellum America* (New Haven: Yale University Press, 1993), 114-15.

14. *JLFA* 3:332.

one who felt the call. It was under Methodist auspices that religious folk music—white and black spirituals—prospered.[15]

Methodism also had a measure of success in bridging ethnic and language barriers. In Pennsylvania in the 1830s and 1840s several Methodist sects introduced lively gospel music and vernacular preaching to German immigrants. The complicated German chorale tradition with its solemn tunes and baroque wording had trouble competing with the rousing songs and lively preaching of Methodist revivalists. The success of these folk traditions among the Germans led Philip Schaff to complain in 1849: "There is a stamping and bouncing, jumping and falling, crying and howling, groaning and sighing, all praying in confusion, a rude singing of the most vulgar street songs, so that it must be loathing to an educated man, and fill the serious Christian with painful emotions."[16] Methodism had great appeal for the outsider and prospered as a genuine grassroots movement.

Methodism fostered social mobility. The movement appealed to petty bourgeoisie, people on the make. Although Methodist hierarchy may have seemed out of step with the democratic stirrings of the times, the vital spring of Methodism under Francis Asbury was to make Christianity profoundly a faith of the people. From preachers like themselves, people received an invitation to join a movement promising dignity of choice and beckoning them to involvement as class leader, exhorter, local preacher, and circuit rider. Lay preaching, the hallmark of American Methodism, served as a powerful symbol that the wall between gentlemen and commoner had been shattered. Methodism had great appeal for upstarts who hungered for respect and opportunity. In the founding of Dayton, Ohio, for instance, the initial elite of the town, Federalist and Presbyterian, were challenged economically and politically by ambitious new arrivals who had a base in the Methodist church.[17] A recent study has shown that

---

15. Assessing this kind of evidence, John Wigger argues that the defining characteristic of American Methodism under Francis Asbury was not a theological abstraction like Arminianism, but a quest for the supernatural in everyday life. John Wigger, "Taking Heaven by Storm: Enthusiasm and Early American Methodism, 1770–1820," *Journal of the Early Republic* 14 (1994): 167-94.

16. Philip Schaff quoted in William Nast, "Dr. Schaff and Methodism," *MQR* 31 (1857): 431. On these themes see Don Yoder, "The Bench Versus the Catechism: Revivalism and Pennsylvania's Lutheran and Reformed Churches," *Pennsylvania Folklife* 10 (1959): 14-23; and Nathan O. Hatch, *The Democratization of American Christianity* (New Haven: Yale University Press, 1989), 102-13, 153-54.

17. Emil Pocock, "Popular Roots of Jacksonian Democracy: The Case of Dayton, Ohio, 1815–1830," *Journal of the Early Republic* 9 (1989): 489-515.

Methodist artisans in Philadelphia in the 1830s were more successful than their peers, more likely to end up as master craftsmen and small retailers.[18]

As a movement, Methodism became a powerful symbol of social mobility, a beacon of aspiring respectability. Leaders like Nathan Bangs and Wilbur Fisk, who began their ministry defiantly outside the religious establishment, later aspired to educational respectability, social standing, and genteel refinement—the former as an urbane New Yorker, the latter as president of Wesleyan University.[19] Between 1840 and 1860, the Methodists founded at least thirty-five institutions of higher education. Between the Civil War and 1900, they founded more than one college or university per year. The leading citizen in antebellum Indianapolis was Calvin Fletcher, a New Englander and Methodist convert, who began with nothing, admitted to being "hungry for advancement," and ended up with great wealth and influence, politically and in Methodist circles.[20] By 1852 eleven of thirteen congressmen from Indiana were Methodists, as well as the governor and one senator. By 1870, twenty-four of thirty-seven states, including ten of the original thirteen colonies, had been governed by a Methodist. In 1880 no denomination could claim the affiliation of more governors than the Methodists. The heirs of Wesley sealed their place as the nation's largest and wealthiest Protestant body in 1896 with the election of Methodist William McKinley, the presidential candidate clearly favored by the wealthy and powerful.

Students of American religion have tended to frame their discussion in terms of models of secularization. Their studies of clergy have long drawn on models of social control and status anxiety, both assuming a story line of elite ministers with established authority fretting about losing the position and status that their profession had once enjoyed but now was being undercut. The study of Methodism reveals the extent to which religion could serve as an avenue of social mobility and gentrification.

Within Methodism, sectarian and churchly traditions have struggled for control. American Methodism in the nineteenth century

---

18. Bruce Laurie, *Working People of Philadelphia, 1800–1850* (Philadelphia: Temple University Press, 1980), 46-48.

19. Abel Stevens, *The Life of Nathan Bangs, D.D.* (New York: Carlton & Porter, 1863); George Prentice, *Wilbur Fisk* (Boston: Houghton Mifflin, 1890).

20. Richard D. Brown, *Knowledge Is Power: The Diffusion of Information in Early America, 1700–1865* (New York: Oxford University Press, 1989), 190-93, 235-40; Calvin Fletcher, *The Diary of Calvin Fletcher*, ed. Gayle Thornbrough et al. (Indianapolis: Indiana Historical Society, 1972–1983), 1:98.

evolved from Francis Asbury's "boiling hot religion" to the Gothic-cathedral Methodism of William McKinley.[21] But Gilded Age Methodism also gave rise to the Holiness movement and to Pentecostalism, what Grant Wacker has referred to as *"the* popular movement" of the twentieth century.[22] Harold Frederic's novel, *The Damnation of Theron Ware* (1896), depicts these deep tensions within Methodism at the dawn of the twentieth century. It is a theme that invites more sustained historical treatment.

The Puzzle of the Scholarly Neglect of American Methodism

Why have scholars found this phenomenal mass movement so uninteresting, so unworthy of attention? Why do we know more about the dynamics of the growth of Fundamentalism and of Pentecostalism, even of Adventism, Mormonism, and the Shakers, than about what was the most dramatic social movement between the Revolution and the Civil War? Several other considerations multiply the force of this question. A problem of sources does not deflect interest in the subject. Methodists were inveterate record keepers and journal writers, and they pioneered the widespread use of the religious press. They were Puritan-like in their obsessive self-chronicling. Why has no one exploited Methodist newspapers, journals, and tracts to trace evolving ideologies within the movement? Bernard Semmel's book, *The Methodist Revolution,* tackles just this kind of question for British Methodism, but the significance and import of Methodist journals in America remains virtually unexplored.[23]

The American scene also stands in striking contrast to the British, where for most of this century historians have wrestled with the broad social and political significance of Methodism. A wide range of scholars—E. P. Thompson, Eric Hobsbawm, James Obelkevich, A. D. Gilbert, W. R. Ward, David Hempton, and Deborah Valenze—have

---

21. The phrase "boiling hot religion" is that of Thomas Wallcut in a letter of 31 October 1789 from Muskingum, Ohio, to James Freeman, a Unitarian minister in Boston. I am grateful to Anthony Stoneburner for bringing to my attention this letter, which is located at the American Antiquarian Society, Worcester, Massachusetts.

22. Grant Wacker, "The Functions of Faith in Primitive Pentecostalism," *Harvard Theological Review* 77 (1984): 353.

23. Bernard Semmel, *The Methodist Revolution* (New York: Basic Books, 1973).

viewed the development of Methodism as central to understanding Britain in the age of democratic revolutions.[24]

The lack of attention to American Methodism is also difficult to understand given the renewed interest of scholars in the early American Republic. Once neglected, this field currently may have become the most fertile and dynamic in American historical studies. Historians are currently probing the complicated dynamics of how the republican society of the Founding Fathers and of artisans and local farmers became the liberal, competitive, market-oriented democracy of the age of Jackson. The most burning questions in early American history concern the emergence of capitalism.[25] How does Methodism, the largest social movement of the period, bear upon these issues? Sociologists such as George Thomas and David Martin have linked the spirit of Methodism and of capitalism, but historians for the most part have not picked up on these cues.[26]

It is also curious that so few feminist scholars have found Methodist sources intriguing. Given the dynamic and entrepreneurial character of early Methodism, the movement provided far greater opportunities for women as active participants. Even if Methodists gave official recognition to very few women preachers, they actively encouraged female speaking and exhorting, even pausing in their sermons to allow inspired women to speak. As Catherine Brekus has pointed out in her recent book on female preaching, the Methodists valued inspiration over theological training and thus gave many more women public leadership roles in exhorting, praying, singing,

---

24. Relevant works include Thompson, *The Making of the English Working Class;* Hobsbawm, *Labouring Men;* James Obelkevich, *Religion and Rural Society: South Lindsey, 1825–1875* (New York: Oxford University Press, 1976); A. D. Gilbert, *Religion and Society in Industrial England: Church, Chapel, and Social Change, 1740–1914* (London: Longman, 1976); W. R. Ward, *Religion and Society in England, 1790–1850* (London: Batsford, 1972); David Hempton, *Methodism and Politics in British Society, 1750–1850* (Stanford, Calif.: Stanford University Press, 1984); and Deborah M. Valenze, *Prophetic Sons and Daughters: Female Preaching and Popular Religion in Industrial England* (Princeton, N.J.: Princeton University Press, 1985).

25. Gordon S. Wood, "The Significance of the Early Republic," *Journal of the Early Republic* 8 (1988): 1-20. See also Robert H. Wiebe, *The Opening of American Society: From the Adoption of the Constitution to the Eve of Disunion* (New York: Alfred A. Knopf, 1984); Sean Wilentz, *Chants Democratic: New York City and the Rise of the American Working Class, 1788–1850* (New York: Oxford University Press, 1984); Joyce Appleby, *Capitalism and a New Social Order: The Republican Vision of the 1790s* (New York: New York University Press, 1984); Alan Taylor, *Liberty Men and Great Proprietors: The Revolutionary Settlement on the Maine Frontier, 1760–1820* (Chapel Hill: University of North Carolina Press, 1990).

26. George M. Thomas, *Revivalism and Cultural Change: Christianity, Nation Building, and the Market in the Nineteenth-Century United States* (Chicago: University of Chicago Press, 1989); David Martin, *Tongues of Fire: The Explosion of Protestantism in Latin America* (Oxford: B. Blackwell, 1990), 21, 43.

and witnessing to their own dreams and visions. Active participation in class meetings provided leadership roles for women that were unavailable in more respectable Calvinist and Episcopalian communions, yet most studies of the role of women in American Protestantism have focused on the latter groups.[27] If one wishes to explore the gendered differences of piety in America, one should concentrate on Methodist experience ranging from Catherine Livingston Garrettson to Jarena Lee to Phoebe Palmer.[28]

The same is true if one wishes to study African Americans as central actors in the unfolding of American Christianity. The development of black preaching and of the African American spiritual took place in a largely Methodist context, as did the formation of African American churches in the North. And if we are ever to explore the question that Donald Mathews has perceptively asked about the South, how white Christianity was affected by black presence, then our attention rightly turns to Methodist distinctions: the camp meeting; the power of folk religious celebrations; of shouting, dancing, and ecstasy; and the musical tradition of the spiritual.[29]

Given these indications of Methodist significance, why have historians not given the movement a more central place? The omission follows three patterns that have shaped the writing of American religious history. The first and most far-reaching is the tradition of studying Christianity largely as intellectual history. Churches typically have interpreted their own history in terms of the evolution of dogma, the development of historical theology. In twentieth-century America this tendency has been reinforced by the orientation of American religious history to New England sources. If intellectual profundity is the standard for religious history—as it is for most who have studied the Puritans and Jonathan Edwards—then the rise of the Methodists may represent a dark age for the American intellect, as Richard Hofstadter implies in *Anti-Intellectualism in America*. Other interpreters of what is important about American religion simply

27. Catherine Brekus, *Strangers and Pilgrims: Female Preaching in America, 1740–1845* (Chapel Hill: University of North Carolina Press, 1998). See also Dee E. Andrews, *The Methodists and Revolutionary America, 1760–1800: The Shaping of an Evangelical Culture* (Princeton, N.J.: Princeton University Press, 2000). Important studies that give little attention to the Methodists include Ruth H. Bloch, "American Feminine Ideals in Transition: The Rise of the Moral Mother, 1785–1815," *Feminist Studies* 4 (1978): 101-26; and Nancy Cott, *The Bonds of Womanhood: "Women's Sphere" in New England, 1780–1835* (New Haven: Yale University Press, 1977).

28. William L. Andrews, *Sisters of the Spirit: Three Black Women's Autobiographies of the Nineteenth Century* (Bloomington: Indiana University Press, 1986).

29. Donald Mathews, "Christianizing the South," in Stout et al., *New Directions*, 84-115.

avoid the Methodists, as in Ann Douglas's book, *The Feminization of American Culture*. In this study, which focuses on the interaction of Congregational and Episcopalian clergy with the literary women in their congregations, the Methodists simply do not measure up.[30]

This tendency to see religious history as intellectual history has also colored the outlook of those who study Methodism. A premier scholar such as Albert Outler returned to the font of the movement, focusing on John Wesley's ideas. Even those who have studied the American experience have construed it in intellectual ways. In an important article, "The Methodist Age in America," Winthrop Hudson characterized the movement in ways that are largely dispositions of thought, such as a belief in instrumental revivalism, a stress on human ability, and a commitment to "popular romanticism." These categories are suggestive, but they place Methodism in a frame of reference that seems sentimental, even inconsequential, when viewed against the backdrop of a Jonathan Edwards.[31]

The one attempt in this century to establish a graduate center that took Methodism seriously was short-lived. William Warren Sweet, who labored at the University of Chicago to bring Methodist sources to light and to train graduate students in this area, was succeeded by Sidney Mead, an equally formidable scholar. But Mead's views of the Methodist contribution could not have been more diametrically opposed to Sweet's. In his highly suggestive set of essays, *The Lively Experiment*, Mead argued that the Revolutionary era is the hinge upon which American Christianity turns, and that the Second Great Awakening terminated the Puritan and inaugurated the pietist, or Methodist, age of American church history. Yet Sidney Mead did not welcome the Methodist onslaught, a "great tidal wave of revivalism." Instead, he saw it as the end of what had been noble about American religion: it "effectively scuttled much of the intellectual structure of Protestantism." Thereafter he lamented, America produced no theology or theologian of the first rank. In the same vein, a student of American politics might decry everything after the age of Jackson because the nation never produced another Thomas Jefferson or John Adams.[32]

30. Richard Hofstadter, *Anti-Intellectualism in America* (New York: Vintage, 1963); Ann Douglas, *The Feminization of American Culture* (New York: Alfred A. Knopf, 1977).

31. Winthrop Hudson, "The Methodist Age in America," *Methodist History* 12 (1974): 3-15.

32. On William Warren Sweet see James L. Ash Jr., *Protestantism and the American University: An Intellectual Biography of William Warren Sweet* (Dallas: Southern Methodist University Press, 1982); and Mead, *Lively Experiment*, 54.

A second reason for the lack of compelling Methodist histories is that Methodist historians have had reasons to sanitize their histories. Modern church historians have chosen to focus on those aspects of their own heritage linked to cultural enrichment, institutional cohesion, and intellectual respectability. William Warren Sweet has done more than any other single scholar in the twentieth century to promote the serious study of Methodists and Baptists on the frontier. He was committed, however, to a vision of these groups as bearers of civilization to the uncouth, unrestrained society of the frontier. Emphasizing the disastrous effects of migration upon civilization and culture, Sweet depicted evangelical denominations as bringing moral order and the first seeds of culture to a rampantly individualistic society. He emphasized how the churches brought order, education, and moral discipline to the frontier. In his hands even the camp meeting became a well-regulated institution. Sweet had little interest in evidence that early Methodism was white-hot with enthusiasm, confrontational and unrefined in its style, and readily dismissed much of John and Charles Wesley's liturgical formality.[33]

Other mainstream Protestant church historians in the twentieth century have also emphasized themes of Protestant solidarity and the church's role in taming the frontier. An unswerving commitment to the unity of the church has made it virtually impossible for church historians, from Robert Baird and Philip Schaff to H. Richard Niebuhr and Winthrop Hudson, to admit that God's ultimate plans could entail the splintering of churches. In his book, *The Great Tradition of the American Churches*, for instance, Winthrop Hudson suggests that the meaning of the American religious experience is the overcoming of sectarian fervor. In the face of disestablishment, he suggests that Protestants closed ranks and embarked upon a powerful counteroffensive to combat the forces of irreligion. There is plenty of room in this scheme for Baptists and Methodists, but only as they shed sectarian dogmatism, ecstatic display, and aggressive proselytizing. Modern church historians, in short, have had difficulty identifying with dimensions of their own ecclesiastical heritage that are

---

33. William Warren Sweet, *Religion in the Development of American Culture, 1765–1840* (New York: Scribners, 1952). According to James L. Ash Jr., Sweet "patronized the multitude of sectarian groups in America as little more than institutional and theological anomalies which attracted the mentally unstable." See "American Religion and the Academy in the Early Twentieth Century: The Chicago Years of William Warren Sweet," *Church History* 50 (1981): 461.

diametrically opposed to the modern embrace of intellectual, liturgical, and ecumenical respectability.[34]

Historians have also passed over the Methodists because the denomination bears the stigma of its petty bourgeoisie origins and identity. The Methodist story, representing the bland, uninspired middle of American society, has not appealed to religious historians who want to study powerful ideas and theologies. Nor has it appealed to social historians intent on studying the disenfranchised—scholars who have real trouble coming to terms with the bourgeoisie.[35] Christopher Lasch has recently noted that American intellectuals of the right and the left express a subtle disdain and distrust of middle America. He suggests that scholars are generally blind to the positive features of ordinary people—their religiosity, respectability, and traditional values of thrift, hard work, and family loyalty.[36] For most of American history, Methodists have been nothing if not moralistic. More than any other denomination they have been identified with the powerful impulse of temperance in American society, a wave cresting in the passage of Prohibition in 1920. Weighed in the balance of Joseph Haroutunian's piety versus moralism, the Methodists come up seriously deficient, the scales tipped on the side of moralism.[37]

No interpretive vision of American religion has arisen organized around Wesleyanism because it so clearly represents that which we take for granted about American society. The Methodist story, replete with perfectionism and cultural accommodation, seems bereft of a prophetic voice, lacks profound insight into the human condition, and is unable to suggest alternatives to the main channels in which American culture has flowed. Perhaps historians ignore Methodists because Wesleyans are too quintessentially American.

The Unique Vantage Point of Methodism for Understanding American Religion

Methodists certainly deserve study like any other American denomination. Yet the movement also provides a crucial vantage

---

34. Hudson, *Great Tradition*. R. Laurence Moore has a superb discussion of this point in "Protestant Unity and the American Mission—The Historiography of a Desire," the introductory chapter to his book, *Religious Outsiders*, 3-21.

35. See Roy Porter, "The Heart of the Country," a review of E. P. Thompson, *Customs in Common* in *The New Republic* (4 May 1992): 35-38.

36. Christopher Lasch, *The True and Only Heaven: Progress and Its Critics* (New York: W. W. Norton, 1991).

37. Joseph Haroutunian, *Piety Versus Moralism: The Passing of the New England Theology* (New York: Harper & Row, 1964).

point from which one can assess the characteristic dynamics of American religion. As Stephen Warner has recently noted, the Christianization of the United States was neither a residue of Puritan hegemony nor a transplantation of a European sacred canopy. It was the striking achievement of nineteenth-century activists.[38] American Methodism, both in its initial flowering and in its institutional growth, is a superb window to understand the characteristic styles, dispositions, and reflexes of the American religious experience. Let me support this argument in four ways.

First, American Methodists reconstructed the church along voluntary lines and welcomed a plural and competitive religious environment. Puritanism grew out of a context of state-sponsored religion, whereas Methodism sprang from the collapse of the monopolistic relationship of religion with the state and with the local community. Methodism aroused the voluntary conscience, calling people to break with religious ties that were hereditary and organic. Methodism in its message and structure embodied a liberal conception of reality that broke decisively with the pre-Revolutionary pursuit of homogeneous community. As a movement of self-conscious outsiders, Methodists embraced the virtues of pluralism, of competition, and of marketing religion in every sphere of life, far beyond the narrow confines of ecclesiastical space. The Methodists invented the American denomination, making obsolete the European reality of church at the cultural center and sect at the periphery.

Second, the Methodists injected vernacular Christianity into the bloodstream of America—faith incarnate in popular culture. In an emerging democratic society, it was the Methodists more than anyone else who were responsible for making Christianity a mass enterprise. Everyday folk rather than college-educated gentlemen scrambled to claim the office of minister. Rejecting the standard reformed sermon, a read discourse with a stiff theological spine, Methodists crafted sermons that were audience-centered, vernacular, and extemporaneous. The resulting religious culture made revivalism a fixture of American religious life. In contrast to Europe and Great Britain, the United States become characterized by populist forms of Christianity, religion that flourished at the periphery of elite culture. American religious discourse, like its political counterpart, excelled at breadth of influence rather than depth of insight. Unlike Europe, American

---

38. Stephen Warner, "Work in Progress Toward a New Paradigm for the Sociological Study of Religion in the United States," *American Journal of Sociology* 99 (1993): 1054-55.

popular culture remained more religious than did high culture. David Martin has argued that Methodists, only a counterculture in England, succeeded in America in defining the core of a democratic culture: "Arminian evangelical Protestantism provided the *differentia specifica* of the American religious and cultural ethos."[39] Martin argues that the dynamic of American religion has remained on the periphery of high culture rather than at the center, and that the whole American style is Methodist, insisting on openness and sincerity rather than on form and privacy.

Third, Methodism resonated with the logic of capitalism and liberal individualism. New England churches to the American Revolution and beyond never gave up the quest to regulate worldly matters along godly lines. Jonathan Edwards, for instance, never divorced religion from public affairs or justified an economic order that ran by its own principles. Edwards denied the possibility of a virtuous market economy and railed against economic individualism.[40] In the early republic, American society became engrossed in commerce and evangelical religion at the same time. Alexis de Tocqueville took note of this striking intermingling of God and mammon within the nation's soul: "I know of no country, indeed, where the love of money has taken stronger hold on the affections of men. . . . There is no country in the world where the Christian religion retains a greater influence over the souls of men than in America."[41] To understand this conflation of materialism and spirituality, we must alter the traditional terms of the debate. In the first generation of the republic, it is not so much the fate of Calvinism and its heirs that sheds light on the American economy. Instead, it is the meteoric rise of American Methodism that offers insight into a society that was awash in religion and in making money—and confident of divine favor upon both endeavors. American Methodism was the prototype of a religious organization taking on market form.

The powerful correlation between Methodism and the shaping of democratic culture has recently been explored by Richard Carwardine. He notes the profound links between revivals and the electioneering that became the norm in Jacksonian America. Both depended upon the existence and exploitation of antitheses, ideolog-

---

39. Martin, *Tongues of Fire*, 21.
40. Mark Valeri, "The Economic Thought of Jonathan Edwards," *Church History* 60 (1991): 37-54.
41. Alexis de Tocqueville, *Democracy in America*, trans. Henry Reeve (New York: Random House, 1945), 1:53, 314.

ical and political. Political organizers learned to raise political excitement to levels commonly associated with religious enthusiasm, and depicted political campaigns as moral crusades. "Party organizers," Carwardine argues, "learnt much from revival preachers about reaching a mass audience through printing press and indoor and outdoor pulpit, about the efficacy of persevering, continuous, and dramatic effort, and about consolidating loyalties."[42] The multiplication of political gatherings directly paralleled "protracted meetings" and the singing of political hymns echoed the catchy melodies of religious folk music. Methodism sprouted from the same cultural taproot that nourished a culture of liberal individualism and mass democracy.

Fourth, the Methodists represent religion in an extremely pliable and adaptable cultural form. Most first-generation Methodists were staunch Jeffersonians. Their children were mostly Whigs, although Methodists were scattered across the political spectrum. Early Methodists stoutly opposed slavery, and the first African American churches took shape in a Methodist context. White Methodists, as a whole, quickly backtracked on the issue with the result that one finds Wesleyans both as leading abolitionists and as leaders in the pro-slavery defense.

As the number of Methodists expanded, what it meant to be Methodist became far less clear. Some Methodists continued the plain-style worship and perfectionism of the early camp meeting. By the 1850s others were building Gothic churches and folding gentility and refinement into the very definition of being religious, as Richard Bushman notes in *The Refinement of America*.[43]

The Methodists are the fountainhead of mainline denominations, professional expertise, and university formation and, indirectly, of twentieth-century Pentecostalism—a movement as stunning in its growth both here and abroad as Methodism was in the early republic. The American conviction of the paramount importance of religious belief, whatever the kind, has a distinct Methodist ring to it.

Puritanism provides a great paradigm for understanding America, if one thinks of transcending ourselves, of imagining what might have been, of finding an alternative vision and source of strength to confront the unpleasant realities of American life. It is like relishing the age of the Founding Fathers and wishing American political

---

42. Carwardine, *Evangelicals and Politics*, 52.
43. Richard L. Bushman, *The Refinement of America: Persons, Houses, Cities* (New York: Alfred A. Knopf, 1992), 313-52.

debate had retained the sophistication and wisdom of Thomas Jefferson, John Adams, and James Madison. The story of Methodism tells us much more about American religion as it actually unfolded— not great, not sophisticated, not awe inspiring, but what it is.

What would American religious history look like if Methodists were nudged closer to the center? From the point of view of theology and educational institutions, Methodists were imitators and followers. Yet they were pacesetters from the point of view of popular mobilization, effective communication systems, participation of women, and empowerment of African Americans. If Methodists were moved to the foreground, we would learn more about class, status, and social structure within religious institutions. We would more readily understand religion as experience and community rather than as abstract ideas. We would comprehend more about how religion has functioned as a powerful instrument of popular education and of vertical mobility. Most important, we would regain a sense of surprise at the ways in which America came to be Christianized between the Revolution and the Civil War. And, in the process, we would gain insight into how religion has so tenaciously gripped the soul of Americans—those on the margins as well as those who have tasted success.

CHAPTER 2

Methodist Growth in Transatlantic Perspective, ca. 1770–1850[1]

David Hempton

In the spring of 1820, a young New England teenager of no great importance underwent one of those life-changing experiences that appear in the records of Methodism wherever it took root in the North Atlantic world in its great era of expansion. His own account of the event, remarkable for nothing but its typicality, is worth repeating at length, for nothing comes closer to the essence of Methodism than its ubiquitous conversion narratives.

I was born in Geensboro Vermont March 27 1802. In the spring of 1820 I was awakened and converted in Middletown, Connecticut under the preaching of Rev John Newland Maffitt. My parents were Christians, but I was a wicked boy, guilty of Sabbath breaking and other sins. I spent the holy day reading novels and playing cards. One Sunday a fellow apprentice came home from meeting and said there was a great preacher at the Methodist church and wanted me to go and hear. But I would not go. Mr. Maffitt preached three times Sunday and Monday, Tuesday, Wednesday and Thursday evenings. Thursday evening I went late. He was preaching when I went in. His remarkably impressive eyes were upon me the moment I entered the door and it seemed to me that an arrow of conviction came to my heart. I was awakened.

1. I am grateful to Mark Noll, Hugh McLeod, Richard Carwardine, John Walsh, and the late George Rawlyk for their comments on earlier drafts of this chapter. I am also grateful to Taylor & Francis for permission to reproduce some material from my *The Religion of the People: Methodism and Popular Religion c. 1750–1900* (London: Routledge, 1996).

My wicked companions saw how I was affected and laughed me in the face. I gave way to shame and went with them to the grog shop. I returned to the church and was found among the scoffers. Mr. Maffitt spoke to me asking me if I had got religion and if I desired. With a scornful tone I replied that I neither had nor desired it. Mark my word young man he said you will kneel at the altar which came to pass the next Sunday night. The Divine Spirit followed me and I was an earnest seeker the next three days. Sunday evening after the sermon, seekers were invited to come to the altar for prayers. A young convert, whom I had promised that I would go forward, came to me to lead me to the altar. I was ashamed to have the large congregation see him talking with me and I sent him away. After sitting two hours I arose to go and looking round I saw the wicked laughing at me. If I had yielded then I should probably have gone on in sin to my eternal ruin. But it had the contrary effect and made me more determined to persevere. I went and bowed before the Lord feeling that I had left the world behind and had confessed to my need of a Saviour.

A brother said if a seeker would tell his feelings, he thought it would help him. I arose trembling and with a faltering voice asked for prayer. Instantly there came a great change in my feelings. There was great peace. The burden of guilt seemed to roll off and I felt as I never did before that I could sing the praise of God from the heart. Now Satan whispered you are not a Christian and it would be wrong for you to sing. I went away from that meeting distressed because I had lost my conviction. I met the pastor and he told me I must not pray for conviction but for conversion and evidence of it. I got up Saturday morning with the determination that I would not eat nor sleep until I had the evidence of pardon. I asked Mr. Warner to give me the day and I would work the 4th of July. I spent the day in the woods in prayer and reading the Bible. In the evening I attended class meeting and was brought out clear. Now I felt that I must make sure work for eternity. There must be no uncertainty in a matter involving bliss or woe forever. I must *know* that my sins were forgiven. But there was no doubt now. The change was so great that I knew that none but God could have made it and whereas before I did not love God, the Bible, the worship of God, the Sabbath and the people of God, now I loved all these. Then I was afraid of death, now I was not afraid to die. I hated the things I once loved. Then I loved sin, now I abhorred it.[2]

Not long before he died, John Edwards Risley reflected that he had preached more than forty-five hundred times to 303 different congre-

---

2. New England Methodist Historical Society, manuscript history collection (Boston University, School of Theology Library). MSS, The Experience of the Rev. John Edwards Risley.

gations over a period of fifty-six years. He estimated that he had spoken to more than thirty thousand people and had been instrumental in the religious conversions of hundreds. Conversion narratives in Methodism are therefore not merely religious experiences confined to the individuals who recorded them, but are links in the chain of the remarkable expansion of the movement in the eighteenth and nineteenth centuries. What then is to be made of Risley's story?

The conversion narrative is a common Methodist genre in which is stressed the drama of the second birth as a means of escaping a world of sin and licentiousness, and of entering a world of faith and godly discipline. Common elements represented in Risley's narrative include the influence of Methodist preachers, the support of prayer and class meetings, the awareness of sensible experience, the desire for assurance, the quest for a subsequent blessing of entire sanctification, the fear of backsliding, and the desire to become a useful instrument of God's grace in the world. The conversion experience was so central to the lives of early Methodists that they are embellished by memory and presented as cosmic dramas. In this case, Risley presents his own conversion as a transition from a world of Sabbath breaking, novel reading, and alehouse frequenting to one of prayer, faith, and Bible reading. The episode is remembered as both a social and a psychological event. He remembers the piercing eyes of the preacher and the social pressures to conform either to the jocular, mocking presence of his friends or to the life of the church community with its mechanisms of corporate insistence. His divided mind is presented as part of a divided society and then as part of a divided cosmology of good and evil, God and Satan. At stake in the transaction are his temporal happiness and his eternal destiny. Fear of death and the implied fear of eternal woe are powerful psychological inducements to come down on the side of the believers against the scoffers, and yet the narrative is presented more as a voluntary submission to the offer of a new life than an escape from a world of threats and torments.

Once the commitment was made there was the customary doubt and indecision. It is at this point that the Methodist machinery of prayer and class meetings offered crucial community support. In addition, Risley's conversion dialectic is soon superseded by another— the desire for the blessing of Christian perfection as against the ever-present fear of backsliding to the world left behind. Out of the heat of dialectical friction emerges his desire to tell the story to others and to work for the triumph of his new principles. Out of the drama of Methodist conversion experiences came the remarkable energy of the movement. Risley's subsequent career as preacher, revivalist, city missioner, and patron of dying Methodist causes is a remarkable tribute to the enduring power of the message he first embraced as a teenager. Risley's narrative of his life's work is not without its tales of hardships and disappointments, but what is striking about it is how a set of experiences in his late teens set a course from which he never deviated and seems never to have regretted. It is not surprising, therefore, that in trying to tell the story of his own life he devotes over a fifth of the narrative to only a few weeks. The memory of those events, simultaneously disturbing and liberating, became the organizing principle of his entire life.

Risley's conversion experience is but one of many thousands of recorded conversion narratives and one of many millions of unrecorded memories in the Methodist tradition. They have a number of common themes. Most occurred during teenage years; most betray some sense of deep psychological distress; most contain within them an explicit or implicit fear of death; many seem to take place in communities experiencing rapid change or an unusual degree of social dislocation; and most converts had some preexisting religious knowledge. Conversion narratives, as with captivity narratives, form a literary genre the conventions of which need to be taken seriously by any investigator. How these documents are decoded will in large measure determine the kind of interpretation of Methodist growth that emerges from them. Whether pitched as the products of social anomie, psychosexual repression, economic dislocation, or religious fervor (by no means exclusive categories), no history of Methodist expansion can afford to ignore them.

Perhaps the most influential historian of Methodism to take seriously the religious conversions and experiences of its followers was Edward Palmer Thompson. Although Thompson described himself as a plain Marxist, he was born into a family with deep Methodist roots. A man of razor-sharp intellect and passionate convictions, Thompson was not only one of Britain's greatest-ever social historians, but also has had a remarkable influence over Methodist historiography since the publication of his great work *The Making of the*

English Working Class in 1963.[3] However, his is a name that will not be regarded with particular fondness by those interested in the history of Methodism as a popular religious movement. The ringing phrase, psychic masturbation, along with his other attempts to get at the heart of Methodist experience through a psychosexual treatment of hymns and images, created an immense stir at the time and has never been forgotten or indeed forgiven by those who felt that a great religious tradition had been immolated on the altar of the sexual faddism of the 1960s.[4]

But Thompson was no mere dedicated follower of fashion. In the midst of the controversy surrounding his interpretation of Methodism, it is easy to forget that Thompson wrote as he did as a result of asking penetrating questions, which seem genuinely to have perplexed him and which still need to be addressed. With a sharp eye for the way the historiography was shifting, he stated that "too much writing on Methodism commences with the assumption that we all know what Methodism was, and gets on with discussing its growth rates or its organizational structures. But we cannot deduce the quality of the Methodist experience from this kind of evidence."[5]

It was in attempting to penetrate to the heart of Methodist *experience*—as opposed to its structures, organization, and theology—that stimulated Thompson to address a number of interlocking questions. Why did working people accept "this passionate Lutheranism" and not the more politically literate and rational faith of the English dissenting tradition, which Thompson considered a more appropriate vehicle for working-class interests in the age of the French Revolution? How should one begin to interpret recorded Methodist experiences when they were so often couched in the most high-flown

---

3. Edward P. Thompson, *The Making of the English Working Class*, revised edition (Harmondsworth, U.K.: Penguin, 1968). Some of Thompson's essays also contain material of interest to historians of Methodism: "The Moral Economy of the English Crowd in the Eighteenth Century," *Past and Present* 50 (1971): 76-136; "Anthropology and the Discipline of Historical Context," *Midland History* 1, no. 3 (1972): 41-55; "Patrician Society: Plebeian Culture," *Journal of Social History* 7, no. 4 (1974): 382-405; and "Eighteenth-Century English Society: Class Struggle Without Class?" *Social History* 3 (1978): 133-65. For an example of the influence of Thompson's work on North American scholars see Gerald W. Olsen, ed., *Religion and Revolution in Early-Industrial England: The Halévy Thesis and Its Critics* (Lanham, Md.: University Press of America, 1990) and Alan Dawley, "E. P. Thompson and the Peculiarities of the Americans," *Radical History Review* 19 (1978-79): 33-59.

4. Thompson dealt with the early critics of his treatment of Methodism in the postscript to the Penguin edition of *The Making of the English Working Class*. These included Robert Currie and R. M. Hartwell, "The Making of the English Working Class?" *Economic History Review*, 2d series, 18, no. 2 (1965).

5. Thompson, *Making of the English Working Class*, 918.

supernaturalistic language about Satan and his demons, and described in the most surreal of images?[6] How can one explain a religion allegedly founded on the principles of a loving sacrifice that nevertheless feared love's effective expression, either as sexual love or in any social form that might irritate relations with Authority? How can the remorseless mechanics of societary discipline be squared with the remarkable outbursts of folk revivalism that seemed to operate on the rawest edge of emotional extremism? How could Methodism simultaneously act as the religion of the industrial bourgeoisie *and* wide sections of the proletariat, given that both Weber and Tawney had confined themselves to explaining why puritanical forms of religion had appealed almost exclusively to the middling sort with economic aspirations?

In answering these questions and in facing up to the many apparent paradoxes of Methodist experience, Thompson imposed several analytical frameworks. I say *imposed* because his conceptual apparatus and sheer power of historical imagination were generally more impressive than his detailed evidence. For convenience he split Methodist history into three epochs: the era of the Wesleyan pastorate, the war years, and "the sober years of ascending respectability and social status."[7] It was the middle period, Methodism's great age of rapid expansion, that interested him most. In this period, he sought to explain Methodist experience in terms of the psychic disturbances occasioned by war, food shortages, and revolutionary political and social changes, which he synthesized in the memorable phrase "the chiliasm of despair." He meant by that, not so much that Methodism was a kind of millenarian sect such as those that came to the fore during the English civil wars and interregnum, but that social and political anomie produced the kind of psychological climate within which a religion like Methodism could flourish. His second broad conceptual framework had to do with Methodism as an inculcator of work discipline and structured leisure at a time when industrial capitalism was eroding the traditional patterns of labor and popular amusement. "The argument is thus complete," he wrote, "the factory system demands a transformation of human nature, the 'working paroxysms' of the artisan or the outworker must be methodized until the man is adapted to the discipline of the machine."[8] It

---

6. Ibid., 402-11.
7. Ibid., 920.
8. Ibid., 397-98.

is here that he quotes with approval D. H. Lawrence's words in *The Rainbow* that the miners "believe they must alter themselves to fit the pits and the place, rather than alter the pits and the place to fit themselves. It is easier."[9] As far as Thompson was concerned, that was the essence of Methodism's impact on the workers in the early industrial revolution.

His third main conceptual framework was based on his view of Methodist theology, and in particular, its doctrine of grace. Grace among the Methodists, according to Thompson, was maintained primarily through service to the church; cultivation of the soul by means of conversion, penitence, and study; and the creation of methodical discipline in every aspect of life. Passion and the workings of the heart were thus to be confined to the religious spheres of dramatic conversions and service to the church, and not to the secular world. In this way "the box-like, blackening chapels stood in the industrial districts like great traps for the human psyche."[10] It was in this psychological disorder that Thompson located the sexual repression and womb imagery of the Methodist hymns. Why then did working people in such large numbers put up with it? The explanation he offered was a combination of indoctrination through Sunday schools and a desperate search for community in a fragmenting social order. Indeed, anything worthy of admiration in Methodism (and in Thompson's scheme there is very little) was owing to the ability of the English working classes to import some of their traditional compassion and common sense into the "religious terrorism" of the Methodist experience.[11]

This is not the time or the place to engage in a point-by-point rebuttal of some of Thompson's arguments. The purpose of describing them at some length is to highlight one of the most imaginative and conceptually fertile attempts to get to the heart of the Methodist *experience* by answering the basic questions, What is it? and Why did it grow where and when it did? In answering these questions Thompson put more stress on the *motives* of the faithful, the *methods* of transmission, and the various *margins* that Methodism exploited than any of his predecessors. What restricted him was not so much the inappropriateness of the questions he asked as his own ideological convictions that since religious belief is essentially irrational, then

9. Ibid., 398, n. 1.
10. Ibid., 404.
11. Ibid., 411-40.

religion must always be explained in terms of displacement and repression. In short, his Methodism could not be allowed to display agreeable characteristics because no religion of any kind has the capacity to do so. Another weakness in Thompson's approach to Methodism, which surfaced also in his influential study of crowd behavior in eighteenth-century England, was his assumption that the essence of the Methodist experience was more or less the same from person to person and from place to place. As with English crowd behavior, he assumes a "unanimity of conceptualization" among Methodists, which fails to do justice to the important variables of age, gender, location, and level of commitment.[12] In particular, his attempt to link Methodist experience to the dynamics of industrial capitalism fails to explain why both the Wesleyan and Primitive connections often made their most spectacular gains in primarily rural or village communities.[13] It would nevertheless be a misjudgment to ignore Thompson's shrewd questions simply because the answers he supplied were unsatisfactory.

What I wish to do, therefore, is to look more closely at motives, methods, and margins in attempting to explain the quite remarkable expansion of Methodism in different parts of the world in the period 1770–1850. I shall begin with some of the implications of Professor William R. Ward's work on the European origins of the Great Awakening before saying something about Methodist growth in Britain, the United States, and Canada. I will then compare those stories with a different and less successful pattern of Methodist growth in Ireland and France during the same period. What accounts for the difference and how can a comparative treatment help answer some of the questions posed by Thompson in a purely English context?

Methodism's European Roots

The roots of the great religious revivals of the eighteenth century—from eastern and central Europe to the middle colonies of America—are to be found, according to Professor Ward, in the resistance of

---

12. Suzanne Desan, "Crowds, Community and Ritual in the Work of E. P. Thompson and Natalie Davis," in Lynn Hunt, ed., *The New Cultural History* (Berkeley: University of California Press, 1989), 47-71.

13. John Walsh made a plea for more serious treatment of rural Methodism in his contribution to James Obelkevich, Lyndal Roper, and Raphael Samuel, eds., *Disciplines of Faith: Studies in Religion, Politics and Patriarchy* (London: Routledge, 1987).

confessional minorities to the real or perceived threat of assimilation by powerful states and established churches.[14] He locates the seeds of future revival in the eighteenth-century Protestant frame of mind, which was a compound of low morale, fear of confessional conflict, eschatological neuroses, and pious devotion—all serviced by an astonishing array of devotional publications and popular preachers. The spiritual life of Europe was quite simply breaking free from confessional control at precisely the time when such control was pursued with renewed vigor. As a result, the pietism of Halle and Herrnhut was fanned into revivals in various Protestant corners of the Habsburg Empire. It was then carried to the British Isles and North America by sweeping population movements and by a remarkable collection of revivalists, who knew of one another's labors and who believed themselves part of a worldwide movement of grace. One of the most attractive and important features of Ward's fine study of the Protestant evangelical awakening is the way in which he is able to bring to life the many sturdy individualists who preached revival, without either etherizing their religious motivation or piously glossing over their most disagreeable qualities. In terms of religious motivation, therefore, we are presented with personalities with mixed qualities of egocentricity and heroism who experienced grace and preached it in ways that Thompson's models of sexual repression and work discipline cannot begin to encapsulate.

Above all, Ward's interpretation is based upon the idea that popular evangelicalism had the capacity to act as a radical and unsettling force in a world order in which the Christianization of the poor was regarded as the exclusive function of politically manipulated and spiritually pragmatic state churches. There are still further radical dimensions to this story that would not surface in an interpretation based on social class alone. The reemergence in theory and in practice of the doctrine of the priesthood of all believers, for example, challenged the notion of a traditional priesthood based on clerical hierarchies and established mechanisms of social control.[15] In addition, the

---

14. This argument is worked out most clearly in William R. Ward, *The Protestant Evangelical Awakening* (Cambridge: Cambridge University Press, 1992), but Ward's earlier articles on the origins of religious revival still retain their value. These have been collected in one volume titled *Faith and Faction* (London: Epworth Press, 1993). The most important are "Orthodoxy, Enlightenment, and Religious Revival" and "Power and Piety: the Origins of Religious Revival in the Early Eighteenth Century." See also Ward, *Christianity Under the Ancien Regime 1648–1789* (Cambridge: Cambridge University Press, 1999).

15. William R. Ward, "Pastoral Office and the General Priesthood in the Great Awakening," *Studies in Church History* 26 (1989): 303-27.

idea that spiritual enlightenment and instruction were not confined to adult males alone, opened up surprisingly influential roles for women and children in early revivalism. Thus, popular Protestantism, for all its carping narrowness and bitter controversies, had the capacity to expand the religious potential of the laity and to have a civilizing and humanizing effect on its humble adherents.[16]

How does all this relate to Methodist expansion in England in the late eighteenth and early nineteenth centuries? The most conceptually integrated alternative to Thompson's interpretation, and the one based on the best command of the evidence, is once again supplied by Ward.[17] With all due attention to Methodist theology, organization, and personal motivation, he nevertheless views Methodism's great age of expansion in English society as part of much wider structural changes in the generation overshadowed by the French Revolution. In this period, a complex of social tensions caused by population growth, subsistence crises, and the commercialization of agriculture—and further exacerbated by prolonged warfare—sharpened class conflict, and undermined the old denominational order. The rising social status of the Anglican clergy and their unprecedented representation on the bench of magistrates cemented the squire and parson alliance at the very time that establishment ideals were most under attack. In such circumstances the Church of England was in no position to resist a dramatic upsurge in undenominational itinerant preaching and cottage-based religion, which even the various Methodist connections struggled hard to keep under control.[18]

Methodism thus made its fastest gains in areas least amenable to paternalistic influence, including freehold parishes, industrial villages, mining communities, market towns, canal and seaports, and other centers of migratory populations. James Obelkevich's classic local study of South Lindsey is a vivid illustration of how the Church of England's attempt to reinforce an older paternalistic, hierarchic, and integrated society was vigorously challenged by more emotionally vibrant and populist forms of religion such as that offered by the

---

16. See for example John Walsh, "Methodism at the End of the Eighteenth Century," in Rupert Davies and Gordon Rupp, eds., *A History of the Methodist Church in Great Britain* (London: Epworth Press, 1965), 1:277-315.

17. William R. Ward, *Religion and Society in England 1790–1850* (London: Batsford, 1972). The main themes are expressed in a more accessible form in "Revival and Class Conflict in Early Nineteenth-Century Britain," in *Faith and Faction*, 285-98.

18. See Deborah M. Valenze, *Prophetic Sons and Daughters* (Princeton, N.J.: Princeton University Press, 1985); Deryck W. Lovegrove, *Established Church, Sectarian People: Itinerancy and the Transformation of English Dissent, 1780–1830* (Cambridge: Cambridge University Press, 1988).

Primitive Methodists.[19] The result was a mixture of class and cultural conflict, which reflected the economic and social structure of the area and led to the growth of an agricultural trade unionism almost entirely under Methodist leadership.[20]

From this perspective, Methodism was a form of popular religion peculiarly well adapted to the kind of economic, social, and political transformations that were changing the face of English society and that were inexorably loosening the control of the established church at the end of the eighteenth century. Religious associations eroded the Church of England, therefore, not primarily by political means, which for long had been the fear of the church's most ardent defenders, but through the cottage prayer meetings and itinerant preaching of a vigorously mobilized laity. In that respect at least Methodism, in its fundamentally religious challenge to the religious structures of England's confessional state, may be seen more as a religious expression of social empowerment than as a reinforcement of *ancien régime* control.[21] Its alternative structure of voluntary religious societies, organized into a connectional system, posed the same kind of threat to the Church of England as the corresponding societies posed to the British state.[22] As Alan Gilbert has stated in his most recent contribution to this old debate:

> The laborers, artisans and tradespeople, the school teachers and other minor professionals, and even (albeit to a much lesser extent) the merchant and manufacturing groups who became Methodists in early industrial England, were the kinds of people who, in matters of politics, industrial relations or social status, often found themselves at odds, in one way or another, with the norms, values and institutions of the ruling classes. . . . Not only were the social groups from which the movement drew the bulk of its members already predisposed towards radical or independent politics, but the very act of becoming a

19. James Obelkevich, *Religion and Rural Society: South Lindsey, 1825–1875* (Oxford: Clarendon Press, 1976).

20. Nigel Scotland, *Methodism and the Revolt of the Field* (Gloucester, U.K.: Alan Sutton, 1981). See also Robert Moore, *Pit-Men, Preachers and Politics: The Effects of Methodism in a Durham Mining Community* (Cambridge: Cambridge University Press, 1974).

21. For rather different interpretations of Methodism's contribution or otherwise to England's *ancien régime* see Jonathan C. D. Clark, *English Society 1688–1832* (Cambridge: Cambridge University Press, 1985), 235-47, and David Hempton, *The Religion of the People: Methodism and Popular Religion c. 1750–1900* (London: Routledge, 1996), 77-90.

22. William R. Ward, "The Evangelical Revival in Eighteenth-Century Britain," in Sheridan W. Gilley and William J. Sheils, eds., *A History of Religion in Britain* (Oxford: B. Blackwell, 1994), 252-72.

Methodist was often interpreted by non-Methodist neighbors and local civil authorities as one of social defiance.[23]

As long as the State and the established church were prepared to acquiesce in a limited toleration for religious enthusiasts, which for all practical purposes hinged on the right to engage in itinerant preaching,[24] and as long as the Methodist leadership was prepared to propagandize its own membership on behalf of the established order, the "social defiance" alluded to by Gilbert was generally kept well within acceptable boundaries.[25]

Equally important in terms of social order was the capacity of Wesleyan Methodism, and subsequently its offshoots, to separate from the established church and then from the main connection in a relatively ordered and disciplined fashion. But the key here is not so much the libertarian sentiments of the sects (that much at least can be conceded to Thompson), as the profound impact of legal and institutional frameworks in helping both to articulate grievances and to manage their consequences. Popular evangelicalism did not create the freeborn Englishman, nor did it single-handedly create the English capacity for disciplined protest. Rather, through Methodism and the connectional system it offered a vibrant religious vehicle for both to operate outside the confines of the established church without seriously destabilizing the British State. Moreover, it was in this period, from 1780 to 1830, that the growth rates of the Methodist membership reached their most spectacular—and from year to year, their most volatile levels in the history of Methodism in England.[26] The most convincing explanation for that pattern is not that Methodism offered a convenient religious vehicle for counterrevolutionary forces, but that it supplied the means by which England's confessional state was eroded from within at the same time as it was challenged from

23. Alan D. Gilbert, "Religion and Political Stability in Early Industrial England," in Patrick K. O'Brien and Roland Quinault, eds., *The Industrial Revolution and British Society* (Cambridge: Cambridge University Press, 1993), 89, and Gilbert, "Methodism, Dissent and Political Stability in Early Industrial England," *Journal of Religious History* 10, no. 4 (1979): 281-99.

24. David N. Hempton, "Methodism and the Law, 1740–1820," *Bulletin of the John Rylands University Library of Manchester* 70, no. 3 (1988): 93-107.

25. All the major surviving collections of Methodist correspondence from the period 1790 to 1820 and the private minutes of the Committee of Privileges after 1803 testify to the efforts made to keep Methodists loyal to the established order. See David Hempton, *Methodism and Politics in British Society 1750–1850* (London: Hutchinson, 1984), 55-115.

26. Robert Currie, Alan Gilbert, and Lee Horsley, *Churches and Churchgoers: Patterns of Church Growth in the British Isles Since 1700* (Oxford: Clarendon Press, 1977), 40-42.

without by pressure from Roman Catholics in Ireland.[27] Ironically, it was when the Methodist leadership self-consciously acted as agents of social control in the Peterloo years, from 1817 to 1820, that Methodist expansion sustained its most serious check before the crippling internal disputes of the late 1840s and early 1850s.[28] Nevertheless, the extent to which Methodism had refashioned the religious landscape in England in the period of the industrial revolution was made clear by the religious census of 1851. The number of Anglican attendants was just over half the total number, and the number of Methodist attendants outstripped all the other nonconformist denominations put together.[29] By 1851 the Church of England was still the only religious denomination in England with a truly national coverage, but it had taken a fearful pounding in those parts of the country where the population was growing most rapidly.

The Rise of American Methodism

An even more dramatic transformation of the old denominational landscape took place in the United States in the period 1776–1850. In 1776 Methodists accounted for only 2.5 percent of religious adherents, comfortably behind the established colonial denominations, whereas by 1850 the Methodist share was 34.2 percent, which was almost double the proportion of Presbyterians, Congregationalists, and Episcopalians put together.[30] In a period of remarkable demographic expansion, Methodist growth rates considerably outstripped those of the population as a whole.[31] By the 1840s a veritable army of over ten

27. Thomas Bartlett, *The Fall and the Rise of the Irish Nation: The Catholic Question 1690–1830* (Dublin: Gill & Macmillan, 1992).

28. See the revealing graph of Methodist membership growth rates in Currie, Gilbert, and Horsley, *Churches and Churchgoers,* 41. The best interpretation of Methodism in the troubled districts of the north of England in these years remains Ward, *Religion and Society.* See also Edward P. Stigant, "Wesleyan Methodism and Working-Class Radicalism in the North, 1792–1821," *Northern History* 6 (1971): 98-116.

29. David M. Thompson, *Nonconformity in the Nineteenth Century* (London: Routledge, 1972), 147-55. See also Bruce I. Coleman, *The Church of England in the Mid–Nineteenth Century* (London: Routledge, 1980), and John D. Gay, *The Geography of Religion in England* (London: Duckworth, 1971).

30. Mark A. Noll, *A History of Christianity in the United States and Canada* (Grand Rapids: Eerdmans, 1992), 153.

31. James C. Deming and Michael S. Hamilton, "Methodist Revivalism in France, Canada and the United States" in George A. Rawlyk and Mark A. Noll, eds., *Amazing Grace: Evangelicalism in Australia, Britain, Canada and the United States* (Grand Rapids: Eerdmans, 1993), 124-53.

thousand itinerant and lay preachers was servicing the fastest growing religious movement between the American Revolution and the Civil War.[32]

In the most recent history of Christianity in the United States, Mark Noll states that "the Protestant churches that flourished most decisively in the first half of the nineteenth century were the Baptists and the Methodists, the two bodies that succeeded in joining most efficiently a democratic appeal with effective leadership."[33] Similarly, Nathan Hatch in an important book calls this period of Methodist expansion "the democratization of American Christianity," which "has less to do with the specifics of polity and governance and more to do with the incarnation of the church into popular culture."[34] The popular religious movements of the early republic, in their refusal to defer to the clergy and learned theologians and in their willingness to take the religious experiences of ordinary people at face value, articulated a profoundly democratic spirit. The rise of a popular religious culture of print, the place of origin of which shifted from eastern seaboard cities to west of the Alleghenies, together with the widespread dissemination of personal stories of transforming religious experience, further contributed to the notion that the religion of the people no longer depended upon clerical mediation.

The style of religious communication and worship also changed. There was a move away from refined sermons of doctrinal exposition to populist addresses employing humor, sarcasm, and popular wisdom. Similarly, the content and expression of religious hymns, ballads, and verse became more accessible to popular taste. "Better than any other source, popular poems and songs capture the force of the early republic's populism," states Hatch, "they translate theological concepts into language of the marketplace, personalize theological abstractions, deflate the pretension of privileged church leaders, and instill hope and confidence in popular collective action."[35] The most common themes are anticlericalism, anti-Calvinism, antiformalism, anticonfessionalism, and antielitism. Empowerment was from God, knowledge was from the scriptures, salvation was available to all, and the spirit was manifested—not in structures and ecclesiastical

---

32. Nathan O. Hatch, *The Democratization of American Christianity* (New Haven: Yale University Press, 1989).

33. Noll, *History of Christianity*, 153.

34. Hatch, *Democratization of American Christianity*, 9.

35. Ibid., 227.

order, but in freedom and heart religion. There were, of course, raw edges to populist religious enthusiasm. Frenetic revivalism, apocalypticism, and sectarian fragmentation were all in evidence as an energetic lay leadership of both men and women struggled free from the control of traditional religious structures. Methodism, with a relatively coherent Wesleyan theology and with its distinctive combination of ecclesiastical authoritarianism and connectional discipline, was in a good position to accommodate popular enthusiasm without capitulating to its most bizarre manifestations. The paradox at the heart of Methodism in the United States in this period is of the creation of an authoritarian religious structure empowered by the authority of the people—an egalitarian spiritual message that did not result in democratic ecclesiastical structures. Methodism in the United States after the Revolution was therefore a form of popular religion that successfully attacked social, ecclesiastical, and professional elites rather than a genuine movement of political or ecclesiastical democracy. How then is this remarkable growth of Methodism to be explained?

As with explanations for the growth of English Methodism in the same period, historians of American Methodism have approached the problem of causality from a bewildering, but by no means mutually exclusive, variety of perspectives. An older generation of scholars, whose work is in danger of being ignored entirely by their more conceptually fertile successors, drew attention (partly from motives of self-interest and inherited pride in a great religious tradition) to Methodism as a civilizing and ordering movement in a disorderly and potentially savage environment. Hence William Warren Sweet, writing mostly in the 1950s, painted a picture of Methodism as a tiered structure of moral courts supervised by a self-educated and disciplined cadre of local and itinerant preachers. Even the apparent wildness of frontier camp meetings had, according to Sweet, an internal discipline imposed by ritual, architecture, hymn singing, and even spring shoots of literacy in a predominantly noisy setting. "Frontier Methodism was far more solidly based than is usually pictured," he wrote, "it was by no means all froth. The long lists of books, Bibles, hymn books, Disciplines, and church periodicals sold to the people by the circuit-riders, all of whom were agents for the Methodist Book Concern, is evidence that the amount of religious instruction afforded the people of the frontier was not inconsiderable."[36] There are clear echoes here of the work of Robert Wearmouth, the distinguished historian of English Methodism and working-class political movements in the nineteenth century. Writing in the period from the 1930s to the 1950s, Wearmouth, in the words of Harold Laski, showed "that the psychological influence of Methodism was to teach its votaries self-confidence, the ability to organize and the ability to formulate their ideas."[37] Methodism was thus the midwife of social and political progress by bringing self-discipline, order, and organizational skills to the working classes of early industrial England. For Wearmouth and Sweet, therefore, Methodism was explicitly a movement of moral and social discipline, which appealed to those in search of an ordered community against the confusion of early industrialization in England and the chaos of the frontier in North America.

That Methodism could serve such functions is not seriously in doubt. There are important local studies of Methodism on both sides of the Atlantic that have shown in a more sophisticated way how popular Protestantism could impose a degree of cultural order on its adherents.[38] But there is another side to the story of early Methodist expansion that does not show up in such tidy categories. The white heat, passion, physical prostrations, and sheer "noise" of the early Methodist revivals were not, on a superficial level at least, characteristics associated with order and civility. Compare, for example, the following contemporaneous and hostile descriptions of Methodist revivals in Yorkshire and North Carolina at the turn of the century:

36. William W. Sweet, *Religion in the Development of American Culture 1765–1840* (New York: Scribners, 1952), 150. See also Sweet, *Methodism in American History* (Nashville: Abingdon Press, 1953). For an assessment of Sweet's strengths and weaknesses see Kenneth E. Rowe, "Counting the Converts: Progress Reports as Church History," in Russell E. Richey and Kenneth E. Rowe, eds., *Rethinking Methodist History: A Bicentennial Historical Consultation* (Nashville: Kingswood Books, 1985), 11-17.

37. The comment is taken from a review by J. Harold Laski of Robert F. Wearmouth, *Methodism and the Working-Class Movements of England 1800–1850* (London: Epworth Press, 1937) in *The New Statesman and Nation* (n.p., n.d.). Wearmouth was a prolific writer on all aspects of the impact of Methodism on the English working classes. See Wearmouth *Methodism and the Common People of the Eighteenth Century* (London: Epworth Press, 1945); *Some Working-Class Movements of the Nineteenth Century* (London: Epworth Press, 1948); *Methodism and the Struggle of the Working Classes* (Leicester: Leicester University Press, 1954); *The Social and Political Influence of Methodism in the Twentieth Century* (London: Epworth Press, 1957); and *Methodism and the Trade Unions* (London: Epworth Press, 1959).

38. Curtis D. Johnson, *Islands of Holiness: Rural Religion in Upstate New York 1790–1860* (Ithaca, N.Y.: Cornell University Press, 1989); Obelkevich, *Religion and Rural Society*. See also John Rule, "Methodism, Popular Beliefs and Village Culture in Cornwall, 1800–50," in Robert D. Storch, ed., *Popular Culture and Custom in Nineteenth-Century England* (London: Croom Helm, 1982): 48-70. For a bibliography of other local studies of British Methodism, particularly in an urban setting, see Davies et al., *History of the Methodist Church* 4:744-45.

Their meetings are frequently noisy and long continued, often till midnight, frequently till morning. It is not unusual for persons to be crying out in distress in various parts of the chapel, and others praying for them. Now a number of stout fellows, kneeling around a sinner in distress, cry aloud, "Come Lord Jesus, come quickly." Anon, the captive being set free, they seem to shake the very house with crying, "Glory be to God." The noise and confusion sometimes are very great, and one could wish it otherwise. . . . They had gone beyond all bounds of decency, such screaming and bawling I never heard. Divided into small companies in different parts of the chapel, some singing, others praying, others praising, clapping of hands, etc., all was confusion and uproar. I was struck with amazement and consternation.[39]

About a week past there was a methodist conference in this place which lasted 7 or 8 days & nights with very little intermission, during which there was a large concourse of people of various colors, classes & such, assembled for various purposes. Confusion, shouting, praying, singing, laughing, talking, amorous engagements, falling down, kicking, squealing and a thousand other ludicrous things prevailed most of the time and frequently of nights, all at once—In short, it was the most detestable farcical scene that ever I beheld.[40]

American scholars, on the whole, have been more sensitive interpreters of what is going on in such gatherings than their British counterparts for whom such "events" have been a more marginal expression within the English religious tradition than has been the case in North America. Donald Mathews, for example, in his creative exploration of the "psychodynamics of orality" in Methodist revivals concludes that it was preaching and its manifold congregational responses "that actually brought the interior life of each person out into a communal sharing of the drama of salvation and commitment."[41] The "liberty" of the New Birth and the shared enthusiasm of the community of the faithful were, literally, "sensible experiences"

39. Thomas Entwistle, *Memoir of the Reverend Joseph Entwistle* (London: Wesleyan Conference Office, 1867), 111-12. See John Baxter, "The Great Yorkshire Revival 1792–6: A Study of Mass Revival Among the Methodists," *A Sociological Yearbook of Religion in Britain* 7 (1974): 46-76; David Luker, "Revivalism in Theory and Practice: the Case of Cornish Methodism," *Journal of Ecclesiastical History* 37, no. 4 (1986): 603-19; John M. Turner, *Conflict and Reconciliation: Studies in Methodism and Ecumenism in England 1740–1982* (London: Epworth Press, 1985); and Hempton, *Methodism and Politics*, 92-98, 277-78.

40. Thomas B. Houghton to James Iredell Jr., 2 February 1807, James Iredell Papers, Duke University. In Donald G. Mathews, "Evangelical America—the Methodist Ideology," in *Perspectives*, 19.

41. Ibid., 20-24.

that translated the intensity of private faith into the most sensuously prolific of public encounters—the revival meeting. E. P. Thompson, in his work on English revivalism, thought that human sexuality was at the heart of such experiences, as did many contemporary observers; but why should sexuality be the only available category for the expression and interpretation of profoundly sensuous experiences? Some fresh light has been shed on this problem by the new historical writing of women who were, after all, allegedly the chief "victims" of the psychosexual peculiarities of Methodist revivalism. Diane Lobody has suggested that it was "the very subversive spirituality of Methodism" that "coaxed women into speech" and that the strikingly eclectic use of the word *liberty* in early Methodist discourse is not merely incidental, but is suggestive of much deeper resonance for both men and women. Women were therefore "the hearers, the receivers, and the bearers of liberty, just as the preachers were."[42] Popular religious enthusiasm, for women and men, was as much a vehicle for personal freedom as it was for social discipline or social control.

What this brief discussion of the carnival of the revival meeting has tried to show is that, notwithstanding the proper emphasis on discipline and order in Methodist spirituality brought out by Sweet, Wearmouth, and others, there was also a sensuous and subversive dimension to it, which lay at the heart of the raw emotions described in the accounts of revival in South Carolina and Yorkshire. What is particularly striking about such accounts is the sheer vitality and variety of oral and bodily expression that onlookers at the time, and religious historians ever since, have struggled unsuccessfully to interpret. The repeated use of the word *confusion* by contemporary observers shows the extent to which the traditional boundary lines of time, gender, decency, noise, and emotional restraint were blown away by the libertarian implications of the New Birth. There is also a powerful element of mutuality in this experience, which was sustained by the corporate expressions of praise and prayer as they were transmitted through hymn singing and communal "noise" of all kinds.

The attempt to come to terms with the interior dialectic of

---

42. Diane H. Lobody, " 'That Language Might Be Given Me': Women's Experience in Early Methodism," in *Perspectives*, 134; and Lobody, "Lost in the Ocean of Love: the Spiritual Writings of Catherine Livingstone Garrettson," in Richey and Rowe, *Rethinking Methodist History*, 175-84. See also A. Gregory Schneider, *The Way of the Cross Leads Home: The Domestication of American Methodism* (Bloomington: Indiana University Press, 1993).

Methodist experience—its combination of spiritual freedom and order—goes some way toward explaining what kind of a movement it was in its pioneering phase, but it does not in itself explain the geographical and chronological patterns of Methodist expansion. In each country in which it took root, Methodism never attracted more than a minority of the host population and was clearly stronger in some areas than in others. The English pattern has been alluded to already, but Methodist expansion in the United States was also quite distinctive. On the eve of the American War of Independence, Maryland and New Jersey accounted for more than half of the entire Methodist membership in the colonies, a fact which caused Edwin Gaustad to conclude that "if Methodism had not been able to adapt itself readily to the conditions of the settled East, it would never have survived to share so boldly in the conquest of the beckoning West."[43] By 1790 Methodist societies were most thick on the ground around the Chesapeake, in northern New Jersey, eastern Connecticut, and the Albany Valley, and there were significant beginnings in southern Virginia, northern North Carolina, and eastern and western South Carolina. There were also considerable numbers of African American Methodists in Maryland, Virginia, and North Carolina. Some of the reasons for the remarkable success of Methodism in the Chesapeake area have been clearly presented by William H. Williams in his classic regional study of the Delmarva Peninsula.[44] Methodism developed a formidable ascendancy in this area due to the compelling power of its message, its attraction to primarily English settlers (especially in the wake of the American Revolution when the appeal of Episcopalianism diminished for obvious reasons), its disciplined espousal of an alternative values system, and its ability to attract African Americans and women in large numbers. In short, Methodism, by substituting "seriousness for frivolity, co-operation for competition, compassion for brutality, and egalitarianism for deference," was a religion ideally suited to the social, political, and economic conditions of rural Delmarva toward the end of the eighteenth century. Moreover, the Methodist ascendancy around the Chesapeake gave the movement a solid base from which to move south and west, and, according to Russell Richey, enabled it to establish a religious

43. Edwin S. Gaustad, *Historical Atlas of Religion in America* (New York: Harper & Row, 1976), 76.
44. William H. Williams, *The Garden of American Methodism: The Delmarva Peninsula, 1769–1820* (Wilmington, Del.: Scholarly Resources, 1984), and Williams, "The Attraction of Methodism: The Delmarva Peninsula as a Case Study, 1769–1820," in *Perspectives*, 31–45.

and cultural pattern that was subsequently exported inland to the demographically growing states of Middle America.[45] Part of that pattern was a characteristically Methodist ambivalence about race and gender. Although Methodism's early repudiation of slavery was not sustained, and although women preachers were thin on the ground, there were nevertheless sufficient opportunities for both African Americans and women to find an emotionally satisfying niche within a movement led and directed principally by white men.

Methodists were able to reap a particularly rich crop among African Americans in the southern states in the half century after the American Revolution.[46] As with other Methodist traditions, mission, revivalism, and migration helped spread African American Methodism. Black members comprised 9 percent of American Methodists in 1786 and over 20 percent by 1810. By then, the thirty-five thousand or so black members of the Methodist church were mostly slaves. Moreover, the membership figures almost certainly underestimate the strength of African American Methodism. Seekers, children, and hearers were not counted in the figures, nor were the many thousands who were not allowed to become members of societies by their white masters.[47] Methodism clearly benefitted from its early denunciation of slavery and from its more radical approach to race relations than the majority of southern whites was prepared to countenance. But there was more to it than that. Methodism offered African American slaves a sense of community, an extended family, an opportunity to meet neighbors, and a way of building some kind of ethnic solidarity. To social function was added the attractiveness of an alternative value system in which African Americans could help one another sustain a dignified morality based on freedom of choice as against the ruthless compulsion and ethical corruption of slavery. But all this still bypasses the essentially religious content of African American spirituality and its emphasis on revival, conversion, experience, and the Bible. The evidence suggests a particular commitment to the ecstatic rituals of conversion and baptism and, at least for some, an eager aspiration for entire sanctification. After all, nothing could

45. Russell E. Richey, "The Southern Accent of American Methodism," *Methodist History* 27 (1988): 3-24. See also his essay included in this volume.

46. Sylvia R. Frey and Betty Wood, *Come Shouting to Zion: African American Protestantism in the American South and British Caribbean to 1830* (Chapel Hill: University of North Carolina Press, 1998), 118-48.

47. Cynthia Lynn Lyerly, *Methodism and the Southern Mind 1770–1810* (New York: Oxford University Press, 1998), 56.

offer a more complete recasting of the slave's sense of diminished humanity than the possibility of Christian perfection on earth as in heaven.

The creative attempt by Lawrence Levine to come to terms with the revivalism of the antebellum slaves through their spiritual and sacred songs shows a close match with enduring aspects of Methodist spirituality. The religious revivals that swept large numbers of slaves and free blacks into the Methodist movement were based upon "a practical (not necessarily theological) Arminianism": salvation is open to all, not a select few; the songs are dominated not by feelings of depravity or unworthiness, but of personal worth and affirmation; there is less concentration upon the terrors of hell than on the deliverance of a chosen people; and the emphasis is not so much on escape from this world as an embattled engagement with it.[48] Moreover, it is important to appreciate the culture and context of spirituals. They were rhythmical, improvisational, communal, and repetitive. They gave new life to old biblical narratives and treated biblical heroes and antiheroes as personal friends or enemies. The spiritual songs of African Americans not only helped mediate the transition from Africa to America, but also built mental bridges between white populist evangelical enthusiasm and black oppressed humanity. It is as inaccurate to say that the bridges never went down as it is to suggest they never existed, for there was, especially before the 1820s, more cross-fertilization between African American and Euro-American popular evangelicalism than some accounts would allow.[49]

The culture of African American religiosity was unashamedly oral and physical. Although literacy was a pearl of great price among pre– and post–Civil War African Americans, its subversive potential was enjoyed by less than 10 percent of the black population.[50] But language was far from unimportant to the rest. Vigorous traditions of orality underpin African American spirituality, from the Motherwit tradition of transmitting female wisdom and knowledge to the extensive memorization of the Bible by black preachers; and from the powerful rhythms of the ring-shout tradition to the ecstatic and exotic

---

48. Lawrence W. Levine, "Slave Songs and Slave Consciousness: An Exploration in Neglected Sources," in Timothy E. Fulop and Albert J. Raboteau, eds., *African-American Religion: Interpretive Essays in History and Culture* (New York: Routledge, 1997), 75.

49. See Alonzo Johnson and Paul Jersild, eds., *"Ain't Gonna Lay My 'Ligion Down": African American Religion in the South* (Columbia: University of South Carolina Press, 1996), 4 and 91.

50. Janet Duitsman Cornelius, *When I Can Read My Title Clear: Literacy, Slavery, and Religion in the Antebellum South* (Columbia: University of South Carolina Press, 1991), 9.

orality of the camp meetings. Noise sometimes militated against secrecy in the "brush arbor" tradition of black spirituality as African Americans sought out sacred spaces away from the offended ears of plantation disciplinarians. One young girl recollected how the elders would go among the people and "put dey han' over dey mouf an' some times put a clof in day mouf an' say 'spirit don talk so loud or de patterol break us up.' "[51]

Cynthia Lynn Lyerly has shown how the early countercultural thrust of Methodism in its religious empowerment of African Americans, slaves, and women capitulated by the early 1800s to the male codes of honor, which emphasized wealth, social status, and conventional gender and color boundaries. Methodism in the South, which had never been able to ignore its cultural context, eventually capitulated to it. But African American evangelical spirituality both predated and survived white Methodism's accommodation to its culture. Although there was no mistaking the narrow ground of racial inferiority to which they had been confined, African Americans were still able to take control of their own classes, societies, and churches. Remarkably, in the main, their religion was employed neither as mere consolation for social injustice nor as a foundation for millenarian speculation, but had an altogether more positive and liberating effect on their lives. The oft repeated idea that Methodism was a dehumanizing sop for the oppressed, whether the white proletariat in England or African slaves in America, has to explain away a good deal of evidence to the contrary.[52] Sensitive observers of how Methodism could challenge white patriarchal authority in households, churches, and broader social settings show just how revolutionary the evangelical message could appear.[53]

Methodism not only sank deep roots within the southern states, but also its powerful itinerant-led expansionism ensured that it was well placed to take advantage of the opportunities presented by the western march of the frontier. By 1800 the Methodist system had been established in western Pennsylvania, Kentucky, and Tennessee and had begun to push its way north into New England. Fifty years later there were more Methodist than any other churches in twenty states of the union, a proportion unmatched by any other religious denom-

---

51. Fulop and Raboteau, *African-American Religion*, 76-77.
52. Ibid., 89-130. See also, Albert J. Raboteau, *A Fire in the Bones: Reflections on African-American Religious History* (Boston: Beacon Press, 1995).
53. For a brilliant description of these processes at work see Christine Leigh Heyrman, *Southern Cross: The Beginnings of the Bible Belt* (New York: Alfred A. Knopf, 1997).

ination.[54] The seventh census of the United States, carried out in 1850, conveys the extent of Methodist success.[55] There were 38,183 buildings returned as used for purposes of religious worship in the United States, supplying accommodation for 14,270,139 persons. Methodists accounted for just over a third of all churches and the Baptists for about a quarter. Thus, the combined numbers of Methodist and Baptist churches comfortably outstripped all the other churches put together. Even allowing for the fact that Presbyterian, Congregational, Episcopal, and Roman Catholic churches were mostly larger than their more humble Methodist and Baptist counterparts, the proportions are still significant. What is equally striking about the figures, by comparison with the British Isles, is that although Methodists were somewhat underrepresented in all of the New England states and somewhat overrepresented in the southern and midwestern states, they had nevertheless achieved a remarkable national coverage. Methodism was therefore not a regional denomination in the United States in the way it undoubtedly was in Britain and Ireland. From that perspective, its ability to influence national culture was even greater than in the British Isles.

A remarkable revolution in religious practice had taken place in the United States by the middle of the nineteenth century, but the gnawing question *why* still remains to be addressed. As with the historiography of British Methodism in the same period, there has been an almost unseemly rush for a single narrative, the "big idea," within which Methodist growth in all kinds of different social and cultural contexts can be interpreted. The most intellectually influential idea is that of the market revolution, and its most striking presentation is from the pen of Charles Sellers in his book on Jacksonian America. The essence of the argument is that religious enthusiasm of the evangelical and Methodist kind was a way of managing the shock of the market. Methodism, in particular, became the main bearer of "antinomian universalism" (as against the grim, sovereign selectivity of Calvinism), and established a system at odds with the competitive, consumerist, flesh-ridden, usurious, and egotistical values of the market place. Methodists were thus spiritual "come-outers"—millennial visionaries—in a world increasingly at odds with their spiritual values. Only later, and partly as a result of the "ethical athleticism" of

---

54. Gaustad, *Historical Atlas*, 43-82.
55. J. D. B. DeBow, *A Statistical View of the United States Being a Compendium of the Seventh Census* (Washington, D.C.: Beverly Tucker, 1854), 132-45.

Methodism's theology of entire sanctification (echoes here of Thompson), did Methodists capitulate to the capitalist imperatives of the market. "Eventually capitalist transformation," wrote Sellers, "would obliterate from the memory of both great popular denominations [the Methodists and the Baptists] their origins in a massive cultural mobilization against the market and its ways."[56]

Religious historians will blink and rub their eyes with puzzlement at Sellers's cavalier and often inappropriate use of theological terminology, but a far more serious problem is that his concept of the market as applied to religion explains at once too much and too little; too much in the sense that his sequential approach to Methodism and the market (from early repudiation to later accommodation) simply does not do justice to the evidence in both Britain and America that early Methodists were by no means consistently pious opponents of enterprise and competition. The failure of Wesley's early experiments with the primitive church's ideal of sharing resources, along with his almost hysterical warnings against the perils of accumulation, show how inured many of his followers were to the vision of material renunciation.[57] In both Britain and the United States, Methodists exhibit a spectrum of opinion from radical suspicion of the grinding ethics of the market—as represented by men like Stilwell and Hersey in the United States and Stephens and Skevington in Britain—to a welcome embrace of the opportunities afforded by an expanding economy.[58] That there were more of the latter breeds of Methodists as a proportion of the whole by the middle of the nineteenth century than there had been at the start of it is not seriously in doubt on either side of the Atlantic. But it would be a mistake to conclude from such a proposition that Methodism as a religious movement was either a puller or a pusher in some kind of metaphorical tug of war with the values of the market. Indeed, if secession is the ultimate litmus test of

---

56. Charles Sellers, *The Market Revolution: Jacksonian America, 1815–1846* (New York: Oxford University Press, 1991), 157-61.

57. The most authoritative discussion of Wesley's views on the ownership and distribution of property is to be found in John Walsh, "John Wesley and the Community of Goods," in Keith Robbins, ed., *Protestant Evangelicalism: Britain, Ireland, Germany and America, c. 1750–c. 1950*, Studies in Church History, Subsidia 7 (Oxford: B. Blackwell, 1990), 25-50; and Walsh, "Methodism and the Common People," in Raphael Samuel, ed., *People's History and Socialist Theory* (London: Routledge, 1981), 354-62.

58. William R. Sutton, *Journeymen for Jesus: Evangelical Artisans Confront Capitalism in Jacksonian Baltimore* (University Park: Pennsylvania State University Press, 1998). For comparisons with popular politics in Britain, see Hempton, *Methodism and Politics*, 208-16. See also, Geoffrey E. Milburn, "Piety, Profit and Paternalism: Methodists in Business in the North-East of England, c. 1760–1920," *Proceedings of the Wesley Historical Society* 44 (1983): 45-92; and David Martin, "Faith, Flour and Jam," *Times Literary Supplement* (1 April 1983): 329-30.

strength of feeling within the Methodist polity, embourgeoisement stirred up a great deal more trouble in Britain than in the United States. The reason for that is not that the two Methodisms were essentially different species, but that class conflict and establishment religion operated far more powerfully in the British environment than they did across the Atlantic.[59]

If Sellers's application of the market to popular evangelicalism attempts to explain too much, it also succeeds, because of its essentially *economic* imperatives, in explaining too little. Where the metaphor of the market really does apply to American Methodism (to a much greater degree than its British counterpart) is in the realm of denominational competition on the one hand and the marketing of religion itself on the other. The Methodists not only engaged in cutthroat competition with the Baptists and other popular enthusiasts for the souls of the masses, but the very fact of doing so, in the words of Lawrence Moore, "committed revivalism to a market logic and ultimately to market strategies."[60] Moreover, whereas the emotional heat of American Methodism remained hotter for longer than its British sister movement, Americans were also better (and still remain so) at presenting popular religion as a form of mass entertainment. They had not the same neurotic fear of vulgarity and disorder as obsessed British Christians of all denominations in the nineteenth century. Methodism, as a religious movement rooted in itinerancy and conversionism, and with a structure designed for growth and flexibility, had therefore more to gain than to lose from the market revolution. But, as the preceding discussion has tried to elucidate, the cultural exchanges that took place in both British and American Methodism in the early nineteenth century do not easily yield their secrets to the crude application of economic metaphors.

59. Benjamin Gregory, *Side-Lights on the Conflicts of Methodism 1827–52* (London, 1898); John H. S. Kent, *The Age of Disunity* (London: Epworth Press, 1966); Robert Currie, *Methodism Divided* (London: Faber & Faber, 1968); John C. Bowmer, *Pastor and People* (London: Epworth Press, 1975); David A. Gowland, *Methodist Secessions: The Origins of Free Methodism in Three Lancashire Towns* (Manchester: Manchester University Press, 1979); John T. Wilkinson, "The Rise of Other Methodist Traditions," in Davies et al., *History of the Methodist Church*, 2:276-329. For interpretations located more distinctly in the social and political conditions of the period see Ward, *Religion and Society*, 236-78 and Hempton, *Methodism and Politics*, 197-208.

60. R. Laurence Moore, *Selling God: American Religion in the Marketplace of Culture* (New York: Oxford University Press, 1994), 64; and Richard J. Carwardine, "'Antinomians and Arminians': Methodists and the Market Revolution," in Melvyn Stokes and Stephen Conway, eds., *The Market Revolution in America: Social, Political, and Religious Expressions, 1800–1880* (Charlottesville: University Press of Virginia, 1996), 282-307.

Another approach to the problem of accounting for the remarkable growth of Methodism, particularly in the United States, is to borrow explanations of processes of social change from the sociologists. In a rapidly expanding society like the United States with its relatively fluid and inadequate structures of institutional control, there was virtually unlimited social space—without hardened distinctions of social class or religious denomination—within which dynamic new religious movements could take root.[61] Methodism, by appealing both to the authenticity of religious experience and to the disciplines of class and church membership, offered an attractive combination of individual assurance and corporate responsibility for those experiencing the fearful exhilaration of rapid social change. In the words of Richard Carwardine, Methodism, within a generation, became the largest religious denomination within the United States due to the "appeal of an Arminian theology whose individualistic, democratic, and optimistic emphases found a positive response in an expanding society where traditional patterns of authority and deference were succumbing to egalitarian challenge."[62] The parallels with England, and indeed Wales where evangelical nonconformity flourished in the expanding crevices of an industrial frontier society, are striking.[63]

Nathan Hatch's recent attempt to assess the significance of American Methodism in four propositions could therefore, with minor modifications, be applied with equal validity to England.[64] In both countries Methodist reconstruction of the church along voluntary lines contributed to a more pluralistic and competitive religious environment. Equally, in both countries, Methodism was able to construct a vernacular religiosity that could appeal, at least in the short term, both to those who were at the raw edges of social change and to those who stood to profit from it. Finally, Methodism, as the sheer complexity and variety of its political expressions in England and the United States clearly demonstrate, was an infinitely flexible and adaptable religious species. Methodists were to be found supporting each of the main political parties in both countries in the 1830s and 1840s, though the majority was democrat in the United States and liberal in England. Moreover, the various pressures thrown up by anti-

61. Deming and Hamilton, "Methodist Revivalism," 127-32.

62. Richard Carwardine, *Transatlantic Revivalism: Popular Evangelicalism in Britain and America, 1790–1865* (Westport, Conn.: Greenwood Press, 1978), 10.

63. See Philip Jenkins, *A History of Modern Wales 1536–1990* (London: Longman, 1992), ch. 10; Ieuan G. Jones, *Communities* (Dyed: Gomer Press, 1987); and Glanmor Williams, *Religion, Language and Nationality in Wales* (Cardiff: University of Wales Press, 1979).

64. Nathan O. Hatch, "The Puzzle of American Methodism," *Church History* 63, no. 2 (1994): 175-89; reprinted as chapter 1 in this volume.

Catholicism, legal disabilities, moral reformism, and social, ethnic, and denominational competition produced a rich mosaic of political allegiances.[65] Environment, context, and locale shaped (and were shaped by) Methodism. It was in recognition of that reality that I stated back in 1984 that, notwithstanding the well-known homogenous features of the Methodist revival in England, there were in fact "many Methodisms in many places at many times."[66] Those who prefer their religious history encased in tidy theories will no doubt find this dispiriting, but sooner or later it will have to be admitted that the capacity for variety and adaptability within the Methodist tradition in Britain and the United States was one of its most marketable features. It proved to be a very adaptable species, capable of reflecting the religious and social characteristics of the regions in which it took root.[67] It swept over rural areas, established footholds in towns and cities, and appealed to sections of populations whose other interests were sometimes antithetical to one another. Above all it changed over time, not monochromatically as is often assumed, but in relation to its date of arrival in a particular locale, and the speed with which it acquired social and cultural power.

Comparison of English and North American Methodism

In both England and the United States Methodism not only grew faster than the total population in the first half of the nineteenth century, but its growth resulted in a dramatic reconfiguration of the old denominational order. It nevertheless remains to be explained why both the numerical growth and cultural penetration of Methodism in the United States was so much more dramatic than in England.[68] It must be stated at the outset that there is a deep-seated disagreement among scholars of English Methodism about the reasons for the limits and the deceleration of Methodist growth. Some emphasize the part played by the preachers and wealthy chapel trustees of Bunting's generation who pushed inexorably for connectional control at the

---

65. Richard J. Carwardine, *Evangelicals and Politics in Antebellum America* (New Haven: Yale University Press, 1993), 113-32.

66. Hempton, *Methodism and Politics*, 230.

67. For an excellent example of how this can be worked out for a particular region see Lyerly, *Methodism and the Southern Mind*.

68. See the explanations offered by Hatch, "Puzzle of American Methodism," 187. See also the pioneering attempt to account for Methodist expansion in America in the late eighteenth century by Dee E. Andrews, *The Methodists and Revolutionary America, 1760–1800: The Shaping of an Evangelical Culture* (Princeton, N.J.: Princeton University Press, 2000).

expense of ranters, radicals, and revivalists.[69] As Methodism became more centralized, more bureaucratic, more clerical, and more respectable, it became less attractive to the increasingly class-conscious proletariat of early Victorian cities. Others, with a more jaundiced view of the potential religiosity of the English poor, combined with a much less jaundiced view of those who had to run the Wesleyan connection in the early nineteenth century, take the view that the Methodists could not have achieved very much more than they did.[70] The most insightful studies of urban Methodism incline more to the former view than to the latter.[71] But perhaps the main reason for the relative weakness of Methodism in England by comparison with the United States was a combination of the remarkable resilience of the frail old established church and the inability of early Victorian Methodism to articulate the class and cultural aspirations of most English urban workers. The former effectively denied Methodism a truly national coverage and access to the emerging mechanisms of welfare policy, whereas the latter set boundaries to its social appeal and political utility.

The Church of England was a formidable competitor for English Methodism, for it had a centuries-old parish system and deep traditions of popular devotion (and indeed a peculiarly English and Anglican lack of devotion) that helped balance its well-known structural and pastoral deficiencies.[72] Moreover, Anglicanism in places such as Lancashire and the West Riding displayed a capacity to recover from early shocks to become modest Anglican strongholds.[73]

69. William R. Ward, "The Religion of the People and the Problem of Control, 1790–1830," *Studies in Church History* 8 (1972): 237-57; and Hempton, *Methodism and Politics*, 85-115.

70. John H. S. Kent, "The Wesleyan Methodists to 1849," in Davies et al., *History of the Methodist Church* 2:213-75; and Kent, *The Age of Disunity*.

71. The best treatment of urban Methodism in the north of England remains Ward, *Religion and Society*. See also David Colin Dews, "Methodism in Leeds from 1791 to 1861," 2 vols. (M. Phil. Dissertation, University of Bradford, 1984); Gowland, *Methodist Secessions*; and Theodore Koditschek, *Class Formation and Urban Industrial Society: Bradford 1750–1850* (Cambridge: Cambridge University Press, 1990), chap. 10.

72. John Walsh, Colin Haydon, and Stephen Taylor, eds., *The Church of England c. 1689–c. 1833: From Toleration to Tractarianism* (Cambridge: Cambridge University Press, 1993); Peter Virgin, *The Church in an Age of Negligence: Ecclesiastical Structure and Problems of Church Reform 1700–1840* (Cambridge: James Clark, 1989); and David Hempton, "Religion in British Society 1740–1790," in Jeremy Black, ed., *British Politics from Walpole to Pitt 1742–1789* (London: Macmillan, 1990), 201-21.

73. Mark Smith, *Religion in Industrial Society: Oldham and Saddleworth 1740–1865* (Oxford: Clarendon Press, 1994); David Hempton, "Bickersteth, Bishop of Ripon: The Episcopate of a Mid-Victorian Evangelical," *Northern History* 17 (1981): 183-202. For more general treatments of urbanization and religion in Britain see Steve Bruce, ed., *Religion and Modernization: Sociologists and Historians Debate the Secularization Thesis* (Oxford: Clarendon Press, 1992); Hugh McLeod, *Religion and Irreligion in Victorian England* (Bangor, Gwynedd: Headstart History, 1993); and Callum G. Brown, "The Mechanism of Religious Growth in Urban Societies: British Cities Since the Eighteenth Century," in Hugh McLeod, ed., *European Religion in the Age of Great Cities* (London: Routledge, 1995), 239-62.

Patriotism, paternalism, and privilege gave Anglicanism access to control mechanisms that were simply not available to any comparable church in North America.[74] At the other end of the scale of piety, Methodism also experienced formidable competition from an alternative parish structure, in the shape of a centuries-old alehouse culture, which performed many of the same functions of sociability and management of information as American Methodism brought to western settlers. Americans were of course not free from the terrors of the demon drink and its institutional manifestations, but its role in the transmission of culture was not as powerful as it was in England. These external factors, together with the inexorable institutionalization of the English Methodist tradition, ensured that while Methodism was able to shake the old English denominational order to its foundations, it was unable to establish a nationwide hegemony of its own.

Methodism in the United States was also transformed from "a socially despised sect of the poor, 'the offscouring of all things,' into a respected denomination of some power and influence," but by mid-century it was the largest single denomination in the country and had a truly national constituency.[75] Moreover, far from struggling for cultural survival among large sections of the population, Methodism was the most numerous, if not always the most influential, tradition within a rampant evangelical Protestantism that Richard Carwardine and Nathan Hatch have argued in their different ways was the principal subculture in antebellum America.[76] Methodism in both Britain and the United States, perhaps because of its populist origins, world-denying piety, and suspicion of abstract theological debate, was more influential in shaping culture by stealth than by the display of a vigorous intellectual and social leadership. Unfortunately for Methodism, the same process happened in reverse.

The different patterns of Methodist growth in Britain and the United States were both reflected in the Canadian evangelical experience, which owed something to each of the other two countries. As the Canadian political economy was transformed by population migrations from the Old and New Worlds, Methodism appropriated something of the populist influence of the American republican

74. John Wolffe, *God and Greater Britain: Religion and National Life in Britain and Ireland 1843–1945* (London: Routledge, 1994); and Keith Robbins, *Nineteenth-Century Britain: Integration and Diversity* (Oxford: Clarendon Press, 1988), 63-96.

75. Carwardine, *Evangelicals and Politics*, 130-31.

76. Ibid., 1.

tradition and something of the reform impulse of British popular evangelicalism.[77] As the control mechanisms imposed by established churches and colonial governors proved hopelessly inadequate for the task of regulating Canadian society, ferociously revivalistic itinerants (both Baptist and Methodist) preached a gospel of individual salvation and communal piety that swept through the out-townships and rural areas of Canada between the American Revolution and the War of 1812.[78] There was little to stand in their way. The predominantly Anglican established churches responded with a disastrous mixture of arrogance, contempt, sporadic military and legal coercion, patient forbearance, and enlightened toleration. With local political culture less sophisticated in colonial Canada than in the postrevolutionary United States, radical evangelicalism brought not only religious revivalism, but also an alternative set of cultural experiences for those on the outer edges of the empire.[79] Popular evangelicalism supplied "firm and divinely sanctioned boundaries and co-ordinates in a society that was desperately searching for explicit boundaries and firm co-ordinates. For believers, moreover, there were new worship communities to which they could be attached—communities that provided fellowship, solace, and emotional support in times of crisis and disorientation."[80] By 1812, itinerant preachers, camp meetings, "a rage for dipping," and evangelicalism's genius for social reorganization had transformed the ecclesiastical landscape of the Canadas and the Maritimes.[81] But the landscape was not altered in the same way as it was in Britain or the United States. Canadian Protestantism was less imprinted with the politics of class conflict than the former, and was less prone to sectarian fragmentation and religious pluralism than the latter. What it shared with both, however, was a religious and cultural revolution promoted by populist preachers that eroded, more relentlessly than any political movement could have done, the hier-

77. Michael Gauvreau, "Protestantism Transformed: Personal Piety and the Evangelical Social Vision, 1815–1867," in George A. Rawlyk, ed., *The Canadian Protestant Experience 1760–1990* (Montreal: McGill-Queen's University Press, 1990), 48-97.

78. George A. Rawlyk, *The Canada Fire: Radical Evangelicalism in British North America 1775–1812* (Montreal: McGill-Queen's University Press, 1994), 102-40.

79. Nancy Christie, "'In these Times of Democratic Rage and Delusion': Popular Religion and the Challenge to the Established Order, 1760–1815," in Rawlyk, *Canadian Protestant Experience*, 9-47.

80. Rawlyk, *Canada Fire*, 121. See also, William Westfall, *Two Worlds: The Protestant Culture of Nineteenth-Century Ontario* (Montreal: McGill-Queen's University Press, 1989).

81. George A. Rawlyk, *Wrapped Up in God: A Study of Several Canadian Revivals and Revivalists* (Burlington, Ontario: Welch Publishing Company, 1988), and *Ravished by the Spirit: Religious Revivals, Baptists, and Henry Alline* (Montreal: McGill-Queen's University Press, 1984).

archical and establishmentarian foundations of colonial society. Canadian culture, as its historians have now demonstrated, was shaped more by the revivalistic pulses of its peripheries than by the ecclesiastical and military power of its core. Methodism, as in the other countries where it took root, was stronger in some areas (Upper Canada) than in others (the Maritimes), and "progressed" over time from raw enthusiasm to cultivated piety. It helped fire other denominations and traded creatively on the cultural exchanges (not least of personnel) between evangelicalism in Canada and the United States. In a not altogether harmonious partnership with the Baptists, Methodism reshaped the old denominational order and spread new forms of religious community through the ubiquitous utility of voluntary associations. Social divisions based on the saved and the unsaved, or the churched and the unchurched, came to mean as much as those based on ranks, orders, and degrees. In short, colonial society had been transformed. But as in Britain and the United States, Canadian Methodism's upward social mobility helped it make peace with the very establishments it had once so vigorously challenged.[82]

Methodism in Ireland and France

However one accounts for the respective strengths and weaknesses of North American and British Methodism, a dramatically less impressive pattern of Methodist expansion was evident in other parts of the North Atlantic world in the same period. This is particularly true of Ireland and France, whose social and political conditions proved much less receptive to the same kind of evangelical Arminianism as made such sweeping gains in England and North America. What accounts for the difference?

Methodism in Ireland took root initially in southern market towns along the routes of Wesley's preaching tours, but it then began to develop more strongly in the north of the country and in two quite specific areas in the southern and southwestern border counties of the province of Ulster.[83] The reasons given for Methodist growth by the preachers who produced it are the familiar Methodist cocktail of itinerant preaching, cell groups, love feasts, hymn singing, the spiritual

---

82. Westfall, *Two Worlds*, 50-81.
83. David Hempton and Myrtle Hill, *Evangelical Protestantism in Ulster Society 1740–1890* (London: Routledge, 1992); Hempton, "Methodism in Irish Society, 1770–1830," *Transactions of the Royal Historical Society*, 5th series, 36 (1986): 117-42.

influence of women, and manifold special providences, which played a vitally important role in persuading Methodists that God was indeed clearing the paths before them.[84] The Methodist emphases on conversion and free association brought new features to the Irish religious landscape, which until then had been dominated by churches—Roman Catholic, Church of Ireland, and Presbyterian—ministering to preassigned communities.[85] Such explanations do not do justice to the peculiar geographical and chronological pattern of Methodist expansion in Ireland. Growth was particularly rapid in the changing and expanding economy of southern Ulster in which a rough sectarian equilibrium between Protestants and Catholics led to increased competition for land, employment, and ultimately, for social and political power. These were also old centers of predominantly English settlement. Ward's statement that one of the reasons for the breakneck expansion of American Methodism was that it offered the English in America "a way of affirming their Englishness without being Anglican" has an obvious application to the English settlements of southern Ulster (echoes here of Delmarva).[86] Thus, in this part of Ireland a powerful mixture of economic competition, cultural and religious conflict, and ethnicity all played their part in the remarkable growth of Methodism at the turn of the century.

The chronology of Methodist growth is as important as its geography. The main growth spurt comes in the period 1770–1830, after which date the pace of growth slowed quite dramatically due to population migration, political conflict, and structural changes within the Methodist community itself. But the growth of Irish Methodism is also more volatile than that of English Methodism in the same period. A chart of annual growth rates shows intense pulses of revivalism at roughly twenty-year intervals, including a particularly dramatic surge in the years immediately after the Rebellion of the United Irishmen in 1798. As in England and the United States, there seems to

---

84. William Arthur, *The Life of Gideon Ouseley* (London: Wesleyan Conference Office, 1876); W. G. Campbell, *"The Apostle of Kerry," The Life of the Rev. Charles Graham* (Dublin: Moffat & Co., 1868); F. J. Cole, *The Cavalry Preachers* (Belfast: n.p., 1945); C. H. Crookshank, *A Methodist Pioneer: The Life and Labours of John Smith* (London: Wesleyan Conference Office, 1881); A. Stewart and G. Revington, *Memoir of the Life and Labours of the Rev. Adam Averell* (Dublin: Methodist Book Room, 1848). An even more revealing picture emerges from the letters of early itinerants and missionaries, which are unfortunately spread out between the Northern Ireland Public Record Office in Belfast, the School of Oriental and African Studies (Methodist missions) in London, and the John Rylands Library in Manchester.

85. David W. Miller, "Presbyterianism and 'Modernization' in Ulster," *Past and Present* 80 (1978): 66-90.

86. Ward, "Evangelical Revival in Eighteenth-Century Britain," 268.

be no very clear link between Methodist expansion and economic indices, and growth slows down after 1830 despite the increase of clerical manpower and the provision of more elaborate buildings.

In many accounts of Methodist growth in the British Isles and North America, the so-called endogenous and exogenous features are usually kept quite separate, even when both are alluded to, but it is increasingly clear that there is a symbiotic relationship between the two. In Ireland, for example, there is a correlation between the religious ideals of evangelical Arminianism and the cultural ideals of an expanding society, and between notions of religious improvement and social progress. In frequent displays of popular enlightenment chauvinism, Methodists expressed their sense of superiority over those allegedly enslaved either to Romish superstition or to the spiritual mediocrity of the established church. More prosaically, the cheapness and flexibility of the Methodist system was well adapted to a society undergoing profound social changes, and the connexional system facilitated the transfer of resources from wealthier urban congregations to sustain pioneer work in poorer rural areas.

As the class membership lists for southern Ulster make clear, Methodism grew spectacularly quickly in one of the last frontiers of the European Reformation at a time of acute sectarian competition. This both opened up space for its growth and development in the short term, and ultimately closed it down in the long term, as Irish Protestants became more nervous about eroding their homogeneity through denominational fragmentation. This is essentially why a large proportion of Irish Methodists chose to remain within the established church, and why Irish Methodism could find little growing space within areas controlled by the Roman Catholic and Presbyterian churches.

Methodist growth in France, though on a much smaller scale, has some interesting parallels with the pattern in Ireland. In the second quarter of the nineteenth century Methodism grew almost exclusively in the department of the Gard, the region with the strongest concentration of French Protestants.[87] Although Protestants comprised almost a third of the Gard's population, the proportion was even higher in the Cantons to the west and north of the city of Nimes and higher still in the Garrigues and the hills of the Cevennes. Although

---

87. I am indebted to Dr. James C. Deming for allowing me to read his doctoral dissertation entitled "Protestantism and Society in France: Revivalism and the French Reformed Church in the Department of the Gard, 1815–1848" (University of Notre Dame, 1989). See also James L. Osen, "The Theological Revival of the French Reformed Church, 1830–1852," *Church History* 37 (1968): 36–49.

primarily an agricultural region, the economic and social structure of the Gard was affected by major changes in the structure of its textile production and by the growth of mining and metallurgical industries. Demographic mobility further added to the capacity for social conflict, but despite these changes Gardois society was divided less by economic issues than by matters of religion. James Deming has shown that "though the Reformed community of the Gard experienced the same social and economic stresses that placed the social question at the forefront of public debate, religious identification continued to unite the Protestant merchant, artisan, peasant and landlord against the menace from the Catholic majority."[88]

The existence of old Moravian settlements in the Gard, a tradition of illuminism sustained through isolation and persecution, and the decline of Calvinism within the French Reformed Church all seemed to indicate that this region would yield significant fruit to the Methodist missionaries who labored there in the years after the Napoleonic Wars. Motivated in part by English chauvinist zeal to redeem the French from their secular excesses, and perhaps even from their residual Roman Catholicism, Methodist missionaries contributed valiantly to a spiritual awakening within Gardois Protestantism in the period from the mid-1830s to the mid-1850s. But when the dust settled, "four decades of Methodist preaching in France yielded a stagnant church of only 1200 members by 1857."[89] Why then were the gains so modest?

As was the case in Ireland, there was an initial desire to proselytize French Catholics, but this was never a practicable proposition. Many within the Reformed Church had no desire to antagonize French Catholics or to renew ancient hostilities. Moreover, as Methodism in France moved from a societary renewal movement with missionary support toward a more settled denomination, it created all sorts of tensions with the Reformed Church. As separatism bred denominational competition, it soon became obvious that the religious market was simply not large enough to accommodate new forms of Protestantism. A powerful combination of government restriction, French Reformed opposition, and popular antipathy further eroded the available space for French Methodism. In a cultural sense the French Reformed Church was as much of a religious establishment as the Irish Episcopal Church or indeed the Irish Presbyterian Church in its cultural heartland of northeastern Ulster. As one French Reformed

---

88. Deming, "Protestantism and Society," 53.
89. Deming and Hamilton, "Methodist Revivalism," 139.

pastor put it, "he did not want to see French Protestantism fracture into small sects without strength or means of existence."[90] In short, voluntarism and revivalism threatened the cultural homogeneity of French Protestantism that had been built up over centuries of determined opposition to Catholic assimilation and state persecution. The price of adopting Methodism was simply too high to pay. Methodism thus made a profound impact on the religious vitality of the Reformed Church, but it was able to carve out only a distinctly small niche for its own particular brand of religious enthusiasm.

Mark Noll in his survey of evangelical religion in North Atlantic societies in the age of revolution has written that "it was the presence of social crisis—compounded of political, intellectual, and often military upheaval—that created the circumstances in which evangelicalism rose to cultural influence."[91] Put another way, evangelical religion seemed to thrive in the expanding crevices and margins of societies undergoing profound change of one sort or another. In England, and more particularly in the United States and Canada, in the period after 1780 the social, cultural, and political space for Methodist expansion seemed almost unlimited. In England a complex of changes eroded both the social and cultural foundations of the confessional state and, crucially, its powers of religious coercion. In the United States and Canada a more flexible, demographically mobile, and pluralistic society offered immense potential for any religion that could combine an egalitarian appeal with an efficient organizational structure. In both Britain and North America religious revival "helped to create a situation of theological and religious pluralism, which was the minimum condition of any sort of progress."[92] In both areas the margins that Methodism was able to exploit were expanding, but the reverse was the case in Ireland and France where the crevices were old ones left over from the Reformation and from the settlement patterns of the sixteenth and seventeenth centuries. These crevices were temporarily widened in south Ulster and in the Gard region, largely as a result of new social tensions grafted on to old confessional conflicts, but the sheer weight of inherited cultural hegemonies soon closed them up. The available space, if anything, narrowed, and Methodism emerged as no more than the religion of an exotic minority.

90. Ibid., 147.
91. Noll, "Revolution and the Rise of Evangelical Social Influence," 113-36.
92. William R. Ward, "Reasonable Enthusiast," *Proceedings of the Wesley Historical Society* 47 (1990): 125-27.

Methodist Motives and Experiences

So far the analysis has concentrated on a comparative treatment of Methodist expansion in different parts of the North Atlantic world in the age of revolution. What is lacking in this, as in almost all historical accounts of Methodism, is some kind of investigation of the religious motives both of those who propagated its message and those who committed themselves to it. There is no lack of interest in the careers of the great leaders of the Methodist revival, but this has not filtered down, with a few distinguished exceptions, to those energetic foot soldiers of Methodist expansion, the itinerant and local preachers, and still less to the great mass of the laity.[93] Both the institutional historians of Methodism and their vigorous Marxist critics have shared a disconcerting diffidence in approaching the "boiling hot religion" of early evangelical enthusiasm.[94] One can understand why the cultural interpreters of Methodism in its twentieth-century forms would have little interest in recovering a potentially embarrassing past, but professional historians have less reason to be so selective. The problem, in essence, lies with the evidence—both in finding it, and in knowing what to do with it.

Methodism, although ultimately the bearer of literacy and self-discipline in almost all the geographical areas it penetrated, was, in its pioneering phase, a movement characterized more by orality and physical expression. It was also assiduous in its record keeping, but the records it kept, for obvious reasons, had more to do with the stationing of preachers, the listing of members, and the building of churches than with the chronicling of experience in class meetings, love feasts, or camp meetings. But Methodist experience, as Edward Thompson shrewdly observed a generation ago, is at the heart of the matter.

---

93. Examples of good recent biographies of revival leaders include Henry Rack, *Reasonable Enthusiast: John Wesley and the Rise of Methodism* (London: Epworth Press, 1989); and Harry S. Stout, *The Divine Dramatist: George Whitefield and the Rise of Modern Evangelicalism* (Grand Rapids: Eerdmans, 1991); but little attention has been paid to the lower tiers of preachers in the period 1770–1830. For an indication of what can be done, see Kenneth D. Brown, *A Social History of the Nonconformist Ministry in England and Wales 1800–1930* (New York: Oxford University Press, 1988). See also Donald Lewis, *The Blackwell Dictionary of Evangelical Biography* (Oxford: B. Blackwell, 1995).

94. The phrase is taken from an excellent chapter on popular evangelical enthusiasm by John H. Wigger, *Taking Heaven by Storm: Methodism and the Rise of Popular Christianity in America 1770–1820* (New York: Oxford University Press, 1998).

It has to be admitted at the outset that the investigation of religious experience and motivation is fraught with difficulties. If Marxist historians have tended to promote notions of displacement and repression, historians with religious convictions have too readily assumed that there is a pure and consistent essence of religious experience, regardless of time, place, and culture.[95] The problem is compounded by the fact that most narratives of religious experience are based on borrowed language either from the scriptures or from other forms of religious literature, including the spiritual biographies of predecessors. Many employ language rich in symbol and imagery drawn mostly from the Bible or from nature, and choose the most highly colored and dramatic forms of expression. Recorded conversions, as with later public testimonies, were designed not only to reinforce the commitment of the recorder, but were also constructed with a wider audience in mind. The better the story, the more dramatic the effect.[96]

The recording of religious experience in Methodism's age of expansion deserves a much fuller treatment than is possible here. All I wish to do in the short space available is to highlight some common themes from the recorded experiences of the American and Irish itinerant preachers, and make some connections with similar materials from other locations. The most striking feature of these accounts is the space devoted to direct "supernatural" interventions, not only in the drama of religious conversion, but also in the manifold special providences that protected the faithful from the evil intentions of the rich, the powerful, and the lewd. This sense of direct divine interest in the affairs of the world helps explain the pietist enthusiasm for keeping spiritual journals and for maintaining historical records as authentic accounts of God's dealings with the community of the faithful.[97] The most complete collection of materials that I know of relating to the life of an itinerant preacher is that of the Irish rural revivalist Gideon Ouseley, whose stated ambition was to preach to every human settlement in Ireland.[98] His career as an itinerant preacher, stretching over

---

95. I try to address this problem using the insights of early modern historians in "'Popular Religion' 1800–1986," in Terence Thomas, ed., *The British: Their Religious Beliefs and Practices 1800–1986* (London: Routledge, 1988), 181-210.

96. Flora Thompson, *Lark Rise to Candleford* (London: Penguin, 1973), chap. 14.

97. See William R. Ward, introduction to *The Works of John Wesley*, R. P. Heitzenrater, ed. (Nashville: Abingdon Press, 1988), 18:1-79; and Ward, "The Renewed Unity of the Brethren: Ancient Church, New Sect or Interconfessional Movement?" in *Faith and Faction*, 124.

98. The collection is located in the Northern Ireland Public Records Office and contains transcriptions of Ouseley's letters, reproductions of his journal, and records of interviews conducted by his nephew shortly before Ouseley's death. See David Hempton, "Gideon Ouseley: Rural Revivalist, 1791–1839," *Studies in Church History* 25 (1989): 203-14.

some fifty years, was rooted in a profoundly painful conversion experience during which he described himself as "harassed, perplexed and hopeless." His resultant release from fear and despair acted as the main psychological motor for his preaching career and was appealed to in virtually every sermon. It supplied him with an unshakable faith in his status as God's messenger both to save the lost and to proclaim judgement against the wicked. He also jealously protected his right of private judgement and freedom of action even to the extent of refusing to sign Wesley's larger minutes, regarding them as mere human compositions. He was remorselessly anticlerical, which manifested itself in an unremitting anti-Catholicism, and, on occasions, antiepiscopalianism. Above all, he never doubted that a supernatural presence guided his every movement in every place in every day.

The experiences of Ouseley and the Irish itinerants closely match those of Methodist preachers in the United States in the same period. "An unprecedented wave of religious leaders in the last quarter of the eighteenth century," states Hatch, "expressed their openness to a variety of signs and wonders, in short, an admission of increased supernatural involvement in everyday life. Scores of preachers' journals . . . indicated a ready acceptance to consider dreams and visions as inspired by God, normal manifestations of divine guidance and instruction."[99] The same is true of the Canadian revivalists brought to life in the work of George Rawlyk, including the intriguingly named Freeborn Garrettson who brought religious revivalism to Nova Scotia in the 1780s.[100] Apart from the traditional conversion experiences, what is striking about these accounts is their sense of emotional ecstasy; "the enmity of my heart was slain, and the plan of salvation was open to me. I saw a beauty in the perfections of the Deity, and felt that power of faith and love that I had been a stranger to. My soul was exceeding happy that I seemed as if I wanted to take wings and fly to heaven."[101] Whatever psychological mechanisms are at work in these intense conversion experiences, mere repression and displaced sexuality do not seem to offer persuasive explanations. What is not in dispute is that such experiences, especially among those who then went on to become itinerant and local preachers, operated as great chain letters of evangelistic transmission in Methodism's age of expansion.

---

99. Hatch, *Democratization of American Christianity*, 10.
100. Rawlyk, *Wrapped Up in God*; and Rawlyk, *Ravished by the Spirit*.
101. Rawlyk, *Wrapped Up in God*, 58.

They not only require a more subtle psychological treatment than has frequently been the case, but they need to be rooted in the specific cultural settings that conditioned their expression.

The North American itinerants, given the distances that had to be covered, were a particularly remarkable collection of preachers. Primarily young white males from artisan and farming backgrounds, their religious enthusiasm was unleashed by vivid religious conversions.[102] Mostly unmarried (in the first generation at least), with little formal education and on remarkably low pay, this energetic fellowship of preachers helped sustain one another's devotion and established an easy familiarity with their audiences. Part of that familiarity was based on a shared enthusiasm for direct supernatural interventions—from dreams and visions to prophecies and physical prostrations—and on bonds of mutuality cemented by hardship, hospitality, and hymn singing. The religious fervor and genuine dedication of the preachers communicated a sense of brotherhood and provided a model of sacrificial holiness to their listeners.[103] The demands on body and spirit were exceptional, and many fell by the wayside, but the striking fact is that, despite almost no material rewards worth speaking of, supply more or less kept pace with demand until predictable pressures emerged to dilute the itinerant part of the preaching. The same had happened at an earlier stage in Britain and for roughly the same reasons: money, marriage, and material comforts.[104] But at the peak of its efficiency, itinerant preaching was a remarkably effective device for Christianizing individuals and their communities, and for bringing a powerful combination of supernatural excitement and iron discipline to those who embraced both.

Although it is now recognized, in some quarters at least, that the most basic prerequisite for religious revival was the existence of a corps of dedicated revival preachers, more attention also needs to be paid to the religious conversions of the rank and file in Methodist

---

102. Wigger, *Taking Heaven by Storm*; Wigger, "Taking Heaven by Storm: Enthusiasm and Early American Methodism, 1770–1820," *Journal of the Early Republic* 14, no. 2 (summer 1994): 167-94; Katharine L. Dvorak, "Peter Cartwright and Charisma," *Methodist History* 26, no. 2 (1988): 113-26; and Cynthia L. Lyerly, "Francis Asbury and the Opposition to Early Methodism," *Methodist History* 31, no. 4 (1993): 224-34.

103. New England Methodist Historical Society, manuscript history collection. This fine collection of itinerant reminiscences needs to be handled with care, but it does offer fresh insight into the motivation of the preachers and the nature of their message. In particular, see the accounts by John Dow, William Gordon, Samuel Kelly, Thomas Marcy, and Walter Wilkie. See also the sermons by John Dow and Daniel Webb.

104. William R. Ward, "The Legacy of John Wesley; the Pastoral Office in Britain and America," in *Faith and Faction*, 225-48.

societies. The main problem here is again lack of suitable evidence beyond the sprinkling of journals, diaries, and obituaries, which naturally contain their own built-in distortions. Valiant attempts have nevertheless been made by Julia Werner and Michael Watts to analyze the religious conversions of English Methodists. Although they display a bewildering eclecticism of age, denomination, and occupation, it seems that most converts had some sort of religious background on which to draw; most were servants, farm laborers, unskilled workers, and artisans; and most converts—though not in the overwhelming proportions conventionally assumed—were likely to be female and relatively young.[105] However, regional variations clearly demonstrate here, as in other studies, that the pattern of Methodist recruitment was more likely to reflect the social and occupational structure of the regions in which it took root than to match the familiar monochromatic categories devised by social historians.[106] That alone should persuade us of the continuing value of microhistories of Methodist growth in town and country to set alongside the burgeoning regional, national, and international studies.[107]

What is striking, however, about the materials analyzed by Werner and Watts is the proportion of Methodist converts who "had had a premonition of death, had died within a year of joining, or had been in very poor health."[108] In addition, Werner is able to relate pulses of Primitive Methodist revivalism to particular times and regions where outbreaks of disease and the predominance of hazardous occupations supplied an urgent social backdrop to religious enthusiasm. There seems little doubt that religious revivalism thrived on the perceived vulnerability of individuals and social groups when confronted by rapid social change or by threats to health and personal security. In such circumstances, Thompson's "chiliasm of despair" and Werner's emphasis on the dynamics of hope offered by Methodist revivalism

---

105. Clive D. Field, "The Social Composition of English Methodism to 1830: A Membership Analysis," *Bulletin of the John Rylands University Library of Manchester* 76 (1994): 153-69.

106. Clive D. Field, "The Social Structure of English Methodism: Eighteenth–Twentieth Centuries," *British Journal of Sociology* 28 (1977): 199-225; and J. Q. Smith, "Occupational Groups Among the Early Methodists of the Keighley Circuit," *Church History* 57 (1988): 187-96.

107. Such studies are valuable not only for explaining Methodist success in some areas, but also its failure in others. See for example, Jeremy N. Morris, "The Origins and Growth of Primitive Methodism in East Surrey," *Proceedings of the Wesley Historical Society* 48 (1992): 133-49. See also, Robert Currie, "A Micro-Theory of Methodist Growth," *Proceedings of the Wesley Historical Society* 36 (1967–68): 65-73. For a remarkably comprehensive account of the various influences operating on the rise and development of Methodism in a particular setting see Dews, "Methodism in Leeds."

108. Julia Stewart Werner, *The Primitive Methodist Connexion: Its Background and Early History* (Madison: University of Wisconsin Press, 1984), 155. See also, Michael R. Watts, *The Dissenters, Volume II: The Expansion of Evangelical Nonconformity* (Oxford: Clarendon Press, 1995).

are but different ideological sides of the same coin. What we need to know more about is the way in which fearful attitudes to death and uncertainty were capable of being alleviated by religious revivalism, both in the short term and over the life of a generation. On the one hand, appeals to the terrors of judgment and eternal punishment (more commonly made by the uncultivated rough diamonds than by the more educated revival preachers) increased anxieties, while on the other, the deeply personal emphasis on the experience of assurance offered immediate release. The distinctive Methodist combination of assurance and perfection offered both emotional satisfaction and, crucially, the means and the way to a better life in this world as well as the next. Moreover, religious conversion offered not only a degree of personal assurance of sins forgiven, but also a ticket (literally in the case of the Methodists) to new forms of community. Class membership tickets were collected and prized as tangible signs of new community identities at a time when old patterns of social and religious organization were no longer adequate.[109] In that sense, the Methodist quarterly ticket was as much a symbol of the demise of the English confessional state as the Toleration Act of 1812 or the constitutional revolution of 1828–32.

Conclusion

It is time to attempt some broad conclusions from this short excursion into the territory marked out by Thompson. In his valiant efforts to bring together Methodist *experience* and *methods* and to locate them in the social *margins* of industrializing England, Thompson was asking the right kind of questions, but he was predisposed by his Marxist assumptions and Weberian methods to give ideologically slanted and incomplete answers. In particular, his inability to conceive of a popular religion that was in any sense a radical expression of popular sentiment against educated and clerical elites restricted the scope of his historical imagination and resulted in the kind of "condescension of posterity" he so vigorously opposed in his treatment of the political characteristics of the English working class.

The tide of Methodist historiography on both sides of the Atlantic is slowly moving away from explanations based on social change alone, which was the intellectual fashion of the 1970s and 1980s,

---

109. Ibid., 156.

toward a more sensitive approach to the analysis of religious motivation and to a new awareness of the importance of the supply side of the equation of Methodist growth.[110] Recent local studies show that the intensity of religious investment in terms of human resources matters as much to the spread of Methodism as does the existence of a favorable economic and social climate. Second, it is clear that the potency of the Methodist *message*, whether borne by sermons, hymns, or testimonies, was an important factor in the movement's expansion. Although there are unlimited books about Methodist theology and how it might be edited and applied to the modern world,[111] it is difficult to think of a single impressive study of how the Methodist message was *spoken* and *heard* in the context of the eighteenth and nineteenth centuries. Although it is not difficult to find examples of hellfire sermons in the Methodist corpus, my own sampling of manuscript sermons given by Methodists in New England reveals a much greater emphasis on the blessedness of faith than on the accursedness of infidelity. The power of the voluntary request, as against the logic of the Calvinist emphasis on election, is one of the most powerful features of Methodist spirituality. Evidence of it can be found in countless hymns and sermons. If indeed modern psychologists are correct to argue that long-term behavioral transformation is more likely to be brought about by positive inducements than by fear of bad consequences, then Methodist spirituality may well have had more to offer than simply offering a way to flee the wrath to come.

There is need for care here. My intention is not to shift the debate away from one kind of incomplete explanation in favor of another equally incomplete alternative. Similarly, in the search for a convincing framework for understanding religious motivation in Methodism's age of expansion, the argument is not for some kind of decontextualized spiritual illuminism, which no historian should tolerate, but for a sensitive exploration of religious experience and motivation within a convincing mental and social landscape of populations in different parts of the world in the period 1750–1850. It is as pointless arguing that Methodism was a hermetically sealed creed of essentially identical characteristics wherever it appeared in

---

110. See, for example, William R. Ward, ed., *Parson and Parish in Eighteen-Century Surrey: Relies to Bishops' Visitations, Surrey Record Society*, XXXIV (Castle Arch, Guilford: Surrey Record Office, 1994), vii–xxii; and Judith Jago, *Aspects of the Georgian Church: Visitation Studies of the Diocese of York, 1761–1776* (London: Associated University Presses, 1997).

111. For an admirable recent example, see Randy L. Maddox, *Responsible Grace: John Wesley's Practical Theology* (Nashville: Kingswood Books, 1994).

the world in its great age of expansion, as it is foolish not to accept that in its distinctive Arminian theology, organizational structure, and religious rituals, Methodism offered a peculiarly attractive and distinctive form of religion to expanding societies breaking free from old patterns of confessional control.

Whatever one says about religious motivation and the essence of Methodism, international comparisons of Methodist growth convincingly demonstrate that some kinds of societies were more receptive to this kind of religion than others. For a religion that itself chipped away at conventional boundary lines of clericalism, gender, age, and education, the most conducive environments were those interstitial and marginal areas where traditional hierarchical structures were either absent or perceived to be antithetical to new interests. From the Kingswood collieries to the American frontier, and from the border counties of southern Ulster to the Welsh valleys, Methodism offered individual assurance and community disciplines. As Noll has written of the Great Awakening in the age of revolution, "Evangelicalism was at its most effective in revolutionary situations because, with unusual force, it communicated enduring personal stability in the face of disorder, long-lasting eagerness for discipline, and a nearly inexhaustible hope that the personal dignity affirmed by the gospel could be communicated to the community as a whole."[112] Here is a more optimistic fusion of motivation, discipline, and community than was offered by Thompson, and one that does justice to a wider range of sympathy, evidence, and geographical location than was available to Thompson some thirty years ago.

It has nevertheless been the argument of this chapter that Thompson, with all his prejudices about the baleful effects of popular religious enthusiasm, intuitively made the connection between the motives of the Methodist faithful, the methods they used to transmit their enthusiasm, and the social margins they were able to exploit in Methodism's age of expansion. Moreover, as he well understood, these were not independent variables or separate exhibits, rather they were like fused chemical elements whose catalytic power operated on one another in a quite remarkable way.[113] In that respect,

---

112. Noll, "Revolution and the Rise of Evangelical Social Influence," 130.

113. Richard O. Johnson, "The Development of the Love Feast in Early American Methodism," *Methodist History* 19, no. 2 (January 1981): 67-83; Russell E. Richey, "From Quarterly to Camp Meeting: A Reconsideration of Early American Methodism," *Methodist History* 23, no. 1 (1985): 199-213. Such evangelical enthusiasm, though characteristic of the Methodists, was not unique to them. See Rawlyk, *The Canada Fire;* and Leigh E. Schmidt, *Holy Fairs: Scottish Communions and American Revivals in the Early Modern Period* (Princeton, N.J.: Princeton University Press, 1989).

Methodism's inner tensions—between assurance and perfectionism, grace and works, liberty and discipline, and "methodism" and spontaneity—manifested themselves in a kind of dialectical spiritual energy that leaps out from the pages of recorded religious experience. Conversely, wherever in the world Methodism took root, its disciplined and respectable piety inexorably eroded the primitive supernatural excitement that accompanied its own growth. As love feasts and quarterly conferences departed from the inner dynamics of the old revivalism, and as class meetings and itinerant preaching were diluted in scope and intensity, neither motives nor methods quite had the old vitality.[114] Even so, the Methodist *system* held together and adapted itself to new social conditions with admirable realism. In both Britain and North America such adaptability did not bring denominational expansion to an end, but it did set more careful boundary lines beyond which it was deemed imprudent to go.

What then of the future for the study of Methodism in its great age of expansion? There is cause for optimism that the creative work of women and African American historians in particular will further shift the balance of interpretation away from the ecclesiastical structures controlled by men, to the religious experiences—however they are to be interpreted—of men, women, and children of different ethnic origins in different parts of the world.[115] In the meantime it remains a sobering fact that there have been dozens more books on the various components of Methodism's ecclesiastical bureaucracies of one kind or another than there have been on the lives and experiences of those who paid for them.[116] There is also a growing awareness that the application of generic causal mechanisms without due sensitivity to the specifics of time and place has done more harm than good to the history of Methodist scholarship on both sides of the Atlantic. Only more sophisticated local studies showing what the Methodist message was and how it was heard and appropriated, together with more wide-ranging comparisons illuminating the variety of the Methodist experience in different places and at different

114. Wigger, *Taking Heaven by Storm;* Henry D. Rack, "The Decline of the Class-Meeting and the Problem of Church Membership in Nineteenth-Century Wesleyanism," *Proceedings of the Wesley Historical Society* 39 (1973–74): 12-21; and Rack, "Wesleyanism and 'the World' in the Later Nineteenth Century," *Proceedings of the Wesley Historical Society* 42 (1979–80): 34-54.

115. Compare, for example, the spread and content of the essays in *Perspectives* with the essays commissioned for the Davies et al., *History of the Methodist Church in Great Britain,* which was initiated by the Methodist Conference in 1953 and finally completed in 1988.

116. See, for example, the splendid bibliography in part two of Davies et al., *History of the Methodist Church,* 4:651-830.

times, can do justice to the complexity of the task in hand. Historians of Methodism could do worse than take to heart Natalie Zeman Davis's appeal for a more rigorously contextual (family, parish, and locality), comparative (sex, social class, and denomination), and relational (both inside and outside religious structures) history of popular religion in the late medieval and early modern periods.[117] Only then will it become clearer what exactly was distinctive about the peculiar Methodist branch of the Great Awakening, and what it was in the social, economic, and political conditions of the eighteenth and nineteenth centuries that enabled popular evangelicalism to make such sweeping gains in so many different parts of the world.

117. Natalie Z. Davis, "Some Tasks and Themes in the Study of Popular Religion," in C. Trinkaus and H. A. Oberman, eds., *The Pursuit of Holiness in Late Medieval and Renaissance Religion* (Leiden: E. J. Brill, 1974), 307-36; and Davis, "From 'Popular Religion' to Religious Cultures," in S. Ozment, ed., *Reformation Europe: A Guide to Research* (St. Louis: Center for Reformation Research, 1982), 321-41.

CHAPTER 3

Fighting Bees: Methodist Itinerants and the Dynamics of Methodist Growth, 1770–1820[1]

John H. Wigger

When I see a man preach I like to see him act as if he were fighting bees.

—*Abraham Lincoln*

The vernacular is the real test. If you can't turn your faith into it, then either you don't understand it or you don't believe it.

—*C. S. Lewis*

In many respects William Ormond was a typical early Methodist preacher. Joining the itinerancy in 1791 at about age twenty-two, he continued to ride circuits until his death in 1803. While riding the Goshen, North Carolina, circuit in January 1792, Ormond was invited to stay at an inn by a "kindly" landlady. But when her husband returned home, he brought several "half drunk" friends and a bottle of rum. As the men continued to drink and grow more boisterous, Ormond left the house hoping to find a hollow "fodder stack" to sleep under. Finding none, he returned to the house and, kneeling, asked the men to join him in prayer, but they only "laughed hearty"

---

1. An earlier version of this essay appeared in *Taking Heaven by Storm: Methodism and the Rise of Popular Christianity in America* by John Wigger, copyright © 1998 by John Wigger. Used by permission of Oxford University Press, Inc.

at his "praying for them." Later, after he had gone to bed, one of the "Sinners" wore Ormond's shoes outdoors and "nastied them." Eight days later Ormond put up with a Methodist family where his "Soul was happy," but where he had to sleep with three of the children "in an indifferent bed," while the husband and wife "lay on the dirt floor before the fire." In between, Ormond traveled on horseback almost every day, preached five sermons, and spent the night in the homes of six different Methodist families. His sermons were from biblical passages that he knew well and would preach from at least 103 times over the course of his career. This small slice of Ormond's career illustrates some of the demands early itinerants faced, and suggests why they were so successful at drawing large numbers into the Methodist movement.[2] Though ignored and rebuffed by many, these preachers knew their audience well, interacting daily with supporters, critics, and potential converts. Predominantly young, single-minded, and remarkably dedicated, the influence of these preachers grew dramatically in the years following the American Revolution, permanently altering the appearance and tone of much of American religion. In short, they were a different kind of clergy than had ever been seen before in America.

Common Roots

Methodist preachers of the early republic represented a distinct social class and came from remarkably similar backgrounds. Educationally and socially, these preachers were cut from the same fabric as their predominantly middling and artisan audiences. Hence, unlike their college-educated Congregationalist, Presbyterian, and Episcopalian counterparts, they were not burdened with the task of spanning social boundaries and comprehending unfamiliar anxieties and aspirations. They began with the advantage of a natural social affinity with their listeners. In many instances the only real distinction between a Methodist preacher and the bulk of his audience was which side of the pulpit each was on. Almost none of the first- or second-generation itinerants had anything more than a common school education. Until 1800 the church limited even a full-time itinerant's

---

2. William Ormond, "William Ormond Jr.'s Journal" (TMS, Duke Divinity School Library, Durham, North Carolina), vol. 1, 15-17; *Minutes MEC* (1840) 1:116.

salary to a mere sixty-four dollars a year. In that year it was increased to eighty dollars a year for an unmarried preacher. By comparison, a Congregationalist minister in 1800 earned an average annual income of four hundred dollars.[3]

Many, or perhaps even most, of the early itinerants and local preachers came from artisan and petty-merchant backgrounds. Before turning to preaching, Francis Asbury, Jacob Gruber, and Noah Levings were metalworkers; Benjamin Abbott was apprenticed to a hatter and then farmed for a time; Henry Boehm was apprenticed in a grist mill, as was Nicholas Snethen; John Campbell Deem was a tanner, as were his father and the Methodist preacher who led him to conversion; James P. Horton, Alfred Brunson, and Enoch Mudge were shoemakers; Samuel Parker, known as the "Star of the West," was a cabinetmaker; John Littlejohn was a shopkeeper and saddlemaker; John B. Matthias was a carpenter, as were Sampson Maynard, who also spent some time at sea, and Robertson Gannaway, who also worked as a shopkeeper, blacksmith, and innkeeper; Thomas Morrell was a shopkeeper and Revolutionary War soldier; Thomas Rankin was a brewer and merchant; Henry Smith was a wagoner, while his father was a blacksmith; Dan Young, Benjamin Paddock, and Ebenezer Newell were common school teachers, the first in New Hampshire, the second in New York, and the third in Maine, New Hampshire, and Massachusetts; and Jacob Young was raised on the Pennsylvania and Kentucky frontiers and built brick houses for a time.[4] In 1802, in Winchester, Virginia, alone, the itinerant James

---

3. Robert Emerson Coleman, "Factors in the Expansion of the Methodist Episcopal Church from 1784 to 1812" (University of Iowa Ph.D. dissertation, 1954), 208-9; Nathan Hatch, *The Democratization of American Christianity* (New Haven: Yale University Press, 1989), 88. On common schools in the early republic see Carl F. Kaestile, *Pillars of the Republic: Common Schools and American Society, 1780–1860* (New York: Hill & Wang, 1983), 13-61.

4. W. P. Strickland, The Life of Jacob Gruber (New York: Carlton & Porter, 1860), 17; Benjamin Abbott, *The Experience and Gospel Labours of the Rev. Benjamin Abbott* (Philadelphia: Ezekiel Cooper, 1801), 1-7; Henry Boehm, *Reminiscences, Historical and Biographical of Sixty-Four Years in the Ministry* (New York: Carlton & Porter, 1866), 16; on Nicholas Snethen see: Boehm, *Reminiscences*, 232; John Campbell Deem, Untitled autobiography, MSS, Ohio Wesleyan University, Delaware, Ohio; James P. Horton, *A Narrative of the Early Life, Remarkable Conversion, and Spiritual Labours of James P. Horton* (n.p.: printed for the author, 1839), 4-5; Alfred Brunson, *A Western Pioneer: Or, Incidents of the Life and Times of Rev. Alfred Brunson* (Cincinnati: Hitchcock & Walden, 1872), 37; on Samuel Parker see Jacob Young, *Autobiography of a Pioneer: Or, the Nativity, Experience, Travels, and Ministerial Labors of Rev. Jacob Young* (Cincinnati: Cranston & Curts, 1857), 338, and Boehm, *Reminiscences*, 263; John Littlejohn, "Journal of John Littlejohn," TMS, Trans. Annie L. Winstead (Nashville: The Upper Room, n.d.), 3-6; John B. Matthias, "The Journal of John B. Matthias," MSS, Drew University library, Madison, N.J., 3-4; Sampson Maynard, *The Experience of Sampson Maynard, Local Preacher of the Methodist Episcopal Church (Written by Himself.) To Which is Prefixed an Allegorical Address to the Christian World, or, a Thimble Full of Truth to Blow Up the World of Error* (New York: printed for the author, 1828), 130-46;

Quinn befriended two carpenters, two shoemakers, and a gunsmith, all of whom eventually became Methodist preachers.[5]

The only striking exception to this pattern was a group of preachers from the deep South. In contrast to the artisan beginnings of their northern counterparts, some of the preachers from the Carolinas and Georgia came from slaveholding families who were part of the minor gentry. Examples of this brand of preacher include William Capers, James Jenkins, and Joseph Travis, all from South Carolina. But most southern Methodist preachers probably came from backgrounds more like those of their northern counterparts. Lovick Pierce, for example, came from a "poor, humble" South Carolina family that "lived by personal daily labor" and "never owned slaves."[6]

Robertson Gannaway, "Autobiography of Rev. Robertson Gannaway," *Virginia Magazine of History and Biography* 37 (1929): 316-22; 38 (1930): 137-44; Thomas Morrell, *The Journals of the Rev. Thomas Morrell* (Madison, N.J.: Historical Society, Northern New Jersey Conference, MEC, 1984), 2-3; Thomas Rankin, "The Diary of Reverend Thomas Rankin, One of the Helpers of John Wesley," TMS, Garrett Evangelical Theological Seminary Library, Evanston, Ill., 21-23, 52-57; Henry Smith, *Recollections and Reflections of an Old Itinerant*, ed. George Peck (New York: Lane & Tippett, 1848), 234-36; Dan Young, *Autobiography of Dan Young* (New York: Carlton & Porter, 1860), 35; Zachariah Paddock, *Memoir of Rev. Benjamin Paddock, with Brief Notices of Early Ministerial Associates. Also, an Appendix, Containing More Extended Sketches of Rev. George Gary, Abner Chase, William Case, Seth Mattison, Isaac Puffer, Charles Giles, and Others* (New York: Nelson & Phillips, 1875), 74; Ebenezer F. Newell, *Life and Observation of Rev. E. F. Newell, Who Has Been More Than Forty Years an Itinerant Minister in the Methodist Episcopal Church, New England Conference* (Worcester, Mass.: C. W. Ainsworth, 1847), 16, 53, 67, and 87; Jacob Young, *Autobiography*, 23-37, 55. On Noah Levings see Joseph Hillman, *The History of Methodism in Troy, N.Y.* (Troy, N.Y.: Joseph Hillman, 1888), 33. On Enoch Mudge see: Mary Orne Tucker, *Itinerant Preaching in the Early Days of Methodism. By a Pioneer Preacher's Wife* (Boston: B. B. Russell, 1872), reprinted in *The Nineteenth-Century American Methodist Itinerant Preacher's Wife*, ed. Carolyn De Swarte Gifford (New York: Garland Publishing, 1987), 83-86. Enoch Mudge published a sermon entitled *An Oration, Pronounced at Orrington, July 4th, 1808* (Boston: Pr. by B. Parks, 1808); and *The American Camp-Meeting Hymn Book. Containing a Variety of Original Hymns, Suitable to be Used at Camp-Meetings; and at Other Times in Private and Social Devotions* (Boston: Joseph Burdakin, 1818).

5. James Quinn, *Sketches of the Life and Labors of James Quinn*, ed. John F. Wright (Cincinnati: Methodist Book Concern, 1851), 65.

6. Though Capers's father was a plantation owner, Capers confessed that "I had never done an hour's work in a field in my life," until he quit the itinerancy and located in 1814. On Capers, Jenkins, and Travis see William Capers, "Autobiography," in *Life of William Capers, D.D.*, ed. William Wightman (Nashville: Southern Methodist Publishing, 1859), esp. 182; James Jenkins, *Experience, Labours, and Sufferings of the Rev. James Jenkins of the South Carolina Conference* (n.p.: printed for the author, 1842; reprint, Columbia, S.C.: State Commercial Printing Company, 1958); and Joseph Travis, *Autobiography of the Rev. Joseph Travis, A.M., a Member of the Memphis Annual Conference. Embracing a Succinct History of the Methodist Episcopal Church, South; Particularly in Part of Western Virginia, the Carolinas, Georgia, Alabama, and Mississippi*, ed. Thomas O. Summers (Nashville: Stevenson & F. O. Owens, 1856). On Capers also see Albert M. Shipp, *History of Methodism in South Carolina* (Nashville: Southern Methodist Publishing House, 1884), 397-435; and William B. Sprague, *Annals of the American Pulpit*, vol. 7, *Methodist* (New York: Robert Carter & Brothers, 1865; reprint, New York: Arno Press, 1969), 454-64. On Pierce see George Gilman Smith, *The Life and Times of George Foster Pierce . . . With His Sketch of Lovick Pierce, D.D., His Father* (Nashville: Hunter & Wellburn, 1888), 6-8. Green Hill, a prominent North Carolina local preacher at whose home the first conference of the MEC was held in 1785, and

Far from being backward-looking traditionalists, most early Methodist preachers were products of post–Revolutionary America and felt comfortably at home among its rising middling classes. In particular, they knew the importance of mobility in an era of unprecedented expansion. Before entering the itinerant ranks most already had an extensive history of geographic mobility themselves. They understood its economic promise for those seeking to better themselves, as well as the risks and hardships frequent relocations entailed. Increasingly longer migrations not only physically removed both preacher and people from established religious structures, but also provided the psychological distance necessary to embrace new ideas and institutions.

From the 1770s until Bishop Francis Asbury's death in 1816, the typical appointment for a Methodist itinerant was only one year on any given circuit. In contrast, the ideal of New England clergy had always been lifetime tenure at a single parish. Of the 550 graduates of Yale College who entered the Congregationalist ministry between 1702 and 1794, a remarkable 71 percent ministered for their entire career at only one church. Only 4 percent served more than three pastorates. In colonial New England, both pastor and people saw ordination as a long-term commitment to a single congregation.[7] Nothing could have been more foreign to the Methodist concept of an itinerant ministry.

A vivid example of the mobility and artisan training that charac-

who later moved to Kentucky, came from a relatively wealthy background and was himself a slave owner. See undated speech in Green Hill Papers, Southern Historical Collection, University of North Carolina at Chapel Hill. After he left the itinerancy, Edward Dromgoole (1751–1835) became a relatively wealthy North Carolina slaveholder, a pattern that was probably repeated by a number of southern preachers. See tax records, 1798–1804, Edward Dromgoole papers, Southern Historical Collection, University of North Carolina at Chapel Hill. On southern Methodist itinerants also see Christine Leigh Heyrman, *Southern Cross: The Beginnings of the Bible Belt* (Chapel Hill: University of North Carolina Press, 1997); and Cynthia Lynn Lyerly, *Methodism and the Southern Mind 1770–1810* (New York: Oxford University Press, 1998).

7. Donald M. Scott, *From Office to Profession: The New England Ministry 1750–1850* (Philadelphia: University of Pennsylvania Press, 1978), 3-5. Moreover, as Scott points out, far from being the cream of the crop, those ministers who were forced to move a second or third time usually had a history of scandal or contentiousness, and each successive move was "almost always from bad to worse" (9). There was, however, a significant transition under way between the 1740s and the American Revolution. Prior to the Great Awakening, itinerancy was seen as an aberration and a threat to social order. But by the time of the Revolution, as Timothy Hall has recently shown, itinerant preachers had become an accepted part of the religious landscape. In a limited sense, these itinerants helped American religion initiate the transition from the colonial era to the mobile, egalitarian, voluntaristic, and market-oriented world of the early republic. See Timothy D. Hall, "Contested Boundaries: Itinerancy and the Reshaping of the Colonial American Religious World" (Ph.D. diss., Northwestern University, 1991).

terized the early lives and careers of so many Methodist preachers is that of John B. Matthias (1767–1848). Born in Germantown, Pennsylvania, the sights and sounds of the war years were among Matthias's most poignant childhood memories. "I had the prinsebels of liberty stambt in my soul boath of state and church," recounts Matthias, "for my father insruckted me in all those princebeals."[8] Before leaving home Matthias followed his parents' wish by joining the Dutch Reformed Church at age eighteen, though he professed to have little understanding of its doctrines. Soon thereafter he began serving a four-year apprenticeship to a carpenter in Philadelphia, where he left off attending church and became a "great sinner." Before his apprenticeship was complete, Matthias quit Philadelphia for New York City and joined the Freemasons.[9]

Hearing of the Methodists' reputation for loud and passionate preaching, Matthias sought out the John Street Methodist Church. There he heard "thundering" John Dickins, "a plain dreast man and When he spock it came with all his might, and it suted me very well, for I allways love'd to hear preashears spack as if thay whar in ernest." For about a year Matthias attended Methodist preaching with a growing sense of conviction, before he suddenly became convinced that God had accepted him and that his conversion was complete. "This testomoney within was as plane to me as the phiseckel operations of the wind apon my Body without," recalled Matthias. "I becam varey zelous and I beleved that I should one day becom a travling preaser [preacher]." He was then twenty-three years of age.[10]

Matthias immediately joined a class meeting and began to exhort in public. Though many New Yorkers found his exhortations too boisterous and jarring, the stationed preachers often sent him to the outposts of Fort Lee and Brooklyn to hold meetings. But it would be more than two decades before Matthias realized his dream of becoming

---

8. Matthias, "Journal," 2.

9. It is not surprising that someone like Matthias would be attracted first to the Masons and then the Methodists in the immediate post-Revolutionary years. Both were, in a sense, idealistic and both offered a form of stability and community in a mobile, expanding society. The growing recent scholarship on Freemasonry includes: Steven C. Bullock, "A Pure and Sublime System: The Appeal of Post-Revolutionary Freemasonry," *Journal of the Early Republic* 9 (fall 1989): 359-74; Bullock, "The Revolutionary Transformation of American Freemasonry, 1752–1792," *William and Mary Quarterly* 47 (July 1990): 347-69; and Paul Goodman, *Towards a Christian Republic: Antimasonry and the Great Transition in New England, 1826–1836* (New York: Oxford University Press, 1988).

10. Matthias, "Journal," 6-8 and 12. John Dickins was stationed in New York City during the conference years 1786–88. Robert Cloud held that post during 1789 and 1790, and Thomas Morrell during 1791 and 1792. See *Minutes MEC* (1840) 1:25, 28, 31, 34, 38, 42, and 46.

a full-time circuit rider. In 1790 Matthias married Sarah Jarvis, a member of the John Street Church, and in 1793 he was licensed as a local preacher. Soon after he moved to Peekskill, on the Hudson River, where he worked as a ship's joiner and preached up to three times each Sunday.[11]

In 1796 Matthias and his family moved to Tarrytown, New York, where he continued as both a joiner and local preacher. Since there was no Methodist preaching in Tarrytown at the time, Matthias announced a meeting in the village shortly after his arrival. When the townspeople "heard of this thay sead to one another[,] com and let us hear our Joiner preash, for som of them thought it streansh [strange] for a man to preash that work't all the weeck, and had not com from a colledge."[12] Indefatigable as he was, it still took Matthias four years to form a class meeting in Tarrytown. Subsequently, Tarrytown became a regular circuit appointment.

Not long thereafter Matthias spent a summer working on a sloop in Haverstraw, New York, where there also was no Methodist preaching. In a short while he succeeded in forming a class of nine members. That fall he "gave the church to sister wondil [Wendel], for she was the only one amongs them that knew anything about exsperemental godleness." He advised the class to meet at least once a week, and returned to Tarrytown. When he returned to Haverstraw the following year to work on another ship, Matthias found the new class "in a vearey prospreas [prosperous] state." With encouragement from the presiding elder of the district, Elijah Woolsey, Matthias expanded the Haverstraw work into a two weeks' circuit, joined forty new members into a society, and eventually formed the outlines of a four weeks' circuit.[13]

By 1810, with three of his sons serving apprenticeships, Matthias was finally able to fulfill his dream of riding a circuit as a regular Methodist preacher. As such, he traveled various New York circuits until his retirement in 1841. His preaching was most effective in the rural frontier areas of upstate New York. In 1825, for example, Matthias volunteered to pioneer a circuit in the remote Highlands

---

11. On John B. and Sarah Matthias, see Sprague, *Annals of the American Pulpit*, 224-30; Samuel A. Seaman, *Annals of New York Methodism: Being a History of the Methodist Episcopal Church in the City of New York from A.D. 1766 to A.D. 1890* (New York: Hunt & Eaton, 1892), 248.

12. Matthias, "Journal," 19.

13. Matthias, "Journal," 23-26. Elijah Woolsey was presiding elder over the Albany district in 1804 and 1805. William Vredenburgh was appointed to the newly organized Haverstraw circuit in 1805. See *Minutes MEC* (1840) 1:121, 133.

region. In that year alone he took in 248 new members. In many ways the Highland mission represented the apex of his career. "Thre are no popel [people] better than those Highlanders," wrote Matthias. "The state of Religion is at presend vary prsperris [prosperous,] the classis are vary livly[,] thay are seeking for Holiniss of hart[,] som are mead perfcte in Love and othris groning so to be—I naver in joy'd my self so well in all my life."[14]

Matthias's career is remarkable when one considers how different it was from the traditional conception of the ministry. He obviously had little formal education and almost no contact with society's elites. For the more than two decades that he labored as a local preacher he received little or no financial support even from his own church, and after he joined the itinerancy he was given mostly difficult, back-country circuits. Yet for Matthias these issues were of relatively little concern. If anything, he turned these circumstances to his advantage, using first his occupational freedom to blaze new trails in areas of New York beyond the reach of the regular circuit riders, and then his affinity with common folk to reach frontier settlers.

Whereas Matthias entered the itinerancy relatively late in life, the early life and career of Alfred Brunson (1793–1882) was more typical in this regard. Though Brunson was a thoroughgoing Yankee who always retained a deep pride in his heritage, he, like Matthias and hundreds of other Methodist preachers of his time, led a peripatetic life both before and after entering the ministry. Born in Danbury, Connecticut, Brunson was apprenticed to a shoemaker, but ran away at age fifteen. Determined to work his way to Ohio, he instead experienced conversion at a Methodist meeting in Carlisle, Pennsylvania. Returning to Connecticut, Brunson bought out his apprenticeship, settled in Bridgeport, obtained a license to exhort, and married Eunice Burr, all by the age of eighteen. Believing that he had been called to preach by an audible divine voice, Brunson applied to enter the full-time itinerancy, but was turned away because he was married and judged to be too brash even for a Methodist preacher. Disappointed, Eunice and Alfred moved to Trumbull County, Ohio, in 1812. Soon after their arrival, Brunson joined the army as a sergeant and spent a year in campaigns on the shores of Lake Erie. In 1817 he began traveling as something of an adjunct circuit rider in the Ohio Conference before the conference admitted him on trial in 1821.

---

14. Matthias, "Journal," 56; *Minutes MEC* (1840) 1:495-96.

Thereafter, he itinerated extensively in Ohio and Western Pennsylvania, eventually settling in Wisconsin. Brunson was popular for his pithy and combative preaching and for his prowess at handling camp meeting rowdies. Known in his younger days as the "boy preacher," he never lost the shop-mechanic edge that made him a favorite with many on his circuits.[15]

Like the majority of their colleagues, John B. Matthias and Alfred Brunson began their preaching careers not with a classical education, but with a firsthand knowledge of the challenges facing ordinary people in the volatile post-Revolutionary years—their daily hopes and fears, their ultimate aspirations. Their pilgrimages into the Methodist itinerancy followed a familiar pattern of artisan training, broken apprenticeships, and emotion-laden conversions. Like Matthias and Brunson, most early circuit riders were accustomed to frequent relocations and understood the sense of rootlessness engendered by the unprecedented geographic expansion of the early American republic. It was from this base of understanding that Methodism launched its campaign to evangelize the nation.

Memorable Conversions

Not only did most of the early Methodist preachers begin life in similar social circumstances, they also by and large shared a common beginning to their religious lives. Most experienced conversion at a relatively young age, often in dramatic fashion, and subsequently began preaching early in adult life. The vast majority could remember the exact date and time of day on which they were converted. Their conversions formed a base of experience without which no Methodist could hope to obtain a public platform.[16] The conversion of Jacob Young (1776–1859) was typical in many respects.

Born in Allegheny County, Pennsylvania, of "poor but respectable parents," Young moved with his family to Kentucky in 1797 where they purchased a tract of uncultivated land. Although his father was "violently opposed to the Methodists," Young began attending

---

15. Brunson, *Western Pioneer*, 13-230; *Minutes MEC* (1840) 1:353. The first Methodist preacher that Brunson ever heard was John "Barney" Matthias in 1804.

16. For a related discussion of the role of gender in Baptist and Congregationalist conversion accounts between 1800 and 1830, see Susan Juster, "'In a Different Voice': Male and Female Narratives of Religious Conversion in Post–Revolutionary America," *American Quarterly* 41 (1989): 34-62.

Methodist preaching out of "curiosity" soon after his arrival in Kentucky. He quickly discovered that these meetings were unlike anything he had ever witnessed before. At one gathering "the congregation was melted into tears; I could compare it to nothing but a storm of wind . . . the congregation nearly all rose from their seats, and began to fall upon the floor like trees thrown down by a whirlwind." Young looked on with amazement: "My tears flowed freely, my knees became feeble, and I trembled like Belshazzar; my strength failed and I fell upon the floor."[17]

The next evening Young sought out the woman at whose house the meeting had been held and asked her to pray and sing with him. No sooner had they begun to sing than Young once again fell to the floor, lying there for "many hours, having no recollection of any thing that passed, only that my mind was dark, and my soul greatly distressed." Then, about midnight, a "light appeared to shine from the south part of heaven, and God, in mercy, lifted up the light of his countenance upon me, and I was translated from the power of darkness into the kingdom of God's dear son." Recovering his senses, Young stood up and began to shout and cry aloud. A few days later he gained assurance of his conversion through a prophetic dream in which Christ showed him his name written in the Book of Life.[18]

All of these elements—family opposition, boisterous meetings, falling in a swoon, shouting, and prophetic dreams—were common parts of early Methodist conversions. Indeed, few preachers of Young's day passed through this stage without similar experiences.

Perhaps no Methodist experienced a more dramatic conversion than did Benjamin Abbott (1732–1796). Born on Long Island, New York, Abbott was apprenticed to a hatter in Philadelphia after the death of both his parents. Leaving the hatter before his term had expired, he next went to work on his brother's farm in New Jersey. Later he married, rented a farm of his own, and joined a Presbyterian church.

At age thirty-three Abbott had a startling dream in which he died and was carried to hell, "a large place, arched over, containing three apartments with arched doors to go from one apartment to another."

> I was brought into the first, where I saw nothing but devils and evil spirits, which tormented me in such a manner, that my tongue or pen

17. Jacob Young, *Autobiography*, 23-42.
18. Ibid., 42-47.

cannot express. I cried for mercy, but in vain. . . . Being hurried into the second apartment, the devils put me into a vice, and tormented me until my body was all in a gore of blood. —I cried again for mercy, but still in vain. . . . I was soon hurried into the third apartment, where there were scorpions with stings in their tails, fastened in sockets at the end thereof: their tails appeared to be about a fathom long, and every time they struck me, their stings, which appeared an inch and a half in length, stuck fast in me, and they roared like thunder. . . . I was hurried through this apartment to a lake that burned with fire: it appeared like a flaming furnace, and the flames dazzled like the sun. The devils were throwing in the souls of men and women . . . and the screeches of the damned were beyond the expression of man. . . . When it came my turn to be thrown in, one devil took me by the head and another by the feet, and with the surprise I awoke and found it a dream. But oh! what horror seized my guilty breast.[19]

Five or six weeks later Abbott had a second dream in which an angelic guide conducted him on a tour of heaven. There, peering through a door, he "saw the Ancient of Days sitting upon his throne, and all around him appeared a dazzling splendour. I stood amazed at the sight; one stepped forward to me arrayed in white, which I knew to be my wife's mother and said to me, 'Benjamin, this place is not for you yet,' so I returned, and my guide brought me back. I awoke with amaze at what I had seen, and concluded that I should shortly die."[20] Despite their vividness, these dreams had little immediate impact on Abbott. Then, seven years later, in 1772, he attended the preaching of a Methodist itinerant at the urging of his wife. "The preacher was much engaged, and the people were crying all through the house," he later recalled. "This greatly surprised me, for I never had seen the like before."[21] Immediately the memory of his dreams seven years previous returned, and his sense of conviction grew.

Abbott and his wife now became devotees of Methodist preaching in their area. At one meeting "the word reached my heart in such a powerful manner that it shook every joint in my body," recalled Abbott. "Tears flowed in abundance, and I cried out for mercy." On another occasion he was "taken with fainting fits," and neighbors began to fear that he was going mad. Yet another intricate prophetic dream finally led to Abbott's conversion shortly thereafter.[22]

---

19. Abbott, *Experience*, 6-7. On Abbott, see Sprague, *Annals of the American Pulpit*, 41-46.
20. Abbott, *Experience*, 7-8.
21. Ibid., 8.
22. Ibid., 9-15.

Conversions such as those of Abbott and Young laid the foundation for a deep sense of personal piety characteristic of virtually all late-eighteenth- and early-nineteenth-century Methodist preachers. Like Wesley before them, American Methodists continued to see salvation as a progressive journey. John Littlejohn (ca. 1756–1836) was typical in this regard. Born in England, Littlejohn arrived in Maryland in 1767 with his new master, storekeeper Thomas Broomfield, on a brig whose company included sixty-five indentured servants and fourteen convicts. After leaving Broomfield, Littlejohn worked as a saddlemaker, storekeeper, and shop foreman in Norfolk, Annapolis, and Alexandria. A prophetic dream led to his conversion in 1774.[23] At the beginning of his preaching career in November 1776, Littlejohn listed the following nine resolutions in his journal:

> 1st Every night to exam[ine] myself.
> 2d To rise every morng before or by the peep of day, & to have family prayr where practicable the 1st thing that the Blacks may attend; & to engage heads of Families to do so.
> 3rd To avoid talkg of Worldly things as much as possible[;] others may yea must[,] I need not.
> 4th To converse with all I can on the Salvatn of their souls. Rich & poor.
> 5th Never to stay at any place longer than necessary.
> 6th To avoid lightness & reprove those who joke & laugh to excess.
> 7th Strictly to enforce the rules on every membr of Society Rich or poor.
> 8th Never to triffel or while away time, & to guard ag[ain]st talkg too much.
> 9th To read the Bible & notes every Morng & eveng wth prayr to God & to read other books occasionally[.] O Lord do thou be my helper.[24]

These kinds of resolutions appear frequently in the journals of early Methodist circuit riders. The first *Discipline* of 1785 advised preachers to rise at 4:00 in the morning and spend an hour in prayer, meditation, and reading the writings of John Wesley, and to do the same again from 5:00 to 6:00 in the evening. When possible, the *Discipline* further urged preachers to spend the entire morning in reading and study.[25] This was essentially the pattern followed by the South Carolina itinerant James Jenkins. "It was my usual practice to read the Bible in the

---

23. Littlejohn, "Journal," 2-10; *Minutes MEC* (1840) 1:8-9; and Obituary of John Littlejohn, *Minutes MEC* (1840) 2:486-87.

24. Littlejohn, "Journal," 23.

25. *Discipline*/MEC 1784, in John J. Tigert, *A Constitutional History of American Episcopal Methodism*, 3rd ed. (Nashville: Publishing House of the MECS, 1908), 562.

morning, and spend some time in prayer and meditation before going to my appointments," wrote Jenkins. "In the afternoon I read other religious books, and, sometimes, retired into the woods for prayer and meditation." Jenkins often spent evenings talking with whomever he was lodging with, noting that "in these private exhortations, I have frequently seen the power of God manifest in the awakening and conversion of souls."[26]

A Rigorous Vocation

The combination of a peripatetic artisan background and a deeply felt practice of piety created a potent mixture. The early itinerants rode their circuits with the belief that bringing the lost to Christ was the highest calling on earth, that their reward in heaven would more than compensate for their sufferings on earth. Spurred on by this belief, they willingly ventured into unfamiliar regions of the country, far from family and friends, often enduring a grueling pace of riding and preaching, prayer and class meetings, all for a meager salary that often barely covered their expenses. For these men, the itinerancy held many allures, including the appeal of being recognized as a minister, albeit a Methodist preacher. Though the foundations of ministerial authority had begun to crack in the post-Revolutionary years, ministers were still among the most respected people throughout the new nation. Moreover, though opponents often ridiculed and threatened Methodist preachers, they were seldom ignored. It must have been exhilarating for a former carpenter or blacksmith to ride into town and instantly draw a larger audience than the local Congregationalist or Episcopalian minister. Few other endeavors offered middling-born men the potential for such instant recognition. Nonetheless, this kind of explanation alone falls short of explaining the tenacity of the early itinerants without an appreciation for their heartfelt religious motivations and their affinity to common folk.

In many parts of the new nation Methodist preachers suddenly seemed to be everywhere, leading one New Yorker to exclaim in 1788, "I know not from whence they all come, unless from the clouds."[27] Their exploits soon became the stuff of legend among their supporters,

---

26. Jenkins, *Experience*, 52-53.

27. Freeborn Garrettson, *American Methodist Pioneer: The Life and Journals of the Rev. Freeborn Garrettson, 1752–1827*, ed. Robert Drew Simpson (Rutland, Vt.: Academy Books, 1984), 135.

and the cause of deep foreboding among their competitors.[28] The Presbyterian minister Joseph Huber was amazed as he traveled the mountains of southeastern Kentucky to discover how thoroughly Methodist circuit riders had canvassed the region. "I at length became ambitious to find a family whose cabin had not been entered by a Methodist preacher," recalled Huber. "For several days I traveled from settlement to settlement, on my errand of good, but into every hovel I entered, I learned that the Methodist missionary had been there before me."[29]

According to another account, on the Tombigbee, Alabama, circuit in 1812 or 1813, Richmond Nolley followed fresh wagon tracks to the camp of a family newly arrived in the area. "What!" exclaimed the father when he discovered Nolley's identity, "have you found me already? Another Methodist preacher!" The man had already left Virginia and Georgia in hopes of breaking the church's hold on his wife and daughter and was dismayed to encounter a circuit rider on the upper reaches of the Tombigbee River "before my wagon is unloaded." Nolley offered him small comfort, telling the man that not only were the Methodists everywhere in this world, but that there would undoubtedly be Methodist preachers both in heaven and in hell.[30]

The Methodist onslaught embraced nearly every region of America's demographic periphery. In 1806 the family of John Campbell Deem (1802–1879) moved from Kentucky to Butler County, Ohio, to escape the "curse of slavery" and an uncertain land title. At that time, Butler County was an "almost unbroken forrest" containing so many wolves that shortly after their arrival the family's two large dogs chose to return to Kentucky, swimming both the Miami and Ohio Rivers on the way. Deem's father built a sixteen-by-twenty-foot log cabin on their new tract of land, which at the time that they moved in did not have a chimney, windows, or a floor. Yet within days of their arrival, a solitary figure on horseback rode up in the

---

28. Donald E. Byrne Jr. has chronicled much of the folklore of American Methodism in *No Foot of Land: Folklore of American Methodist Itinerants* (Metuchen, N.J.: Scarecrow Press, 1975).

29. A. H. Redford, *The History of Methodism in Kentucky*, 3 vols. (Nashville: Southern Methodist Publishing House, 1870), 3:530. I first discovered this episode in Johnson, *Frontier Camp Meeting*, 19.

30. S. R. Beggs, *Pages from the Early History of the West and North-West: Embracing Reminiscences and Incidents of Settlement and Growth, and Sketches of the Material and Religious Progress of the States of Ohio, Indiana, Illinois, and Missouri, with Especial Reference to the History of Methodism* (Cincinnati: Methodist Book Concern, 1868), 298. This story appears in a number of nineteenth-century Methodist histories. On Nolley, see also *Minutes MEC* (1840) 1:275-6. Tombigbee is sometimes spelled Tombeckbee in Methodist records.

rain, asking "if there was a Methodist family living there." According to Deem, his mother's "heart was swelled with emotion" to discover that one of the twin pillars of her life (the other being her family) had preceded her into the new country. As was customary, the preacher stayed for dinner and then led the family in prayer and singing. Not only did the Deems remain staunch Methodists, but John Campbell eventually became a circuit rider himself.[31]

Half a continent away, Nancy Caldwell (1781–1865) recalled that there was no regular preaching in North Yarmouth, Maine, until the itinerant Joel Ketchum made a foray into the area in 1795. Deeply affected by the preaching of Ketchum and subsequent itinerants, Caldwell, her parents, and siblings all joined the Methodists. "I valued a meeting more than my necessary food," remembered Caldwell. For the Caldwells and thousands like them, the Methodist church became the one social institution outside the family that gave meaning to their daily struggles, and on which they could depend. It offered not only the hope of eternal salvation, but also the prospect of entertainment and the promise of someone to turn to in times of crisis.[32]

But this kind of growth did not come without risk. First-generation preachers were often threatened with physical attack, particularly during the Revolutionary War, when many Americans suspected Methodists of loyalist sympathies, and before the movement had attained any appreciable degree of social legitimacy. American-born Philip Gatch was attacked and beaten on several occasions. In 1775 he was tarred near Baltimore, the hot tar permanently damaging one eye. Between 1778 and 1780 Freeborn Garrettson was beaten, nearly shot, threatened with hanging, and thrown in jail. In 1778 John Littlejohn came close to being tarred and feathered "by some of the bettr sort, as they suppose they are," because they mistakenly assumed he was a Tory. "Being denounced from the pulpit as illiterate, unsound in our principles, and enthusiastic in our spirit and practice—in a word, every way incompetent, and only to be despised," wrote the itinerant Thomas Ware reflecting on this early

---

31. Deem, Untitled autobiography, 1-5. Obituaries of Deem can be found in the *Minutes of the 28th Session of the Cincinnati Annual Conference of the MEC* (Cincinnati: MEC, 1879), 84-86; and the *Minutes/MEC/1879*, 17-18.

32. Nancy Caldwell, *Walking With God: Leaves from the Journal of Mrs. Nancy Caldwell*, ed. James O. Thompson (Keyser, W.Va.: For Private Distribution, 1886), 20-21. In 1794 Joel Ketchum was appointed to the Marblehead circuit in Massachusetts; in 1795 to the Middletown, Connecticut, circuit, and in 1796 to the Pomfret, Connecticut, circuit. See *Minutes MEC* (1840) 1:56, 63, 70.

period, "the multitude, men and women, were imboldened to attack us; and it was often a matter of diversion to witness how much they appeared to feel their own superiority."[33]

No less a concern for many early itinerants was the disapprobation of family members who thought that the young man in question could do better than to become a Methodist preacher, or who feared the consequences of challenging powerful ecclesiastical hierarchies. Dan Young's mother urged him to join the Presbyterians or Baptists rather than the Methodists, and John Littlejohn's mother threatened to disinherit him if he persisted in his preaching. Benjamin Paddock's father found the Methodists to be "about as distasteful to him as any thing well could be." Word that his son planned to join the itinerancy "frenzied him." John Cooper's father "threw a shovelfull of hot embers" on Cooper when he discovered him at prayer, but Cooper became a Methodist preacher anyway.[34]

Even the audacious Billy Hibbard had his early doubts about the Methodists. The son of a tanner and shoemaker, Hibbard was born in Connecticut in 1771. Following his conversion, Hibbard was torn between his desire for respectability and his attraction to Methodism. "I wanted to be a Congregationalist, and to be respectable. But I wanted the love and seriousness of the Methodists," wrote Hibbard. His wife opposed his early public speaking because she was embarrassed by her husband's hubris, as was his father, who threatened to disinherit him and who "reproved me for preaching, because I had not been educated at college."[35] Whatever else might be said in this regard, it is clear that most early itinerants were not pushed into joining the traveling connection by parents or family.

---

33. Philip Gatch, *Sketch of Rev. Philip Gatch*, ed. John McLean (Cincinnati: Swarmstedt & Poe, 1854), 32-55; Garrettson, *Methodist Pioneer*, 69-100; Littlejohn, "Journal," 97; and Thomas Ware, *Sketches of the Life and Travels of Rev. Thomas Ware* (New York: T. Mason & G. Lane, 1840), 104. Philip Gatch was born near Baltimore, Maryland, in 1751, converted in 1772, itinerated in New Jersey, Delaware, Maryland, and Virginia beginning in 1773, and died in 1835. Billy Hibbard recalled that as late as 1800 when he rode the Granville, Massachusetts, circuit, "some threw stones at me, and some set their dogs on me as I rode along." See Billy Hibbard, *Memoirs of the Life and Travels of B. Hibbard, Minister of the Gospel* (New York: printed for the author, 1825), 167. On Garrettson's imprisonment, also see E. C. Hallman, *The Garden of Methodism* (n.p.: Peninsula Annual Conference of the Methodist Church, n.d.), 300-301. On early opposition to Methodism in Virginia, see Robert A. Armour, "Opposition to the Methodist Church in Eighteenth-Century Virginia" (Ph.D. diss., University of Georgia, 1968), chaps. 2, 4, and 6. Armour points out that in Virginia, Methodists faced less persecution during the war than in neighboring states, and that opposition to Methodism in Virginia usually focused on charges of enthusiasm.

34. Dan Young, *Autobiography*, 32; Littlejohn, "Journal," 115; Paddock, *Memoir*, 19-20; and Elizabeth Connor, *Methodist Trail Blazer Philip Gatch 1751–1834: His Life in Maryland, Virginia, and Ohio* (Rutland, Vt.: Academy Books, 1970), 44.

35. Hibbard, *Memoirs*, 60, 66, and 93; and Sprague, *Annals of the American Pulpit*, vol. 7, *Methodist*, 299.

A further risk stemmed directly from the grueling pace of traveling and preaching undertaken by early itinerants. Inevitable risks included sickness and accident. Richmond Nolley died from exposure in 1814 after falling from his horse while fording a stream in a remote area of Louisiana. John Brooks labored so intensely during his first three years in the itinerancy that, he recorded, "I lost my health and broke a noble constitution, so that I have never seen one day since, clear of pain, and sometimes of indescribable sufferings." During one tempestuous revival Brooks lay "sick in bed," but the people "literally forced me out, and made me preach."[36]

The sheer size of many circuits and the number of appointments they included added a dimension of hardship. Freeborn Garrettson claimed to have traveled over one hundred thousand miles between 1776 and 1793, while sometimes preaching up to four times a day. Benjamin "Green" Paddock's first two full circuits—the Lyons, New York, circuit in 1810 and the Northumberland, Pennsylvania, circuit in 1811—were both four weeks' circuits of three to four hundred miles with some thirty preaching appointments per round. In 1812 his appointment was to the Chautauqua circuit, a vast charge covering all or parts of Cattaraugus and Chautauqua Counties in western New York, and Erie, Venango, Crawford, and Warren counties in northwestern Pennsylvania. Like Paddock's previous two appointments, Chautauqua was a four weeks' circuit of some four hundred miles with few roads, numerous streams to cross, and more than thirty preaching appointments.[37]

---

36. John Brooks, *Life and Times of Rev. John Brooks* (Nashville: Nashville Christian Advocate, 1848), 53 and 67.

37. Garrettson, *Methodist Pioneer,* 59, 69, 80, 86, and 293. On Freeborn Garrettson's whirlwind campaign in Nova Scotia, 1785–1787, see George A. Rawlyk, "Freeborn Garrettson and Nova Scotia," *Methodist History* 30 (1992): 142-58. On Paddock, see Paddock, *Memoir,* 82-94, 123; and *Minutes MEC* (1840) 1:215. Chautauqua was spelled "Shetockway" in early Methodist records. In 1792 Elijah Woolsey took a similar appointment in upstate New York, as did Thomas Smith in 1805. Smith's appointment was to the Seneca circuit in Genessee county, New York, situated between the Cayuga and Seneca Lakes. "It has been said by some people that ministers preach for the sake of ease and profit," lamented Smith in 1805. Referring either to himself or an acquaintance, Smith continued:

"I know one that has rode four thousand miles, and preached four hundred sermons, in one year; and laid many nights on wet cabin-floors, and sometimes covered with snow through the night, and his horse standing under a pelting storm of snow or rain; and at the end of that year receiving his traveling expenses and *four* silver dollars of his salary. Now if this be a life of pleasure, ease, and profit, pray what is a life of labor and toil?"

See Elijah Woolsey, *The Supernumerary: Or, Lights and Shadows of Itinerancy. Compiled from the Papers of Rev. Elijah Woolsey, by George Coles* (New York: Lane & Tippett, 1845), 24-26; and Thomas Smith, *Experience and Ministerial Labors of Rev. Thomas Smith . . . Compiled Chiefly from His Journal* (New York: Lane & Tippett, 1848), 126.

In 1799 Billy Hibbard rode the Cambridge, New York, circuit, a five- hundred-mile, four weeks' circuit with up to sixty-three preaching appointments plus the responsibility of meeting classes. During the same conference year Thomas Smith estimated that he traveled a remarkable 4,200 miles, preached 324 times, exhorted 64 times, and met classes 287 times on the Flanders, New Jersey, circuit.[38] Likewise, Jacob Young's first assignment was on the Salt River, Kentucky, circuit, a six weeks' circuit of some five hundred miles. On his first round the new itinerant delivered fifty sermons in addition to meeting classes and holding prayer meetings. By the conference year 1806 Young routinely reported that he was averaging thirty sermons a month, in addition to class meetings, prayer meetings, and family visitations.[39]

The combination of preachers drawn from artisan backgrounds and integrated into a national network was unique to Methodism. In contrast, the Baptists relied on farmer-preachers, particularly in newly settled regions, who functioned on much the same level as a Methodist local preacher, preaching on Sundays and occasionally at weekday meetings or funerals. Often a Baptist preacher earned a dollar per meeting, or about the going daily wage for many skilled workers.[40]

Though the Baptists organized some state and regional home-missionary societies in the first decade of the nineteenth century, it was not until much later that they effectively banded together on a national level. Hence, the Baptists simply could not match the canvassing power of the Methodist itinerants who preached nearly every day. This was a major reason that, while the Baptists grew impressively during the early national period, Methodist expansion was even more

---

38. Hibbard, *Memoirs*, 145; Smith, *Experience*, 55.

39. Jacob Young, *Autobiography*, 74 and 207. A map of Young's Salt River circuit can be found in Dickson D. Bruce, *And They All Sang Hallelujah: Plain-Folk Camp-Meeting Religion, 1800–1845* (Knoxville: University of Tennessee Press, 1973), 40. Over the course of more than fifty years in the ministry, Peter Cartwright estimated that he preached 14,600 sermons, received 10,000 new members into the church, baptized 8,000 children and 4,000 adults, and preached 500 funerals. See Peter Cartwright, *Autobiography of Peter Cartwright. The Backwoods Preacher* (New York: Hunt & Eaton, 1856), 522-23.

40. A. H. Newman, *A History of the Baptist Churches in the United States* (New York: Christian Literature Company, 1894), 336; William Warren Sweet, *Religion on the American Frontier*, vol. 1, *The Baptists* (New York: Henry Holt, 1931), 36-57; and O. K. Armstrong and Marjorie M. Armstrong, *The Indomitable Baptists: A Narrative of Their Role in Shaping American History* (Garden City, N.Y.: Doubleday, 1967), 104. Like Methodist itinerants and local preachers, a Baptist preacher could be either "ordained" to administer the sacraments, or only "licensed" to preach. Also see Gregory A. Wills, *Democratic Religion: Freedom, Authority, and Church Discipline in the Baptist South, 1785–1900* (New York: Oxford University Press, 1997).

remarkable. Sociologists Roger Finke and Rodney Stark have estimated that while the Baptist share of religious adherents increased from 16.9 percent in 1776 to 20.5 percent in 1850, the Methodist share increased from 2.5 percent to 34.2 percent during the same interval.[41]

Along with a frenetic pace of traveling, preaching, and conducting quarterly, class, and prayer meetings, the circuit riders of this period frequently had to contend with poor or uncertain lodging. Most often, the itinerants stayed with sympathetic families along their route, though they sometimes lodged at inns or slept in the open. At the end of one weary day in the western Virginia backcountry, Thomas Ware sought shelter at the isolated cabin of a young couple. "The man gave me to understand, at once, that I could not stay there," recalled Ware. "I looked at him, and smiling, said, that would depend upon our comparative strength." Unwilling to wrestle the preacher, the couple relented, and in the morning Ware baptized their children.[42]

Like most of the itinerants, Henry Smith made it a policy to lodge at the homes in which he preached. But after preaching a funeral sermon in Ohio in 1801, even Smith's resolve was put to a "severe trial." "For when bed-time came I was conducted to the room from which the corpse had been taken a few hours before, to sleep on the bedstead, perhaps the very bed, on which the young man had died, without the house having been scrubbed and properly aired." Smith stuck it out, but fleas and barking dogs kept him awake all night. Thomas Smith had a similar experience while riding the Asbury, New Jersey, circuit in 1807. On this occasion Smith found himself in the uncomfortable situation of having to sleep in the same room with the body of a man who had died that morning. Unlike Henry Smith, he did not last the night, choosing instead to sleep outdoors curled up next to a tree root.[43]

Similar experiences led Jacob Young to eventually give up on the policy of always staying where he preached, but not without being challenged by a colleague who accused him of excessive pride and ambition. Young replied that he "would visit the people as far as practicable, catechise them, and pray with them, but, when I could

---

41. Roger Finke and Rodney Stark, *The Churching of America 1776–1990: Winners and Losers in Our Religious Economy* (New Brunswick, N.J.: Rutgers University Press, 1992), 55; Robert G. Torbet, *A History of the Baptists*, rev. ed. (Valley Forge: Judson Press, 1963), 246-47. For a thorough history of the development of Baptist missionary societies during the first two decades of the nineteenth century see Albert L. Vail, *The Morning Hour of American Baptist Missions* (Philadelphia: American Baptist Publication Society, 1907), 86-156.

42. Ware, *Sketches*, 156-57.

43. Smith, *Recollections*, 67; Smith, *Experience*, 156.

avoid sleeping among fleas and bed-bugs, I intended to do it."[44] The fact that Young had to defend this decision at all indicates the strength of the early circuit riders' commitment to maintaining a close rapport with the people to whom they preached. It was this commitment, perhaps more than anything else, that endeared them to their listeners. Looking back on his career, Henry Smith observed: "If I was but poorly qualified for a missionary in every other respect, I was not in *one thing;* for I had long since conquered my foolish prejudice about eating, drinking, and lodging. I could submit to any kind of inconvenience when I had an opportunity of doing good. . . . My call was among the poor, and among them I could feel myself at home."[45]

The popularity of Methodist preachers among the church's adherents was also, no doubt, in part the result of their small salary. Even so, there were frequent shortfalls. For the fifteen years James Jenkins itinerated, he received $22, $44, $64, $54, $64, $64, $64, $64, $64, $64, $64, $64, $80, $160, and $140, respectively. The longtime itinerant James Quinn traveled for more than forty years beginning in 1799, mostly in and around the Ohio country. He estimated that at the end of his career the church owed him some twenty-six hundred dollars in unpaid salary and expenses. Dan Young likewise realized a two hundred dollar shortfall in five years in the itinerancy, and Peter Cartwright calculated his shortfall over the course of his career at sixty-four hundred dollars. Nor were things likely to improve with retirement. "I have long since learned that a superannuated Methodist preacher is usually a much more welcome guest in heaven than any where on earth," concluded Quinn at the end of his career. But in the end the financial uncertainty of the itinerancy was perhaps no worse than that faced by most Americans of the period. In many instances, shared hardships only served to strengthen the bond between both the preachers themselves, and between preacher and people. "I have observed," wrote the itinerant Benjamin Lakin in 1810, "that where I have suffered most, I always find it hardest to part with the people."[46]

---

44. Jacob Young, *Autobiography,* 262.

45. Smith, *Recollections,* 313.

46. James Jenkins, *Experience,* 229; Quinn, *Sketches,* 209 and 233; Dan Young, *Autobiography,* 94; Cartwright, *Autobiography,* 522; and Benjamin Lakin, "The Journal of Benjamin Lakin, 1749–1820," in William Warren Sweet, ed., *Religion on the American Frontier, 1783–1840: The Methodists* (New York: Cooper Square, 1964), 240. While presiding elder over the Albany, New York, district in 1804, Elijah Woolsey was dismayed to discover that one of his preachers who had seven children had received only fifty cents quarterage. But even this was more than the eight cents Billy Hibbard received for one quarter of 1811. See Woolsey, *Supernumerary,* 87; Hibbard, *Memoirs,* 310. On Quinn, also see Sprague, *Annals of the American Pulpit,* 314-21.

Perhaps Freeborn Garrettson captured the essence of the resiliency of the early itinerants when he wrote in reference to upstate New York, "I feel for the preachers in these back settlements, for although the people are kind, yet they often have hard fare, and seldom a private room; but it is a most growing country."[47] Growth, that was the measure of success. It required sacrifice, but it also held great promise. Offsetting the rigor of the itinerancy was the potential of getting in on the beginning of something big. As a group, the early Methodist preachers were well suited for reaching newly politicized middling Americans. Willing to endure the hardships of the itinerant life, they kept pace with the nation's territorial expansion, remaining both geographically and socially close to their constituents and to potential converts.

A National Brotherhood

As a result of their common social background, similar religious experience, and shared adversity, the itinerants of the early national period not surprisingly developed close personal ties with one another.[48] Separated from family and community, they turned to one another for fellowship, solace, and advice. For many, these friendships lasted a lifetime. "Of all beings on earth, Methodist preachers should love each other," wrote the southern itinerant Joseph Travis. "Their toil, their privations, their self-sacrificing and laborious calling, should ever create a unison of feeling and of sentiment towards each other."[49] The longtime Methodist preacher William Burke, who began his preaching career in 1791 in western Virginia and Tennessee, concluded that the early circuit riders were "like a band of brothers."[50] Sentiments such as these abound in the journals and memoirs of Methodist preachers from every region. "We loved one another," wrote New York's Elijah Woolsey. "We felt willing to live, to suffer,

---

47. Garrettson, *Methodist Pioneer*, 285.

48. Drawing on the work of anthropologist Victor Turner, Lawrence Foster suggests that the sense of *communitas* and fellow feeling among early Shakers, Oneida Perfectionists, and Mormons—all highly committed movements—was extremely intense, and had something to do with their liminal status in society. The early Methodist itinerants arguably experienced a similar kind of liminal status, and hence developed interpersonal relationships of similar intensity. See Lawrence Foster, *Religion and Sexuality: Three American Communal Experiments of the Nineteenth Century* (New York: Oxford University Press, 1981), 8-9.

49. Travis, *Autobiography*, 222.

50. William Burke, "Autobiography of William Burke" in James B. Finley, *Sketches of Western Methodism* (Cincinnati, 1865; reprint, New York: Arno, 1969), 58.

and to die together."[51] Methodist preachers may have ridden their circuits alone, but through camp meetings, quarterly and annual conferences, and, perhaps most important of all, through a vast correspondence network, they developed and maintained close friendships.[52]

A rare window into how this communications network functioned is afforded to us by a collection of letters written to Daniel Hitt. Born in 1770, Hitt was, throughout much of his career, a thoroughly average Methodist preacher. He entered the itinerancy in 1790 and traveled extensively in western Pennsylvania, Virginia, and Maryland. In 1795 he was appointed presiding elder over the region encompassing most of western Pennsylvania. In 1807 Hitt became Francis Asbury's traveling companion for one year, and then for eight years served as one of the church's book agents. Thereafter he served as presiding elder over various districts in or near Pennsylvania.[53]

The surviving collection of letters to Daniel Hitt includes 335 letters written between 1788 and 1806 by some one hundred people. Some of the letters are from family or former parishioners, but most are from some fifty colleagues. Whereas a small portion of the letters are short notes concerning preaching appointments or other points of business, most are more personal in tone. More than anything else they reveal a vast fraternal network spanning the length and breadth of the United States. For the circuit rider who changed locations every one or two years, the fellowship of the preachers often provided his most important reference point.

Along with family news and reports on their health, those who wrote to Hitt communicated news of revivals and hard times from across the new nation. In 1794, for example, the Methodist preacher Thomas Lyell wrote concerning the Lancaster, Virginia, circuit (a circuit Hitt himself had ridden in 1790): "I can with sorrow inform you that a great declension (greater than ever I expected) prevails:—The friends (if I may call them) are much in the spirit of *Slavery*.—some

---

51. Woolsey, *Supernumerary*, 57.

52. On at least one occasion Francis Asbury claimed to have written as many as one thousand letters a year. Although this was clearly not the case for his first years in America, it may not have been an exaggeration for his later career. Certainly Asbury wrote as many letters as Wesley, and probably a great many more. See *JLFA* 3:vii. A portion of this correspondence flowed through America's fledgling postal system. On the development of the postal system see Richard R. John, *Spreading the News: The American Postal System from Franklin to Morse* (Cambridge, Mass.: Harvard University Press, 1995).

53. Matthew Simpson, *Cyclopedia of Methodism* (Philadelphia: Louis H. Everts, 1881), 446; Sprague, *Annals of the American Pulpit*, 184-86.

buying & others repenting that they ever let theirs go free."[54] Lyell's views on slavery were at odds with many on the Lancaster circuit, but he knew he could count on Hitt for a sympathetic ear. And for Thomas Lyell, in many respects, this was more important. His association with the people of the Lancaster circuit was, after all, temporary and local; that with his fellow itinerants was lasting and national in scope.

Hitt's correspondents freely shared their setbacks and triumphs, revealing a clear sense of individual and communal mission. In September 1796 the itinerant Jesse Stoneman wrote to Hitt from his new circuit in Connecticut. Raised on the Ohio frontier, Stoneman's first appointment in 1793 had been to the Clarksburg circuit in western Virginia. Connecticut was quite a shock for Stoneman, but he did not intend to give up easily. "My resolutions, & determinations are at the present, to spend and be spent in the glorious cause, I have embarked in. . . . Brother, this is a fine school; I am not sorry that I came to this land; I am satisfied the hand of GOD was in it; I have seen good days, & hope to see greater." Stoneman knew that he could count on Hitt to understand his situation. Less optimistic, but no less open and straightforward in tone, is a letter from the itinerant Michael H. R. Wilson, then riding the Tioga, Pennsylvania, circuit. "My circuit was & is in a disagreeable condition: I turn out ten, where I take in one," wrote Wilson in February 1797. "My labor is not much blest in this place, unless it is blest in turning out disorderly persons." Daniel's brother Samuel Hitt, himself an itinerant, was even less delicate in his assessment of the Harford, Maryland, circuit. "I have accomplished a round on the circuit," wrote Samuel in January 1797, "& find it wants a great deal of pruning and manuring."[55] Despite their difficulties, Michael Wilson and Samuel Hitt could take solace in knowing that there was someone else who understood their situation and approved of their choices.

54. Thomas Lyell to Daniel Hitt, 13 January 1794, "Letters to Daniel Hitt," trans. Annie Winstead, Special Collections, Ohio Wesleyan University, Delaware, Ohio. Thomas Lyell was received on trial as a Methodist itinerant in 1792. He eventually became an Episcopalian minister. See Thomas Lyell, "Autobiography," Aldert Smedes Papers, Southern Historical Collection, University of North Carolina at Chapel Hill; *Minutes MEC* (1840) 1:43; and Travis, *Autobiography*, 79.

55. Jesse Stoneman to Daniel Hitt, September 1796; Michael H. R. Wilson to Daniel Hitt, 6 February 1797; Samuel Hitt to Daniel Hitt, 4 January 1797, "Letters to Daniel Hitt." Wilson died in 1798 in Lancaster County, Pennsylvania. He was born in Maryland in 1770 and had joined the itinerancy on trial in 1796. See *Minutes MEC* (1840) 1:65 and 1:79. Born in the East, Stoneman early in life migrated with his family to the Ohio frontier. He joined the itinerancy on trial in 1793, located in 1806, settling in or near Fairfield County, Ohio. He died in 1840 and is buried in the Thornville, Ohio, cemetery. See *Minutes MEC* (1840) 1:48 and 1:136; "Ministers File," Ohio Wesleyan University, Delaware, Ohio; William Ryan, Obituary of Jesse Stoneman, *WCA* 6 (24 January 1840), 160.

Hitt's correspondents also sought and gave advice freely. In February 1796 the Methodist preacher Seely Bunn wrote to Hitt from Baltimore, lamenting his own "bashfulness." "I have the greatest power over them in the pulpit & class room: but when I attempt to discharge my duty to individuals in private, they beset me. Is it so with thee brother?" asked a perplexed Bunn.[56] Whereas Bunn was looking for advice on how to handle contentious members, the itinerant Amos Garrett Thompson was ready to dish out some advice in a May 1790 letter to Hitt. Thompson, who fancied himself something of a homegrown poet, closed his letter with a composition designed to admonish Hitt and to warn him against the temptation to marry.

> John saith to the Christians, Live in Love
> And I the saying must approve:
> Love is the prize I hope to gett.
> The prize is free for Daniel Hitt.
> Paul saith believe, but oh for faith,
> That I may find the narrow path;
> Some times I fear I've not a bit,
> How is it with you Brother Hitt?
> James saith believe & work also,
> One by itself will never do:
> Both in concert are sure to get,
> True peace for me & Brother Hitt . . .
>
> If I creep slow, let Daniel know;
> It's dangerous for to Tarry;
> Think of this too, it will not do.
> For you or me to marry.
>
> Vexation & strife, and probation & Life,
> Our all here on earth is but short;
> But a sharp Edged knife, or if you please a Wife:
> If it cuts us, it will make us to snort.
> Let me & thee, or Hitt or miss,
> Go see & be, an heir of bliss
> And cry & die, & Spout & stamp,
> And try & fly, and rout the camp.

---

56. Seely Bunn to Daniel Hitt, 18 February 1796, "Letters to Daniel Hitt." Bunn joined the itinerancy on trial in 1792. In 1796 he was stationed on the Baltimore circuit. See *Minutes MEC* (1840) 1:43 and 1:69.

The Devil is a suttle fox
He'll try to get us in a box;
To get our feet into the stocks
And then to shear us of our locks.[57]

Marriage was one of the few immediately perceptible threats to the bond that existed between the traveling preachers. Hence, it is not surprising to find that Thompson was not the only one who wrote to Hitt on this subject. In 1794 Caleb J. Taylor wrote from Kentucky decrying a "marriage Fever" that seemed to be sweeping the ranks of the preachers. "Though I expect you are no misagomist," wrote Seely Bunn later that same year, "[I hope] you will remain in a state of celibacy, yet awhile."[58] Whatever the effect of these persistent warnings, Daniel Hitt never married.

The open and unguarded tone reflected in Thompson's poetry is evident throughout the Hitt letters. These were men closely involved in one another's lives, or who had been at one time. At least two correspondents wrote to tell Hitt that they were naming their newborn sons after him. "I often think of you brother Daniel, & the happy moments we have spent together; & the many miles we have rode together; how sweet is the thought of friendship past," wrote Thornton Fleming in January 1797, in a passage typical of many in the Hitt collection. "I have not forgot the hours, days, weeks, months, & may I not say years, that we have spent together," wrote Robert Manley in September 1801. "How many fatigueing rides over the hills, thro mud & water, thro. heat & cold in order to discharge our duty to God, ourselves & fellowmen, how many meetings have we attended together?" Friendships built in this way could be enduring.[59]

The degree of collegiality reflected in the letters to Daniel Hitt persisted as long as the itinerancy remained a viable institution. But over time, the itinerancy underwent a gradual transformation, beginning first in the cities and more densely populated regions. By the middle third of the nineteenth century, as fewer preachers willingly moved outside their immediate regions and some even demanded long-term

57. A. G. Thompson to Daniel Hitt, 25 May 1790, "Letters to Daniel Hitt." Thompson joined the traveling connection on trial in 1785; he located in 1796. See *Minutes MEC* (1840) 1:23 and 1:66.

58. Caleb J. Taylor to Daniel Hitt, 11 April 1794, Seely Bunn to Daniel Hitt, 26 August 1794, "Letters to Daniel Hitt."

59. Thornton Fleming to Daniel Hitt, 29 January 1797; Robert Manley to Daniel Hitt, 30 September 1801, "Letters to Daniel Hitt."

or virtually permanent appointments, the sense of a truly national fellowship among the traveling preachers began to fade.

The Problem of Marriage

Marriage represented a special challenge for the itinerant system. Most of the first-generation Methodist preachers considered celibacy a necessity, if not a duty. Marriage usually necessitated locating, since the people on most circuits either could not or would not provide enough extra financial support for a preacher's wife or children, as Pleasant Thurman learned when he was appointed to the Edenton, North Carolina, circuit in 1811. That September, Thurman made a motion at the circuit stewards' meeting "that all the residue of the money after the payment of his own board and church expences should be applied to the board & salary of his wife." The stewards rejected the motion "unanimously." When Thurman continued to press his case, the circuit's October 1811 quarterly meeting conference affirmed the stewards' decision, noting that "the Society are not bound to support P. Thurman's wife."[60]

So, although marriage was not an outright sin, many considered it an abdication of a higher calling. A preacher who married and located usually continued as a local preacher, though as such he forfeited membership in their conference, becoming something of a second-class citizen. William Capers captured the antagonism toward marriage among first-generation preachers in a speech by the presiding elder Lewis Myers at the South Carolina conference of 1811:

> A young man comes to us and says he is called to preach. We answer, "I don't know." He comes a second time, perhaps a third time, even a fourth time, saying, "A dispensation of the gospel is committed unto me, and woe to me if I preach not the gospel." Then we say to him, "Go and try." He goes and tries, and can hardly do it. We bear with him a little while, and he does better. And just as we begin to hope he may make a preacher, lo, he comes again to us, and says, "I must marry." We say to him, "If you marry, you will soon locate: go and preach." "No, I must marry, I *must* marry." We say to him, "A dispensation of the gospel is committed to you, and woe be unto you if you preach not the gospel." "But no," he says, I *must marry*." And he marries. It is enough to make an angel weep![61]

---

60. Edenton, North Carolina, MEC Papers, Southern Historical Collection, University of North Carolina at Chapel Hill.
61. Capers, "Autobiography," 143-44.

"In those days of long rides and little quarterage, with no allowance for family expenses, it was deemed vastly imprudent for a young preacher to marry, should he even get an angel for his wife," concluded Capers. Indeed, he discovered just how true this was after marrying Anna White in January 1813. That year the Capers were stationed in Wilmington, North Carolina. Their expenses for "subsistence of the most frugal kind" was three hundred dollars, while their income was less than two hundred dollars. Capers located the next year and took up farming. As late as 1809 the Virginia Annual Conference was known as the "Bachelor Conference," since of the eighty-four preachers present only three were married.[62]

Hence, the decision of whether or not to marry was a difficult one for many preachers and their prospective wives. Some, such as Freeborn Garrettson in the north and James Jenkins in the south, delayed marrying for many years so as not to impede their ministries. Though Jenkins was "strongly tempted" to marry and locate in 1795, in the final analysis, "when I looked over the work and saw the harvest so great, and the labourers so few, I could not reconcile it to my conscience to quit while I was able to hold on." Similarly, Garrettson withdrew a marriage proposal in 1775 after he received what he believed to be a divine impression in the night, saying, "You are about to do your own will; I have a greater work for you: you must go out and preach the gospel."[63] Henry Boehm likewise waited until he was forty-three to marry Sarah Hill in 1818, Thomas Ware did not marry until age thirty-eight, and Henry Smith waited until sixty.[64] All the same, many more married at a more customary age and located to farm or practice a trade. Perhaps no one agonized over this decision more than John Littlejohn.

Almost from the beginning of his itinerant career in 1776 Littlejohn had been considering the possibility of marrying and settling down. Early on he wrote to the veteran preacher George Shadford asking his advice. Shadford wrote back that "he did not approve of my locating."[65] In June 1778 Littlejohn made a dangerous pilgrimage (dangerous because many regarded Methodists as Tories at the time) to see

---

62. Capers, "Autobiography," 115, 160, and 178-80; and Boehm, *Reminiscences*, 221.

63. Jenkins, *Experience*, 72; Garrettson, *Methodist Pioneer*, 51. Jenkins eventually married in 1805 and located in 1806; and Garrettson married Catherine Livingston in 1793, though he continued in the itinerancy.

64. Boehm, *Reminiscences*, 470; Ware, *Sketches*, 226; and Smith, *Recollections*, 287.

65. Littlejohn, "Journal," 58. Shadford was sent to America by Wesley in 1773 along with Thomas Rankin. He returned to England in 1778 and died in 1816. See Simpson, *Cyclopedia*, 794.

Francis Asbury in Delaware and open his heart to him on the matter. Whatever else he may have said, Asbury promptly sent Littlejohn back to preach on the Baltimore circuit. Soon after, Littlejohn consulted Philip Otterbein, who "gave it as his opinion that I ought to preach, that my call was sufficient," and also the Methodist preacher Philip Gatch, who "wrote to me, to let me know, he wished it was with him as in times past, meaning before his marriage."[66] Indeed, about the only person who did not want Littlejohn to continue itinerating was his mother, who threatened to disinherit him if he continued. Not surprisingly, amid all this dithering his prospective bride grew "much dissatisfied with my intentions."[67]

His doubts notwithstanding, Littlejohn married Monica Talbott of Fairfax County, Virginia, in December 1778, settling soon thereafter in Leesburg, Virginia. "My purpose was to follow my Trade for a support," wrote Littlejohn. "I had no difficulty in deciding to Locate as I then reviewed it improper for a Methodist Preecher to travel the Circuit after they were married."[68] In all likelihood, more than two-thirds of the late-eighteenth- and early-nineteenth-century itinerants followed a course similar to John Littlejohn's.[69]

But as time went on, more and more preachers continued to itinerate even after marrying. Some of their wives became more involved in their ministries, rather than simply living with relatives or friends while their husbands traveled, whereas others single-handedly ran their households during their husbands's long absences. Most were as committed to the spread of the Methodist message as their husbands were, if not more so. A case in point is Betsey Roye Lakin. In February 1796, Benjamin Lakin wrote in his journal, "Was much exercised about Marrying, an object presented herself before my mind, many delights appeard in that state of life; But I believe I can serve

---

66. Littlejohn, "Journal," 108 and 114. Philip Gatch's marriage was, apparently, a relatively happy one. "My wife's heart was given up to God," wrote Gatch at one point. "When I went out preaching, we parted in peace, and when I returned, we met in love." See Connor, *Methodist Trail Blazer*, 90-91. Philip William Otterbein was a major figure in the formation of the Church of the United Brethren in Christ, and a supporter of the MEC. Otterbein came to America in 1752 and pastored the German Evangelical Reformed Church in Baltimore from 1774 until his death in 1813. See Frederick Norwood, *Story of American Methodism* (Nashville: Abingdon Press, 1974), 103-6.

67. Littlejohn, "Journal," 119.

68. Littlejohn, "Journal," 124. Littlejohn continued as a local preacher in Leesburg until 1818 when he and his family moved to Kentucky, eventually settling in Logan County. Littlejohn died in Kentucky in 1836. See *Minutes MEC* (1840) 2:486-87.

69. This estimate is based on the statistics of Jesse Lee and William Warren Sweet. See Lee, *Short History*, 316-25; and Sweet, *Methodists*, 50.

God and be more useful in my present state." But by March 1798 Lakin had changed his mind, and in April of that year he married Betsey Roye and located. Two years later, at Betsey's urging and following a series of prophetic dreams and omens, Lakin rejoined the traveling connection, accepting appointment to the Limestone, Kentucky, circuit. Lakin continued to travel for the next twenty years, with Betsey often accompanying him. Frequently plagued by self-doubts, it is unlikely that Lakin would have reentered or remained in the itinerancy without Betsey's unflagging support. Once, after a run-in with his presiding elder, he decided to quit the itinerancy. "But when I came to inform my wife of my intentions she opposed me in my plan, and insisted that I was not traveling for the President Elder But for God and if God had called me to the work I aut [ought] not to quit it."[70]

Much as Benjamin Lakin had done, Elijah Woolsey married in 1797 and reentered the traveling connection in 1800. Woolsey's wife often assisted in his meetings by "praying with and comforting the mourners." Similarly, Joseph Travis continued to itinerate after marrying Elizabeth Forster in 1811, as did Jacob Young after marrying Ruth Spahr, and Lovick Pierce after marrying Ann Foster, both in 1809. In 1812, while Young was in charge of the Ohio district, he noted that, because of the economic impact of the war, some of the itinerants "felt discouraged, and some thought of retiring from the work, but their courage revived again, their wives were zealous for the good cause, and exhorted their husbands to weather the storm."[71]

Sibbel Hibbard consistently offered this kind of support to her husband, the itinerant Billy Hibbard. Though she opposed Billy's public speaking early on, by the time he launched his itinerant career in 1797 Hibbard could write: "My dear wife instead of desiring me to stay at home, exhorted me to trust in the Lord, and be faithful to do my duty; she assured me that nothing could induce her to give me up." During the succeeding years Sibbel took in weaving and spinning, earning $300 over one three-year stretch, and briefly ran a school for thirty children. Alfred Brunson, whose wife once ran a boarding house to augment the family income, even argued that marriage was an advantage for a Methodist itinerant because it served to more firmly

---

70. Lakin, "Journal," in Sweet, *Methodists*, 214-27. For a similar account of the itinerant James Kelsey and his wife, see C. D. Burritt, *Methodism in Ithaca: A History* (Ithaca, N.Y.: Andrus, Gauntlett & Co., 1852), 156-57.

71. Travis, *Autobiography*, 70; Woolsey, *Supernumerary*, 64-70; Smith, *Life of Pierce*, 27; and Jacob Young, *Autobiography*, 265 and 299.

"fasten" him to the local community. Writing in the 1840s, the longtime itinerant Henry Smith also argued in favor of itinerants marrying:

> We take up a young, inexperienced man, and admit him on trial, with the expectation that he will lay aside the spirit and study of the world, and devote himself wholly to his religious studies, and the work of the ministry, to which he solemnly professes to be called. But the first or second circuit he goes to, he seems to forget his solemn pledge, and enters prematurely into matrimonial engagements, and fills the circuit with more talk about his courtship than his usefulness, or the number of souls converted through his instrumentality. This may afford some amusement to the young and chaffy professors, but it rolls trouble upon the hearts of the more serious and zealous of the flock of Christ, over which he is made an overseer, and thus ends his call to itinerate; for he drives down his stake, and enters into other business.

"Better take one well made, well married, laborious, enterprising minister of Jesus Christ, than half a dozen such fickle-minded boys," concluded Smith.[72]

Analyses such as Smith's and Brunson's represented a subtle yet profound shift in American Methodism, and indeed in much of the larger culture as well.[73] The post-Revolutionary years had been a period of unprecedented upheaval in which only the most basic elements of past religious structures and practices seemed immune to change. In this atmosphere, American Methodism both nurtured and relied on a cadre of zealous young preachers willing, at least for a time, to sacrifice all in their quest to evangelize the nation. Methodist preachers were liminal figures in regard to their celibacy, but, unlike the Shakers, Mormons, and Oneida Perfectionists of the 1830s and 1840s, their practice did not lead to some new, radical concept of marriage and the family.[74] The celibacy of the itinerants was never an overt attempt to redefine sexual relations and the family, but rather a matter of pragmatic expediency during the movement's most volatile, formative years. When the immediate need for celibacy faded, so did the practice among Methodist preachers.

---

72. Hibbard, *Memoirs*, 137, 161, and 236; Brunson, *Western Pioneer*, 174 and 268; and Smith, *Recollections*, 136-37.

73. In fact, when Smith reflected on Methodism's earlier history he could come to just the opposite conclusion. "I would humbly say to the present race of preachers and members in the Methodist Church, that the church owes much, almost everything, under God, to the labors of unmarried preachers," wrote Smith on another occasion. See Smith, *Recollections*, 90.

74. On the development of Shaker, Mormon, and Oneida Perfectionist views and practices concerning marriage, sexual relations, and the family, see Foster, *Religion and Sexuality*.

In their marriage practices and attitudes toward the family, Methodist preachers never operated very far outside the prevailing values of middling Americans. By the 1810s and 1820s, as Methodist societies became more numerous and more prosperous, and the church in general became more socially respectable, fewer preachers were willing to forgo marriage and a settled home life, and fewer of their parishioners saw it as a preacher's duty to do so. Married preachers were able to continue itinerating, but only because in most regions of the country circuits became more compact, closer to one another, and less difficult to travel, while salaries increased and became more dependable—in short because the itinerancy did not demand the same sacrifices that it once had.

This transition can be seen in the autobiography of Mary Orne Tucker (1794–1865), a rare first-person memoir by the wife of a Methodist preacher. Born in Corinth, Vermont, Tucker's parents farmed out their children to relatives early on because of financial pressures. Mary was thus raised by a relatively well-to-do aunt and uncle on a farm near Charlestown, New Hampshire. Tucker's religious curiosity was first aroused when Francis Asbury visited her home, and later stimulated by an elderly wayfarer whom the family took in on a stormy winter night. Before retiring to bed, the man sang from a Methodist hymn book, prompting Mary to ask, "Do tell me, old man, what makes you look so happy? You are poor, and you came here on foot in this severe storm; I am certain that you possess but little to render life cheerful, yet you seem perfectly so." The man simply replied that he was a Methodist, but this was enough to arouse Mary's curiosity about what at that time seemed a mysterious and shadowy sect.[75]

Mary was converted in 1812, and in 1816 married Thomas Wait Tucker (1791–1871), despite the "opposition of near and dear friends who . . . thought me rash and foolish in uniting my destiny with that of a penniless Methodist preacher."[76] That year Thomas was appointed to the Athens, Vermont, circuit, a three weeks' circuit of 160 miles. During Thomas's first tour of the circuit, Mary boarded with a family in Athens. But when Thomas returned, she insisted on accompanying him, over his objections, by riding two to the horse. "We set out

75. Tucker, *Itinerant Preaching*, 9-23. Also see Leonard I. Sweet, *The Minister's Wife: Her Role in Nineteenth-Century American Evangelicalism* (Philadelphia: Temple University Press, 1983). Sweet suggests four models to illustrate the roles open to ministers' wives from the sixteenth to the nineteenth centuries: the Companion, the Sacrificer, the Assistant, and the Partner (3-11).

76. Tucker, *Itinerant Preaching*, 36.

in rather awkward style, which afforded a little amusement to some of the lookers on, but it did not disconcert me, as I expected to improve by practice. It was not a very comfortable mode of traveling, but a perfectly safe one for me, as I was young and nimble as a squirrel. . . . We were every where received with the greatest cordiality, and my first essay at circuit travelling was successful."[77]

Combative and energetic, Mary would need these qualities to persevere through the trials of the early rural itinerancy. At one house, holes in the walls and roof allowed enough snow to blow into their bedroom that it became ankle-deep by morning. On another occasion the Tuckers were invited to share a dinner being cooked on the same fire over which an old horse that "had recently died a natural death" was being boiled for soap grease. Mary noted with dismay that the contents of the two kettles occasionally frothed over into one another.[78]

In time, material circumstances gradually improved for the Tuckers, though Thomas never rose above ordinary stature as a preacher and often suffered from poor health. Stage travel became more widespread, and the Tuckers were routinely appointed to one after another of the rapidly multiplying city stations in New England. In 1818 and 1819 Thomas was stationed in Bristol, Rhode Island, and in 1820 and 1821 in Somerset, Massachusetts, followed by appointments in New London, Connecticut; Milford, Massachusetts; Lisbon, New Hampshire; Weymouth, Massachusetts; Newport, Rhode Island; and Wilbraham, Massachusetts. In 1837 Mary, who wanted to be near her grown children, accompanied Thomas to the annual conference in Springfield, Massachusetts. When Thomas's station was announced as a town in lower Rhode Island, she went to bishop Elijah Hedding and had the appointment changed to Millbury, Massachusetts.[79] This, of course, was a far cry from the way things had been done in the days of Francis Asbury, as Tucker herself fully realized, and was indicative of how settled and comfortable Methodism was becoming by the second quarter of the nineteenth century.

Shifts in Francis Asbury's attitude about marriage also reflect this same trend toward a settled clergy. Always concerned with maintaining the movement's popularity and its ability to reach the broadest

77. Ibid., 49.
78. Ibid., 52-54.
79. Ibid., 92.

possible audience, Asbury initially opposed his preachers marrying. "No man I ever knew cherished a higher Christian regard for the female character than he," wrote Thomas Ware concerning Asbury's stance on marriage circa 1790, "yet, for the sake of the itinerancy, he chose a single life, and was doubtless well pleased with those preachers who, for the same reason, followed his example."[80] "Some men marry fortunes, and go to take care of them; some men marry wives, and go to make fortunes for them; and thus, when, for the time, we should have age and experience in the ministry, we have youth and inexperience," Asbury remarked to James Quinn in 1803.[81] As late as 1805 when Asbury heard of Thomas Coke's marriage in England, he wrote, "Marriage is honourable in all—but to me it is a ceremony awful as death. Well may it be so, when I calculate we have lost the travelling labours of two hundred of the best men in America, or the world, by marriage and consequent location."[82] But as it became easier for a married preacher to itinerate, and indeed as the people began to expect their preachers to marry, Asbury at times gave his blessing to a circuit rider's marriage. Hence, in 1803, he gave his blessing to James Quinn's marriage at the age of twenty-eight, and at the 1804 Virginia Annual Conference Asbury defended admitting the married Samuel Monnett on trial, stating, "Better take preachers well married, than be at the trouble of marrying them after you get them."[83]

However strong his misgivings about a settled clergy may have been, Asbury could not deny that, like Mary Tucker, many preachers' wives worked tirelessly in support of their husbands and the church. "With youthful ardor and sanguine expectations," wrote Tucker after thirty years of marriage and itinerancy, "I set out upon life's great journey, determined if I could not labor like my husband in a public manner, I would devote all my energies to smooth his rough paths, and strengthen his hands for the great work of saving souls." However confining this role may seem from our perspective, it was one that Tucker readily and gladly accepted. Despite the sacrifices demanded of an itinerant's wife, she enjoyed a strong relationship with Thomas throughout their marriage. "It may be thought by some, of cold practical natures, that the old and gray headed should have done with romance . . . that the happiness of wedded love is a thing

---

80. Ware, *Sketches*, 183.
81. Quinn, *Sketches*, 78.
82. *JLFA* 2:474 (9 July 1805).
83. Smith, *Recollections*, 126.

of the past," wrote Mary in the late 1840s. This, she admitted, might be true for those whose marriage was based only on "sentiment." But, "those whose affections are founded upon true love and esteem, and nurtured by constancy and unselfishness, grow in strength with each succeeding year . . . the silken cord that first bound such hearts together is gently drawn tighter, and the crosses and afflictions shared in common bind them the more firmly."[84]

Indeed, by the 1820s and 1830s the strong but domesticated faith of Mary Tucker was in many ways more representative of American Methodism than was that of Francis Asbury. It is telling that, after Asbury's death in 1816, the two men elected bishops in his place, Enoch George and Robert R. Roberts, had both married.[85]

An Education Fit for a Preacher

The development of close personal ties between the preachers formed the foundation of Methodist ministerial training. In many respects the Methodist system was based on the artisan concept of apprenticeship. Unwilling to submit to lengthy traditional programs of theological education, newly licensed Methodist preachers were tutored on the job by more experienced colleagues. In place of any kind of seminary or college training, less experienced preachers were often paired with better-seasoned itinerants on the same circuit.

Though early Methodists rejected traditional theological education, they by no means rejected learning *per se*. "We do not despise learning," declared the itinerant Thomas Ware, "on the contrary we hold it to be desirable. But we do not deem it an essential qualification of a gospel minister. Grace, rather than human learning, qualifies a man to preach." And grace, as the itinerant William Beauchamp was fond of pointing out, could most readily be measured by the conversion of souls. Hence, from the very start, colleagues and congregations judged Methodist preachers by the results of their preaching. Early

---

84. Tucker, *Itinerant Preaching*, 141-42. For a similar firsthand assessment of the rewards of marrying a Methodist preacher, see Julia A. Tevis, *Sixty Years in a School Room: An Autobiography of Mrs. Julia A. Tevis, Principal of Science Hall Female Academy. To Which is Prefixed an Autobiographical Sketch of Rev. John Tevis* (Cincinnati: Western Methodist Book Concern, 1878), 262.

85. Quinn, *Sketches*, 122-23. On this topic, also see Sweet, *The Minister's Wife*, 47-50; and A. Gregory Schneider, "From Democratization to Domestication: The Transitional Orality of the American Methodist Circuit Rider," in Leonard I. Sweet, ed., *Communication and Change in American Religious History* (Grand Rapids: Eerdmans, 1993), 141-64.

Methodist sermons invariably emphasized the practical, the immediate, and the dramatic. "People love the preacher who makes them feel," concluded Ware.[86]

Despite their aversion to formal schooling, one of the by-products of conversion and entrance into the ministry for many of the early itinerants was a newly awakened desire to read. "Such was my thirst for knowledge," wrote Alfred Brunson, reflecting on his early career, "that when I could not get lights in the house, I have sat for hours out-of-doors and read by moonlight." Similarly, following his conversion, Jacob Young "began to feel an intense thirst for knowledge . . . the desire to improve my mind increased daily." He pored over the Bible, read Freeborn Garrettson's journal, Fletcher's *Appeal* and *Works*, Baxter's *Saint's Everlasting Rest*, and Wesley's *Sermons*.[87] Like Young and many of his contemporaries, Billy Hibbard embarked on a similar course of reading early in his career. "Though I had only a small degree of education, barely a common school education," wrote Hibbard, "yet I could sometimes read one hundred pages in a long winter's evening, and the next day work hard at farming business, dressing flax, threshing grain, chopping wood; working with my hands, that I might not be chargeable to any, and have something good to feed the Methodist preacher and his horse."[88] From the beginning, Wesley had placed a premium on encouraging his preachers and people to read, and literacy remained an important part of the Methodist experience in America. Like Wesley, Asbury and his colleagues believed strongly in the power of the written word. If a preacher claimed, "I have no *Taste* for Reading," the 1784 *Discipline* advised him to "Contract a Taste for it by Use, or return to your Trade."[89]

86. Ware, *Sketches,* 189 and 175; Beauchamp, *Letters on the Call and Qualifications of Ministers of the Gospel* (Richmond, Va.: John Early, 1853), 54-57, 60-61, 65, 67, 75, and 89.

87. Brunson, *Western Pioneer,* 64, also see p. 219; Jacob Young, *Autobiography,* 51. Contemporary editions of the works listed by Young include: Freeborn Garrettson, *The Experience and Travels of Mr. Freeborn Garrettson, Minister of the Methodist Episcopal Church in North America* (Philadelphia: John Dickins, 1791); Richard Baxter, *The Saints Everlasting Rest: Or, A Treatise of the Blessed State of the Saints in Their Enjoyment of God in Glory: Extracted from the Works of Mr. Richard Baxter by John Wesley, M.A. late Fellow of Lincoln College, Oxford* (Philadelphia: John Dickins, 1791); John Wesley, *Sermons on Several Occasions,* 4 vols. (Philadelphia: John Dickins, 1794–1801); John Fletcher, *The Works of the Rev. John Fletcher,* 3 vols. (Philadelphia: John Dickins, 1791–92); and John Fletcher, *An Appeal to Matter of Fact and Common Sense; or, A Rational Demonstration of Man's Corrupt and Lost Estate* (Philadelphia: John Dickins, 1794).

88. Hibbard, *Memoirs,* 128 and 96. The scope of Francis Asbury's reading over the course of his career is truly impressive given his educational background. See Robert C. Monk, "Educating Oneself for Ministry: Francis Asbury's Reading Patterns," *Methodist History* 29 (April 1991), 140-54; and Edward M. Lang, *Francis Asbury's Reading of Theology: A Bibliographic Study* (Evanston, Ill.: Garrett Theological Seminary Library, 1972).

89. *Discipline*/MEC 1784, in Tigert, *History,* 563.

Indeed, an impressive number of the late-eighteenth- and early-nineteenth-century preachers improved their literacy dramatically following their conversions, as the life of Sampson Maynard illustrates. The son of a carpenter, Maynard was born in England about 1757. Early on he was apprenticed to a butcher, but soon ran away, eventually learning carpentry from his father. When the Revolutionary War broke out, Maynard again ran away, this time to join the British navy. After five years at sea he returned to England, leaving the navy to return to carpentry once again. "I rambled from town to city, and worked at my trade," he wrote, "for I hated the name of a lazy fellow, nor could I bare to go in rags as I saw some of my shop-mates. . . ."[90] He experienced conversion as a result of an intense visionary experience in which Satan confronted him in his shop. In 1795 Maynard left England for New York, where he was ordained a deacon and then an elder, all as a local preacher, while still working at his trade. Maynard reported that he could barely read when converted, but by the end of his career he was able to compose an autobiographical work of some two hundred fifty-two pages. Likewise, Benjamin Abbott's autobiography is nearly two hundred pages, Billy Hibbard's is 368 pages, Jacob Young's is 528 pages, and Alfred Brunson's stretches to more than eight hundred pages.

What is perhaps most important to understand in this respect is that though almost none of the early Methodist preachers had a classical education, most were at least as well educated as the bulk of their audience. They had enough learning to make them respectable to their listeners, but not so much as to make them seem distant or irrelevant.

The autobiography of William Capers (1790–1855) sheds additional light on the training of young Methodist preachers and the bonds that formed between them. Capers's account is particularly valuable because, though he became a thoroughgoing Methodist preacher, his upbringing, conversion, and career were in many respects atypical. Hence, his background demanded that he reason through what most early itinerants took for granted. The son of a slaveholding plantation owner and former Revolutionary War officer, Capers was born in January 1790 near Charleston, South Carolina. Unlike most Methodist itinerants, he grew up in relative affluence. As a youth, he attended boarding schools, entering South Carolina College in 1805 with the

---

90. Maynard, *Experience*, 144.

ability to read some Latin and Greek. Eager to make a name for himself in local politics, he dropped out of college in 1808 and began studying law.[91]

Prior to this time, Capers had attended camp meetings in 1802, 1803, and 1806 near his home. At the first two of these meetings he witnessed first hand the "jerks," the "jumping exercise," and other forms of convulsive enthusiasm often associated with turn-of-the-century revivals. At all three meetings Capers saw large numbers fall in a swoon, appearing "senseless, and almost lifeless, for hours together; lying motionless at full length on the ground, and almost as pale as corpses." He came away from these meetings with a deep sense of conviction, but remained unconverted. "I did not fall at any time, as I saw others do," he later recalled. "I kept myself aloof, I knew not why."[92]

In 1808 Capers was again convicted of his lost spiritual state following yet another camp meeting. As a result, he gave up studying law and looked for an opportunity to join the Methodists. "I longed with intense desire for the time to arrive when, by joining the Church, I should formally break with the world, and identify myself with those who . . . for being the most spiritual and least worldly, were regarded the most enthusiastic and least rational of all the sects of Christians." Capers did in fact join the Methodists in August 1808, but an incident from this event reveals how little he actually understood of the movement at the time. Following the meeting, Capers, who was dressed "in the point of fashion, with a deep frill of linen cambric and a full-sized breastpin at my bosom," went to the home of an "old Methodist." There he was advised that he should quit wearing ruffles and breastpins, or at least find a way to "hide them." At first Capers was "profoundly puzzled"; Why would anyone want to hide fine clothes? But he soon caught on, and proceeded to "rip off the frill from my bosom, which my sister kept, as a memorial of those simple-hearted times, for many years." Later, Capers would even forgo wearing suspenders because they struck some of his listeners as too pretentious.[93]

---

91. Capers, "Autobiography," 11-70. On Capers, also see Shipp, *Methodism in South Carolina*, 454-64.

92. Capers, "Autobiography," 51-55.

93. Capers, "Autobiography," 71-76, and 118. The itinerant Lovick Pierce had a similar experience with suspenders. After arriving on the Augusta, Georgia, station in 1806, Pierce realized that his country clothes would not do in town. So, "I got me a new suit—of course, cut Methodist fashion—and, among other things, I got a *pair of suspenders,* for, really, I could not get along without them; but I had to hide them out of sight when Brother Myers came my way, or he would have thought me sinfully worldly." Smith, *Life of Pierce,* 26.

On the day that Capers joined the church, the itinerant William Gassaway asked him to accompany him on his circuit. Capers agreed and, much to his surprise, was immediately called on to exhort following Gassaway's sermons. Why would someone who was still unsure of his conversion be afforded such treatment? Most likely Gassaway simply could not resist the temptation to have a member of the local gentry by his side, or pass up the opportunity to draw someone of social distinction further inside the Methodist orbit. If so, the tour had the desired effect. As he traveled with Gassaway, Capers gradually became confident of his own conversion, though he never had the kind of dramatic encounter so typical of early Methodist preachers. He also felt increasingly called to preach, and proposed that he should embark on "a regular course of divinity studies, which I should pursue without interruption for several years." Gassaway objected, telling him that the Methodist way was "to study and preach and preach and study, from day to day."

> He admitted that on my plan he might learn more theology, and be able to compose a better thesis, but insisted he would not make a better preacher. In this argument he insisted much on the practical character of preaching: that to reach its end, it must be more than a well-composed sermon, or an eloquent discourse, or able dissertation. It must have to do with men as a shot at a mark; in which not only the ammunition should be good, but the aim true. . . . And the force of preaching must largely depend, under the blessing of God, on the naturalness and truthfulness of the preacher's postulates; arguing to the sinner from what he knows of him. . . .

"The true question was as to usefulness, not eminence," concluded Capers.[94]

Capers eventually came to accept what most new itinerants realized up front: Methodist preachers were literally trained on the job, learning by observation and through coaching from their more experienced colleagues to preach forceful, pragmatic, vernacular sermons. "The traveling preacher finds himself providentially initiated into a great theological school, where study and practice move on together," wrote Charles Giles. "What he gains by study is brought into daily

---

94. Capers, "Autobiography," 76-85; Sprague, *Annals of the American Pulpit,* 462. Gassaway joined the traveling connection on trial in 1788, spent the bulk of his career preaching in Georgia and North and South Carolina, and located in 1814. In 1808 Gassaway was on the Santee, South Carolina, circuit. See Abel McKee Chreitzberg, *Early Methodism in the Carolinas* (Nashville: MECS, 1897), 100-101; Shipp, *Methodism in South Carolina,* 191-98; *Minutes MEC* (1840) 1:161.

use; and hence it becomes deeply printed on the memory. . . . So he must pursue his course of learning through life, and graduate on the day of his death."[95]

Seasoned preachers like Gassaway often made a practice of taking junior colleagues under their wings. Alfred Brunson looked to Shadrach Bostwick as his mentor. Bostwick had begun itinerating in 1791 and located in 1805. Thereafter, "his house was a theological school," wrote Brunson, "where he gave many lectures and model sermons, from which we [the younger preachers] obtained much useful knowledge pertaining to our holy calling."

In addition to mentoring by senior colleagues and presiding elders, the younger itinerants also evaluated and advised one another. While appointed to the same circuit, Brunson and Calvin Ruter agreed to critique each others sermons. "No one step in my life contributed so much to correct my language in public speaking as this," wrote Brunson. According to William Capers, the younger preachers of his day rarely met together for any length of time without exchanging this kind of advice. "It might be in their pronunciation of such or such a word, some article of dress, or the way the hair was combed," recalled Capers, "or it might be something more serious, touching their spirit or manners; so that we were always watching over each other, and, as I believe, for good."[96]

Some of the better-educated and more experienced preachers were of course capable of producing subtle, well-crafted sermons. Ezekiel Cooper (1763–1847) was known as one of early American Methodism's outstanding preachers and debaters. Born in eastern Maryland, Cooper left home in 1783 to become a joiner, but reluctantly agreed, at the insistence of Francis Asbury, to take up the Caroline, Maryland, circuit in 1784. Like many itinerants, he kept both a journal and a circuit notebook. For each year, the notebook contains a listing of each preaching place, plus the dates and sermon texts for each appointment. These notebooks reveal that on rural circuits Cooper preached up to four hundred times a year. On the East Jersey circuit in 1786–87 he preached 345 times, but used only seventy-three scripture passages, or texts. Cooper used twelve of these texts ten or more times. Mark 13:37 and 1 Thessalonians 5:19 were his

95. Giles, *Pioneer*, 288-89.

96. Brunson, *Western Pioneer*, 235 and 204; Capers, "Autobiography," 134. On education and the early circuit riders, also see Raymond P. Cowan, "The Arminian Alternative: The Rise of the Methodist Episcopal Church, 1765–1850" (Ph.D. diss., Georgia State University, 1991), chap. 10.

favorites that year; he used each at least twenty times. Both Mark 13:37 ("And what I say unto you I say unto all, Watch.") and 1 Thessalonians 5:19 ("Quench not the Spirit.") are short, cryptic passages that could no doubt be turned to several purposes. Nonetheless, Cooper's sermons on these passages could be memorable events. Elijah Woolsey distinctly remembered Cooper preaching from Mark 13:37 more than four decades after the event, describing the sermon as "a dagger to my heart."[97]

After Cooper had spent only four years on rural circuits, Asbury began stationing him in important town pulpits. In these settings Cooper honed his skills as an orator. Here he spent more of his time meeting classes and calling on members, and less time preaching. He also did not have the luxury of being able to repeat himself as often. In Annapolis, Cooper preached only 185 times during the conference year 1789–90, but used 120 texts.[98]

But most of the early itinerants were less inventive than Ezekiel Cooper. Thomas Smith recorded twenty-nine of his preaching texts for the years 1798 through 1802 in his memoirs. Of these, nine are from the book of Matthew. Indeed, during Smith's first year of itinerating it seems he read or preached from little else! In the ensuing years Smith expanded his sights to include the writings of Paul, the other Gospels, and a handful of Old Testament books, but the majority of the Bible never found its way into his preaching.[99] Thomas Morris's journal for January 1816 to February 1817 on the Marietta, Ohio, circuit reveals a similar pattern of repetition and selectivity.

---

97. Lester B. Scherer, *Ezekiel Cooper, 1763–1847: An Early American Methodist Leader* (n.p.: Commission on Archives and History of the UMC, ca. 1965), 1-16, 21, and 166; Woolsey, *Supernumerary*, 9. On Cooper also see George A. Phoebus, *Beams of Light on Early Methodism in America: Chiefly Drawn from the Diary, Letters, Manuscripts, Documents, and Original Tracts of the Rev. Ezekiel Cooper* (New York: Phillips & Hunt, 1887); Sprague, *Annals of the American Pulpit*, 108-12.

98. Scherer, *Ezekiel Cooper*, 167. Similarly, Thomas Morrell's journal reveals that between 1796 and 1809, during which time he preached mostly in and around Elizabethtown, New Jersey, Morrell used a relatively extensive number of texts from both the Old and New Testaments. Morrell, *Journals*, 29-50. Thomas Morrell was born in 1747 in New York, fought in the Revolutionary War as an officer, and worked in his father's mercantile business both before and after the war. In 1786 he became a local preacher and in 1789 was ordained an elder. Morrell married three times and lived during most of his career in Elizabethtown, New Jersey. He died in 1838. On Morrell see Simpson, *Cyclopedia*, 630; Sprague, *Annals of the American Pulpit*, 145-50.

99. Smith, *Experience*, 20-175. Cooper, for his part, dreaded the prospect of seminary educated ministers. Such a class of preachers, he feared, would inevitably become focused on obtaining "dignity, ease, and fortune." Scherer, *Ezekiel Cooper*, 187-88.

Apart from the Psalms, the newly licensed Morris preached almost exclusively from a limited number of New Testament passages.[100]

William Ormond's journal contains one of the most complete records of sermon texts left by an itinerant. His journal extends from July 1791, shortly after Ormond began itinerating, to October 1803, a few months before his death (with the exception of a missing volume for December 1792 to August 1795). For the nearly 10 years covered in the journals, Ormond preached 1,823 sermons from 262 identifiable biblical passages. But, as with Smith and Morris, Ormond had his favorites. His 10 favorite texts, along with the number of times he preached from each, were: 2 Timothy 2:11-12 (83); Psalm 40:1-4 (73); 1 John 4:18-19 (65); Genesis 19:17 (58); Matthew 24:13 (54); 1 Peter 2:4 (54); 2 Corinthians 13:5 (44); 1 Peter 4:18 (44); Isaiah 21:5 (43); and Hebrews 4:9 (43). Indeed, Ormond's 27 favorite texts, from which he preached at least 20 times each, account for 56 percent of all his sermons. As with Thomas Smith, most of the Old Testament and much of the New never found their way into Ormond's preaching. Excluding Ormond's 10 favorite Old Testament passages, the remaining Old Testament texts account for only 18 percent of his sermons. He preached on only 4 passages from Acts, and only 22 times from Romans, but 86 times from Revelation, 117 times from 1 Peter, and 126 times from Isaiah.[101]

Ormond clearly knew many of his favorite texts by heart, often quoting them in his journal rather than giving the chapter and verse reference. His favorite texts were the sort that could be used in a variety of settings. Second Timothy 2:11-12 reads, "It is a faithful saying: For if we be dead with him, we shall also live with him; If we suffer, we shall also reign with him; if we deny him, he also will deny us." Psalm 40:1 reads, "I waited patiently for the LORD; and he inclined unto me, and heard my cry," and 1 John 4:18-19 reads, "There is no fear in love; but perfect love casteth out fear: because fear hath torment. He that feareth is not made perfect in love. We love him, because he first loved us." These passages, dealing with faithfulness, death, the Resurrection, patience, mercy, fear, and love could be used to address a variety of situations. Considering that Ormond rode

---

100. Thomas A. Morris, "A Diary Referring to the Text or Texts of Each Day; Also the Time & Place of Delivering the Same, and the Nos. Received Into Society by Tho. A. Morris," MSS, Ohio Wesleyan University, Delaware, Ohio, 1-22. Born in 1794 near Charleston, West Virginia, Morris joined the Ohio Conference on trial in 1816 and was elected a Bishop of the MEC in 1836. He died in 1874. See Simpson, *Cyclopedia*, 630-31.

101. Ormond, "Journals," vols. 1-5.

eleven circuits during the years covered by his journal, he probably never preached the same sermon twice in the same place. But it is also clear that he made little attempt to guide his listeners through any sort of systematic or extended study of the scriptures.[102]

Of itself, this pattern did not represent a failing on the part of Smith, Morris, or Ormond. The first *Discipline* of 1785 stated that the goal of Methodist preaching was to deal with an audience "so as to get within them, and suit all our Discourse to their several Conditions and Tempers: To chuse the fittest Subjects, and to follow them with a holy Mixture of Seriousness, and Terror, and Love, and Meekness."[103] In other words, as Philip Gatch pointed out, the goal was to aim "more at the heart than the head," to link the concerns of everyday life to the ultimate fate of one's eternal soul. Gatch's sermons relied heavily on anecdotes, leading Henry Smith to describe him as a "close home preacher." "Sound Wesleyanism," according to James Quinn, was best represented by "a truly evangelical sermon—no philosophical chaff or metaphysical froth."[104] Charles Giles remembered that the early Methodist preachers in upstate New York spoke "plainly and forcibly." "Experimental religion was a lucid theme to them. They spoke from the deep emotions of their own hearts—told us what they knew and how they felt." Their sermons were rarely "formal and lifeless, but close, alarming; pointed, and practical." Added Giles: "It is a lamentable fact, which cannot be concealed, that there are many ministers in the different churches, famed for their talents and learning, who have attracted much attention, and often obtained the applause of men, but never have made a Felix tremble, or caused an infidel to blush, or converted one sinner from the error of his ways. No signs follow them but worldly honours, pride, affluence, and moral death."[105]

However partisan this assessment may be, the early Methodist preachers were clearly cut from different cloth than many of their counterparts in the established churches. Anning Owen, an itinerant who spent most of his twenty-year career from 1795 to 1814 in western New York, was known as "Bawling Owen" because of his vociferous

---

102. Ibid.

103. Tigert, *History*, 539-40.

104. Gatch, *Sketch*, 102, 183, and 189; and Quinn, *Sketches*, 136. Likewise, Francis Asbury "had a remarkable method of making an unexpected use of observations he had dropped in preaching," according to one of his traveling companions. See John Wesley Bond, "Anecdotes of Bishop Asbury [1817]," MSS, Drew University Library, Madison, N.J.

105. Giles, *Pioneer* (New York: Lane & Sandford, 1844), 58-62 and 129.

preaching style. Lovick Pierce reportedly could preach three three-hour sermons in a day, "and then sing the doxology with as clear a tone as when he rose in the morning." James Meacham most often used the word *cry* in his journal to describe his own sermon delivery, as in, "many precious souls, to whom I cryed . . ." Likewise, when the itinerant Jimmy Jenkins prayed, it was said that his "soul, voice, strength, all went in. The sound was as the roar of a tempest, ablaze with lightning, and pealing with thunder." In this regard, Owen, Pierce, Meacham, and Jenkins were simply following the advice of Francis Asbury, who once urged one of his preachers to "feel for the power, feel for the power, brother."[106]

Following Wesley, American Methodists were Arminians who believed that God's grace is resistible. Though God first reaches out to us, we are free to accept or reject eternal salvation. From the Methodist point of view, no choice could be more important. Moreover, conversion was a vocation, not a one-time event; it was possible for believers to turn from God and lose their salvation. This is why Methodist sermons were often so passionate and direct. When Joseph Crawford preached Nabby Frothingham's funeral sermon in 1809, his text was 1 Corinthians 15:55-57 ("O death, where is thy sting? O grave, where is thy victory? The sting of death is sin; and the strength of sin is the law. But thanks be to God, which giveth us the victory, through our Lord Jesus Christ.") and his three points were:

I. Sin, that brought Death into the world, and is in our text declared to be the sting of Death!
II. The several kinds of Death produced by sin.
III. The victorious exclamation, Through Jesus Christ our Lord.

After expounding on these points, using Frothingham's life as an illustration, Crawford declared to his audience in typical Methodist fashion, "your time may be very short; you know not who next may be swept away." "Let all ask the question, My merciful God, am I prepared should I be next; all stand in the gap—all are exposed—let all take the alarm."[107]

---

106. Samuel G. Ayres, *Methodist Heroes of Other Days* (New York, 1916), 35; Smith, *Life of Pierce*, 31; James Meacham, "A Journal and Travel of James Meacham," ed. William K. Boyd, *Annual Publication of Historical Papers of the Historical Society of Trinity College* 9 (1912): 66-95; 10 (1914): 87-102; Smith, *Life of Pierce*, 12; and Boehm, *Reminiscences*, 441.

107. Joseph Crawford, *The Substance of a Sermon Delivered at the Funeral of Miss Nabby Frothingham, of Middletown (Conn.), February 24, 1809, to a Numerous Crowd of Attentive Hearers, in the Methodist Meeting-house* (New York: John C. Totten, 1809), 5-27.

Sometimes a preacher's illustrations could be dramatic. Benjamin Abbott once preached a funeral sermon to the accompaniment of a violent thunderstorm: "I lost no time, but set before them the awful coming of Christ, in all his splendour, with all the armies of heaven, to judge the world and to take vengeance on the ungodly! It may be, cried I, that he will descend in the next clap of thunder! The people screamed, screeched, and fell all through the house." Abbott's sermons (at times he claimed to be given sermon texts in his dreams) were often the occasion of such emotional outbursts. At one particularly boisterous meeting, people shouted and fell to the floor while others rushed the door or jumped out of windows to escape the mayhem inside. In the midst of it all a woman cried out that Abbott must be a devil to cause such a stir, but Abbott himself was quite pleased with the whole affair.[108] Similarly, Joseph Everett once preached a sermon during a storm in which he twice entreated God to "send thy thunder still nigher." According to one account, the next day a man attempted to get a legal injunction against Everett's preaching, stating that "he verily believed that had Mr. Everett called the third time, they would all have been struck dead."[109] This last embellishment may well be apocryphal, but it nonetheless illustrates the emotional appeal associated with early Methodist preaching.

Clearly the Methodist style of preaching was new and even shocking at first for many Americans. According to Jesse Lee, when Robert Williams first preached in Norfolk, Virginia, in 1772, "The general conclusion was, that they never heard such a man before: for they said, sometimes he would preach, then he would pray, then he would swear, and at times he would cry." Explained Lee: "The people were so little used to hearing a preacher say hell, or Devil in preaching, that they thought he was swearing, when he told them about going to hell." But by the early nineteenth century the Methodists had helped alter the tone and appearance of sermon and preacher to such a degree that this kind of preaching was widely recognized, if not universally welcomed. According to Abner Chase, two lawyers once happened upon a meeting at which the itinerant William Keith was about to preach. Seeing Keith, one lawyer quipped, "If that is the preacher, I think we shall get but little to-night." "Don't be hasty in

---

108. Abbott, *Experience*, 89, 22, and 51.
109. Travis, *Autobiography*, 37.

making your conclusion," replied the other, "you can never tell how far a toad will hop from his appearance."[110]

Because audiences largely judged Methodist preachers by their ability to evoke a heart-swelling response and their willingness to endure the rigors of itinerant life, rather than for their theological polish, many began their preaching careers at a remarkably young age. Seth Crowell and Benjamin Paddock began exhorting at ages fourteen and sixteen, respectively, and were appointed to their first circuits at eighteen and twenty; George Gary began itinerating in 1809 at age fifteen, as did Martin Ruter in 1800 at sixteen, both in New England; Lovick Pierce joined the South Carolina conference as a traveling preacher in 1804 at the age of nineteen, despite never having attended school more than six months in his life; and Seth Mattison was licensed to exhort in 1805 at age seventeen and as a local preacher at nineteen.[111] In June 1801 Laban Clark attended his first annual conference in New York City. As he gazed at the assembled preachers, Clark noted with approval that "the conference was composed mostly of young men in the prime of life and none past the meridian and vigour of manhood . . . looking at them I said to myself[,] with such men we can take the world."[112]

Conclusion: An Alluring Combination

The typical early circuit rider preached from a basic set of scripture texts embellished with anecdotes and analogies from everyday life. The doctrinal content of his sermons was no doubt consistently Wesleyan, and both his character and beliefs were subject to an annual

---

110. Jesse Lee, *A Short History of the Methodists* (Baltimore, 1810; Rutland, Vt.: Academy Books, 1974), 40; Abner Chase, *Recollections of the Past* (New York: published for the author, 1848), 40. William Keith (1776–1810) was born in Easton, Massachusetts, and first joined the itinerancy in 1798. Keith died while stationed in New York City, leaving a widow and three children. See William Keith, *The Experience of William Keith (Written by Himself) Together With Some Observations Conclusive of Divine Influence on the Mind of Man* (Utica, New York: Asahel Seward, 1806); *Minutes MEC* (1840) 1:193-94.

111. Seth Crowell, *The Journal of Seth Crowell: Containing an Account of His Travels as a Methodist Preacher for Twelve Years* (New York: J. C. Totten, 1813), 10-12; Paddock, *Memoir*, 52 and 80; and Smith, *Life of Pierce*, 12 and 18. On Gary, see Boehm, *Reminiscences*, 247; and Paddock, *Memoir*, 296; on Ruter, see Dan Young, *Autobiography*, 70; and Simpson, *Cyclopedia*, 770; and on Mattison, see Paddock, *Memoir*, 332-34. John Fidler was apparently only fifteen years old when he began preaching as an itinerant in 1784. See Leonard T. and Carolyn E. Wolcott, *Wilderness Rider* (Nashville: Abingdon Press, 1984), 15; and *Minutes MEC* (1840) 1:19.

112. Laban Clark, *Laban Clark: Circuit Rider for the Methodist Episcopal Church*, trans. E. Farley Sharp (Rutland, Vt.: Academy Books, 1987), 30.

review. But what few expository skills he may have utilized were largely gleaned from the sermons of his colleagues. He learned to preach with what the itinerant Henry Smith referred to as an irresistible "holy knock-'em-down power."[113] Nothing would have been more unthinkable to a Methodist itinerant than the dispassionate reading of a prepared sermon. They invariably preached extemporaneously, without the aid of notes or manuscript. In the ardently egalitarian and turbulent post-Revolutionary years, the itinerants succeeded in both establishing a rapport with their audiences and stunning them with an apocalyptic vision of impending divine judgment. Largely self-educated, they instinctively understood the importance of speaking in the vernacular. They were both familiar and frightening—homespun heralds of a gospel that was attune to everyday life and common experience, and unsettling in its larger implications. This proved to be an alluring combination.

The appeal of the circuit rider was something the famous evangelist Charles Finney clearly understood. "Look at the Methodists," wrote Finney, "Many of their ministers are unlearned, in the common sense of the term, many of them taken right from the shop or the farm, and yet they have gathered congregations, and pushed their way, and won souls every where. Wherever the Methodists have gone, their plain, pointed and simple, but warm and animated mode of preaching has always gathered congregations." "We must have exciting, powerful preaching, or the devil will have the people, except what the Methodists can save," concluded Finney.[114] Writing two decades later, the historian Philip Schaff came to much the same conclusion. Schaff noted that the emergence of Methodism was almost as important a step in the development of Protestantism as the Puritan revolution of the seventeenth century. Though he had little sympathy for the popular nature of American Methodism's early phase, he was a keen observer who could not help but acknowledge some of the factors that led to the movement's vitality and growth. Schaff, like so many commentators before and since, was particularly impressed by the effectiveness of the Methodist preachers. What Methodist preachers lacked in higher education they made up for with "a decided aptness for popular discourse and exhortation," and by "fidelity and

---

113. Smith, *Recollections*, 31. On the background, education, and preaching of the early circuit riders, also see Frederick V. Mills, "Mentors of Methodism, 1784–1844," *Methodist History* 12 (October 1973), 43-57.

114. Charles G. Finney, *Lectures on Revivals of Religion* (New York: Leavitt, Lord & Company, 1835; reprint, Cambridge, Mass.: Harvard University Press, 1960), 273.

self-denial." Added Schaff: "They are particularly fitted for breaking the way in new regions . . . and for laboring among the lower classes of the people."[115] Early Methodist preachers popularized American religion not so much out of ideological conviction but because it was the only world they knew. They were natives in the early republican world of egalitarianism, geographic mobility, and the religious free market—a world in which the older denominations were still but immigrants.

---

115. Philip Schaff, *America: A Sketch of the Political, Social, and Religious Character of the United States of North America* (New York: C. Scribner, 1855; reprint, Cambridge, Mass.: Harvard University Press, 1961), 135-38.

CHAPTER 4

Female Evangelism in the Early Methodist Movement, 1784–1845

Catherine A. Brekus

In 1836, an African Methodist woman named Jarena Lee published the first edition of her religious memoir. Her book told the astonishing, inspiring story of an uneducated, "poor coloured woman" who rose to fame as an evangelical preacher during the early decades of the nineteenth century.[1] In 1819, certain that God had divinely inspired her to preach, Lee left the security of her home and family in Philadelphia for the lonely, self-sacrificing life of an itinerant evangelist. Traveling by horseback, by boat, or on foot, she crisscrossed the

---

1. Lee published two editions of her memoir, the first in 1836 and an expanded version in 1849. See Jarena Lee, *The Life and Religious Experience of Mrs. Jarena Lee, A Coloured Lady, Giving an Account of her Call to Preach the Gospel* (Philadelphia, 1836), reprinted in William L. Andrews, ed., *Sisters of the Spirit: Three Black Women's Autobiographies of the Nineteenth Century* (Bloomington: University of Indiana, 1986), and Jarena Lee, *Religious Experience and Journal of Mrs. Jarena Lee, Giving the Account of Her Call to Preach the Gospel* (Philadelphia: printed for the author, 1849), reprinted in Sue Houchins, ed., *Spiritual Narratives* (New York: Oxford University Press, 1988). The quote is from the 1849 edition, p. 27. For more on Lee, see Frances Smith Foster, "Neither Auction Block nor Pedestal: The Life and Religious Experience of Jarena Lee, A Coloured Lady," in Domna C. Stanton, ed., *The Female Autograph* (New York: New York Literary Forum, 1984); Nellie Y. McKay, "Nineteenth-Century Black Women's Spiritual Autobiographies: Religious Faith and Self-Empowerment," in Joy W. Barbre, ed., *Interpreting Women's Lives* (Bloomington: Indiana University Press, 1989), 139-54; Candis A. LaPrade, "Pens in the Hand of God: The Spiritual Autobiographies of Jarena Lee, Zilpha Elaw, and Rebecca Cox Jackson" (Ph.D. diss., University of North Carolina at Chapel Hill, 1994); Gloria Davis Goode, "Preachers of the Word and Singers of the Gospel: The Ministry of Women Among Nineteenth-Century African-Americans" (University of Pennsylvania Ph.D. dissertation, 1990); and Carla L. Peterson, *"Doers of the Word": African-American Women Speakers and Writers in the North* (New York: Oxford University Press, 1995).

country on her mission to spread the gospel, visiting churches in Pennsylvania, New Jersey, New York, Maryland, Delaware, Ohio, and even Canada. Remarkably, in 1827 alone, Lee covered more than two thousand miles and preached several hundred sermons. She created a sensation in antebellum America, often speaking to overflowing crowds at camp meetings and church services. Although her audiences were usually composed of other African Americans, she was reputed to be such a powerful, charismatic speaker that many white Methodists flocked to her meetings as well. As a black woman in the pulpit, Lee often suffered hostility and persecution, but she devoted her career to defending the spiritual equality of the sexes. "As unseemly as it may appear now-a-days for a woman to preach," she explained, "it should be remembered that nothing is impossible with God. And why should it be thought impossible, heterodox, or improper for a woman to preach? seeing the Savior died for the woman as well as for the man."[2]

Jarena Lee met many other Methodist female preachers and exhorters as she traveled across the country. In 1839, she shared a pulpit with Zilpha Elaw, an equally popular preacher for the African Methodists, and in 1841 she met "Sister Tilgham" (Juliann Jane Tilmann) who was returning home after a long absence "preaching the Everlasting Gospel of the Kingdom." She also met at least three other female preachers (none of whom she identified by name) who accompanied her on her travels and lent her spiritual support.[3] Although Lee often felt isolated, she was only one member of a larger community of women—both white and black—who felt called to a life of public evangelism in early national and antebellum America.

Between 1784 and 1845, at least twenty-two women preached for the Methodists and African Methodists, and hundreds of others shared their testimonies during church services, camp meetings, and love feasts. In their early history, the Methodists gave women extraordinary freedom to speak, encouraging them to share their religious experiences by "witnessing" in public. Institutionally, they were opposed to female preaching, but they still allowed women to "exhort" if they felt inspired. Exhorting was spontaneous and informal; it did not require women to explicate biblical texts, but only to tell their own personal stories of repentance and salvation. In con-

---

2. Jarena Lee, *Religious Experience*, 11.
3. Jarena Lee, *Religious Experience*, 88, 93, 61, 63, 94-95. Like Lee, Elaw also published her memoirs. See Zilpha Elaw, *Memoirs of the Life, Religious Experience, Ministerial Travels and Labours of Mrs. Zilpha Elaw, An American Female of Colour* (London, 1846), reprinted in Andrews, *Sisters of the Spirit*, 51-160.

trast, preaching was more authoritative, and it was supposed to be reserved for ordained clergymen alone.[4]

Methodists have only recently begun to recover the history of the female evangelists who filled the churches in the late eighteenth and early nineteenth centuries. Their stories are central to understanding the complicated history of women and religion in America; they reveal that the struggle over women's religious leadership stretches deep into the American past. Studying the lives of these female evangelists—whether preachers or exhorters—also throws light on the character of the early American Methodist movement as a whole. In their treatment of women, the early Methodists revealed their deep ambivalence over the dramatic transformations wrought by the market revolution.[5] In their formative years, they reacted to the dislocations of economic change with fear and suspicion, separating themselves from the secular world in order to preserve a Christian ethic of communal responsibility. Their churches were countercultural and relatively egalitarian, permitting women, laymen, and even slaves to proclaim the gospel. By the 1830s and 1840s, however, the Methodists had embraced the liberal, capitalist values of the middle-class culture they had once shunned. As they became more concerned with respectability, they promoted an ideology of domesticity that deprived women of their earlier freedom of speech. Mixing egalitarianism with conservatism, communalism with individualism, the early Methodists helped define both the possibilities and the limits of female evangelism in nineteenth-century America.

Praying Women: Methodist Women and the Ideology of Domesticity

Many recent historians have noted the central role that female Methodists played in nurturing and sustaining the early

---

4. I have identified the following Methodist female preachers before 1845: Eliza Barnes, Zilpha Elaw, Elizabeth (last name unknown), Rachel Evans, Julia A. J. Foote, Laura Smith Haviland, Sarah Hedges, Rebecca D. Hutchins, Rebecca Cox Jackson, Jarena Lee, Salome Lincoln, Elice Miller Smith, "Sister" Mills, Sarah Orne, Sarah J. Paine, Miss Parker, Julia Pell, Hannah Reeves, Sarah Riker, Ellen Stewart, Sally Thompson, Juliann Jane Tillman. For more information on these women and other female preachers, see Catherine A. Brekus, *Strangers and Pilgrims: Female Preaching in America, 1740–1845* (Chapel Hill: University of North Carolina Press, 1998). Three other women preached for the United Brethren: Laura P. Clemens, L. Courtland, and Lydia Sexton.

5. See Charles Sellers, *The Market Revolution: Jacksonian America, 1815–1846* (New York: Oxford University Press, 1992).

movement.[6] In the Methodist Episcopal Church (MEC), as in other Protestant denominations, women were the core of the church, feeding and housing Methodist itinerants, opening their homes for religious meetings, and encouraging others to convert to the faith. Women such as Barbara Heck and Mary Edwards Helm are still celebrated today as "founding mothers" who helped build the fledgling church into a thriving institution.[7] Although the names of many other Methodist women have disappeared, their memory lives on in the anonymous parade of "pious women" that fill clergymen's memoirs. For example, in his history of the Methodist Church in New Jersey, George Raybold praised a group of nameless "praying women" for "help[ing] much in the Lord."[8]

The African Methodist Episcopal Church (AME), organized by the Reverend Richard Allen in 1816, also owed much of its early success to the efforts of its female members.[9] Besides engaging in traditionally "feminine" activities such as sewing clothes for ministers, visiting

---

6. Beginning as early as the mid-seventeenth century, most Protestant converts were women. For example, in New Haven's First Congregational Church, 65 percent of the new members admitted between 1680 and 1690 were female, and women continued to dominate church membership lists into the twentieth century. See Harry S. Stout and Catherine A. Brekus, "Declension, Gender, and the 'New Religious History,'" in Philip R. VanderMeer and Robert P. Swierenga, eds., *Belief and Behavior: Essays in the New Religious History* (New Brunswick, N.J.: Rutgers University Press, 1991), 27-28. See also Barbara Welter, "The Feminization of American Religion," in *Dimity Convictions* (Athens: Ohio University Press, 1976), 83-102, and Richard D. Shiels, "The Feminization of American Congregationalism, 1730–1835," *American Quarterly* 33 (1981): 46-62.

7. On the legend of Barbara Heck, see Elizabeth Muir, *Petticoats in the Pulpit: The Story of Early Nineteenth-Century Methodist Women Preachers in Upper Canada* (Toronto: The United Church Publishing House, 1991), 165-79. On Helm, see Rosemary Skinner Keller, "Women and the Nature of Ministry in the United Methodist Tradition," *Methodist History* 22 (January 1984): 106. For scholarship on women in the early Methodist movement in America, see Jean Miller Schmidt, *Grace Sufficient: A History of Women in American Methodism* (Nashville: Abingdon Press, 1999); Donald G. Mathews, *Religion in the Old South* (Chicago: University of Chicago Press, 1977); A. Gregory Schneider, *The Way of the Cross Leads Home: The Domestication of American Methodism* (Bloomington: Indiana University Press, 1993); Cynthia Lynn Lyerly, *Methodism and the Southern Mind, 1770–1810* (New York: Oxford University Press, 1998), especially 94-118; Diane Helen Lobody, "Lost in the Ocean of Love: The Mystical Writings of Catherine Livingston Garretson" (Drew University Ph.D. dissertation, 1990); Diane H. Lobody, "'That Language Might Be Given Me': Women's Experiences in Early Methodism," *Perspectives*, 127-44; Joanna Bowen Gillespie, "*The Ladies Repository*, 1841–1861: The Emerging Voice of the Methodist Woman," in Russell E. Richey and Kenneth E. Rowe, eds., *Rethinking Methodist History* (Nashville: Kingswood Books, 1985), 148-58; Dee E. Andrews, *The Methodists and Revolutionary America, 1760–1800: The Shaping of an Evangelical Culture* (Princeton, N.J.: Princeton University Press, 2000); Hilah F. Thomas and Rosemary Skinner Keller, eds., *Women in New Worlds* (Nashville: Abingdon Press, 1981); and John Wigger, *Taking Heaven by Storm: Methodism and the Rise of Popular Christianity in America* (New York: Oxford University Press, 1998).

8. George A. Raybold, *Annals of Methodism or Sketches of the Origin and Progress of Methodism in Various Portions of West Jersey* (Philadelphia: T. Stokes, 1847), 48.

9. On the founding of the AME see Will B. Gravely, "African Methodisms and the Rise of Black Denominationalism," *Perspectives*, 108-26.

the sick, and preparing food for camp meetings, women also helped raise money and recruit new converts.[10] Through their tireless evangelism, women such as Elizabeth Cole and Sophie Murray added scores of converts to the church's growing membership lists.[11] Similarly, in the African Union Methodist Church, formed in Delaware in 1813, women such as Ferreby Draper and Sarah Hall exhorted converts in their homes and taught them the rudiments of Methodist theology.[12] None of these women were slaves, but because they were black, they often faced racial as well as religious persecution. For example, Priscilla Baltimore, a free woman in the slave state of Missouri, aroused white suspicions after organizing the first AME church in St. Louis in her home. When the Reverend William Paul Quinn traveled across the border to preach to black converts there, she repeatedly risked imprisonment by ferrying him across the Mississippi River in the dead of night.[13]

At a time when women's "sphere" was being redefined, these early Methodist women—both black and white—were praised more for their private "influence" over family members and friends than for their public acts of religious leadership. In the late eighteenth and early nineteenth centuries, a new ideology of female domesticity was gradually beginning to take shape. As the consumer revolution transformed the traditional subsistence economy, men's and women's work became increasingly differentiated.[14] Instead of laboring side by side in self-sufficient households, men were expected to make their living in the competitive world of the marketplace while women cared for children in the sheltered environment of the home. In practice, of course, many lower-class women went to work for wages, and even those who did not earn money for their labor continued to perform backbreaking chores within their households. Nevertheless, the

---

10. See "The Great Part Taken by the Women of the West in the Development of the AME Church," chapter XXXV of Lawson A. Scruggs, *Women of Distinction: Remarkable in Works and Invincible in Character* (Raleigh, N.C.: L. A. Scruggs, 1893), 148-53. Sarah Allen, the wife of the Reverend Richard Allen, organized a female sewing circle to make clothing for male itinerants. See L[ewellyn] L[ongfellow] Berry, *A Century of Missions of the African Methodist Episcopal Church* (New York: Gutenberg Printing Company, 1942), 36.

11. See Jualynne Dodson, "Nineteenth-Century A.M.E. Preaching Women," in Keller et al., *Women in New Worlds*, 278-79.

12. See Lewis V. Baldwin, "Black Women and African Union Methodism, 1813–1983," *Methodist History* 21 (July 1983): 225-37.

13. On Priscilla Baltimore, see L. L. Berry, *Century of Missions*, 37; James A. Handy, *Scraps of African Methodist Episcopal History* (Philadelphia: AME Book Concern, 1901), 345-46; and Alexander W. Wayman, *Cyclopaedia of African Methodism* (Baltimore: Carroll, 1882), 18.

14. See Nancy F. Cott, *The Bonds of Womanhood: "Woman's Sphere" in New England, 1780–1835* (New Haven: Yale University Press, 1977).

new emphasis on domesticity had profound consequences for both men and women. In the seventeenth and eighteenth centuries, women had been perceived as weak and morally irresponsible, but in the wake of the Revolution, they were elevated as "republican mothers" who were expected to be more virtuous and selfless than men.[15] In sermons, religious periodicals, and popular magazines, they were told that they had enormous power to shape the lives of their husbands and children. As one woman confided to her diary:

> All men feel so grand and make such a pother [sic] about their being lords of the world below—if their mothers had not taken such good care of them when they were babies, and instilled good principles into them as they grew up, what think you would have become of the mighty animals—oh every man of sense must humbly bow before woman. She bears the sway, not man as he presumptuously supposes.[16]

Women, not men, were the moral guardians of the American republic.

The Methodists both reflected and shaped this emerging ideology of domesticity by praising women for their influence within their families.[17] The journals of Methodist ministers are filled with accounts of pious women who single-handedly converted their sinful husbands, brothers, and fathers. In these stories, "weak" women inevitably triumphed over hard-hearted men, conquering men's passions through gentleness and meekness rather than physical force. On one hand, many of these stories seem contrived: they seem to reflect the Methodists' embrace of domestic ideology as much as reality. By the 1840s, narratives of devout, long-suffering wives and repentant husbands had become standard fare in Methodist magazines such as *The Ladies Repository.* Yet undoubtedly many women *did* lead their male family members into the church. As John Bangs remembered, he experienced conversion soon after his "pious sister" took him by the hand and begged him to seek salvation, tearfully reminding him that "if you die in your sins, where God and Christ is you will never come." Years later, after becoming a preacher, Bangs recalled that her

---

15. See Linda Kerber, *Women of the Republic: Intellect and Ideology in Revolutionary America* (Chapel Hill: University of North Carolina Press, 1980), 269-88.

16. Mehitable May Dawes (Goddard) diary, 12 June 1815, Arthur and Elizabeth Schlesinger Library on the History of Women in America, Radcliffe College, quoted in Cott, *Bonds of Womanhood,* 99.

17. See two works by A. Gregory Schneider: *Way of the Cross,* esp. 122-35, and "Social Religion, the Christian Home, and Republican Spirituality in Antebellum Methodism," *Journal of the Early Republic* 10 (summer 1990): 163-89.

parting words had "wounded my heart, and had a thunderbolt literally struck me I could not have felt much worse."[18] Like many other men, he attributed his initial "awakening" to the influence of a woman's example.[19]

Within the family, women's religious faith enabled them to overturn traditional relationships of authority. Instead of obeying men in Christian subjection, they questioned their fitness to serve as heads of their households. Some men reacted angrily, trying to reassert their authority through verbal or even physical abuse. For example, James Erwin, a Methodist circuit rider, remembered meeting a woman in 1831 who had been badly beaten by her husband after being "born again" on the mourners' bench. Her neighbors found her with "disheveled hair, clothes torn to tatters, bruised and bleeding."[20] However, many other men seem to have willingly turned to their wives and daughters for spiritual instruction, temporarily reversing accepted gender roles. At first Hosea Brown had ridiculed his daughter Ellen for joining the Methodists—a disorderly sect that encouraged "crying amens, groanings, and loud shouts of praise to God"—but her pious example eventually inspired him to seek grace himself. Kneeling beside her, he begged her to pray for his salvation. Although Brown was clearly perplexed by his sudden dependence on his daughter, he yielded to her greater religious authority, becoming "truly like a little child." Because of her conversion, Ellen and her father had virtually switched roles: she was the parent, and he the child in need of instruction. "It seems strange that Ellen has got to be older than her parents," he commented.[21]

18. John Bangs, *Autobiography of Reverend John Bangs, of the New York Annual Conference* (New York: n.p., 1846), 16-17.

19. For other examples of Methodist women who proved instrumental in converting family members, see Lucy Richards, *Memoirs of the Late Miss Lucy Richards, of Parris, Oneida County, N.Y.* (New York: Lane & Sanford, 1842), 78-82, and Philip Slaughter, *Memoir of Col. Joshua Fry . . . With an Autobiography of His Son, Rev. Henry Fry* (n.p., n.d), 84-85.

20. James Erwin, *Reminiscences of Early Circuit Life* (Toledo, Ohio: Spear, Johnson, & Company, 1884), 90. For other examples, see George Coles, *Heroines of Methodism; or, Pen and Ink Sketches of the Mothers and Daughters of the Church* (New York: Carlton & Porter, 1857), 162, 164. Wives could also react violently when their husbands joined the Methodists. E. F. Newell recounted the story of a woman who would "fret and storm" whenever her husband attempted to read the Bible in the house. "Often, when he went to a Methodist meeting, she expressed the wish that he might be brought home a corpse!" E. F. Newell, *Life and Observations of Rev. E. F. Newell . . . Who Has Been More than Forty Years an Itinerant Minister in the Methodist Episcopal Church* (Worcester, Mass.: C. W. Ainsworth, 1847), 71.

21. Ellen Stewart, *Life of Mrs. Ellen Stewart, Together with Biographical Sketches of Other Individuals. Also, A Discussion with Two Clergymen, and Arguments in Favor of Women's Rights* (Akron, Ohio: Beebe & Elkins, 1858), 10-11.

As these examples illustrate, the Methodists held an ambivalent view of women's place in the family and church. At the same time that they praised women for leading recalcitrant husbands and fathers to Christ, they also insisted on women's "natural" subordination to men. Nevertheless, the Methodists' emphasis on the spiritual equality of the sexes had momentous implications for the female converts who filled the pews. As church leaders soon discovered, women's influence could not be confined to the home.

Witnessing for Christ

In the early years of the movement the Methodists allowed both women and laymen to take on new public leadership roles in the church. Institutionally, they created an authoritarian, hierarchical system of church government, but they still defended every person's ability to experience the divine without clerical mediation.[22] Not only ministers, but women, laymen, and even children believed they had a sacred responsibility to "witness" for Christ. The Methodists, as historian A. Gregory Schneider has noted, placed great value on the liberty of speech.[23]

The early Methodists mixed strong individualistic tendencies with an even stronger streak of communalism. They located ultimate religious authority in the soul of every individual convert, but they also believed that every person had a divine obligation to "testify" to his or her experience of salvation. Although conversion was a profoundly personal, intimate moment, it often took place during church services, and it inevitably drew believers into a community of fellowship. In the first flush of the "new birth" many fledgling Methodists became informal evangelists, telling their neighbors, friends, and even strangers to repent and seek salvation. For example, Benjamin Abbott met a young woman whose experience of grace—"the mighty power of God"—convinced her that she had been called "to go from house to house, and warn her neighbors to flee from the wrath to come."[24] Another woman became so *wild with religious joy* that she went from place to place "exhorting others and praising the Lord."[25]

---

22. On the democratic impulses of the early Methodists, see Nathan O. Hatch, *The Democratization of American Christianity* (New Haven: Yale University Press, 1989).

23. Schneider, *Way of the Cross*, 98.

24. Benjamin Abbott, *Experience and Gospel Labours of the Rev. Benjamin Abbott* (New York: J. Collord, 1832), 79-80.

25. Raybold, *Annals of Methodism*, 21.

Such behavior was frowned upon by clergymen in many other denominations as disorderly and "enthusiastic," but the Methodists believed that new Christians could not control their overwhelming feelings of relief and joy. Instead of silencing female converts, they let them shout, sing, and testify in public.

In class meetings, praying bands, and love feasts, the Methodists encouraged every convert—regardless or race, class, age, or sex—to tell his or her story of salvation to the larger community. Bands were usually quite small, often numbering only two or three, and they were usually segregated by sex. Class meetings were larger, and in the early years of the movement men and women often met together. (This was especially true in towns where the Methodist community was small and there were not enough people to create more than one or two classes.) In these small, intimate gatherings, men and women shared their personal stories, "witnessing" to their faith in God. Similarly, in larger quarterly love feasts, converts were expected to reveal their innermost religious feelings to their "brothers" and "sisters" in Christ. Even though this public scrutiny could be intimidating, circuit riders reported that as many as one hundred or two hundred people could step forward during a single love feast to share their testimonies.[26] "Any person may speak who chooses," Jonathan Crowther reported.[27]

Because love feasts and class meetings were "social" gatherings, women as well as men were permitted to speak publicly. Even though the Methodists were certainly familiar with the Pauline injunction— "Let your women keep silence in the churches"—they chose to interpret it as a warning against female rule and governance rather than female speech. Balancing the words of Paul against the examples of New Testament heroines such as Anna and Priscilla, they argued that women could "prophesy" in public as long as they did not try to usurp male authority. As one clergyman explained, "In *church meetings* for the transaction of the *business* of the church, women should be silent, they should learn in obedience—they should not be meddling with those affairs which are peculiarly designed for the transaction of men." At the same time, however, he claimed that women were perfectly free to pray and exhort in "religious meetings for the

26. Erwin, *Reminiscences*, 16. For accounts of women speaking during love feasts, see Lucy Richards, *Memoirs*, 47, 73; and Ellen Stewart, *Life*, 11.

27. Jonathan Crowther, *A True and Complete Portraiture of Methodism; or the History of the Wesleyan Methodists* (New York: J. C. Totten, 1813), 239.

worship of God."[28] Even though female Methodists such as Rebecca Noyes were not permitted to vote on church business or serve as delegates to the General Conference, they reportedly "melted" their listeners "into tears" because of their eloquence.[29] "Sister" Sally Schuyler, one of the first Methodists in Rhinebeck, New York, so impressed one clergyman that he marveled, "Her gift in prayer, at all times, surpassed all I ever heard, of man or woman."[30] These examples could be multiplied by the dozens; ministers' journals and religious periodicals are filled with descriptions of women such as Fanny Glines, "who used to rise in the congregation and exhort the people to repent and turn to God and live," and Rachel Wilsey, who gained a reputation for being "gifted in prayer."[31]

The evidence suggests that hundreds of women exhorted informally during Methodist services in the late eighteenth and early nineteenth centuries. Since the line between social meetings and regular church services often broke down, both women and laymen spoke during formal worship when they felt divinely inspired. In the 1790s, for example, Benjamin Abbott allowed a female exhorter to speak even though she had interrupted one of his sermons. "I stopped preaching," he explained, "which I always judged was best, in similar instances, and let God send by whom he will send."[32] Ministers such as Abbott believed that women, like men, should not be silenced during moments of ecstatic communion with God. Of course, there were clergymen who disagreed; James Finley was irritated by the custom of allowing any layman or woman to "rise and deliver their impressions" no matter who was preaching. When a "female prophet" rudely interrupted his sermon, he ordered her to sit down and wait until he had finished speaking.[33] Yet Finley was outnumbered by preachers who feared angering God by "quenching the spirit." As one of Finley's colleagues explained, most of the early

---

28. See *Morning Star* (Limerick, Maine), vol. V, no. 18 (1 September 1830). Although this clergyman was a Freewill Baptist, he perfectly summarized the position of the early Methodists.

29. On Noyes, see Elbert Osborn, *Passages in the Life and Ministry of Elbert Osborn, An Itinerant Minister of the Methodist Episcopal Church* (New York: Joseph Longking, 1853), 50.

30. Billy Hibbard, *The Life and Travels of B. Hibbard, Minister of the Gospel* (New York: J. C. Totten, 1825), 237-38. For more on Schuyler, see George Coles, *Heroines of Methodism*, 156.

31. Fanny Glines belonged to a Methodist church in Conway, Maine. She died in 1805. See Newell, *Life*, 100. Rachel Wilsey is one of several "praying women" mentioned in Raybold, *Annals of Methodism*, 55.

32. Abbott, *Experience and Gospel Labours*, 140.

33. W. B. Strickland, *Autobiography of Rev. James B. Finley, or Pioneer Life in the West* (Cincinnati: Methodist Book Concern, 1853), 286-87.

Methodists believed in giving people "free toleration to express their feelings in their own way."[34]

Like their white counterparts, the African Methodists also allowed women to exhort and witness during religious meetings. Although the African Methodists created their own distinct religious community with their own bishops and ruling elders, they also perpetuated many of the traditions begun by their parent church. Class meetings, praying bands, and love feasts were central features of their worship, and women, like men, believed that they had a religious obligation to speak. Some, like Annie Dickerson, tried to stay within their "sphere" by confining their exhortations to other female converts, but others, such as Doritha Hill, addressed mixed groups of men and women.[35] As the wife of a Baltimore minister, Hill not only led class meetings in his absence, but spoke to his congregation before and after Sunday services.[36] In Philadelphia, a woman identified only as "Mrs. Cook" was given clerical permission to hold her own prayer meetings and exhort publicly.[37] As wives and mothers, these women prided themselves on their domestic influence within their families, but as Christians, they broke down the barriers between "public" and "private" by making the world their household.

The Methodists' acceptance of female evangelism made them virtually unique in the late eighteenth and early nineteenth centuries. Besides radical groups such as the Quakers and Shakers, and new dissenting sects such as the Freewill Baptists and Christian Connection, very few Protestant denominations allowed women to speak publicly.[38] Even as late as 1827 the Presbyterians forbade women from praying aloud "in social meetings . . . for religious worship," and during the 1830s, Congregationalist ministers such as Parsons Cooke insisted that it was a "shame" for women to speak in the church.[39]

---

34. John Bangs, *Autobiography*, 165-66.

35. On Dickerson, see Handy, *Scraps*, 344.

36. On Doritha Hill, see L. L. Berry, *A Century of Missions*, 36-37; and Handy, *Scraps*, 344.

37. Jarena Lee, *Religious Experience and Journal*, 11.

38. On female preachers for the Freewill Baptists and Christian Connection, see Brekus, *Strangers and Pilgrims;* and Louis Billington, "Female Laborers in the Church: Women Preachers in the Northeastern United States, 1790–1840," *Journal of American Studies* (U.K.) 19 (1985): 369-94.

39. On Presbyterian opposition to women's public speaking, see Charles C. Cole Jr., "The New Lebanon Convention," *New York History* 31 (1950): 385-97; Lois A. Boyd and R. Douglas Brackenridge, *Presbyterian Women in America: Two Centuries of A Quest for Status* (Westport, Conn.: Greenwood Press, 1983), 93-94; and Page Putnam Miller, *A Claim to New Roles* (Philadelphia: American Theological Library Association, 1985), 48-49. For the Congregationalists, see Parsons Cooke, *Female Preaching, Unlawful and Inexpedient. A Sermon* (Lynn, Mass.: James R. Newhall, 1837).

Indeed, when a Methodist woman in Ohio interrupted a Calvinist worship service by shouting aloud her praises to God, she was forcibly carried out of the building.[40]

Why did the Methodists allow women to testify and witness in public at a time when so many other denominations sharply restricted their speech? In their early years the Methodists seem to have recognized that they could not afford to waste the talents of any of their members, regardless of sex or even race. Since Methodist membership exploded in the early years of the American republic, increasing to a quarter million by 1820, there never seemed to be enough ordained ministers to keep pace with such spectacular growth. In 1784, for example, there were only 125 clergymen to oversee 14,988 members.[41] Given the shortage of qualified men, the Methodists depended on the laity as well as the clergy to help in their mission to "reform the Continent, and to spread scriptural Holiness." To be sure, they did not completely suspend social conventions; for example, they never considered ordaining women or even allowing them to vote. Yet in order to build their small persecuted sect into a thriving denomination, they allowed women as well as laymen to become informal evangelists.

Unlike more conservative denominations such as the Anglicans, the Methodists even allowed substantial numbers of slaves to preach. Although many states forbade blacks to hold their own separate religious meetings, Methodists sidestepped these laws by appointing slave men as "exhorters" rather than full preachers.[42] As a result, southern slaves converted to Methodism in extraordinary numbers. In 1787 there were fewer than four thousand black Methodists, but by 1841, that number had increased to more than one hundred thousand.[43] Although slave women, unlike men, were not officially licensed to exhort, many seem to have felt called to share their faith. As one ex-slave remembered, his mother had "shouted and sung for three days, going all over de plantation and de neighboring ones" after being converted at a camp meeting.[44] In later years, as the

---

40. Strickland, *Autobiography of James B. Finley*, 257.

41. These statistics are cited in Andrews, *Methodists and Revolutionary America*.

42. See Albert J. Raboteau, *Slave Religion: The "Invisible Institution" in the Antebellum South* (New York: Oxford University Press, 1978), 136; and Donald G. Mathews, *Religion in the Old South* (Chicago: University of Chicago Press, 1977), 185-236.

43. See Charles C. Jones, *The Religious Instruction of the Negroes in the United States* (Savannah, Ga.: Thomas Purse, 1842; reprint, Freeport, N.Y.: Books for Libraries Press, 1971), 41, 86.

44. George P. Rawick, ed., *The American Slave: A Composite Biography* (Westport, Conn.: Greenwood Press, 1972), vol. 12, *Georgia*, pt. 2, 227, quoted in Raboteau, *Slave Religion*, 227-28.

Methodists grew more powerful and respectable, they tried to curtail female "enthusiasm," but in their early history, they depended on an active laity because there were simply not enough ministers to fill every Methodist pulpit.

The spontaneity and excitement of Methodist camp meetings and revivals also contributed to the breakdown of traditional proscriptions against women's public speech. Instead of sitting quietly in the pews, converts often cried aloud, wept, and even shouted. Mary Chapman Goodwin, for example, a Methodist who lived in Ohio, "was generally among those who shouted aloud the praises of the Lord." According to her son, "she thought it would be a great sin for her to suppress her feelings and keep silent, when she felt like shouting."[45] Other converts experienced such transports of joy that they lost control of their limbs, jerking their bodies back and forth in convulsions of ecstasy, or fell to the ground in swooning fits.[46] In this ecstatic, emotionally charged environment, boundaries between public and private, the individual and the community, and women and men, all seemed to dissolve.

Besides the shortage of ordained ministers and the turbulence of camp meetings, there were theological reasons for the Methodists' acceptance of women's public evangelism as well. Unlike the Presbyterians, Congregationalists, and Anglicans, the early Methodists believed that the divine inspiration of the "spirit" was the most important qualification for ministry. As the sons of small farmers and artisans, many early Methodist ministers had never been formally educated, and they ridiculed those who believed that diplomas from Harvard or Yale could substitute for the experience of being "called." Men such as "Brother Cushman," widely admired as "a strong and eloquent preacher," freely admitted that they "had never seen the inside of a college, and did not know the first principle of English grammar."[47] By the 1820s and 1830s, Methodist leaders had

---

45. James Mathes, *Life of Elijah Goodwin, the Pioneer Preacher* (St. Louis: John Burns, 1880), 23. For other examples of men and women shouting, see Mathes, *Life of Elijah Goodwin*, 19; Raybold, *Annals*, 32; Joseph Pickering, *Inquiries of an Emigrant: Being the Narrative of an English Farmer from the Year 1824 to 1830; With the Author's Additions, to March, 1832* (London: Effingham Wilson, 1832), 26-27; and Heman Bangs, *The Autobiography and Journal of Rev. Heman Bangs* (New York: N. Tibbals & Son, 1872), 14, 48, 92. See also Winthrop H. Hudson, "Shouting Methodists," *Encounter* 29 (1968): 73-84.

46. For a description of the "jerks," see John Stewart, *Highways and Hedges; or Fifty Years of Western Methodism* (Cincinnati: Hitchcock & Waldren, 1872), 67. Benjamin Abbott recorded numerous examples of men and women fainting or swooning in his *Experience and Gospel Labours*, 69-70, 91, 116, 124, 152-53, 222-23, 243, 245.

47. Charles R. Harding, "Autobiography 1807–1869," American Antiquarian Society.

begun to distance themselves from their earlier anti-intellectualism, but in their formative years they disdained clerical education as less important than the direct experience of God's grace—a message with truly revolutionary implications for lower-class men, women, and slaves. Jarena Lee, a female preacher for the AME, echoed scores of other itinerants by pointing out that Christ's first disciples had been poor and uneducated. If a group of "unlearned fishermen" had been divinely inspired by Christ, why couldn't she—a "weak female"— make the same claim?[48]

The early Methodists seemed to take pride in their flouting of conventional social norms. As many historians have noted, they were countercultural in many of their impulses, deliberately setting themselves apart from the "corruption" of the secular world. In the South, where Methodism was strongest, converts transformed their religion into a scathing indictment of the patriarchal "culture of honor."[49] They questioned the morality of slaveholding, demanded male self-control rather than self-assertion, and adopted a plain style of dress and speech that visibly distinguished them from the planter elite.[50] By allowing women (and slaves) to speak publicly in their religious meetings, they drew even sharper boundaries between their utopian "island of holiness" and the hierarchical culture of the outside world. In this sense, the Methodists' encouragement of female speech was not merely a historical accident, but a deliberate attempt to define what made them different from other denominations in the early republic.

Conventional gender norms were often suspended in the early Methodist community. Women not only took on the "masculine" prerogative of public speaking, but as historians Donald Mathews and Diane Lobody have noted, Methodist men cultivated a "feminine" language of meekness and self-sacrifice.[51] "I am nothing, and helpless as a child!" exclaimed James Finley. He described himself as "weak" and utterly dependent on God's grace, unable to accomplish anything through his own strength.[52] Deliberately identifying himself

---

48. Jarena Lee, *Religious Experience and Journal*, 12.

49. On the "Southern accent of American Methodism," see Russell E. Richey, *Early American Methodism* (Bloomington: Indiana University Press, 1991), 47-64; and his essay in this volume.

50. See Rhys Isaac, *The Transformation of Virginia, 1740–1790* (Chapel Hill: University of North Carolina Press, 1982); Mathews, *Religion in the Old South*; and Schneider, *Way of the Cross*, especially 111-21. Curtis D. Johnson has traced the efforts of northern evangelicals to separate themselves from the world in his book *Islands of Holiness: Rural Religion in Upstate New York, 1790–1860* (Cornell, N.Y.: Cornell University Press, 1989).

51. See Mathews, *Religion in the Old South*, 123; and Lobody, " 'That Language Might be Given Me,' " 141-43.

52. Strickland, *Autobiography of James B. Finley*, 183.

with the image of submissive womanhood, he stressed his passivity rather than his mastery and self-reliance. In their published writings, men such as Finley often described themselves in feminine language as "brides of Christ," and they were not ashamed to shed tears during their sermons.[53] Just as their plain, Quaker style of dress visibly set them apart, their emotionalism, their ethic of self-sacrifice, and their emphasis on their Christlike suffering all distanced them from the ideology of aggressive manhood popular in the early republic. Indeed, by describing themselves with feminine imagery, they symbolically renounced their "male" power and authority in order to become more like Christ.[54] Like men have done in marginal or oppressed groups throughout history, they identified with the "feminine" in order to emphasize their renunciation of the values and mores of the larger culture.[55]

Yet even though Methodist men used images of womanhood to define themselves rhetorically, they did not question the unequal power relations between real men and women in the home. In some ways, their symbolic reversal of conventional gender roles only underscored their greater social and religious authority as husbands and fathers. Ironically, the Methodists expanded women's opportunities for public self-expression, but by helping to formulate and popularize the restrictive ideas about female domesticity that became common during the late 1820s and 1830s, they also set firm limits on the behavior considered appropriate for "virtuous" women. Despite praising women as more pious, "simple," and "tender" than men, they also insisted that their "weakness" made them unfit for the harsh realities of political and economic life.[56] Instead of allowing them to preach, they praised them for "strengthening the hands" of their ministers.[57]

---

53. Philip Embury often began to cry during his sermons. See Albert Gallatin Meacham, *A Compendious History of the Rise and Progress of the Methodist Church* (Hallowell, Canada: n.p., 1832). One male convert claimed that "he had never shed tears" before his conversion, even during times of great sorrow, but after joining the Methodists, he could not forbear "weeping for joy." See Ellen Stewart, *Life*, 10.

54. Caroline Walker Bynum discusses symbolic gender reversals in her fascinating study, *Holy Feast and Holy Fast: The Religious Significance of Food to Medieval Women* (Berkeley: University of California Press, 1987), 284.

55. Sociologist Jacqueline Field-Bibb argues that women become important symbolically whenever there is criticism of authority or an attempt to create a more egalitarian community. See her *Women Towards Priesthood: Ministerial Politics and Feminist Praxis* (Cambridge: Cambridge University Press, 1991), 201-2.

56. For a few examples, see Gardiner Spring, *The Influence and Excellence of the Female Character* (New York: F. & R. Lockwood, 1825), 14-15; "Female Piety," *Mutual Rights and Methodist Protestant* 2, no. 5 (3 February 1832): 36; and J. B. Wakeley, *Lost Chapters Recovered from the Early History of American Methodism* (New York: Carlton & Porter, 1858), 554-55.

57. See the obituary of Mrs. Catherine Mummey in *Mutual Rights and Methodist Protestant*, 2, no. 37 (14 September 1832): 295.

Fearful of trespassing the boundaries between informal witnessing and authoritative preaching, some women never found the courage to speak. When Nancy Caldwell, a Methodist in Poland, Maine, felt called to exhort in front of her congregation, she admitted fearing that her husband would rather see her dead than expose her "ignorance."[58] In 1806, however, at the age of twenty-five, she finally found the courage to begin speaking during religious meetings, sharing her own personal religious experiences rather than "preaching" from biblical texts. As she grew older she gained such renown for her piety that she was celebrated as a "mother in Israel," a respected and beloved pillar of her church. But even though she apparently enjoyed the support of her fellow Methodists, she continued to experience "severe mental suffering" because of her call to "witness in the sanctuary." Whether because of implicit clerical or lay disapproval or her own self doubts, she never overcame her feeling of being an outsider, a misfit in a world where women were expected to "keep silence in the churches." "I felt much alone on account of my peculiarities," she lamented, "much like a speckled bird among the birds of the forest."[59]

Like Caldwell, Fanny Butterfield Newell also struggled with her doubts about the propriety of women speaking in public. Converted in 1808 when she was only sixteen, Newell began speaking in love feasts and class meetings, but almost immediately became convinced that God had called her to preach. Because she viewed herself as nothing more than a "feeble woman," she doubted that her call was genuine, and in 1809, she tried to stifle her ambitions by marrying E. F. Newell, a Methodist circuit rider.[60] Yet to her dismay, she soon found that the usual duties of a minister's wife—visiting the sick, praying with other women, and comforting the spiritually distressed—failed to remove her overwhelming desire to preach. After dreaming one night that she had spoken from the text to a large crowd, "Repent, for the kingdom of God is at hand," she wrote:

> Could I preach as well when awake as when asleep, I should think "wo is me, if I preach not the Gospel";—and even now, if I was a man, I should think it was my duty, and should be willing to go and preach Jesus, and hold a bleeding Saviour up to view before a guilty world of

58. Nancy Caldwell, *Walking with God: Leaves from the Journal of Mrs. Nancy Caldwell*, ed. Rev. James O. Thompson (Keyser, West Virginia, 1886), 47.

59. Ibid., 50, 52.

60. Fanny Newell, *Memoirs of Fanny Newell; Written by Herself, and Published by the Desire and Request of Numerous Friends*, 3rd ed. (Springfield and New York, 1833), 46-47.

sinners. O Saviour! thou art calling me to something, I know not what.[61]

Newell struggled with her call to preach for years, longing to be "like Deborah of old, a mother in Israel," but finally resigned herself to being a helpmate to her husband. Too timid to become a preacher herself, she became the ideal minister's wife, volunteering to sacrifice her own dreams for the good of his flock. "I will go with you," she told her husband, "and hold up your hands, and join to preach the acceptable year of the Lord to perishing sinners." Although she still suffered "awful temptations" about whether she should speak in public, she began exhorting to his congregations after he had finished preaching. To justify herself she affirmed, "Whatever may be said against a female speaking, or praying in public, I care not; for when I feel confident that the Lord calls me to speak, I dare not refuse."[62]

There seem to have been many women who felt called to preach but who never found the courage to defy the Methodist hierarchy. Like Newell, many of these women became the wives of Methodist itinerants, choosing to help their husbands in their ministerial careers instead of embarking on their own. Charles Harding, a circuit rider in Vermont and New Hampshire, usually traveled in company with his wife Nancy, who "had an excellent gift of prayer and exhortation, and was very useful, and much beloved by the people."[63] Similarly, women such as Amey Scott and Elizabeth Cantrell did not dare to hold their own meetings, but spoke at the close of their husbands' sermons instead.[64]

As ministers' wives, Sunday school teachers, home and foreign missionaries, and charitable workers, women found outlets for their talents that did not require them to overstep the boundaries of acceptable female behavior. Many seem to have concluded that it would be easier to channel their religious ambitions into more "feminine" activities than to face public ridicule or clerical sanction. For example, Eliza Barnes traveled across northern New England as an itinerant evangelist for a few brief years in the 1820s, but eventually abandoned her preaching career to become a missionary to the Native

---

61. Ibid., 75.

62. Newell, *Memoirs*, 125, 161, 147, 135. E. F. Newell discussed his wife's popularity as an exhorter in his memoir, *Life and Observations*, especially 149, 184-85.

63. Charles R. Harding, "Autobiography 1807–1869."

64. On Scott and Cantrell, see Muir, *Petticoats in the Pulpit*, 145, and Leonard Sweet, *The Minister's Wife: Her Role in Nineteenth-Century American Evangelicalism* (Philadelphia: Temple University Press, 1983), 118.

Americans in Canada. Instead of facing questions about her right to speak in public, she earned wide praise for her self-sacrificing devotion to the "heathen."[65] Similarly, when Lucy Richards felt called to pray in public, she decided to follow Barnes's example and become a female missionary.[66] Even though all of these women preached informally, they never claimed the authority of ministry by demanding their own pulpits.

Women in the Pulpit

Only a small, courageous group of women stretched the boundaries of Methodist "liberty" to the breaking point by demanding recognition as preachers. Between 1784 and 1845, at least twenty-two Methodist women traveled across the country as itinerants, often attracting huge crowds wherever they preached. Although women such as Hannah Reeves, Elice Miller, and Zilpha Elaw have been virtually forgotten by twentieth-century historians, they caused a sensation among Methodists in early national and antebellum America.

In England, scores of women traveled as Methodist itinerants during the late eighteenth and early nineteenth centuries. In 1771 John Wesley admitted that some women might have an "extraordinary call" to preach the gospel, and by the 1840s more than two hundred women had served as preachers for Methodist sects such as the Bible Christians and the Primitive Methodists.[67] Several of these women

---

65. On Eliza Barnes, see Muir, *Petticoats in the Pulpit*, 108-16. Nancy Towle, a nondenominational female preacher, met Barnes on a preaching tour of New Hampshire in 1825. See Nancy Towle, *Vicissitudes Illustrated, in the Experience of Nancy Towle, in Europe and America*, 2d edition (Portsmouth, N.H.: John Caldwell, 1833), 43-44.

66. Unfortunately, Richards's work with the Oneida Indians was cut short when the Methodist Conference decided it would be cheaper to hire a man. See Lucy Richards, *Memoirs*, 165. Similarly, Margaret Prior, a tireless crusader for the Moral Reform Society in New York City, reportedly visited more than three hundred and fifty families a month, distributing religious tracts and "preaching the gospel" to them, but her church never formally recognized her efforts. See Sarah R. Ingraham, compiler, *Walks of Usefulness, or Reminiscences of Mrs. Margaret Prior* (New York: American Female Moral Reform Society, 1843; reprint, New York: Garland Publishing, 1987), 56, 116.

67. Paul Wesley Chilcote, *John Wesley and the Women Preachers of Early Methodism* (Metuchen, N.J.: Scarecrow Press, 1991), 143, and Deborah M. Valenze, *Prophetic Sons and Daughters: Female Preaching and Popular Religion in Industrial England* (Princeton, N.J.: Princeton University Press, 1985). See also Earl Kent Brown, *Women of Mr. Wesley's Methodism* (New York: Edwin Mellen Press, 1983); D. Colin Dewes, "Ann Carr and the Female Revivalists of Leeds," in Gail Malmgreen, ed., *Religion in the Lives of English Women, 1760–1930* (London: Croom Helm, 1986), 68-87; Field-Bibb, *Women Towards Priesthood*; and F. W. Bourne, *The Bible Christians—Their Origin and History, 1815–1900* (n.p.: Bible Christian Book Room, 1905).

visited the United States on missionary tours, providing American women with inspiring examples of female religious leadership. Ruth Watkins, Ann Warren, and Ann Wearing visited New York City in 1829–30, and H. M. Knowles traveled to Cincinnati in 1831.[68]

In America, female preaching was more widespread in the first few decades of the nineteenth century than most historians have realized. Between 1790 and 1845 a small army of at least one hundred women crisscrossed America as itinerant evangelists dedicated to "saving souls." Besides the Methodists, most belonged to the Freewill Baptists and Christian Connection, new sects that challenged the Calvinist orthodoxy in the wake of church disestablishment. Although these sects did not allow women to be ordained, they often publicized their meetings in the religious press, and most important, they officially licensed women as "female laborers."[69]

In contrast to the Freewill Baptists and the Christian Connection, the MEC and the AME never formally recognized female preachers, but despite their institutional conservativism, individual ministers and congregations sometimes gave women liberty to speak. Elleanor Knight, for example, an itinerant for the Christian Connection, reported that she had received "many calls and invitations [to preach] from . . . Methodist brethren" in New Hampshire and Maine.[70] In the early years of Methodism, local churches were influenced as much by local customs as by official doctrine, and although they were ostensibly subject to episcopal control, in practice they often acted independently. In the 1830s and 1840s, as denominational authority became increasingly centralized, this autonomy began to erode, but it never entirely disappeared.

Because female preachers could not be ordained or installed as settled pastors, they traveled as itinerants instead. Constantly traveling from one town to another, they preached outside in fields and forests as well as in churches, schoolhouses, and private homes. Like male itinerants, many of them seem to have died young, exhausted by the rigors of walking on foot or riding by horseback through icy winters and scorching summers.[71] As women, they also felt particularly

---

68. John H. Acornley, *A History of the Primitive Methodist Church in the United States of America* (Fall River, Mass.: B. R. Acornley, 1909), and Muir, *Petticoats*, 152-61.

69. Brekus, *Strangers and Pilgrims*.

70. *Christian Herald* 9, no. 6 (4 May 1843).

71. For a vivid picture of the challenges of itinerant life see Robert Boyd, *Personal Memoirs: Together With a Discussion Upon The Hardships and Sufferings of Itinerant Life* (Cincinnati: Methodist Book Concern, 1860), 155-57, 184-87.

vulnerable to the dangers they might encounter on the road. When Ellen Stewart considered walking to a neighboring town to accept a preaching invitation, "Satan" tempted her not to go by reminding her, "you are a woman, alone and unprotected; you may meet mad dogs, or what is worse, mad men on the road."[72] For added protection, most women traveled in pairs, but even then they feared being robbed—or worse, sexually assaulted.

Female preachers also faced unique financial difficulties. To be sure, male itinerants were also quite poor, making a maximum of eighty dollars a year at a time when the average Congregationalist clergyman earned five times as much. But because women were not officially licensed, they could not depend on any regular salary at all.[73] Sometimes churches collected contributions for them at the end of their sermons, but since their supporters were typically poor themselves, women were also forced to rely on their own labor. For example, Sarah Orne worked in a New Hampshire cotton mill to help pay her expenses.[74] Sarah Riker, who had once "preached with freedom" in New York City's Wesley Chapel, was eventually forced to ask for poor relief.[75] Without reliable financial support, these women followed their calls in the face of overwhelming odds.

Most female preachers belonged to the MEC or the AME rather than one of the smaller dissenting sects. Between 1784 and 1845, eleven women were affiliated with the MEC, seven with the AME, two with the Reformed Methodists, one with the Methodist Protestants, one with the AMEZ, and one with the Wesleyans.[76] Three

---

72. Ellen Stewart, *Life*, 114.

73. These statistics are from Hatch, *Democratization*, 88. Methodist church records are full of ministerial complaints about meager pay and poor living conditions. For example, see "Journal of the Quarterly Conference, Scarborough Circuit of the Methodist Episcopal Church, 1808–1873," Maine Historical Society, entries for 13 January 1810, 21 July 1810, and 25 January 1840.

74. On Orne, see Charles W. Kern, *God, Grace, and Granite: The History of Methodism in New Hampshire* (Canaan, N.H.: Phoenix Publishing, 1988), 130. Similarly, Salome Lincoln, a former mill worker, helped support herself by sewing clothing. See Almond H. Davis, *The Female Preacher, or Memoir of Salome Lincoln* (Providence, Rhode Island, 1843; reprint, New York: Arno Press, 1972), 97.

75. Richard Whatcoat, "Journal," 8 June 1792, Library of Congress.

76. The Reformed Methodists numbered three thousand members in 1848, and the Wesleyan Methodists claimed six thousand. The Methodist Protestants were much larger, numbering sixty thousand in 1843. See Wesley Bailey, "History of the Reformed Methodist Church," in John Winebrenner, ed., *History of All the Religious Denominations in the United States* (Harrisburg, Pa.: John Winebrenner, 1848), 388; James R. Williams, "History of the Methodist Protestant Church," in *History of All the Religious Denominations in the United States*, 380; and Ira Ford McLeister, *History of the Wesleyan Methodist Church* (Syracuse, N.Y.: Wesleyan Methodist Publishing Association, 1934), 38.

more women belonged to the United Brethren, who resembled the Methodists in worship but did not formally unite with them until the twentieth century.[77] Because the Reformed, Wesleyan, and Methodist Protestant churches were formed in reaction to the Methodists' growing authoritarianism and episcopal form of government, they tended to be the most tolerant of female preaching, allowing women such as Hannah Reeves and Ellen Stewart to preach at their quarterly meetings and other official gatherings. Reeves, for example, was invited to preach in front of the General Conference of the Methodist Protestants on two separate occasions.[78] Yet even as these dissenting sects tried to give laypeople greater representation in decision making, they did not extend the same rights to women as they did to men. When the Methodist Protestants were first organized in 1828, they decided to allow women to vote on church business, but quickly reversed their opinion later the same year.[79] Similarly, the Reformed Methodists complained bitterly about the "despotism" of bishops and clergymen, but they did not allow women to exercise any political power.[80] Even in these supposedly democratic Methodist sects, women were not entitled to vote or serve as delegates to the General Conference, and they certainly could not be ordained.

In response to this institutional resistance, female preachers managed to patch together a network of support from individual male ministers. Sympathetic clergymen opened their pulpits to women, publicized their meetings, and wrote them letters of recommendation to carry with them on their travels. Zilpha Elaw, an African Methodist who traveled to Virginia in 1828, remembered with gratitude that a white Methodist minister there had treated her "with very great

---

77. See Jeffrey P. Mickle, "A Comparison of the Doctrines of Ministry of Francis Asbury and Philip William Otterbein," *Perspectives*, 93-107.

78. "Mrs. Hannah Reeves, Preacher of the Gospel," *MQR* 59 (1877): 440. For more on Reeves, see George Brown, *The Lady Preacher; Or, the Life and Labors of Mrs. Hannah Reeves, Late the Wife of the Rev. William Reeves of the Methodist Church* (Philadelphia: Daughaday & Becker, 1870). See also Ellen Stewart, *Life*, 61, 101.

79. William T. Noll, "Women as Clergy and Laity in the Nineteenth-Century Methodist Protestant Church," *Methodist History* 15 (January 1977): 109; *Constitution and Discipline of the Methodist Protestant Church* (Baltimore: John J. Harrod, 1830), 29; and *Mutual Rights of the Ministers and Members of the Methodist Episcopal Church* (Baltimore) 1, no. 1 (August 1824): 11-12. For more on the Methodist Protestant Church, see Williams, "History of the Methodist Protestant Church," 380-82.

80. On the Reformed Methodists, see *Gospel Luminary* (West Bloomfield, N.Y.), 2, no. 8 (August 1826), and Bailey, "History of the Reformed Methodist Church," 383-90. See also Edward J. Drinkhouse, *History of Methodist Reform*, 2 vols. (Norwood, Mass.: Norwood Press, 1899).

kindness" and had "much promoted [her] labors in that neighbor-hood."[81] Without his approval, few churches would have allowed her to preach.

Even ministers who opposed female preaching on principle some-times made exceptions for women who particularly impressed them. For example, Lorenzo Johnson, an elder for the Reformed Methodists, admitted that he "felt a strong prejudice against female preachers," but after meeting Salome Lincoln he concluded that she "had as great a CALL as myself." In 1832, he wrote a letter of recommendation for her to take with her to neighboring churches.[82] Lincoln also received support from Pliny Brett, the Presiding Elder of the Reformed Methodists, who assured his clerical colleagues that she was "a per-son of unexceptionable character" who was "universally approbated as a laborer in the cause of God."[83]

Like their white brethren, AME ministers were often ambivalent about allowing women into their pulpits, but many were won over by the talents of women such as Jarena Lee, Zilpha Elaw, Rachel Evans, and Juliann Jane Tillman. The Reverend Richard Allen, the founder of the AME, initially refused Jarena Lee's request to become a preacher, advising her to become an exhorter instead, but reversed his decision eight years later. After Lee interrupted a church service by springing to her feet and delivering an impassioned, sponta-neous sermon, she expected Allen to expel her from the church, but to her surprise, he announced that "he now as much believed that I was called to that work, as any of the preachers present."[84] From then on, he was one of her warmest advocates, arranging for her to preach in several AME churches and inviting her to accompany him and several elders to the New York Annual Conference.[85] Similarly, other clergymen welcomed female itinerants into their churches and even raised money to defray their traveling expenses.[86] The Bishop William Paul Quinn, one of the most influential ministers in the denomination, claimed there was no better preacher in the Western Reserve than Rachel Evans, including Rachel's own husband.[87]

Regionally, northern and western Methodists seem to have been

81. Elaw, Memoirs, 93-94.
82. Davis, Female Preacher, 38.
83. Ibid., 41.
84. Jarena Lee, Religious Experience and Journal, 11, 17.
85. Ibid., 29.
86. For one example, see ibid., 34.
87. See Handy, Scraps, 345, and L. L. Berry, Century of Missions, 39.

more tolerant of female preaching than their southern counterparts. Throughout the country, women spoke in class meetings and love feasts, but it was only in New England, the Mid-Atlantic, and the Midwest that significant numbers of women were allowed into Methodist pulpits. Even though the southern Methodists challenged the patriarchal culture of southern honor, they were never able to completely transcend its conservatism. Choosing power over purity, they questioned the morality of slaveholding, yet eventually accepted the right of their members to own slaves. They allowed women and laymen to testify in public, but tightly controlled who had access to the authority of ministry. As a result, women such as Sarah Roszel of Virginia and Sarah Hinton of North Carolina gained local renown as exhorters, but they spoke informally rather than explicating scriptural texts.[88] Even Elice Miller Smith, a New England native who was reportedly "more universally admired, than any other *female* [preacher] of America," met a cold reception when she arrived in Virginia.[89] According to the Reverend George Brown, she was harassed by clergymen who questioned her right to preach.[90] Perhaps because of the opposition that she faced, Smith eventually decided to marry a Methodist minister, trading her itinerant life for a position as a class leader. According to the female preacher Nancy Towle, who visited her in 1832, "since her confinement by marriage,—she had not that religious enjoyment, which she formerly had known."[91]

Of all the Methodist female preachers that I have been able to uncover in my research, only seven preached in the South, and they never ventured farther into Dixie than the border states of Virginia and Maryland. Besides Elice Miller Smith, Hannah Reeves occasionally visited Virginia during the 1830s, and Laura P. Clemens and "Sister" L. Courtland were active in Maryland in the early 1840s.[92] All three of the other women—Zilpha Elaw, Jarena Lee, and Elizabeth (whose last name is unknown)—were African Methodists who

---

88. On Roszel, see Muir, *Petticoats in the Pulpit*, 146. On Hinton, see Schneider, *Way of the Cross*, 129. On the conservatism of southern evangelicalism, see Christine Leigh Heyrman, *Southern Cross: The Beginnings of the Bible Belt* (New York: Alfred A. Knopf, 1997); Mathews, *Religion in the Old South*; and Stephanie McCurry, *Masters of Small Worlds: Yeomen Households, Gender Relations, and the Political Culture of the Antebellum South Carolina Low Country* (New York: Oxford University Press, 1995).

89. Towle, *Vicissitudes*, 200. For a description of a meeting that Elice Miller Smith held in Baltimore, see *Morning Star* 1, no. 15 (17 August 1826).

90. George Brown, *Recollections of Itinerant Life: Including Early Reminiscences* (Cincinnati: R. W. Caroll, 1866), 185-88.

91. Towle, *Vicissitudes*, 196.

92. On Clemens and Courtland, see A. W. Drury, *History of the Church of the United Brethren in Christ* (Dayton, Ohio: United Brethren Publishing House, 1924), 425.

courageously traveled to the southern states to preach to slaves. Heedless of their own safety, they traveled by horseback or on foot to "bind up the brokenhearted" and "proclaim liberty to the captives," frequently facing hostile white crowds in their meetings.[93] None of them were physically injured, but all admitted fearing that they might be imprisoned or sold into slavery because of their message of liberation. Elizabeth, who had been born to slave parents and did not win her own freedom until the age of thirty, remembered angering white authorities because she "spoke against slavery." When the magistrates demanded to know who had given her the authority to preach, she responded that she had not been ordained by "the commission of men's hands," but by God himself.[94]

Although there were no itinerant preachers among southern slave women, who were physically confined to their plantations, many seem to have served as unofficial spiritual leaders. In Louisiana, for example, a Methodist woman known only as "Aunt Hester" prayed aloud, sang hymns, and read the Bible during meetings that she held in the slave quarters. Unfortunately, there is no record of what she said during her informal sermons, but apparently she did not preach an otherworldly gospel. Because her master was so threatened by her revolutionary interpretation of Christianity, he sold her to prevent her from "ruining" his other slaves.[95] Elsewhere in the South, slave women such as "Sinda" and "Clarinda" gained reputations as slave "prophetesses."[96] Although very little evidence of slave female preaching has survived, women often served as spirit mediums in West African religions, and this custom may have survived the voyage to America. When the Scotsman David Macrae visited the South shortly after the Civil War, he found that "The pious negroes delight in prayer; and the women, at some of their religious meetings, are as free to lead as the men. Their prayers are full of fire, and often exceedingly vivid and impressive."[97]

---

93. Jarena Lee preached on this text (Isaiah 61:1) at a meeting for slaves that she held near Baltimore in 1836. See Jarena Lee, *Religious Experience*, 78.

94. *Elizabeth, A Colored Minister of the Gospel, Born in Slavery* (Philadelphia: Tract Association of Friends, 1889), 11.

95. Coles, *Heroines*, 139-41.

96. On Sinda, see Frances Anne Kemble, *Journal of a Residence on a Georgian Plantation in 1838–1839*, ed. John A. Scott (New York: Alfred A. Knopf, 1961), 118-19. On Clarinda, see Henry Holcombe, *The First Fruits, in a Series of Letters* (Philadelphia: Ann Cochran, 1812), 59-60.

97. David Macrae, *The Americans at Home* (Edinburgh, 1870; reprint, New York: E. P. Dutton, 1952), 365.

Whether white or black, northern or southern, female preachers often faced ridicule and hostility from the men and women they tried to convert. Despite the support of individual ministers, they were insulted, locked out of churches where they were supposed to preach, and harassed by spectators who tried to intimidate them.[98] Like male Methodists, they angered many conservatives because of their "disorderly" style of worship and their theological challenge to the Calvinist orthodoxy. (Benjamin Abbott, who bragged that he "tore old Calvin up" in his sermons, barely escaped being tarred and feathered.[99]) Yet because of their sex, female preachers faced even greater animosity than their male colleagues. Instead of being attacked because of the substance of their beliefs, they were forced to answer questions about whether they were "leading men" or trying to usurp clerical authority.[100] When a group of angry men harassed Ellen Stewart during one of her meetings, they did not ask her to explain her theological doctrines, but confronted her with "a book full of filthy, and obscene remarks about women."[101] Other women, especially black women, were threatened with physical violence. Zilpha Elaw remembered that when she preached in Portland, Maine, "an unusually stout and ferocious looking man" approached her in the pulpit "as if he intended to seize or strike me," looming over her "as if he would take my life."[102]

To defend themselves against their critics, women such as Elaw developed elaborate justifications for their right to preach. Scripturally, they often cited the examples of biblical heroines such as Anna, Priscilla, Mary, Phoebe, and Philip's four daughters as proof that God could call women as well as men to preach. Ellen Stewart, for example, described herself as a "modern Anna," and Jarena Lee argued that Mary had been the *"first"* to "preach the risen Saviour" after finding Christ's empty tomb.[103] Like modern-day feminists, they collected as much scriptural evidence as possible of women's evangelism in the early Christian church. Others responded to the Pauline injunction, "Let your women keep silence in the churches," by quoting an equally evocative and powerful verse from Joel: "And it shall

98. For an example, see Davis, *The Female Preacher*, 66.

99. Benjamin Abbott, *Experience and Gospel Labours*, 159, 64.

100. For an example, see Jean McMahon Humez, ed., *Gifts of Power: The Writings of Rebecca Jackson, Black Visionary, Shaker Eldress* (Amherst: University of Massachusetts Press, 1981), 103.

101. Ellen Stewart, *Life*, 80.

102. Zilpha Elaw, *Memoirs*, 128.

103. Ellen Stewart, *Life*, 101, and Jarena Lee, *Religious Experience and Journal*, 11.

come to pass afterward, that I will pour out my spirit upon all flesh; and your sons and your daughters shall prophesy."[104]

Rather than defending their right to preach on the grounds that they had transcended their gender (a common strategy of medieval women mystics), these women described themselves as "Mothers in Israel" or "Sisters in Christ."[105] Drawing on both biblical imagery and the language of republican motherhood, they both reinforced and undermined common ideas about women's domesticity. On one hand, they seemed to root their religious authority in their tradition-al domestic roles as mothers and sisters, but on the other, they also identified themselves with some of the most powerful women in the Bible. As scholars have pointed out, there are only two "Mothers in Israel" mentioned in the Bible, and both were powerful women who took on leadership roles outside of the patriarchal household. Deborah, one of the most renowned military leaders in the Old Testament, rescued the nation of Israel from its enemies, whereas the other "Mother in Israel," a "wise woman" from the city of Avel of Bet Maacah, persuaded one of David's generals not to destroy her city. "Sisters" appear more frequently in the Bible, but they too defied con-ventional definitions of womanhood. In his letter to the Romans, Paul described Phoebe as "our sister," and instructed the church to "assist her in whatsoever business she hath need of you: for she hath been a succourer of many, and of myself also." Although the nature of Phoebe's "business" was disputed by nineteenth-century evangeli-cals, a few of the most progressive suggested that she had been one of the first female evangelists. According to Methodist clergy, Mothers in Israel and Sisters in Christ mixed "feminine" tenderness with "masculine" strength: they were loving nurturers, but also "bold sol-diers" for Christ.[106]

Female preachers also defended themselves by claiming to have been divinely inspired. Besides using scriptural examples to justify their decision to preach, they laid claim to an immediate encounter

---

104. For examples, see the epigraph to Jarena Lee, *Religious Experience and Journal;* Davis, *Female Preacher,* 16-17; Ellen Stewart, *Life,* 17-19; and Zilpha Elaw, *Memoirs,* 124.

105. For examples, see the essays in *Women Preachers and Prophets through Two Millennia of Christianity,* ed. Beverly Mayne Kienzle and Pamela J. Walker (Berkeley: University of California Press, 1998).

106. On "Mothers in Israel," see Rachel Adler, "'A Mother in Israel': Aspects of the Mother-Role in Jewish Myth," in *Beyond Androcentrism: New Essays on Women and Religion,* ed. Rita M. Gross (Missoula, Mont.: Scholars Press, 1977), and Deborah Valenze, *Prophetic Sons and Daughters,* 35-37. The biblical references to "Mothers in Israel" are to Judges 5:7 and 2 Samuel 20:19. The reference to Phoebe is from Romans 16:1-2. "Bold soldier" quoted in Schneider, *Way of the Cross,* 183.

with the divine—a claim that others could question but never ultimately disprove. Like male Methodists, they believed that God not only communicated with humanity through the scriptures, but more immediately through dreams, visions, and voices.[107] As part of this popular strain of religiosity, women such as Julia Foote and Zilpha Elaw claimed that God had directly contacted them during a moment of mystical revelation. According to Foote, she had been visited by an angel of God holding a scroll imprinted with the words, "Thee have I chosen to preach my Gospel without delay."[108] Even Nathan Bangs, one of the primary architects of Methodism's later rise to middle-class respectability, claimed in his early career that God had reassured him through a prophetic dream.[109]

Black women seem to have been especially visionary.[110] Unlike men, who often couched their claims to direct inspiration in ambiguous language, writing that it *seemed* as if Christ had appeared to them by "the eye of faith," black female preachers insisted that they had actually seen heavenly visions or heard angelic voices.[111] For example, Rebecca Jackson, an African Methodist who later became a Shaker eldress, described seeing Christ smiling at her from his cross.[112] Similarly, Jarena Lee reported that she had "distinctly heard" God commanding her, "Go Preach the Gospel!" At first she had plaintively responded, "No one will believe me," but she triumphed over her fears when God insisted, "Preach the Gospel; I will put words in your

107. Historians have often overlooked this intense visionary enthusiasm, but as historian John Wigger has argued, the "quest for the supernatural in everyday life—and not a theological abstraction like Arminianism—was the key theological distinction of early American Methodism." See John H. Wigger, "Taking Heaven by Storm: Enthusiasm and Early American Methodism, 1770–1820," *Journal of the Early Republic* 14 (1994): 167-94.

108. Julia A. J. Foote, *A Brand Plucked from the Fire: An Autobiographical Sketch* (Cleveland: W. F. Schneider, 1879), in Andrews, *Sisters of the Spirit*, 200. See also Zilpha Elaw, *Memoirs*, 56. For more on Foote, who was a member of the AMEZ Church, see Bettye Collier-Thomas, *Daughters of Thunder: Black Women and Their Sermons, 1850–1979* (San Francisco: Jossey-Bass Publishers, 1998), 57-68.

109. Abel Stevens, *Life and Times of Nathan Bangs* (New York: Carlton & Porter, 1863), 82.

110. For an excellent discussion of the visionary experience of black female preachers, see Jean M. Humez, "'My Spirit Eye': Some Functions of Spiritual and Visionary Experiences in the Lives of Five Black Women Preachers, 1810–1880," in Barbara Harris and Jo Ann McNamara, eds., *Women and the Structure of Society* (Durham, N.C.: Duke University Press, 1984), 129-43.

111. Even the "enthusiastic" James Horton usually stopped short of claiming that he had actually seen Christ or heard the voice of God. When he described a particularly powerful religious experience, he wrote, "it *appeared* to me that I could hear the angels around me singing the praises of God—heaven *seemed* to be open in all its immortal beauty before me." See James P. Horton, *A Narrative of the Early Life, Remarkable Conversion, and Spiritual Labors of James P. Horton* (n.p., 1839), 52. The emphases are mine.

112. Humez, ed., *Gifts of Power*, 85.

mouth, and will turn your enemies to become your friends."[113] With little education, money, or social authority, black female preachers were particularly dependent on voices and visions to guide and protect them.

Despite their radical claim to divine inspiration and their impassioned defense of female evangelism, very few of these women ever demanded complete equality to men. Although records are fragmentary, only Ellen Stewart seems to have become involved in the woman's rights movement, and only Laura Clemens—a member of the United Brethren—seems to have asked for ordination. (Her request was flatly refused.)[114] More typical was Salome Lincoln, who repeatedly denied that she was entitled to the same prerogatives as male ministers. Even though Lincoln firmly believed that women as well as men could preach and pray in public, she stopped short of advocating female pastors. There were "diversities of gifts," she explained, and men and women were destined for different roles in the church.[115]

Because female preachers combined their belief in women's spiritual equality with political conservatism, they can best be described as biblical rather than secular feminists. Instead of demanding equality to men, they continued to accept women's "natural" subordination. For example, Zilpha Elaw described women who refused to submit to "the paternal yoke or the government of a husband" as "indecent and impious—conveying a disrespect to the regulations of Scripture."[116] Perhaps because of this conservatism, few Methodist women tried to combine their preaching careers with marriage and motherhood. With the notable exceptions of Hannah Reeves and Sally Thompson, who traveled in company with their husbands, the majority of female preachers were either single or widowed. Although Salome Lincoln continued to speak publicly after marrying Junius Mowry, a Reformed Methodist minister, her appearances in the pulpit gradually dwindled as she devoted herself to raising two children. Even though female preachers anticipated the woman's rights movement by defending their right to preach and speak as equals, they also wanted to protect the sanctity of the family against the dislocations of rapid social and economic change.[117]

---

113. Jarena Lee, *Life and Religious Experience*, 35.
114. Drury, *History of the United Brethren*, 425.
115. Davis, *Female Preacher*, 13.
116. Zilpha Elaw, *Memoirs*, 61.
117. On biblical feminism, see Catherine A. Brekus, "Harriet Livermore, the 'Pilgrim Stranger': Female Preaching and Biblical Feminism in Early-Nineteenth-Century America," *Church History* 65 (1996): 389-404.

In many ways the early Methodists were reactionaries. Instead of embracing the dramatic transformations set in motion by the market revolution, they tried to create countercultural "islands of holiness" to set themselves apart from the rest of the world. Ironically, they became best known for their championing of the liberal values of individualism and free agency, but in their early years they also preached an ethic of communal and familial responsibility. In the tightly knit, intimate atmosphere of love feasts and class meetings, they struggled to preserve traditional Christian values against the centripetal forces of mobility and commercial expansion. Disturbed by the vast economic and political changes that were reshaping everyday life in the early republic, they preached repentance and reformation rather than the triumph of secular progress.

Theologically, female preachers mixed their commitment to biblical feminism with traditional evangelical beliefs. In their most important innovation, they transformed the Bible into a defense of women's spiritual equality, often using their sermons to defend female preaching. During a camp meeting in Ohio, Ellen Stewart riveted her audience by preaching on the text, "She hath done what she could."[118] Yet like Methodist men, female preachers devoted the majority of their sermons to the classic themes of sin, repentance, and salvation. For example, in 1829 Salome Lincoln preached on a popular verse from the apostle John: "Behold the Lamb of God, which taketh away the sin of the world."[119] Similarly, during a sermon that she delivered in Brooklyn, New York, Jarena Lee assured her listeners that "whosoever shall believeth in [Christ] shall not perish, but have eternal life."[120] Contrary to what their critics accused, these women were not theological radicals who were trying to subvert the Methodist orthodoxy. Like the men in their denomination, they were devout evangelicals who took seriously their commitment to "saving souls." Perhaps if they had been more radical, they would have had a more lasting, egalitarian impact on the church, but they also would never have been so widely accepted by rank-and-file believers.

From all accounts, audiences were transfixed by the charismatic, dynamic presence of female preachers in the pulpit. Instead of standing stiffly and reading formal, prepared sermons, women spoke extemporaneously, punctuating their words with shouts, groans, and

118. Ellen Stewart, *Life*, 83.
119. Davis, *Female Preacher*, 54. Her text was John 1:29.
120. Jarena Lee, *Religious Experience and Journal*, 30.

exclamations of praise. Like their male colleagues, who were criticized for using "bad English" and speaking with crude "vehemence and gesticulation," most of these women were celebrated for their "power" and "warmth" in the pulpit rather than their refinement.[121] At a camp meeting in Rhode Island, for example, one woman slapped her hands "with great violence" to emphasize her words, whereas another spoke so loudly that "the veins of her forehead and temples as well as those of her neck, 'swelled up like whip chords.'" Not surprisingly, critics found these women "bold and uncouth," complaining that their loud voices and "contortions of countenance" made them appear shockingly unfeminine.[122] However, female preachers found a much more sympathetic audience among the sailors, factory workers, and farm wives who crowded their meetings. Even though early American Methodism crossed lines of class as well as race, it particularly appealed to the uneducated, working-class poor, and female preachers were skilled at speaking the language of the streets.

These women became extremely popular in the early nineteenth century, often addressing overflowing crowds at churches and camp meetings. When Salome Lincoln announced that she would preach at a schoolhouse near Taunton, Massachusetts, it was so "densely crowded" that the windows were removed so that people could stand outside to hear.[123] "Miss Parker," a nondenominational preacher who was loosely affiliated with the Methodists, reportedly spoke to a crowd of one thousand people in Grasmere, New Hampshire, in 1841.[124] Similarly, Elice Miller sometimes held services outdoors because she could not find buildings large enough to accommodate her audiences. Although many people seem to have been attracted to women's meetings out of curiosity, female preachers remained popular even after their novelty wore off. For example, Hannah Reeves repeatedly visited the same towns as she accompanied her minister husband on his circuit, but during a career that spanned thirty-seven years, she continued to draw large audiences. On one occasion when she was ill, her husband tried to preach in her stead, but he found that "nothing would satisfy the congregation but 'the woman.' "[125]

---

121. Catherine Reed Williams offered this description of a male Methodist in her *Fall River: An Authentic Narrative* (Providence, R.I.: Marshall, Brown, & Company, 1834), 177.

122. Ibid., 188, 181-82.

123. Davis, *Female Preacher*, 66, 69.

124. On Parker, see Kern, *God, Grace, and Granite*, 131. Parker may have also been the unnamed female preacher who organized a Methodist church in Goffstown, New Hampshire, in the same year. See Robert F. Lawrence, *The New Hampshire Churches; Comprising Histories of the Congregational and Presbyterian Churches in the State* (New Hampshire: N. W. Goddard, 1856).

125. Brown, *Lady Preacher*, 122.

Silencing the Female Voice:
The Methodist Quest for Respectability

Through their self-sacrificing zeal, female preachers such as Hannah Reeves helped build Methodism into the single largest Protestant group in America. In revivals across the northern and midwestern states, they helped organize new churches and added thousands of new converts to Methodist membership lists. As the circuit rider Charles Harding noted, "In many places our sisters have been our best, and truest, and most faithful workmen. But for them many of our societies, now strong and flourishing, would have had no existence."[126] Like the male itinerants who were so richly praised for their selfless devotion, female preachers embraced lives of suffering and persecution.

By the 1830s and 1840s, however, these women found that their labors were no longer welcome. As Methodism was transformed from a small, struggling sect into a powerful, middle-class denomination, women were no longer allowed to preach or even exhort in public. Writing in 1833, the Reverend George Coles commented that "the practice of praying in prayer-meetings by our gifted sisters" had become virtually obsolete.[127] Earlier generations of women had filled meetinghouses with their loud exhortations and heartfelt prayers, but as the Methodists strove to attain greater respectability, they tried to suppress this religious "enthusiasm." Class meetings all but disappeared, and church services became more quiet and orderly.

The MEC underwent a dramatic transformation in the first few decades of the nineteenth century. In the early years, most converts had been lower-class farmers and laborers who were attracted to the Methodists' Arminian theology and their popular, egalitarian style of worship. Deliberately setting themselves apart from the values of the larger culture, they questioned the unbridled pursuit of wealth, arguing that riches led to moral temptations that Christians should avoid. Although few were desperately poor, they lacked the niceties that were beginning to appear in more affluent households, such as tables and dinner plates.[128] Ironically, however, the Methodists' commit-

---

126. Harding, "Autobiography."

127. Coles, *Heroines*, 13.

128. See Richard L. Bushman, *The Refinement of America: Persons, Houses, Cities* (New York: Alfred A. Knopf, 1992), 74-78. Ellen Stewart, for example, lived in a log cabin in Ohio that had no floor, no table, and "but few of the necessities of life." See Stewart, *Life*, 75.

ment to moral discipline and hard work eventually led them to unexpected economic success. As historian Nathan Hatch has noted, "Methodism resonated with the logic of capitalism and liberal individualism."[129] When Charles Harding had first joined the Methodists in 1825, most converts were "farmers, mechanicks [sic], or day laborers" who were called "fanaticks," "ignorant," "noisy," and "crazy," but by 1869, they had been replaced by "Methodist lawyers, Methodist Physicians, Methodist merchants," and scores of Methodist politicians.[130]

As the membership of the denomination changed, so did its style of worship. With the help of ministers such as Nathan Bangs, a new generation of educated, upwardly mobile men and women tried to distance themselves from the Methodists' earlier tradition of anti-intellectualism, visionary "enthusiasm," and female evangelism. In New York City, for example, Bangs tried to discourage the "impatience of scriptural restraint and moderation, clapping of the hands, screaming, and even jumping, which marred and disgraced the word of God."[131] In place of these "disorders," he envisioned a more refined form of worship in which educated middle-class clergymen would instruct their silent congregations in the subtleties of biblical exegesis.

Perhaps, as H. Richard Niebuhr once suggested, all sects are eventually destined to mature into denominations.[132] Building on the sociological theories of Max Weber and Ernst Troeltsch, Niebuhr drew a sharp distinction between *sects*, which begin as protest movements against the religious orthodoxy, and *denominations*, which are closely allied to "national, economic, and cultural interests." As "churches of the disinherited," sects set themselves apart from the larger culture, but historically, they tend to be short-lived. Within a generation, converts begin to create more formal institutions in order to pass on their beliefs to their children. As Niebuhr explained, "The sect must take on the character of an educational and disciplinary institution, with the purpose of bringing the new generation into conformity with the

129. Nathan O. Hatch, "The Puzzle of American Methodism," *Church History* 63 (1994): 187.

130. Harding, "Autobiography."

131. Stevens, *Life and Times of Nathan Bangs,* 183. On the "allure of respectability," see Hatch, *Democratization,* 201-6.

132. H. Richard Niebuhr, *The Social Sources of Denominationalism* (1929; reprint, New York: Meridian, 1959).

ideals and customs which have become traditional."[133] If the members of a sect want to perpetuate their vision, if they want to exert an enduring influence on future generations, then they must learn to compromise with their culture.

Yet to suggest that the Methodists' quest for cultural acceptance was inevitable obscures the element of choice involved. In the 1830s and 1840s, many Methodists were tired of being labeled as enthusiastic "fanatics," and they self-consciously *chose* to embrace the values of a culture that they once had opposed. For women preachers, who were marginalized and vilified, such a decision appeared as a decline, a betrayal of the Methodists' early heritage. Yet to many other Methodists, it represented a significant improvement. In one of the most important developments, Methodist colleges were formed, and education was no longer regarded as an impediment to spiritual growth.

Unfortunately, however, the new emphasis on gentility and education had devastating consequences for female preachers and exhorters. By the 1830s even the limited support that they had received from male ministers had begun to disappear. As a result, the number of women who decided to preach began to dwindle, with only eight women beginning their careers during the 1830s and the 1840s. Instead of "testifying" in public, these women were encouraged to conform to a more "feminine," domestic image. As George Coles explained, women's "constitution and sympathies" made them unfit to be "public teachers," but they could still exert influence within their own sphere—a sphere that seemed to be perpetually narrowing. A woman "cannot speak in loud, clarion tones," he explained. "Her voice is rather that of the soft lute, soothing and alluring; but it is not the less powerful for its gentleness."[134] In 1831, the Reverend George Ryerson suggested that women could "preach" by sewing clothing for the poor.[135]

---

133. See Max Weber, "The Protestant Sects and the Spirit of Capitalism," in *From Max Weber: Essays in Sociology,* trans. and ed. Hans Gerth and C. Wright Mills (New York: Oxford University Press, 1946), 302-22, and Ernst Troeltsch, *The Social Teachings of the Christian Churches,* trans. Olive Wyon (London, 1931; reprint, Chicago: University of Chicago Press, 1976), 1:131, 331-43. See also Benton Johnson, "On Church and Sect," *American Sociological Review* 28 (1963): 539-49.

134. Coles, *Heroines,* 17.

135. *Christian Advocate* (April 1831): 122, quoted in Elizabeth Muir, "The Bark School House: Methodist Episcopal Missionary Women in Upper Canada, 1827–1833," in John S. Moir and C. T. McIntire, eds., *Canadian Protestant and Catholic Missions, 1820s–1960s* (New York: Peter Lang Publishing, 1988), 32.

In 1836, the Methodists symbolized their growing commitment to female domesticity by excommunicating Sally Thompson, a popular itinerant who had been preaching in New England for more than ten years. According to contemporary accounts, she had been "encouraged in her labors" by ministers in Boston, but when she moved to New York in 1833, she was greeted with resentment and hostility. She managed to garner enough support to continue preaching for another three years, but after repeatedly refusing to submit to the hierarchy's "limits and rules," she was finally forced out of the church. Thompson could have tried to appeal the ruling, but instead, she decided to join a sect that was more tolerant of female preaching. Shortly after her excommunication in 1836, she became a member of the Christian Connection, traveling as an itinerant for at least another eleven years.[136]

Other women also left the Methodists because they felt frustrated by the growing restrictions on female speech. Some, like Ellen Stewart, simply transferred their allegiance from the MEC to the Reformed, Protestant, or Wesleyan Methodists.[137] Others decided to abandon the denomination altogether, finding new homes with churches that allowed them greater freedom to speak. Like Sally Thompson, Sarah Hedges had traveled as a Methodist itinerant for more than ten years, but in 1821 she joined the Christian Connection in search of greater "liberty."[138]

The AME also tried to push female preachers out of the denomination as they sought greater respectability and middle-class acceptance. Under the leadership of the Reverend Daniel Alexander Payne, they tried to curtail the enthusiastic shouting, dancing, and clapping that had characterized their early worship. Payne was particularly opposed to female preaching, arguing that women's most important

---

136. See Sally Thompson, *Trial and Defence of Mrs. Sally Thompson, On a Complaint of Insubordination to the Rules of the Methodist Episcopal Church, Evil Speaking and Immorality, Held Before A Select Committee of Said Church in Cherry Valley, June 10, 1830* (West Troy, N.Y.: W. Hollands, 1837), pamphlet available in the Drew University Archives. I am grateful to Richard Shiels for this reference. See also *Christian Palladium* 4, no. 21 (1 March 1836): 332-33; *Zion's Herald* 7, no. 12 (23 March 1836); and Philetus Roberts, *Memoir of Mrs. Abigail Roberts; An Account of Her Birth, Early Education, Call to the Ministry* (Irvington, N.J.: M. Cummings, 1858), 145-47. The *Christian Palladium,* a Christian Connection journal, reported her travels on behalf of the denomination during the 1830s and 1840s.

137. Ellen Stewart, *Life,* 54.

138. *Christian Palladium* 12, no. 1 (5 July 1843): 16. See also Evans Williams Humphreys, *Memoirs of Deceased Christian Ministers; or, Brief Sketches of the Lives and Labors of 975 Ministers, Who Died Between 1793 and 1880* (Dayton, Ohio: Christian Publishing Association, 1880), 167.

role lay within the home.[139] In the 1810s and 1820s, women such as Rachel Evans and Zilpha Elaw had managed to convince ministers that their calls were genuine, but by the 1830s and 1840s they found it more difficult to find churches that would allow them to speak. Julia Foote, who did not begin her preaching career until 1845, lamented that "there was no justice meted out to women in those days." As punishment for her refusal to stop speaking publicly, she was excommunicated from her AME congregation in Boston.[140]

In response to the growing restrictions on women's "gifts," AME women formed a group to defend female preaching. In 1844, 1848, and 1852 they lobbied the General Conference in favor of licensing women, but they were defeated each time. According to Julia Foote, the clergymen at the 1844 Conference were so "incensed" by the idea of allowing women to preach that they all "talked and screamed to the bishop, who could scarcely keep order."[141] Frustrated by the pressures of defeat, these women eventually disbanded sometime during the mid-1850s. In the contemptuous words of Daniel Alexander Payne, "They held together for a brief period, and then fell to pieces like a rope of sand."[142]

By the 1840s the domestication of Methodism was complete. Rather than acknowledging the raw emotion that had characterized their early revivals, Methodist historians presented a more genteel, orderly version of their past. Although the names of male luminaries such as Benjamin Abbott and Nathan Bangs were lovingly preserved in clerical biographies, female preachers seem to have been deliberately forgotten. In one prominent exception, Hannah Reeves was memorialized in an article in the *Methodist Quarterly Review,* but the picture that emerged of her was deeply ambivalent. On one hand, Reeves was praised for agreeing to serve as a "helpmeet" to her husband (a clergyman) even though she was "superior to him in gifts" and could have demanded her own circuit. Yet Reeves was also described as a "masculine," "indomitable" woman who was willing to sacrifice her children's welfare to satisfy the demands of her career. Noting that she had given birth to three children, all of whom died in their youth,

---

139. See David W. Wills, "Womanhood and Domesticity in the AME Tradition: The Influence of Daniel Alexander Payne," in David W. Wills and Richard Newman, eds., *Black Apostles at Home and Abroad* (Boston: G. K. Hall & Co., 1982), 133-46.

140. Foote, *A Brand Plucked from the Fire,* 207.

141. Ibid., 216.

142. Daniel Alexander Payne, *History of the African Methodist Episcopal Church* (Nashville: Publishing House of the AME Sunday-school Union, 1891; reprint, New York: Arno Press, 1969), 237, 273.

the author concluded, "they were born but to die thus prematurely; for the maternal profession—and it is such—precludes another set of duties alien to it."[143] According to this article, Reeves may have been a success as a preacher, but she was a failure as a mother. If she had been less selfish, less ambitious, and more "feminine," her children would have survived.

Faced with such overwhelming opposition, Methodist female preachers began to disappear in the late 1830s and 1840s. Although some women continued to preach, obstinately refusing to cave in to denominational pressure, their popularity waned as the Methodists attracted more middle-class converts. Hannah Reeves continued to hold meetings until her death in 1868, but her appearances seem to have become increasingly rare as congregations demanded greater refinement and polish from their ministers. Similarly, during the 1840s Jarena Lee was shunned by the clerical leaders who had once defended her. In 1845, when she asked the AME Book Committee to help her publish an expanded version of her memoirs, they responded with disdain, treating her as an outcast instead of as one of the pillars of the early church. Presumably, few African Methodist clergymen wanted to memorialize a woman who so perfectly symbolized the uneducated, visionary enthusiasm of their early history. According to their report, "the manuscript of Sister Jarena Lee has been written in such a manner as it is impossible to decipher much of the meaning contained in it."[144] In 1849, Lee defied the church by publishing her memoirs at her own expense, but nothing more is known about her subsequent life. Like most of the other Methodist women who preached between 1784 and 1845, she was forgotten by the clerical leadership, leaving few traces of her memory in the historical record.

Conclusion

Recovering the lives of these forgotten female preachers sheds light on a critical and neglected part of Methodist history. For a few brief years, the early Methodists gave women unprecedented freedom to testify, exhort, and even preach in public—freedoms that were sharply restricted as the denomination became more successful and

---

143. "Mrs. Hannah Reeves," 446.
144. Payne, *History of the African Methodist Episcopal Church*, 190.

respectable. Indeed, the disappearance of female itinerants in the 1830s and 1840s marked a profound transformation in Methodist identity. Instead of setting themselves apart as a people unto themselves, the Methodists had become the religious establishment. With more than one and a half million members in 1850, they exerted a powerful force in shaping American culture.[145]

The Methodists continued to struggle with the question of female preaching throughout the nineteenth century. Certainly, the Methodist tradition of female evangelism did not end in the 1840s, and in some ways, the most exciting developments were still to come. But the growing numbers of women who stepped into Methodist pulpits in the 1870s and 1880s were an entirely different breed from the visionary enthusiasts who had caused such controversy in the early years of the movement. Although evangelists such as Phoebe Palmer and Anna Oliver seemed to represent the culmination of an earlier tradition of female preaching, they shared little with the women who had preceded them in the pulpit.

In 1840, at the same time as ministers were discouraging women from speaking publicly, Phoebe Palmer began hosting the Tuesday Meeting for the Promotion of Holiness in her home, launching a public career that would span more than thirty years. Palmer was a charismatic, dynamic leader, but unlike the "coarse," uneducated women who had filled the campgrounds with their loud shouts and fervent hallelujahs, she won the support of conservative ministers such as Nathan Bangs because of her genteel style and her embrace of middle-class values.[146] Even though she spoke to thousands of converts in meetings across the country, she refused to call her work *preaching*. As she explained, "It is our aim, in addressing the people . . . to simplify the way of faith. . . . Preach we do not; that is, not in a *technical* sense."[147] In contrast to the contentious female itinerants who had once roamed the American countryside, she represented a more domestic, motherly style of female religious leadership.

Following in the steps of Phoebe Palmer, the female evangelists of the 1870s and 1880s were eminently respectable. Influenced by the

---

145. Roger Finke and Rodney Stark, "How the Upstart Sects Won America: 1776–1850," *Journal for the Scientific Study of Religion* 28 (1989): 27-44.

146. Stevens, *Life and Times of Nathan Bangs*, 351.

147. Richard Wheatley, *The Life and Letters of Phoebe Palmer* (1881; reprint, New York: Garland Publishing, 1984), 614. See also Harold E. Raser, *Phoebe Palmer: Her Life and Thought* (Lewiston, N.Y.: Edwin Mellen Press, 1987), 76-79, and the essay by Kathryn Long in this volume.

Victorian "cult of true womanhood," they based their claim to ministry on their special "feminine" sensibilities. Unlike earlier female preachers, who had described themselves as spiritual "mothers" or "sisters" who were also "bold soldiers for Christ," they took the language of feminine domesticity to a greater extreme. "Pastoral work is adapted to women," Anna Oliver explained, "for it is motherly work. The mother has her little group, the pastor the flock. As a mother spreads her table with food suited to the individual needs of her family, so the pastor feeds the flock." According to Oliver, she deserved to be ordained because of her "natural qualifications" as a woman.[148]

It would be easy to portray this greater emphasis on female difference and domesticity as a decline for Methodist women. For many historians, the history of early American Methodism appears as a fall from grace, a capitulation to middle-class conformity. To Russell E. Richey, for example, the early Methodists seem to have lived in a kind of Eden, a utopian world that was shattered as they sacrificed their egalitarianism in favor of cultural acceptance.[149] Certainly, many early female preachers would have agreed with his assessment. Despite the sacrifices that they made for their church, and their immense popularity in the early nineteenth century, they were belittled, harassed, and eventually forgotten by their "brothers" and "sisters" in Christ. As the Methodists embraced the ideology of domesticity, they deprived women of their earlier liberty of speech, urging them to "keep silence in the churches." Clearly, the Methodists lost a vibrant part of their heritage when women such as Jarena Lee and Salome Lincoln were forced out of the ministry.

However, history is rarely a record of either absolute progress or absolute decline; it takes unexpected twists and turns, transforming our perceptions at every fork in the road. In the short term, the Methodists' embrace of domesticity had tragic consequences for women, but in the long run, it gave them a powerful language of female uniqueness that made it possible for them to defend their right to vote, own property, and be ordained.

---

148. Barbara Welter, "The Cult of True Womanhood, 1820–1860," *American Quarterly* 18 (1966): 151-74. Anna Oliver, "'Test Case' on the Ordination of Women," reprinted in Frederick A. Norwood, ed., *Sourcebook of American Methodism* (Nashville: Abingdon Press, 1982), 449. On Oliver, see Kenneth E. Rowe, ed., "The Ordination of Women: Round One; Anna Oliver and the General Conference of 1880," *Perspectives,* 298-308. On Methodist women in late-nineteenth-century America, see Rosemary Skinner Keller, "Creating a Sphere for Women: The Methodist Episcopal Church, 1869–1906," *Perspectives,* 332-42; and Nancy A. Hardesty, *Your Daughters Shall Prophesy: Revivalism and Feminism in the Age of Finney* (Brooklyn, N.Y.: Carlson Publishing, 1991).
149. See Richey, *Early American Methodism,* xii.

Future generations of female preachers, no matter how domesticated, possessed a political consciousness of themselves *as women* that their predecessors had lacked. Without this consciousness, the woman's rights movement and the crusade for women's ordination would never have been possible. In the words of historian Nancy Cott, "the ideology of woman's sphere formed a necessary stage in the process of shattering the hierarchy of sex."[150] By demanding political and legal as well as spiritual equality to men, women such as Anna Oliver transformed the Methodist churches in radical and enduring ways.[151] They embraced a refined, domestic style of religious leadership, but unlike earlier women, they also demanded a fundamental transformation in the relationship between the sexes. By fighting for the authority of ordination, they guaranteed that women would never be pushed to the sidelines of the church again. In one of the ironies of history, the domestication of Methodism led to the silencing of women such as Jarena Lee and Hannah Reeves, but it also fueled the rise of a new generation of educated, politically astute women who demanded full equality in the church.

---

150. Cott, *Bonds*, 200.

151. On women's ordination, see Barbara Brown Zikmund, "Winning Ordination for Women in Mainstream Protestant Churches," in Rosemary Radford Ruether and Rosemary Skinner Keller, eds., *Women and Religion in America* (San Francisco: Harper & Row, 1986) 3:339-48; and Virginia Lieson Brereton and Christa Ressmeyer Klein, "American Women in Ministry: A History of Protestant Beginning Points," in Janet Wilson James, ed., *Women in American Religion* (Philadelphia: University of Pennsylvania Press, 1980), 171-90.

CHAPTER 5

" . . . many of the poor Affricans are obedient to the faith"[1]
Reassessing the African American Presence in Early Methodism in the United States, 1769–1809

Will Gravely

A century and a half of largely unchallenged acceptance of African slavery by Europeans in the New World had taken place before the first Wesleyan missionaries from Great Britain preached the Christian gospel to this particular classification of "the poor."[2] Less than three weeks after landing in Pennsylvania, Joseph Pilmore found Methodist societies in Philadelphia formed according to the Wesleyan model. His journal entry for the week of 6 November 1769 forms the epigraph for this essay: "The Lord is making bare his arm in the sight of the heathen, and many of the poor Affricans are obedient to the faith." Pilmore's testimony sets the agenda for this reassessment of the African Methodist presence in the Wesleyan movement on the North American continent for the first generation.[3]

---

1. Joseph Pilmore, *The Journal of Joseph Pilmore, Methodist Itinerant For The Years August 1, 1769 to January 2, 1774*, ed. Frederick E. Maser and Howard T. Maag (Philadelphia: Message Publishing Co., 1969), 26. Appreciation is due the editors of the Lilly Endowment-sponsored project, "An Afro-American Religion Documentary," Professor David Wills of Amherst College, and Professor Albert J. Raboteau of Princeton University for access to some of the sources in this paper. Drs. Jeanne Knepper and Warren Napier were helpful graduate research assistants when they were students in the joint Ph.D. program between the University of Denver and the Iliff School of Theology.</p>

2. My analysis begins with John Wesley's sending of preachers Joseph Pilmore and Richard Boardman to the American colonies in 1769.

3. Pilmore, *Journal*, 26. Since African Americans, slave and free, referred to themselves and were referred to as *Africans*, I commonly use that term, and less occasionally *Negro, black,* and *colored* according to the context. *African Methodist* was a common appellation as late as the 1830s

Along with other contemporary documents, the diaries, journals, letters, and reminiscences of the early British missionaries sent by Wesley and of native colonial Methodist preachers make up the sources for this reconsideration. These "white" sources are clearly secondary.[4] They can, however, indicate to the modern reader in some sense how African Methodist converts apprehended and expressed the transformational energy of the early Wesleyan message, as we shall see in "Spiritual Power Among African Methodist Converts." They also demonstrate in what ways Africans participated in the distinctive Wesleyan means of grace—class meetings, love feasts, watch-nights—alongside the more conventional expressions of faith—praying, singing, exhorting, preaching, baptizing, and receiving holy communion. Those dynamics are our concerns in "African Methodist Participation in Wesleyan Organization and Means of Grace." Such sources, to be sure, are limited by their secondary descriptive accounts of the African "others," but theirs remain the only written primary evidence available for the first quarter century of the American Methodist movement. The hermeneutical challenge is how to see and hear these African Christians refracted through European-American texts. By 1794, direct African voices emerged, new dynamics were present, and the black presence in American Methodism began to move in significantly new directions—issues addressed in "New Forms of African Methodist Presence, 1794–1809."

A comprehensive reconsideration of the early African Methodist presence requires the further step of inquiring how that presence has

to include those who remained in the MEC as well as those who formed the AME, AMEZ, and African Union Methodist denominations between 1813 and 1822. On the general point, see my "Dialectic of Double-Consciousness in Black American Freedom Celebrations, 1808–1863," published originally in 1982 and reprinted in David Hackett, ed., *Religion and American Culture* (New York and London: Routledge, 1995), 109-26. This study does not include the African Methodist societies in Nova Scotia, nor does it engage the interpretive issues of African cultural legacies that were blended with Christian rituals and behavior by the early converts. The best work on these issues, beginning with fifteenth-century missions in Africa and coming to North America is Sylvia Frey and Betty Wood, *Come Shouting to Zion: African-American Protestantism in the American South and the British Caribbean to 1830* (Chapel Hill: University of North Carolina Press, 1998).

4. The construction of whiteness in the early consciousness of European Americans was legalized in the Naturalization Act of 1790, which converted every immigrant from Europe into a free white person. That process did not end legally until the Walter-McCarren immigration reform act of 1952, and its legacy remains part of the racist coding of American discourse and of the designations of the federal census. The impact of white identity on definitions of citizenship and inclusiveness in the political community of the country, especially as it pertains to the stories of various communities of Asian Americans, is the subject of Ronald Takaki's *Strangers from a Different Shore: A History of Asian-Americans* (New York: Penguin, 1989), and *A Different Mirror: A History of Multicultural America* (Boston: Little, Brown, 1993), especially chapters 1 and 14.

been interpreted in Methodist historical narratives, both black and white, and embracing chroniclers of specific denominations as well as of the broader movement. How were the early African Methodists remembered? Were they acknowledged and then forgotten? Were they underrepresented in the depictions of American Methodist origins? Where was their presence ignored or repressed? How has the early African Methodist presence been reasserted? Such an encounter of black and white in Methodism would be to apply to religious history what Nobel prize winner Toni Morrison has proposed for American literary criticism in her book *Playing in the Dark: Whiteness and the Literary Imagination.*[5]

Before denominational historical narratives can be read as primary texts for a Methodist version of *Playing in the Dark*, however, a scrupulous reassessment of the sources of the first generation has to occur. The process could be modeled along the lines that secular historians Sidney and Emma Norgrady Kaplan and James McPherson have done for the American Revolution and the Civil War.[6] That task, whose importance African American scholar Lewis Baldwin has recently underscored, was begun more than two decades ago by the late Harry V. Richardson and the late David H. Bradley Sr.[7] The ongoing recovery of additional contemporary sources from the eighteenth and nineteenth centuries enables this reassessment to be expanded, laying the groundwork for addressing the next level of analysis extending back to earlier historians.[8]

---

5. This book is a collection of the William E. Massey Sr. Lectures in the History of American Civilization at Harvard in 1990, whose university press published them in 1992. Building on the present essay, presented at the Asbury Conference in 1994, I have offered some parallel reflections in "'Playing in the Dark'—Methodist Style: The Fate of the Early African American Presence in Denominational Memory, 1807–1974," in William B. Lawrence, Dennis M. Campbell, and Russell E. Richey, eds., *The People(s) Called Methodist: Forms and Reforms of Their Life* (Nashville: Abingdon Press, 1998), 175-90.

6. The Kaplans' volume is *The Black Presence in the Era of the American Revolution*, revised ed. (Amherst: University of Massachusetts Press, 1989). McPherson's older study, *The Negro's Civil War* (New York: Pantheon Books, 1965) was reprinted in 1991.

7. Richardson's study was *Dark Salvation: The Story of Methodism As It Developed Among Blacks in America* (Garden City, N.Y.: Doubleday, 1976), especially chapter 3. Bradley's essay, "Francis Asbury and the Development of African Churches in America," *Methodist History* 10, no. 1 (October 1971): 3-29, preceded Richardson. Baldwin's proposal is in "Early African American Methodism: Founders and Foundations," in Grant S. Shockley, et al., eds., *Heritage and Hope: The African-American Presence in United Methodism* (Nashville: Abingdon Press, 1991), 23-28.

8. Building on the earlier model for an interactive study of racial dynamics in Methodism, occurring in Donald G. Matthews's *Religion in the Old South* (Chicago: University of Chicago Press, 1977), Frey and Wood have assembled and interpreted a rich array of new sources in *Come Shouting to Zion*. Likewise, John Wigger's recent book, *Taking Heaven by Storm: Methodism and the Rise of Popular Christianity in America* (New York: Oxford University Press, 1998), especially chapter 6, is grounded in manuscript and newly uncovered material to which he gives a creative reading.

Spiritual Power Among African Methodist Converts

The experiential testimonies of early African Methodists occur frequently in the private and published records of the first preachers. Pilmore's companion, Richard Boardman, wrote to Wesley on 4 November 1769 to recount an African woman's spiritual struggle—a woman whose condition of bondage exacerbated her effort to appropriate the Wesleyan evangel. "One . . . came to me to tell me she could neither eat nor sleep, because her Master would not suffer her to come to hear the word. She wept exceedingly," Boardman explained, "saying, 'I told my Master I would do more work than ever I used to do, if he would but let me come; nay, that I would do everything in my power to be a good servant.'"[9] In Philadelphia, Pilmore recorded in his journal in August 1771 that he too heard an African woman convert declare in New York that "her heart was so full of divine love that she could not express it."[10] Francis Asbury's journal contains similar observations. The early New York African Methodists were greatly "affected," he noted in November 1771, by their reception of "the word." He even applied the same language to himself the following September upon observing "the poor Negroes, seeing their sable faces at the table of the Lord" at St. Paul's Chapel in New York where the early Methodists took the sacrament.[11]

The witness to the conversion of Africans spread outside the colonial cities of New York and Philadelphia. In Maryland, Asbury "spoke closely to the poor Negroes" in December 1772. The next August he recorded an incident of dramatic conversion in Kent County. "In public worship, at Mr. Gibbs's," he wrote, "a serious Negro was powerfully struck; and though he made but little noise, yet he trembled so exceedingly that the very house shook."[12] It was in

---

9. "Letter CCCXXIII (From Mr. Richard Boardman, to the Rev. J. Wesley), New York, Nov. 4, 1769," *Arminian Magazine* 7 (1785): 163-64.

10. Pilmore *Journal*, 96 (1 August 1771). I have refrained from pressing the important gender issues necessary to our fullest understanding of African Methodist converts. Jean Miller Schmidt in her new book *Grace Sufficient: A History of Women in American Methodism 1760–1939* (Nashville: Abingdon Press, 1999), 54, 61, 72-73, works with some of these same sources in relation to white and black Methodist women's spiritual experiences and roles. See also Cynthia Lynn Lyerly, "Religion, Gender, and Identity: Black Methodist Women in a Slave Society, 1770–1810," in Patricia Manton, ed., *Discovering the Women in Slavery: Emancipating Perspectives on the American Past* (Athens: University of Georgia Press, 1996), 202-26; and Frey and Wood, *Come Shouting to Zion*, 110, 121-22, 127-28, 165-66, 171-72, 188-89, 210.

11. *JLFA* 1:9-10 (12 November 1771), 43 (13 September 1772).

12. Ibid., 1:56-57 (7-8 December 1772), 89 (5 August 1773). For an early reference to Asbury meeting with African Methodists in Baltimore, see 1:190 (23 June 1776).

Virginia, however, that a revival movement with a significant response by Africans occurred in seven or eight counties more than a decade after 1765. English native Thomas Rankin's account to Wesley about events in the summer of 1776 dramatized their active presence. Preaching at Boisseau's Chapel in Amelia County on 30 June at 4:00 P.M., Rankin evoked a "mighty effusion of the Spirit," which lasted for more than an hour. The "groans and strong cries after God and the Lord Jesus Christ" drowned out his preaching, so that finally he and George Shadford were so overcome that they "sat down in the pulpit." Rankin's letter to Wesley mentioned the racially inclusive nature of the congregation, but the special response of the Africans noted in his journal was excised from the published version of the report. It read: "And what was peculiarly affecting, I observed in the gallery, (appropriated for the black people) almost every one of them upon their knees; some for themselves, and others for their distressed companions." A week later at White's Chapel, Rankin preached on Ezekiel's vision of the dry bones to a full house, with another five hundred people outside braving the threat of rain. Again, he could not get the biracial audience to compose themselves. Many, he wrote to Wesley, cried aloud to God—"some on their knees, and some on their faces"—and Rankin added, "Hundreds of Negroes were among them, with the tears streaming down their faces."[13] In March of the following year, colonial native preacher John Littlejohn spoke to a "much crowded" biracial audience in Richmond. "Towards the close the poor Africans could forbear no longer but w[i]th strong cryes & tears called for mercy," he wrote in his journal. After most whites in the audience left "in confusion & dismay as if the great deep was

---

13. Ibid., 1:207-24 with quoted material on 221-22; and the unpublished "Journal of Thomas Rankin, 1773–78" in its typed transcription by Francis H. Tees at Drew University, 43-44 (30 June and 7 July 1776). Pro-Methodist Anglican clergy Devereux Jarratt and Archibald Roberts, Methodist evangelists Robert Williams, Shadford, and Rankin, and local preachers Thomas Saunders and John Dickins led the Virginia revival. Jarratt's *A Brief Narrative of the Revival of Religion in Virginia. In a Letter to a Friend* was written 10 September 1776 to Rankin. When published it also contained Rankin's letter to Wesley, which was dated 24 June 1778 (revised to 1777 by the editors of *JLFA*). Together they were separately published, but they also came to be included in the early editions of Asbury's *Journal*.

An earlier account at Deer Creek, Maryland, on 8 November 1774 reveals that Rankin experienced similar spiritually powerful services. Making special mention of what was happening in the black section of the chapel and asking the rest of the congregation to look there, Rankin wrote: "I then said, 'See the number of the black Africans, who have stretched out their hands and hearts to God!' While I was addressing the people thus, it seemed as if the very house shook with the mighty power and glory of Sinai's God. Many of the people were so overcome, that they were ready to faint, and die under his almighty hand" (trans. p. 19).

going to overwhelm them," Littlejohn remained behind "to point the Bl[ac]ks to Jesus as their only ark of saf[e]ty f[ro]m the storm."[14]

Besides such accounts by the preachers describing the dramatic collective fervor of Africans, cases of individual spiritual inquiry, of Christian composure in the face of death, and of finding sanctification for leading an exemplary life also continued to occur and be recorded. At Trenton, New Jersey, in May 1772, Pilmore recounted a prayer meeting at the conclusion of which "a poor Negro woman [came] to [him] in great distress of soul, [who] cast herself at [his] feet." Pilmore "raised her up, and encouraged her to trust in the Lord, and he would soon have mercy upon her and pardon all her offences." In Norfolk, Virginia, the next August, "two poor slaves" came to Pilmore and asked to be instructed "in the way of salvation." Giving "a short and plain account of the Plan of the Gospel . . . how sinners may come to God and be saved," he sang and prayed together with them. The two African inquirers "expressed great thankfulness," Pilmore noted, and "seemed determined to be Christians."[15]

An African Methodist woman in New York provided the missionary Boardman with a chance to witness a paradigmatic Christian death in 1771. Writing to Wesley, he found comfort in the way "some poor negroes" had died, "rejoicing in the God of their salvation." To his inquiry as to whether she was afraid to die, the black Christian replied, "O no, I have my blessed Saviour in my heart; I should be glad to die: I want to be gone, that I may be with him forever. I know that he loves me; and I feel I love him with all my heart." Her continuing deathbed witness astonished many "till the Lord took her."[16]

Colonial native preacher Freeborn Garrettson, while traveling the Calvert Circuit in Maryland in 1783, recorded in what is now a fragmented text another African Methodist woman's exemplary Christian dedication. After she struggled "to set her soul at liberty," this woman "received a clear witness of His pardoning love." Not content to miss the Wesleyan potential for perfection, "she earnestly sought it day and night" until she received sanctification. Garrettson's longer description of her and of her situation deserves being read in his own words.

---

14. "Journal of John Littlejohn," trans. Annie L. Winstead, mimeographed publication at The Upper Room, Nashville, n.d., 16 March 1777 (trans. p. 33).

15. Pilmore, *Journal*, 131 (13 May 1772), 149 (2 August 1772).

16. "Letter CCCLVI (From Mr. R. Boardman, to the Rev. J. Wesley), New York, April 2, 1771," *Arminian Magazine* 8 (1785): 113-14.

She appears now to be established. She is a slave, who hires her time of her master. She is very industrious, pays her hire, and keeps herself well clothed. I have frequently seen her at five sermons running. It is uncommon to see her many minutes together idle. She commonly carried her work with her. She hires a room and boards herself and lives alone. She rises several times in the night to pray and particularly at 4 o'clock in the morning. In short this is her experience; my trials are many, but every moment I'm happy in God, having an abiding witness.[17]

The spiritual potency of the African appropriation of Wesleyan preaching did not cease throughout the first generation of the movement. Philip Bruce wrote to Bishop Thomas Coke from Portsmouth, Virginia, in March 1788, claiming that "the greatest work in many parts of this circuit is among the blacks." He described a particular night meeting in Isle of Wight County where "a cry among the poor slaves . . . drowned the preaching. . . . I saw a number," Bruce declared, "(some of who[m] at first appeared to be most stubborn) brought to the floor, and there lie crying till most of them got happy."[18] In nearby Petersburg the same phenomenon was present during a quarterly meeting, where "many scores of black as well as white people fell to the earth, and lay in agonies till evening; and some, especially the blacks, lay struggling till they beat the earth with their hands, head and feet, while others kicked holes in the ground."[19]

Further north the stories of African conversion circulated. Traveling the Chesapeake region in the summer of 1789, Richard Whatcoat's labors were encouraged by a letter describing conversion and sanctification experiences. It included an account of "one Bla[c]k man powerfully Stru[c]k to the ground under Conviction in his Return from Q[uarterly] Meeting when the Lord Spoke peace to his Soul."[20] A year later on the Calvert circuit, William Colbert confided in his journal that as he stood between the black and white congregants, "I wanted to see a move among them, therefore I exerted

17. Freeborn Garrettson, *American Methodist Pioneer. The Life and Journals of The Rev. Freeborn Garrettson 1753–1827*, ed. Robert Drew Simpson (Rutland, Vt.: Academy Books, 1984), 227.

18. "An extract of a letter from PHILIP BRUCE, elder of the Methodist Episcopal church, to Bishop Coke, dated Portsmouth, Virginia, March 25, 1788," *Arminian Magazine* (Philadelphia) 2 (1790): 562-63. The "colored" membership of Portsmouth grew from 57 in 1787, to 259 in 1788, to 473 in 1789, and to 693 in 1790; *Minutes MEC* (1840), 28, 31, 35, 58.

19. R. Garrettson, "An Account of the Revival of the Work of God at Petersburg, in Virginia," *Arminian Magazine* 13 (1790): 300-307.

20. William Warren Sweet, ed, *Religion on the American Frontier, 1783–1840: The Methodists* (New York: Cooper Square, 1964), 77.

myself, and sure enough, there was a move for the blacks behind began to shout aloud jump and fall—the whites to look wild, and go off."[21] Eight years later Richard Allen and Jupiter Gibson wrote to Bishop Asbury by way of Ezekiel Cooper to report on a revival of religion in Philadelphia, especially in the Bethel African Church. "Our congregations," they explained, "nearly consist of as many whites as blacks; many that never attended any place of worship before come; some through curiosity, and many of them are awakened and join the Society, so that nearly as many whites as blacks are convinced and converted to the Lord." The results of such an unprecedented revival in Philadelphia confirmed the ministry of these two local leaders, one black and the other white, and demonstrated that a tentative biracialism could mark their work in the same way that it was present twenty-years earlier in Virginia.[22]

By the time Allen and Gibson could write in 1798 of their roles in a biracial revival in Philadelphia, something significant had occurred over the previous three decades. The public manifestation of spiritual power among Africans was beyond dispute. And it was contagious. Paul Burall, a Cornish native traveling in America in 1783, described being at Methodist gatherings in Philadelphia under Asbury just before the MEC was established. They forged for him a strong identification with the "Negors":

And wen I came hear, Just on the Close of the war, the Methidis was very low, one Meting house In the sitty, and Mr. Asbery the only Preacher that was year (and sum other Com before I left), and most of the Society was the Negors. And to [at] the Mettings I was delighted to hear them tell thear Experance, so sempill, so free, and so Artless, I could often wiling to chainge With them. . . . For at the time I thought the[y] was Very sinsear, that if I was to tarey hear that thease people would be my People.[23]

---

21. "Journal of William Colbert" (5 April 1790), MSS and transcribed versions at the Garrett-Evangelical Theological Seminary.

22. Richard Allen and Jupiter Gibson from Philadelphia, 22 February 1798, to Ezekiel Cooper, in the Cooper Collection, Garrett-Evangelical Theological Seminary, and in George A. Phoebus, ed., *Beams of Light on Early Methodism* (New York: Phillips & Hunt, 1887), 252-54. See also Charles H. Wesley, *Richard Allen Apostle of Freedom* (Washington, D.C.: Associated Publishers, n.d.), 89-90; and Benjamin T. Tanner, *An Outline of Our History and Government for African Methodist Churchmen, Ministerial and Lay* (Philadelphia: AME Book Concern, 1884), 91 (on Gibson being a white member of Bethel Church in Philadelphia).

23. *Cornwall to America in 1783 From the Journal of Paul Burall (1755–1826)*, ed. by his great-great-great niece (London: The Fenland Press, 1932), 13. Dr. Kenneth Rowe of Drew University discovered this passage and shared it with me.

African Methodist Participation in Wesleyan Organization and Means of Grace

Public displays and private spiritual achievements required channeling, so that the second important feature of African converts to Methodism in America can be found in the structure for their religious lives. Their involvement in the distinctive features of the Wesleyan system and of its means of grace became no less striking than did the power of their spiritual experience.

The class meeting, as Pilmore discovered in Philadelphia, was already operative for African Methodists in 1769. Five years before and thus predating Wesley's missionaries, in Robert Strawbridge's society at Sam's Creek in Maryland, a slavewoman, Anne Sweitzer, was a member—perhaps a charter member—and Jacob Toogood, also a bondsman, was an early licensed local preacher. The formation two years later of the John Street society in New York, under Philip Embury, included another African Methodist bondswoman, Bettye. In May 1770 Pilmore wrote to Wesley that the New York society included "a number of black women, who meet together every week; many of whom are happy in the love of God." To another correspondent he called the group a "Class," adding, "I think upon the whole they are as happy as any Class we have got."[24]

Few class lists from the earliest period survive, but it is clear from the preachers' journals that both biracial and racially separate, and gender inclusive and segregated classes were common to the African Methodists from the beginning. Separating classes by race and within racial classification by gender, however, had come to be a pattern in New York by 1793 and in Baltimore by 1800.[25] The move was gradual. On the Talbot circuit in Maryland in 1783, Garrettson mentioned

---

24. Baldwin, "Early African American Methodism," 23-24; on Toogood, see Edwin Schell, "Beginnings in Maryland and America," in Gordon Pratt Baker, ed., *Those Incredible Methodists: A History of the Baltimore Conference of the United Methodist Church* (Baltimore: Commission on Archives and History, The Baltimore Conference, 1972), 13-14, 535-36; "Letter CCCXXVIII (From Mr. J. Pilmoor, to the Rev. J. Wesley and all the Brethren in Conference), New-York, May 5, 1770," *Arminian Magazine* 7 (1784): 222-24; Frederick E. Maser, "Discovery: A Revealing Letter from Joseph Pilmore," *Methodist History* 10, no. 3 (April 1972): 54-58.

25. Samuel A. Seaman, *Annals of New York Methodism Being a History of the Methodist Episcopal Church in the City of New York from A.D. 1766 to A.D. 1890* (New York: Hunt & Eaton, 1890), 464-66 gives an enumeration of twenty gender-separated and one "mixt" classes called "white," and two male and four female "colored classes." By 1802 the "white" classes were thirty-four, with one of both genders, and the "colored classes" were eleven—four for males and seven for females. For Baltimore City and East Baltimore class records at the United Methodist Historical Society at Baltimore, see microfilm at the Hall of Records in Annapolis. For Philadelphia, see Dee Andrews, "The African Methodists of Philadelphia, 1794–1802," in *Perspectives*, 145-58.

holding black classes on 19 June, 6 July, 7 September, and 10 November.[26] Cooper's journal refers to convening separate black classes on four occasions between 1784 and 1790, and Whatcoat records meeting black classes at Richard Allen's house in Philadelphia four times in 1791. Colbert's journal has seventy-three references to separate black classes between 1790 and 1807. The bilingual (German and English) preacher, Henry Boehm, regularly convened separate classes for the Africans in his ministry in Delaware and Maryland, and in his travel as Asbury's companion elsewhere—especially in South Carolina.[27]

The class meeting structure was, therefore, the earliest separate African Methodist group experience. As racial separatism increased and the number of African converts grew, the class gave way to the racially distinct congregation or society. The developments for separate African societies in Philadelphia, New York, and Baltimore by 1796 are well-known stories, but there were also some all-black congregations emerging outside those urban centers. In 1794 Colbert praised the Oxen Hill African society opposite Alexandria, Virginia, which was led by free blacks but whose numbers came mostly from the enslaved population. They had built a meeting house and had become a station on the Montgomery circuit. Colbert's journal entry expressed his admiration:

> [T]heir society is very numberous, and very orderly, and to their great credit with pleasure I assert, that I never found a white class so regular in giving in their Quarterage, as these poor people are, and the greater part of them are slaves, of whom [I] never request anything. But they will enquire when the Quarterly Meetings are from time to time, and by the last time the preacher comes round before the Quarterly Meeting they will have five Dollars in silver tied up for him: as they are

---

26. Garrettson, *Methodist Pioneer*, 225-26, 229, 232. The 6 July class meeting was "a little after sunrise," obviously scheduled to harmonize with the work schedule of the black participants.

27. "Journal of Ezekiel Cooper," unpublished MSS, 26 December 1784, 28 February 1785, 20 January 1790, 29 December 1790; "Journal of Richard Whatcoat," unpublished MSS, 10 January, 4 April, 11 April, 17 April, 1791; and the numerous references in Colbert's "Journal"—all at Garrett-Evangelical Theological Seminary. The best discussion of Colbert's ministry among and the impact upon him by African Methodists is in Warren S. Napier, "Formed for Friendship: Revisioning Early American Circuit Riders Through the Journal of William Colbert, 1790–1833" (Ph.D. dissertation: the Iliff School of Theology and the University of Denver, 1996), chap. 4. The MSS "Journal of Henry Boehm," microfilm copy at Drew University, contains more than one hundred references to separate black classes or services between 1800 and 1808. See also Joseph B. Wakeley, ed., *The Patriarch of One Hundred Years: Being Reminiscences, Historical and Biographical, or Sixty-Four Years in the Ministry by Rev. Henry Boehm* (New York: Nelson & Phillips, 1875), 62-64, 69.

so numberous the circuit preacher cannot meet them all, there are 2 leading characters among them, that fill their station with dignity. They not only have Class meetings, but their days of examination in order to find out anything that may be amiss among them and if they can settle it among themselves they will, if not . . . so would these people bring matters of the greatest moment before the preacher.[28]

The class meeting, for all its usefulness in recruitment, building of community, and maintenance of discipline depended upon the supplemental forms of Wesleyan spirituality—especially the means of grace in the love feasts and watchnight services. These distinctive Wesleyan rituals often occurred at the quarterly meetings when the preachers rounded up the laity in the classes from the surrounding circuits for a time of spiritual renewal. African Methodists made their presence felt in these increasingly popular gatherings. At a love feast in Philadelphia in September 1770, Pilmore commented that "even the poor Negroes came forth and bore a noble testimony for God our Saviour." Fourteen months later from the same Methodist community, Pilmore received a letter from "a poor Negro slave" whose "bondage is such" that the class member was unable to receive the ticket needed to participate in the love feast. Requesting that it be sent by another member, the African explained an absence from the "Watch-night" service by saying, "But I bless God that night, I was greatly favoured with the spirit of prayer, and enjoyed much of his divine presence."[29] In November, four years later, Rankin found the

---

28. Colbert's "Journal" (23 January 1794). For his continuing ministry among the Oxen Hill African society, see 7 February, 20 February, 20 March, 3 April, 1 May, 15 May, 26 June, 10 July 1794. The African membership on the Montgomery circuit grew from 340 to 392 between 1794 and 1795; *Minutes MEC* (1840), 57, 61. On the controversy over whether the Oxen Hill meetinghouse, which may have been constructed as early as 1791, is the predecessor for St. Paul United Methodist Church in Oxen Hill, Md., see William B. McClain, *Black People in the Methodist Church: Whither Thou Goest?* (Cambridge, Mass.: Schenkman Publishing Company, 1984), 41-42 n. Wigger (*Taking Heaven by Storm*, 240 n. 33) suggests the possibility that James Smith's description of a somewhat similar society and its meetinghouse "in the old fields, not far from Bladensburg" on the Prince George circuit in Maryland in 1816 was the same as the Oxen (Smith spells it *Oxin*) Hill society. A careful reading of Smith's description of the preaching points on the circuit confirms their distinction, while not giving us a date of origin for the Bladensburg African Methodist society and meetinghouse. See Smith, *Recollections and Reflections of an Old Itinerant* (New York: Lane & Tippett, 1848), 296. In 1791 James Meacham discovered in Cumberland, Md., "a good meetinghouse," which "the poor blacks . . . built." "A Journal and Travel of James Meacham, Part II, 1789–1797," ed. William K. Boyd, *Annual Publication of Historical Papers of the Historical Society of Trinity College* 10 (1914): 91.

29. Pilmore, *Journal*, 58 (5 September 1770), 107 (10 November 1771). The letter from the slave member is quoted in the latter entry. The watchnight service was not limited to the New Year's Eve tradition of celebrating the John Wesley covenant service, but it occurred throughout the year in relation to the needs of the circuit and the classes, and to the willingness of enslaved members to attend during their hours of rest from labor.

opposite case when "the watchnight was attended with a peculiar blessing . . . in particular to those black people who could not attend the love feast" on the Kent circuit in Maryland.[30]

As with the case of the composition of the classes, there were both biracial love feasts and racially separated meetings for the ritual. Whatcoat recorded eight love feasts for Africans in 1794 and 1795, including services at Chestertown, Pennsylvania, and Milford, Delaware.[31] Asbury held two such love feasts in Charleston in 1795 and 1796. Colbert's journal contained twenty references to African love feasts between 1790 and 1806. Boehm listed seven occasions of the ritual for Africans between 1800 and 1803.[32]

The class meeting, preaching and exhortation, and the special Wesleyan forms of corporate fellowship were training a corps of black leaders who slowly emerged in the African societies. As early as 1773, Asbury named one of the "poor Negroes . . . deeply affected with the power of God" as "fit to send to England soon, to preach."[33] Six years afterward in Delaware, he identified a recently liberated "black man" who "gave such an extraordinary account of the work of God in his soul, and withal displayed such gifts in public exercises" that he seemed ripe for "peculiar usefulness to the people of his own colour."[34] Slightly more than two years later, Henry or Harry Hosier was speaking alongside Asbury in Virginia to launch a career of twenty-five years as a Methodist lay preacher.[35]

Despite Asbury's early interest in identifying African exhorters or preachers, and his cooperative work with Hosier (who was also a valet and servant to the bishop), in the early years the records do not mention many licensed African Methodists approved for exercising

---

30. Rankin, "Journal," 21 November 1775. For earlier references to many blacks that could attend a love feast at the Henry Waters Chapel in Maryland, see 7 November 1774 and 16 April 1775.

31. Whatcoat, "Journal," 8 June, 20 July, 3 August, 10 August, 21 September, 12 October 1794; 19 August, 27 September 1795.

32. JLFA 2:43, 77 (25 February 1795 and 3 February 1796). On Colbert, see Napier, "Formed For Friendship," 252-84. See also Boehm, "Journal," 19 July, 19 December 1800; 8 February, 12 March, 8, 17 April 1802; 14 April 1803.

33. Asbury (to his parents), Baltimore, 24 January 1773, in JFLA 3:15.

34. Ibid., 1:298 (25 March 1779).

35. Ibid., 1:403 (21 May 1781). See also 1:362, 413, 494 n., 539 n., 681-82 n., 689 n., and 2:389 n. For a note on Hosier's sermon in Virginia on Christmas night 1787, where he was described as "a negro who rides with Mr. Asberry," see John S. Moore, ed., "Richard Dozier's Historical Notes, 1771–1818," Virginia Baptist Historical Register 28 (1989): 1415. Asbury's Journal (1:556) records the context, but without mentioning Hosier's presence. The most thorough study of almost all the primary and secondary references to Hosier is Warren Thomas Smith, "Harry Hosier: Black Preacher Extraordinary," Journal of the Interdenominational Theological Center 7 (1980): 111-28.

their gifts in public.[36] By the last decade of the century, however, and from an unusual source for church history, fugitive slave advertisements in Maryland and North Carolina listed the names of five men who were identified as Methodist exhorters or preachers. Sam, absent from "the service of Charles Gosnell" in Baltimore County, had been "RAISED IN A FAMILY OF RELIGIOUS PERSONS, COMMONLY CALLED METHODISTS, AND HAS LIVED WITH SOME OF THEM FOR YEARS PAST, ON TERMS OF PERFECT EQUALITY," the ad for 1793 read. "HE HAS BEEN IN THE USE OF INSTRUCTING AND EXHORTING HIS FELLOW CREATURES OF ALL COLORS IN MATTERS OF RELIGIOUS DUTY," it continued with emphasis. Jem, a runaway from James Brice in Annapolis in 1797, "IS OR PRETENDS TO BE OF THE SOCIETY OF METHODISTS. HE CONSTANTLY ATTENDED THE MEETINGS, AND AT TIMES EXHORTED HIM-SELF." Jacob, who stole himself away from Thomas Gibbs, near Queen Anne in 1799, professed "TO BE A METHODIST, AND HAS BEEN IN THE PRACTICE OF PREACHING OF NIGHTS." Simbo, formerly the property of the late Frances Burns of Onslow County, North Carolina, was a literate Methodist preacher when he became a fugitive in 1799. The ad for his capture said he "speaks very distinct" and that most probably he could be caught "at Methodist meetings." The last of the list, Dick, ran away in Anne Arundel County, Maryland, in February 1800. The ad to recover him merely read, "HE IS A METHODIST PREACHER."[37]

In Methodist documents, however, only the names of Hosier and Richard Allen, who wrote in his autobiography that he began preaching at the end of the American Revolution, occurred significantly in the first twenty-five years of the movement. Allen, who was not ordained by Asbury until 1799 and then only as a local deacon with no annual conference ties, traveled with Benjamin Abbott, Jonathan Forest, Leari Coal, Peter Moriarty, Irie Ellis, Whatcoat, and Colbert—

---

36. Since licensing exhorters and preachers occurred at the local circuit and quarterly conference levels, there is no register of such names in annual conference minutes in early Methodism. Even as they were in leadership roles, preachers and exhorters were not ordained. Preaching and exhorting were roles for laity in the Methodist system as Wigger carefully distinguishes them; *Taking Heaven by Storm,* 29.

37. "Colored Methodist Preachers Among the Slaves," *Journal of Negro History* 1 (1916): 202-5. Citations are from *The Maryland Journal and Baltimore Advertiser* (14 June 1793), *The Maryland Gazette* (4 January 1798 and 4 September 1800), and *The Newbern Gazette* (15 August 1800). Two other African Methodist laypersons with no mention of preaching activity were Jem, in Baltimore County in 1789, and Allick, in Baltimore in 1790. See Lathan A. Windley, compiler, *Runaway Slave Advertisements: A Documentary History from the 1730s to 1790* (Westport, Conn.: Greenwood Press, 1783), 2:376, 402.

among the "white" Methodist elders. But he refused the role that Hosier assumed when accompanying Asbury, since it would have required that he not mix with the slaves, that he sleep separately, and that he perform the role of personal servant. One document from 1785 that Allen filed with the Pennsylvania Abolition Society has him traveling south and even preaching among Native Americans before he settled in Philadelphia for the rest of his career, but that ministry has not been separately verified.[38] Hosier was also the traveling companion of other white preachers besides Asbury, particularly Thomas Coke, Cooper, Colbert, and Garrettson. With the latter he made a tour of New England in the summer of 1790, where he usually exhorted after Garrettson's sermon. His presence, partly as a curiosity to New Englanders, brought large crowds, as in Providence, Rhode Island, when more than a thousand people came on Sunday evening, 11 July, to hear him.[39]

Hosier appears less frequently in the sources in the 1790s, perhaps because of his reported struggle with alcoholism. The modern reader might speculate about what factors of his peculiar situation in Methodist circles contributed to his disability. But by 1803 he had returned to an active informal traveling ministry, preaching "with life and power," according to Colbert and Boehm, in Philadelphia and in the Chesapeake District. In May 1805, Colbert sought to recognize his special place in early Methodism and his restored effectiveness in spreading the Wesleyan message by petitioning the Philadelphia

38. Absalom Jones, who became the first African in the priesthood of the Protestant Episcopal Church, may also have been a licensed local preacher in Methodism before 1794, though Allen claimed that he was the only "colored preacher in Philadelphia" in 1793. See *The Life Experience and Gospel Labors of the Rt. Rev. Richard Allen,* introduction by George Singleton (New York: Abingdon Press, 1960), 19-24. The document from 1785 at the Pennsylvania Historical Society reads: "After the War he Believed it to be his Duty to Travel abroad as a Preacher of Righteousness, and for the first six months Traveled at his own Cost, and the Remainder of his Religious Journeys his expences was for the most Part defrayed by the Religious Society of which he was a Member; he Traveled into various parts of New York, New Jersey, Pensilva., Delaware, Virginia, Maryland, North and South Carolina; and also spent two Months visiting the Indian Natives." See Gary B. Nash, ed., "New Light on Richard Allen: The Early Years of Freedom," *William and Mary Quarterly,* 3d series, 46 (1989): 332-40.

39. *Extracts of the journals of the Rev. Dr. (Thomas) Coke's Three Visits to America* (London: New Chapel, City-Road, 1796), 16, 18-19. Cooper, "Journal," 16 May 1785, 4 June 1787; Colbert, "Journal," has fifteen references between 1803 and 1806, including Hosier's funeral; Garrettson, *Methodist Pioneer,* 237-38, 266-70. Garrettson's plan to have Hosier preach in Nova Scotia to compete with Countess of Huntingdon African minister, John Marratt, mentioned in a letter to John Wesley (*Methodist Pioneer,* 251), apparently never materialized.

Conference for a formal appointment for the veteran folk-preacher. The move failed, and the next May Hosier died.[40]

After the formation of separate African congregations with their own church buildings, the need for class leaders, exhorters, preachers, and ordained clergy (even if only local deacons as in the case of Allen between 1799 and 1816) dramatically increased. When the MEC General Conference of 1800 actually authorized the ordination of black deacons, thus confirming Asbury's independent initiative of the previous year, the bishops moved cautiously in implementing the rule. It was conspicuously left out of the *Discipline*, in part to mollify opposition in the southern annual conferences. By 1806, Asbury elevated to the diaconate "three Africans"—June Scott, Abraham Thompson, and James Varick—in the Zion African Church in New York. Two years later he extended the office to Daniel Coker and William Miller in New York, and a year afterward to Jacob Tapsico and James Champion in Philadelphia. In 1808 the Philadelphia Conference elected Jeffery Beulah "a Colour'd Local Deacon," but suspended him two years later for breach of discipline.[41]

At the same time, at quarterly conference levels, African Methodist leaders were being licensed as exhorters and local preachers. In 1800 the Sharp Street Church in Baltimore licensed James Cole, James Carlbin, and Thomas Dublin as local preachers, five other men as exhorters, and three additional leaders of public prayer.[42] On the Annamessex circuit in Maryland, attached to the Philadelphia Conference, an exhorter named Shadrach earned Boehm's attention in January 1802 by speaking "with life & pow[e]r" though "deprived of his natural rights." Six weeks later in the same vicinity "Br[other] Jacob a Bl[ack] man preacht," Boehm noted in his journal.[43] Up the

---

40. Colbert, "Journal," 8 June 1803, 16 September 1804, and 12 January, 19 January, 20 January, 26 January, 27 January, 19 February, 21 February, 1805. His 25 January 1805 entry reads: "I was very much affected at some of part of the experience of Harry Hoshure, which he in private conversation related." Colbert visited Hosier regularly in his final weeks (22 March, 30 April, 1 May 1806). African Methodists Christopher Atkinson and Jeffrey Beulah spoke at Hosier's funeral on 18 May 1806. The failed petition by Colbert and eighteen other signatories "to the Methodist Episcopal Bishops and Philadelphia Conference at Chestertown, May 1, 1805 in behalf of Henry Hosure" is in the Philadelphia Conference Historical Society papers at Old St. George's Church. Henry Boehm recorded in his "Journal," 4 May 1803, that Hosier had made a comeback, noting "I belief he has the spirit again to assist him to declare the council of God."

41. Reginald F. Hildebrand, "Methodist Episcopal Policy on the Ordination of Black Ministers, 1784–1864," *Methodist History* 20, no. 3 (April 1982): 124-27; Philadelphia Conference MSS minutes, beginning 1802, 21, 74 (26 March 1808), 102 (26 April 1810).

42. List of Black Speakers, 20 April 1800, vol. I, Sharp Street MEC Records, United Methodist Historical Society, Baltimore, as cited in Frey and Wood, *Come Shouting to Zion*, 167, 242 n. 89.

43. Boehm, "Journal," 31 January, 5 March 1802. Whatcoat heard a slave preacher named Joe preach in Curry Tuck County, Virginia, in the late spring of 1799. See "Journal," 1 June 1799.

coast, George White, who was first a trustee in the Zion Society in New York as it began to meet separately in 1796, got the call to preach after attending a camp meeting in 1804. Apprenticed as a traveling exhorter on Long Island and in New Jersey, White finally won approval, after four disappointing rejections, as a licensed preacher.[44]

On the frontier, other patterns emerged. At Fishing Creek, Kentucky, a Methodist society had as its local preacher and leader, Jacob, who, though an illiterate African American slave, Jacob Young noted, "could preach a pretty good sermon." His organizational skills, aided by several local women, Young praised by saying, "His society is in excellent order." Whether the slave preacher, Jacob, had official authorization from a quarterly conference before Young appeared on the scene in 1802 is not clear, but the black Methodist congregation was added to his circuit.[45] Further south in the Carolinas roles and authority for black Methodist leaders varied by circumstance. Henry Evans, a free African Methodist preacher, planted Methodism and built the first meetinghouse in Fayetteville, North Carolina, before 1810. Further east in the same state, presiding elder Thomas Mann found "Jeremiah's Society" as the only Methodist congregation in Chatham County. Headed by Jeremiah, who may have been a free African American, the society's meetings attracted a biracial audience.[46] The African Methodists in Charleston's Bethel Church, before the secession of 1815, had black class leaders who held Sunday meetings in rural locations in the South Carolina low country. William Capers, the white Methodist who would later be associated with the southern mission to the slaves, called them "our agents." They were given authority, he said, "to admit and exclude members," keep "regular lists of their classes," and report back to church officials in the city on Mondays.[47]

---

44. Graham Russell Hodges, ed., *Black Itinerants of the Gospel: The Narratives of John Jea and George White* (Madison, Wis.: Madison House, 1993), 13-15. Hodges attributes racial prejudice, which surely existed, to White's difficulties when it may have been a misreading of how quarterly conferences licensed exhorters and preachers, black and white. The original publication is *A Brief Account of the Life, Experience, Travels, and Gospel Labours of George White, an African: Written by Himself, and Revised by a Friend* (New York: John C. Totten, 1810).

45. Jacob Young, *Autobiography of a Pioneer; or the Nativity, Experience, Travels, and Ministerials Labors of Rev. Jacob Young; with Incidents, Observations, and Reflections* (Cincinnati: Cranston & Curts, 1857), 97-99.

46. Frey and Wood, *Come Shouting to Zion*, 157 and 193 on Evans, and 163 on Jeremiah, citing Thomas Mann, "Journal," between 1805 and 1813, in the Manuscript Division, Perkins Library, Duke University; William M. Wightman, *Life of William Capers, D.D. One of the Bishops of the Methodist Episcopal Church, South; including an Autobiography* (Nashville: Southern Methodist Publishing House, 1859), 124-28.

47. Wightman, *Capers*, 124, 138-40.

Although we cannot, because of the inconsistent nature of the surviving sources in local Methodist contexts, have a comprehensive record of the number of licensed preachers, exhorters, prayer leaders, and itinerating class leaders, the documentation of African Methodist participation statistically makes a convincing case. Prior to 1786 there were no racial distinctions in data, but that year the largest number of African members were in the Talbot (332), Calvert (316), and Carolina (243) circuits with no black members, curiously, reported in Philadelphia, and only twenty-five in New York. From that point forward the growth rate of "colored" members was spectacular, from 3,893 in 1787 to 16,227 in 1793. The African membership was concentrated in Maryland, Virginia, North Carolina, and Delaware. Following four years of a decrease reaching 30 percent (for which there is no documented evidence for an explanation), the growth resumed. The total numbers reached 18,659 in 1802 and 31,884 by 1809, with the same areas of strength retaining their membership, but now extended to South Carolina. Of the seven annual conferences only New England's numbers were insignificant in 1809. In the urban areas, Charleston had 1,650, Philadelphia 826, Baltimore 700, New York 469, and Frederick, Maryland, 303. The largest collection of African Methodists, however, was in the circuits, eleven of which in the Delaware District numbered 6,106 members. There were 1,438 on the Calvert circuit in the Baltimore District, 2,640 in four circuits of the Chesapeake District, 2,443 in the Camden, South Carolina, District, and 2,368 in the Norfolk District. From 1796 until the denominational separations in 1813–22, African Methodists composed 20 percent of the total membership of the MEC.[48]

New Forms of African Methodist Presence, 1794–1809

With the dedication of the African Bethel Church in Philadelphia in 1794, at which white clergy Bishop Asbury, John Dickins, and Thomas Morrell preached, sang, and prayed, the pattern of racially separate congregations with their own buildings forecast a different kind of African Methodism for the future.[49] Until 1813 in Wilmington,

---

48. *Minutes MEC* (1840), 28, 51-52, 57, 61, 69, 102-4, 169-71, and annually for the ratios after 1796.

49. Allen, *Life Experience*, 31; *JLFA* 2:18 (29 June 1794); Thomas Morrell, *The Journals of the Rev. Thomas Morrell*, ed. Michael J. McKay (Madison, N.J.: Historical Society of the Northern New Jersey Conference of The United Methodist Church, 1984), 24. Morrell, who preached at the dedication on 1 Peter 2:5, later held a love feast at Bethel, which he called "a remarkable lively time," 25 (10 September 1794).

Delaware, until 1816 in Philadelphia, Baltimore, and Charleston, and until 1822 in New York, the traditional forms of African Methodist presence could be retained within the MEC system of governance, though African church trusteeism had made inroads in the Bethel and Zion societies in 1796 and 1800, respectively. Especially in urban centers of African Methodist life, what was new was a growing independence and sense of autonomy that could not be contained within Episcopal Methodism. The white leadership of the MEC never moved to consider the ordained black deacons regular members of annual conferences or to extend the office of elder to such veteran pastors as Allen. The spiritual power of the African converts and their sometimes massive presence at local levels were not sufficient to overcome white dominance in the councils of the clergy.

The spirit of independence for African American Methodists was nourished generally by the success of the First Emancipation—the ending of slavery in New England, New York, Pennsylvania, and New Jersey between 1783 and 1827. It was also manifested in the development of a network of separate black institutions in an increasingly autonomous community. Those positive forms of self-assertion, however, always emerged in the context of racial exclusion and discrimination by white Americans against the people of color.[50]

The formation of separate African churches grew out of these social contexts. In addition, the legal grounds for religious belonging in the new nation shifted from established churches to religious freedom as organized religious groups incorporated themselves as voluntary associations. African Methodists participated in these changes, along with African Baptists, African Presbyterians, and African Episcopalians before 1810. In the Methodist case, a shift to three separate African Methodist denominations by 1822 was distinctive. Only Baptists, with a more localized basis for being denominational, made similar separations into African church associations, but that only came later in the next generation of the black independent church movement.[51]

---

50. The standard older studies of these developments are Arthur Zilversmit, *The First Emancipation: The Abolition of Slavery in the North* (Chicago: University of Chicago Press, 1967); and Leon F. Litwack, *North of Slavery: The Negro in the Free States* (Chicago: University of Chicago Press, 1961). More sophisticated accounts of the evolution of status from slavery to freedom include Shane White, *Somewhat More Independent: The End of Slavery in New York City* (Athens: University of Georgia Press, 1991); and Gary B. Nash and Jean R. Soderlund, *Freedom By Degrees: Emancipation in Pennsylvania and Its Aftermath* (New York: Oxford University Press, 1991).

51. I have discussed some of these developments in "African Methodisms and the Rise of Black Denominationalism," *Perspectives*, 108-26, 519-25. See also my "The Rise of African Churches in America (1786–1822): Re-examining the Contexts," in Timothy E. Fulop and Albert J. Raboteau, eds., *African-American Religion: Interpretive Essays in History and Culture* (New York and London: Routledge, 1997), 133-51.

In 1794 there also appeared the first autonomous African Methodist publication, Allen's and Absalom Jones's *A Narrative of the Proceedings of the Black People, During the Late Awful Calamity in Philadelphia, in the Year, 1793*. Although not an explicitly religious document, the text defended the behavior of African citizens who nursed others during the yellow-fever epidemic. It also contained in the appendix, however, three addresses—to slaveholders, to slaves, and "to the Friends of Him who hath no Helper"— and a hymn of five stanzas. Cosigned, these writings were retained by Allen in his posthumous autobiography in 1833, so that the *Narrative*, especially the addresses and verses, can be seen as the first publication by an African Methodist in the United States.[52] Four years later, former African American Methodist Boston King published his life story in *The Methodist Magazine* in England, and the next year the contract between the Bethel African Society of Philadelphia and the MEC, drawn up in 1796, was in print. It contained some supplementary material written by Richard Allen who, two years later, issued the first edition of his hymnal.[53]

With the appearances of publications like these, African Methodists were creating a voice for themselves in a literary sense to extend their presence beyond the oral forms of preaching, praying, singing, and shouting in Methodist revivalism. The sources for comprehending this African Methodist presence, therefore, shift from secondary "white" documentation to primary accounts. By 1810, Daniel Coker, who moved from New York to be a leading minister in the Baltimore African American Methodist community, issued the first African American Methodist publication attacking slavery—*A Dialogue Between a Virginian and An African Minister*.[54] It appeared, ironically, two years after the last major effort to establish an antislavery norm for the MEC had failed.[55]

---

52. The *Narrative* is reprinted in Dorothy Porter, ed., *Negro Protest Pamphlets* (New York: Arno Press, 1969). A copy of the 1833 edition of Allen's *Life Experience* is in the Library Company of Philadelphia. British Methodist knowledge of the role of Allen and Jones came in *Arminian Magazine* 17 (1794): 363-68.

53. King's "Memoirs" are serialized in (the British) *Methodist Magazine* monthly from March to June in 1798 (105-10, 157-61, 209-13, 262-65). See also *The Articles of Association of the African Methodist Episcopal Church, of the City of Philadelphia, in the Commonwealth of Pennsylvania* (Philadelphia: John Ormrod, 1799). Allen's hymnal was called *A Collection of Spiritual Songs and Hymns Selected from Various Authors* (Philadelphia: John Ormrod, 1801). A second edition was issued the same year with ten additional hymns. See Eileen Southern, *The Music of Black Americans: A History*, 2d. ed. (New York: W. W. Norton, 1983), 73-81, 86, 168, 173, 176.

54. The pamphlet is reprinted in Porter, *Negro Protest Pamphlets*. Its original publication was *A Dialogue . . .* (Baltimore: Benjamin Edes, for Joseph James, 1810).

55. See Mathews, *Slavery*, for the standard account. My own earlier work focused on this story in "Early Methodism and Slavery: The Roots of a Tradition," *The Drew Gateway* 34 (1964): 150-65; and in "Methodist Preachers, Slavery and Caste: Types of Social Concern in Antebellum America," *Duke Divinity School Review* 34 (1969): 209-29.

In an appendix to his *Dialogue* Coker compiled a list of eight ordained Methodists out of thirteen African ministers that he knew about, another eleven African local preachers (all Methodist), and another fifteen African churches (eleven of which were Methodist). Although the tabulation was incomplete, as Coker admitted, it did dramatize the African Methodist presence in an emerging profile of independence. Coker also quoted from the statistical compilation of African Methodist membership for the previous year of 31,884, but he let that number stand alone without comparing it with other African Protestant communions.[56]

Independence would not be the only pattern for the future, however, for the largest segment of the African Methodist membership would remain with the MEC and, after 1845, with the MECS.[57] That kind of persistent presence echoing older patterns of the first generation and surviving white domination in the church has been an unbroken link for black Methodists who remained in the MEC, the MC, and the UMC in the United States.[58] Their ongoing presence ensured that, bracketing the MECS after 1870, the major trajectory of Methodism in America has never been "white" as we say, but some form of biracialism even at the cost of the racially defined Central Jurisdiction of the MC from 1939 to 1968.[59]

From the first generation, however, the biracial character of the Methodist movement had its own complexity. We are required to see simultaneously (a) the substantial fact of the African presence, which made Methodism essentially biracial, (b) the social reality of white dominance over enslaved and free blacks, and the various modes of discrimination in ecclesiastical organization and practice, (c) the spaces where that dominance was challenged, ignored, or compromised by both Africans and white churchfolk, (d) the spiritual men-

---

56. Coker, *Dialogue,* 40-42.

57. I have written on the origins of the Colored (later Christian) Methodist Episcopal Church in *Methodist History* 18, no. 1 (October 1979): 3-25.

58. The black presence in mainline Methodism after the formation of the three African Methodist denominations can be pieced together from the little-known history, Lewis Y. Cox, *Pioneer Footsteps with introduction by C. A. Tindley* (Cape May, N.J.: Star & Wave Press, 1917); L. M. Hagood, *The Colored Man in the Methodist Episcopal Church* (Cincinnati: Cranston & Stowe, 1890); and I. L. Thomas, ed., *Methodism and the Negro* (New York: Eaton & Mains, 1910). Richardson's *Dark Salvation,* McClain's *Black People,* and the anthology by Shockley, *Heritage and Hope,* bring the story into the twentieth century.

59. Wigger errs on this point when he describes his study as focusing "primarily on the white Methodist Episcopal Church" in *Taking Heaven by Storm,* 202 n. 5. See James S. Thomas, *Methodism's Racial Dilemma: The Story of the Central Jurisdiction* (Nashville: Abingdon Press, 1992).

toring that went in both directions from African to European-American and vice versa, and (e) the rise of a more direct African American Methodist voice accompanying the formation of separate classes, societies, congregations, conferences, rituals, roles, and in time, denominations. To honor the choices, however proscribed, of the early African converts requires that we do not risk reifying the dominance of whites as if it were acceptable to or accepted by African Americans. Otherwise, we will invalidate the authenticity of their spiritual achievements and relegate their presence once again to a secondary or subordinate place not worthy of being featured in the main Methodist story.

If this survey furthers the goal of changing the perceptions of the first generation of American Methodism so that no future history will be written without confronting the significant African presence, my task has been achieved. Such a change means that we will not discuss, as I formerly did in my work on Methodism and slavery, the denominational struggle over that issue as if it were not occurring in the presence of African Methodist members, class leaders, exhorters, and preachers, or as if the conflict did not hold special significance for them. But there is another more subtle interpretive challenge that this essay does not address directly, except in the quotation from Paul Burall and by inference in the journal entries of the early Wesleyan missionaries and native preachers. That challenge is to ask what difference did it make to the white Methodists for there to be this African presence? To ask that question is to focus not on Pilmore's "Africans," but on what their presence and contact meant to whites. That question returns us to the related agenda of *Playing in the Dark,* Methodist style, alluded to in the beginning of this essay. When we have begun to do that, we will have learned better how to think interactively in historical work, which Ashis Nandy and Charles Long do so deftly in their quest for a postcolonialist, postracist hermeneutic for studying religion and society.[60]

60. Nandy's *The Intimate Enemy: Loss and Recovery of Self Under Colonialism* (Delhi: Oxford University Press, 1983); and Long's *Significations* (Philadelphia: Fortress Press, 1986) acknowledge that systems of domination have damaged everyone, and that we all continue to be in various modes of denial or recovery from them. Even though the focus is on African American Protestantism, Frey and Wood in *Come Shouting to Zion* masterfully demonstrate an interactive historical method, both around the categories of race and gender, and embracing Methodist developments in the American South and the British Caribbean.

CHAPTER 6

The Formation of American Methodism: The Chesapeake Refraction of Wesleyanism

Russell E. Richey

The Chesapeake was the heart and soul of early Methodism, its center, its capital, its place of greatest strength, its site of holiest memories, its Jerusalem.[1] There, perhaps, Methodism made its earliest significant impact; there it became, for a time, the dominant Protestant denomination.[2] There Methodism was black and white, rich and poor, free and slave, professional and artisan, German- and English-speaking, young and old, urban and rural.[3] There it had the numbers, the leadership, and increasingly the resources to affect social policy and

1. An earlier variation of this essay was delivered at a joint World Methodist Historical Society/ Wesley Historical Society meeting in Cambridge, England, in July 1993, and appeared as "The Chesapeake Coloration of American Methodism," in *Methodism in Its Cultural Milieu*, ed. Tim Macquibban (Oxford: Applied Theology Press, 1994), 111-29, and is republished with permission. On this point, see William H. Williams, *The Garden of American Methodism: The Delmarva Peninsula, 1769–1820* (Wilmington, Del.: Scholarly Resources Inc., 1984).

2. Terry D. Bilhartz, *Urban Religion and The Second Great Awakening. Church and Society in Early National Baltimore* (Rutherford, N.J.: Fairleigh Dickinson University Press; London: Associated University Presses, 1986); William R. Sutton, *Journeymen for Jesus: Evangelical Artisans Confront Capitalism in Jacksonian Baltimore* (University Park: Pennsylvania State University Press, 1998); Robert J. Brugger, *Maryland: A Middle Temperament* (Baltimore: Johns Hopkins University Press, 1988); and Gordon Pratt Baker, ed., *Those Incredible Methodists: A History of the Baltimore Conference of The United Methodist Church* (Baltimore: Commission on Archives and History, 1972).

3. Barbara Jeanne Fields, *Slavery and Freedom on the Middle Ground: Maryland During the Nineteenth Century* (New Haven: Yale University Press, 1985); Christopher Phillips, *Freedom's Port: The African American Community of Baltimore, 1790–1860* (Urbana: University of Illinois Press, 1997); William H. Williams, *Slavery and Freedom in Delaware, 1639–1865* (Wilmington, Del.: Scholarly Resources Books, 1996); and Charles G. Steffen, *The Mechanics of Baltimore: Workers and Politics in the Age of Revolution, 1763–1812* (Urbana: University of Illinois Press, 1984).

the social order; there also Methodism's contradictions and tensions came to focus; there its commitments to holiness and reform, to evangelism and influence, came early to clash. In the contradictions and tensions that were Maryland and the Chesapeake, "a middle temperament" or "the middle ground" of American society, Methodism participated actively.[4] And in those contradictions and that Chesapeake origin and the peculiar Chesapeake refraction of the Wesleyan spirit lie some of the pieces to the puzzle of American Methodism.[5]

By "Chesapeake" I intend not just the Delmarva Peninsula, but really the world of early Methodism, including the colonies/states in and around the Chesapeake.[6] "Middle colonies/states" might serve as an alternative designation, but to the popular mind dissociates the region from the South and the peculiar institutions thereof, though rightfully imaging the religious pluralism of the territory into which Methodism entered. I have previously argued for "southern or Upper South" to describe Methodism's heartland.[7] "Chesapeake" suggests a region embracing both slavery and religious pluralism, and serves to convey more of the complexity of Methodist origins. Also, by "refraction" I intend not simply the events we associate with the founding decade, particularly those of 1784, portentous though they were; rather I want to discuss the religious system that those events solidified, the way in which Chesapeake Methodism refracted distinctive

---

4. Brugger, *Maryland: A Middle Temperament*; Fields, *Slavery and Freedom on the Middle Ground*; and Phillips, *Freedom's Port*.

5. The image of the puzzle is Nathan Hatch's, whose *The Democratization of American Christianity* (New Haven: Yale University Press, 1989) and "The Puzzle of American Methodism" in *Reflections* (summer-fall 1993), 13-20, and reprinted in this volume, reclaim a place for Methodism in the formation of American society. Since Hatch's statements, a number of scholars have dealt in groundbreaking fashion on early Methodism and its place in American society. Among them are A. Gregory Schneider, *The Way of the Cross Leads Home: The Domestication of American Methodism* (Bloomington: Indiana University Press, 1993); Christine Leigh Heyrman, *Southern Cross: The Beginnings of the Bible Belt* (New York: Alfred A. Knopf, 1997); John H. Wigger, *Taking Heaven by Storm: Methodism and the Rise of Popular Christianity in America* (New York: Oxford University Press, 1998); Cynthia Lynn Lyerly, *Methodism and the Southern Mind, 1770–1810* (New York: Oxford University Press, 1998); and Dee E. Andrews, *Religion and the Revolution: The Rise of the Methodists in the Greater Middle Atlantic, 1760–1800* (Princeton, N.J.: Princeton University Press, 2000).

6. The usage depends upon Jack P. Greene, *Pursuits of Happiness* (Chapel Hill: University of North Carolina Press, 1988), and refers to patterns or trajectories of development common in the Chesapeake colonies in the decades preceding independence, and sharply contrasted with those of New England. The larger commonalities, it should be conceded, should not obscure the differences that existed among the Chesapeake colonies, with their different political structures and social patterns.

7. See my earlier book, *Early American Methodism* (Bloomington and Indianapolis: Indiana University Press, 1991), especially the chapter "The Southern Accent of American Methodism."

aspects of the Wesleyan message, how Methodism in that region colored the whole movement. I want to understand what Freeborn Garrettson meant when on returning to his home on the western shore in 1818 and finding the Methodist work to have actually deteriorated, he proclaimed it a nursery of American Methodism.[8] The nursery of Methodism? What might we mean by calling the Chesapeake the nursery of Methodism? Or by calling it the "garden of American Methodism," to employ the image from Henry Boehm and of William Williams's important book?[9]

Such images point us toward a reformulation of the American religious saga, and specifically, of the Methodist story. To appreciate that "reformulation" and to grasp how the Chesapeake has colored American religion and American Methodism, we need to remind ourselves of some historiographical commonplaces.

Historiographical Assumptions That Have Obscured Methodism's Chesapeake Origins

The first commonplace, now highly contested but still operative in the popular mind, is that the American religious story begins with the

---

8. In a journal entry for 16 January 1818, Garrettson had affirmed: "I rode to Boosby Hill, and preached in a school house. The Society here is not as large as it was 45 years ago. I was comforted under an impression that it had been a nursery in which many trees of righteousness had been raised many of whom had been transplanted in heaven, whilst others had removed to different parts of the back settlements where they have invited the gospel, and have been a means of establishing other nurseries than this—for this was among the first Methodist Societies on the continent." Freeborn Garrettson, *American Methodist Pioneer: The Life and Journals of the Rev. Freeborn Garrettson, 1752–1827*, ed. Robert Drew Simpson (Rutland, Vt.: Academy Books, 1984), 325.

9. Williams, *Garden of American Methodism.* See also his related essay, "The Attraction of Methodism: The Delmarva Peninsula as a Case Study, 1769–1820," in *Perspectives*, 31-45. My analysis depends on this marvelous and seminal book, a model exercise in conference history. Williams addresses himself at various points to the Delmarva coloration of Methodism. These comments simply elaborate and extend his judgments to the Chesapeake generally. Critical in that elaboration are the equally valuable volumes: Bilhartz, *Urban Religion;* and Sutton, *Journeymen for Jesus.* There are two other authorities I ought to acknowledge. One is Donald G. Mathews, whose *Religion in the Old South* (Chicago: University of Chicago Press, 1977) probes the dimensions of the evangelicalism we will have under review. Mathews has more recently returned to deal explicitly with Methodism. See "Evangelical America—The Methodist Ideology," in *Perspectives*, 17-30; and "United Methodism and American Culture: Testimony, Voice, and the Public Sphere," in *The People(s) Called Methodist*, ed. William B. Lawrence et al. (Nashville: Abingdon Press, 1998), 279-304. The second is Jack P. Greene, whose *Pursuits of Happiness* (Chapel Hill: University of North Carolina Press, 1988), forcefully enunciates and synthesizes criticisms of the older New England–biased reading of American development.

Puritans, perhaps specifically with the Pilgrims.[10] Historians adopt other starting points, construct different metanarratives, and concede that other forms of Christianity, not to mention Native American religions, preceded Puritanism on the North American landscape. Anglicans and Roman Catholics, in particular, had planted their standards by the time the Puritans came on the scene. However, in American cultic life it is the Puritans and their sense of destiny, their notions of an errand into the wilderness, their belief that this new world belonged in God's providential plans for the Christianization of the world, and their embrace of those plans in formal covenants that is privileged—it is the Puritan story that we recall at Thanksgiving as the national saga. And with Sydney Ahlstrom and others, the American story has been made the extension of the Puritan story.[11]

Against that narrative and a world that Calvinists had built, Methodists indeed contended in making their way into and sustaining their own claims to legitimacy within American society. In negotiating their way into legitimacy, Methodists chose to challenge Calvinist theology (predestination and election particularly), but to respect, indeed to privilege, the Puritan metanarrative. They did so— as did other evangelical denominations—by owning the Puritan covenant and joining the errand toward a Christian America. They did so, more ironically, by writing the Puritan narrative into their own. A succession of Methodist historians, beginning with Jesse Lee in 1810 and continuing through Frederick Norwood in 1974, fit the Methodist story into the Puritan framework.[12] In so doing, they tended to honor the New England imprint on American Protestantism as a whole, and simply lose sight of the peculiarities of their own regional origins. Here, then, is one commonplace that stands in the way of our understanding of the Chesapeake refraction of American Methodism—the American religious story is a Puritan one.

A second commonplace complements this and differentiates southern religion from northern. Northern religion, we are taught, so

---

10. See especially Thomas A. Tweed, ed., *Retelling U.S. Religious History* (Berkeley: University of California Press, 1997). The utility of the older narrative convention might be seen in the starting point and selections of David A. Hollinger and Charles Capper, eds., *The American Intellectual Tradition: A Sourcebook*, 2d ed., 2 vols. (New York: Oxford University Press, 1993).

11. Sydney E. Ahlstrom, *A Religious History of the American People* (New Haven: Yale University Press, 1972).

12. See my "History as a Bearer of Denominational Identity: Methodism as a Case Study," in *Beyond Establishment: Protestant Identity in a Post-Protestant Age*, ed. Jackson W. Carroll and Wade Clark Roof (Louisville: Westminster John Knox Press, 1993), 270-95.

informed by the Puritan aspiration toward a redeemed social order (and whiggish or republican visions of a moral political order), yielded the American ethic, its sense of moral purpose, its capacity for prophetic self-criticism, its moments of corporateness or social awareness, and its reforming impulse. Southern religion, on the other hand, has tended more toward individualism, spiritualizing of faith, and acquiescence in societal norms and ethos.[13] Northern religion transforms and reshapes the social and political order; southern religion accommodates to the social and political order. Northern religion activates the community to common moral endeavor; southern religion puts the individual alone with his or her god, so southerners could be oblivious to the moral dilemmas of race and caste and business and law and society.

Given this bifurcation, the Chesapeake story has to be divided into its northern and southern versions; or it must be told as a chapter of the one or the other—as a chapter of the northern story or the southern story. Into such a bifurcation Methodist historians have pressed Methodism's first schism, that of Fluvanna (1779–80), construing as "southern" the Virginia wing that pushed for ordinations, sacraments, and Americanization without Wesley's authorization, and construing as "northern" the Baltimore contingent that remained loyal to Asbury and Wesley.[14] Such a reading, however, obscures the fact that both wings belonged to the world of the Chesapeake, to the world of slaves and slaveholders.

Neither that episode nor much of early Methodism follows the stereotype of "southern." Nor does such a North-South construction appreciate that early Methodists bore witness against slavery in the midst of slaveholding, contributed materially to the rapid growth of the population of "freedmen," and carried on their preaching and teaching in a world of slaves and free persons of color, and of slaveholders and whites committed to manumission. But a North-South reading readily came to dominate Methodist historiography; a reading reinforced by the rivalry between Baltimore and New York over claims to have been the first founded, and by the sectional crisis that swept Methodism and the country in the 1820s and 1830s. Here, then, is the second commonplace that stands in the way of our under-

---

13. For an attempt to distinguish these patterns see Samuel Hill, *The South and the North in American Religion* (Athens: University of Georgia Press, 1980), 7, 26-27.

14. For the earliest such reading see Jesse Lee, *A Short History of the Methodists* (Baltimore: Magill & Clime, 1810; reprint, Rutland, Vt.: Academy Books, 1974), 69-74.

standing of the Chesapeake refraction of early American Methodism—the southern religious story, or the Methodist chapters thereof, is to be told in the singular and as a tale writ back from the long saga of compromise; the northern story as a more corporate and ethical one; the Methodist saga as almost immediately incorporated into or divided into the one or the other; and Methodism's "middle ground" as simply lost.

A third historical commonplace concerns Methodist chronology. It holds that a national church emerged, relatively immediately, from the events of 1784. Wesley's ordinations, the planning at Barratt's Chapel, and the Christmas Conference accomplished the transformation that Fluvanna had sought, transformed the Methodist society into a church, and "Americanized" the Wesleyan movement—but without Fluvanna's division south and north, and with John Wesley's blessing at that. And so Methodism quickly became what this blueprint envisioned, a national church, because of the providential fit of Methodism and the new nation.

That "fit," the church's historians thought, lay in the Wesleyan blueprints, in the details of the Methodist master plan: in Methodism's national vision to reform the continent and spread scriptural holiness over the land; the principles of class-meeting, itinerancy, and connection, which transmitted the vision and sinewed Methodists into one people; Arminian theology, which taught responsibility and morality; hymnody and popular literature, which met individuals on their own terms; a missionary zeal, which impelled Methodists toward every new frontier; and an itinerant general superintendency, which kept the "great iron wheel" in motion. Narrators might have expanded or contracted these details (the marks of Methodism's providential design for the New World), but they recounted them faithfully in moving quickly from the Baltimore events of late 1784 to a national level. So the events at Barratt's Chapel and the Christmas Conference made a church possible and made it a national church. This is the third commonplace.[15]

These three historiographical commonplaces have effectively obscured the place of the Chesapeake in the Methodist saga. They have lulled Methodists and the historians who have recounted their story into a misreading of the play of region in Methodist experience and of the place of Methodism in American experience. Methodism

---

15. My essay "History as a Bearer of Denominational Identity" elaborates these points.

and its interpreters have been prone to such false consciousness—prone to ignore the Chesapeake through claiming immediate "nationality" for the movement; prone to obscure Methodism's regional character by pitting the claims of New York and Philip Embury against those of Maryland and Robert Strawbridge, and/or by reading later sectionalism back into the earlier movement; prone to discount the special Chesapeake refraction in terms of southern individualism; tempted to ascribe Methodist idealism, social passion, and corporate vision to something else than Chesapeake origins.

In an earlier essay I spoke to these tendencies, particularly the third, trying to revise this misestimation and counter these commonplaces by speaking of "The Southern Accent of American Methodism."[16] I recognize now that "Chesapeake" rather than "southern" would better describe the social location and ethos of early Methodism. And so I would insist over against the third commonplace, that the story of Methodism's emergence as a national church needs to begin by recognizing its initial regional contours and character; against the second commonplace, that the religious ethos that evolved in the Chesapeake differed significantly from what we think of as typically "southern"; and against the first commonplace, that through Methodism and other movements whose origins lay around the Chesapeake—specifically Roman Catholicism, Quakerism, and perhaps Presbyterianism—this region contributed materially to the American religious story. These three points, then, counter the commonplaces in terms of which we have usually told our story, and make Barratt's Chapel, Delaware, and adjoining colonies/states not just the stage, but really the substance, of the Methodist drama.

How Chesapeake Became National Methodism

Before describing the *what* of the Chesapeake refraction of Wesleyanism, I should remark briefly on the *how*, the mechanisms by which the Chesapeake shaped American Methodism. Five points concerning early Methodism deserve mention: (1) the sheer number of Methodists in the Chesapeake and the high percentage they came to constitute of the whole population; (2) the Chesapeake as Methodism's place

---

16. This now constitutes a chapter in my book *Early American Methodism*. The essay appeared initially in *Methodist History* 27 (October 1988): 3-24.

of concentration, of settlement, of development; (3) the outmigration of Chesapeake Methodists to found churches throughout the nation; (4) the significant leadership drawn from the Chesapeake; and (5) leadership from elsewhere formed by its deployment there.[17] William Williams covers these factors quite nicely but focuses on Delmarva; I appeal to his arguments, but would suggest they extend to the entire Chesapeake.

For instance, Williams notes that Methodists numbering 253 on the Delmarva Peninsula in 1775 reached 4,604 in 1784,[18] constituting, then, 6 percent of the adult population, and already the largest denomination—perhaps as large as the others combined.[19] Eight years later Delmarva Methodism had doubled to 9,911, its high-water mark for the decade. Then it exploded again, reaching 18,985 in 1805 and reaching almost 25,000 by 1807.[20] Methodists, then, constituted a high proportion of the total Delmarva population, roughly 20 percent.[21] Similarly, on the Western Shore and particularly around Baltimore, Methodism grew rapidly, constituting roughly 20 percent of the total Protestant population in 1790 and sustaining such growth even while Delmarva tapered off, so that by 1810 almost a third of Baltimore Protestantism was Methodist and by 1830, almost half.[22]

---

17. Each of these points, by their insistence on the relative importance of the Chesapeake, contain within them a qualification that we will reiterate but that is obviously not the emphasis of this essay. The qualification is that Methodism was also present very early in other sections, that it fit into the ethos of those places as well, and that those regions also contributed to the peopling, leadership, and equipping of the national movement. The emphasis here on the Chesapeake refraction of Wesleyanism does not intend to posit no roles for other sections, but rather to suggest that this region had a peculiarly important role. Implicitly suggested here, but not fully developed, is the argument that as it moved west, Methodism was to succeed in what would be a succession of America's "middle grounds"—in the border areas between north and south.

18. At that point, 5,288 of the total Methodist membership of 14,988 resided in Maryland, two-thirds of these Marylanders on the Eastern Shore. See *Those Incredible Methodists*, 60.

19. Williams, *Garden of Methodism*, 58-59.

20. Ibid., 76, 81. By 1800 Peninsula Methodism had declined to 8,705.

21. Ibid., 87.

22. "In 1790 about one in five Baltimore Protestants was a Methodist. By 1810 the ratio had climbed to nearly one in three and by 1830 to nearly one in two. For many years the rate of Methodist growth within the city exceeded that of the denomination as a whole. Whereas nationally The Methodist Episcopal Church expanded an impressive 293% between 1800 and 1820, in Baltimore the percentage increase was 350%, notwithstanding the fact that hundreds of Baltimore blacks left the denomination for the schismatic African Methodist Episcopal Church" (Bilhartz, *Urban Religion*, 85). The percentages of the total population were, of course, lower. Bilhartz estimates roughly one-tenth of the population was Methodist-affiliated in 1810 and one-sixth in 1830. He contrasts this pattern of prominence and growth with the much touted frontier reading of Methodist history and suggests that growth had "little to do with the system of traveling ministers" and that doctrines did not differ markedly from competitors. "Baltimore Methodists of the era achieved revival principally because they labored so diligently to promote it. . . . Methodists made evangelism their top priority and unhesitatingly pursued all means available to achieve this goal" (Bilhartz, *Urban Religion*, 86).

These were numbers and proportions to constitute a real nursery, a population worth spending time with and caring for.

Correspondingly, during this period Chesapeake Methodism constituted a huge proportion of the Methodist total. Delmarva alone counted for huge percentages—in 1781, 27 percent of Methodism was concentrated in Delmarva and by 1784, 31 percent. Thereafter it grew less rapidly than the church nationally, but it still constituted 19 percent of the total as of 1804 and 8 percent in 1820.[23] Here, too, the import of such concentration should not be underestimated.

After 1810 Delmarva Methodism declined both absolutely and relatively—in actual numbers and as a percentage of the total Methodist population. Or, to put the matter differently, Delmarva Methodism transplanted itself west, south, and north, and so occupied a larger territory. What Williams affirms of Delmarva applied with even more force to the larger Chesapeake area. Here Methodism did loom large, constituting virtually an establishment around Baltimore, as on the Peninsula, and enjoying similar strength elsewhere around the waterway. Here Methodism took shape. And from here Methodism spread west. Asbury's journal and travels dramatize that spread; he follows the Methodist people west, discovering old friends in what he terms "new Virginia" (Ohio); he might well have spoken also of "new Delaware" or "new Maryland." His "brothers" and "sisters" had taken the family religion west.[24] The Chesapeake had expanded to become national Methodism.[25] So Chesapeake Methodism stretched itself west, making a Methodist belt across the middle of the country.

We have always known that the older sectors of Methodism contributed leadership to the national movement. Class leaders, local preachers, and itinerants were credited with their roles in making new settlements into moral communities. Here too, though, we should note from where leadership derived. Henry Boehm certainly knew. He affirmed: "The peninsula produced some of the strongest men of Methodism: Shadrach Bostwick, Caleb Boyer, William Beauchamp, Ezekiel Cooper, Hope Hull, Dr. William Phoebus, Stephen Martindale, Lawrence McCombs, Lawrence Lawrenson, Bishop Emory, and many others."[26] To

---

23. Williams, *Garden of Methodism*, 3 56, 59, 77, 87. By this point Methodism had become extremely strong on the western shore, particularly on the Baltimore District, which included Georgetown and Annapolis; see *Those Incredible Methodists*, 98-112.

24. *JLFA* 2:55-56, 481, 554, 573, 615, 684, 694.

25. On that religiosity, see Schneider, *Way of the Cross*.

26. J. B. Wakeley, *The Patriarch of One Hundred Years; Being Reminiscences, Historical and Biographical, of Rev. Henry Boehm* (New York: Nelson & Phillips, 1875); reprint by Abram W. Sangrey (Lancaster, Pa., 1982), 79.

that list we would certainly add Richard Allen and Peter Spencer, architects of African American Methodism. And others, not native, received their decisive formation there, perhaps Asbury among them. In Chesapeake Methodism new recruits learned what Methodism could be and do; here they received nurture in leadership. Illustrative was Thomas Ware, who in 1783 was taken in and taught by the good Methodists on the Dover circuit.

> I was kindly received by the people on Dover circuit, and soon saw that that was the place for me. I was made to forget that I was among strangers. The simplicity, urbanity, and fervent piety, of the Methodists, on Dover circuit, were such that, after visiting a society once, it seemed long before I was to return to it again. Some of the members were wealthy and in the higher circles of life; but they were not ashamed to bear the cross. Among these were some, particularly a number of females, distinguished for piety and zeal, such as I had never before witnessed. The lady of Counsellor Bassett, and her two sisters, Mrs. Jones and Ward, possessed an uncommon degree of the true missionary spirit, and greatly aided the young preachers, by whom principally, the Lord was carrying on his work on that favoured shore. To these might be added others, and especially the wife of Judge White, who was a mother in Israel in very deed.[27]

(Note the formulation "a mother in Israel"; we will return to it.) The following year, Ware's education in ministry still incomplete, he was sent to Kent circuit: "Here, as on Dover circuit, I found a great number of young people, some of them connected with the first families; and I witnessed the pleasure of seeing many of them leading lives of piety and adorning the doctrine of God our Saviour in all things."[28]

Here, then, are five factors to consider in thinking about how Chesapeake Methodism affected the whole: (1) the sheer number of Methodists in the Chesapeake and the high percentage they came to constitute of the whole population; (2) the Chesapeake as Methodism's place of concentration, of settlement, of development; (3) the outmigration of Chesapeake Methodists to found and stock churches throughout the nation; (4) leadership drawn from the Chesapeake; and (5) leadership from elsewhere formed by its deployment there.

---

27. Thomas Ware, *Sketches of The Life and Travels of Rev. Thomas Ware* (New York: G. Lane & P. P. Sandford, 1842; facsimile edition, Holston Conference, 1984), 80.
28. Ibid., 87.

Facets of Methodism Reflecting a Chesapeake Coloring

What might be meant by a Chesapeake coloring or refraction? Certainly it must mean taking seriously the stage on which Methodism emerged. But must it not also mean the drama acted out on that stage, the *what* as well as the *how*, the regional shaping and the substance that was shaped there? The substance of Methodism can indeed be seen in Delmarva or Chesapeake terms. In this section I will explore nine facets of Chesapeake religion, of the Methodism that emerged there, and later of American Methodism.[29] These facets gave Methodism a distinctive regional character. However, they also refracted, I will argue, characteristically Wesleyan impulses. Thus, the Chesapeake colors of American Methodism were refractions of hallmarks of Wesleyanism itself. And each of these contextual factors possessed intrinsically religious, even theological, hues. Through each facet the Chesapeake gave Methodist distinctives cultural expression and praxis form. The Chesapeake made Wesleyan principle into American practice.

Pluralism

In the Chesapeake, as in England, Methodism set out to reform the church, but found Anglicanism weak and competitively disadvantaged. Anglican discomfort and Methodist vitality were affected by two great religious currents that fed the region—first, the Quaker and to some extent Roman Catholic watershed policy of toleration, which welcomed nonconformists, dissenters, and sectarians of every stripe and language; and second, the freshets of pietism,[30] which animated the Protestants among these groups with a vision of God amid the Babel. They called these freshets "awakenings" or "revivals," and through them brought new communities—of Moravians, Presbyterians, Baptists, Mennonites, and Nicholites—into being. Methodism thus found itself in a more genuinely pluralistic situation in the colonies and new nation than it had in England. It was religiously pluralistic and ethnically pluralistic. Here Wesley's catholicity would envelop not just Irish and Scotch-Irish, but also Germans and Africans.

---

29. No one of these points would perhaps be unique to Chesapeake religiosity. It is the gestalt that strikes me as characterizing.

30. On the international contours of pietism see W. R. Ward, *The Protestant Evangelical Awakening* (Cambridge: Cambridge University Press, 1992), and Ted A. Campbell, *The Religion of the Heart: A Study of European Religious Life in the Seventeenth and Eighteenth Centuries* (Columbia: University of South Carolina Press, 1991).

Catholicity? Henry Boehm recalled the Philadelphia Conference of 1803, at which he was ordained deacon: "Throughout the whole this was a comfortable and profitable conference; the business was done in love and harmony." Boehm remembered several who preached powerful sermons, Bishop Whatcoat among them. He noted also Black Harry: "His sermon was one of great eloquence and power. The preachers listened to this son of Ham with great wonder, attention, and profit."[31] In the Chesapeake, a German like Boehm and an African like Hosier would team with Asbury or Coke or Garrettson to take the Methodist message to all. Here Methodism had pluralism within and catholicity without; and catholicity within and pluralism without. Pluralism gave Wesley's catholicity social coloration. In the Chesapeake, Methodism learned to speak in a family of many tongues and took on new vernaculars. So the "old Methodist" dialect claimed a hearing. It emerged as an ethnically pluralistic, perhaps the first ethnically pluralistic, mass movement—an achievement really possible in the Chesapeake. So the Chesapeake stamped Methodism with an aspiration that it has continued to chase—to make Wesley's catholicity a social reality.

Quarterly Corporate Drama

Methodism gained its hearing in the Chesapeake by various means, including finding an American counterpart to Wesley's field preaching: Quarterly Corporate Drama.[32] Outdoor meetings were not new to the region. Presbyterians had made good use of the tradition of Scottish sacramental occasions;[33] Germans had found big meetings useful; Quakers had their counterparts. In the Chesapeake, Methodists drew crowds that forced them outdoors. They turned inconvenience into a convention, circuit business into a religious festival, quarterly meeting into a protracted revival. The region, Rhys Isaac has taught us, defined community more by event than by place.[34] The community gathered itself at dance, muster, horse race, election, and the like. American Methodists found in the quarterly

---

31. Wakeley, *Patriarch of One Hundred Years*, 89-92.
32. See Lester Ruth, *A Little Heaven Below: Worship at Early Methodist Quarterly Meetings* (Nashville: Kingswood Books, 2000).
33. Leigh Eric Schmidt, *Holy Fairs: Scottish Communions and American Revivals in the Early Modern Period* (Princeton, N.J.: Princeton University Press, 1989).
34. Rhys Isaac, *The Transformation of Virginia, 1740–1790* (Chapel Hill: University of North Carolina Press, 1982).

meeting—which they lengthened to two days—an event that would define religious community. In August 1791, in Maryland, Ezekiel Cooper "being accompanied by more than twenty person . . . set off for the quarterly meeting at Joseph Pigman's."

> At twelve o'clock we began public service. The congregation was very large—about two thousand—the greatest number, I think, that ever I saw at a quarterly meeting on Saturday. We went into the woods under an excellent shade. I preached from Matt. xxiv, 14; Brother Pigman and Brother Bruce exhorted. It was a time of great tenderness among the people. After preaching we gave the sacrament in the preaching house. . . .
>
> *Sunday* 14. At eight o'clock A.M. love-feast began; the preaching-house, though pretty roomy, would not hold nearly all the friends. The Lord was very precious to us. At eleven o'clock it was laid upon me to preach again. I opened our Lord's words in John (ix.4), to an uncommonly large concourse of people—some think six or seven thousand; I judge, at a moderate calculation, there were four or five thousand—I had to speak very loud. The Lord helped me; word fell with power on the congregation; truly it was an awful time! The word was like a sword in the hearts of some who cried out aloud to God; tears flowed on every hand; the countenances of the people bespoke the effect of the truth in their souls. Brothers Forest and Reed exhorted. There were three or four other traveling preachers who had not time to say anything. This was a grand quarterly meeting. I hope great good was done. It was wonderful where the people could all come from; but such a concourse was hardly ever seen in those parts before.[35]

Thereafter, it was frequently seen in those parts. And for a decade before the emergence of the camp meeting, Chesapeake Methodists made the quarterly meeting a great religious festival, a time when persons traveled for miles to be together, an event for the circuit, of course, but also for the larger community—a psychodrama in Arminian terms, sweeping sinners into the play of God's redeeming grace. Or as Thomas Ware put it:

> Camp meetings had not yet been introduced; and we knew not what to do with the thousands who attended our quarterly meetings. Sometimes we were forced to resort to the woods, and even to hold our

---

35. George A. Phoebus, comp., *Beams of Light on Early Methodism. Chiefly Drawn from the Diary, Letters, Manuscripts, Documents and Original Tracts of the Rev. Ezekiel Cooper* (New York: Phillips & Hunt, 1887), 135-36, for Saturday, 13 August 1791.

love-feasts in the grove. Our membership increased rapidly; but we refrained from urging any to join the Church until they had taken time to reflect and examine whether they had fully made up their minds to be religious, and could unreservedly take upon themselves the vows of their God.[36]

On Delmarva, in the Chesapeake, quarterly meeting gave Wesley's revival and his business conference an American camp-meeting coloration.

Voluntarism of the Heart

Methodism defended a voluntarism of the heart, an evangelical Anglicanism that invited rich and poor, free and slave, men and women, old and young into a new community of discipline and spiritual growth. It was an Episcopal church defined by conversion. And conversions did come. Emory Pryor provides a typical account in a letter to Ezekiel Cooper on 23 March 1790:

MY DEAR BROTHER: May peace attend you forever! Through mercy I enjoy a degree of health, and my soul is happy in God. I received your letter the 21st ultimo. There is a gracious work in this circuit—sinners coming home to God. Since our quarterly meeting there appears to be a considerable stir among the people. I see as gracious times as I have ever seen since I have been in Dorset. The devil is roaring in a wonderful manner. My God, I trust, will bruise his head.

I suppose you heard of the work among the rich in this place. Henry Ennalls and wife and sister have been converted to God since our quarterly meeting; yea, his house-keeper and all his Negroes down to those but eight years old. Glory be to God for his goodness to the children of men! Cambridge appears to be up in arms about it. We have permission to preach in the Courthouse at last. . . .

Emory Pryor

---

36. Ware, *Sketches*, 235. About a meeting in Dover in 1800, which was appointed to extend a week, Ware said: "There were but few of the principal houses in this metropolis in which there were not some converted during the meeting; and more than once the whole night was employed, both in the church and private houses, in prayer for penitents, and in rejoicing with those who had obtained an evidence of pardon, or were reclaimed from their backslidings" (ibid., 234).

N. B. Our quarterly meeting will be the 22d and 23d of May. I should be glad if you could come over, if it should be out of my power to attend yours.[37]

Upon his conversion, Ennalls, like Garrettson, freed his slaves.[38]

That act was very un-Anglican—and very Methodist. Methodists presented themselves as "episcopal" but called for a conversion that turned the Anglican world upside down. This "Methodist" version of Anglicanism found itself at war with the world around it: at war with war; at war with slavery; at war with the genteel world with its elaborate rituals of fashion, display, gambling, and combat; at war with the "old" Anglicanism that embraced the world. But it created its own new world—a pietist one, a Wesleyan one, effectively entered by the conversion experience and then lived out by Wesleyan norms. And since, as Bill Williams has shown, Methodism countered the Anglican world and its norms with invitations to all—albeit on these new terms—it could and did become "churchlike," an evangelical alternative to Anglicanism, a pietist movement that invited the whole social system to a new profession and new self-understanding. It succeeded, at least in part, because it looked like, but differed from, the Anglicanism the region knew.[39]

A Social Ethic Defined Over Against Gentility

As an evangelical Anglicanism, Chesapeake Methodism elaborated a social ethic defined over against gentility.[40] It derived from Wesley an elaborate social ethic, a set of guidelines for the good life, a pathway to holiness. One negative referent in Wesley's social ethic was gentility—that elaborate code that governed the genteel life. American Methodists also saw gentility as the exact inversion of the gospel, particularly gentility lived out by the slaveholders. Indeed, the power of *gentility* as metaphor may have been more expressive in the Chesapeake than in England because the social contrasts were

---

37. Phoebus, *Beams of Light*, 116.

38. Asbury noted in his journal for 9 November 1790 (*JLFA* 1:656) that he "lodged with brother Henry Ennalls, who, with his wife, has been powerfully brought to God; his slaves were freed immediately."

39. Williams, *Garden of American Methodism*, 89-90, 94-98.

40. For elaboration of this assessment of Methodist style, see Schneider, *Way of the Cross;* Heyrman, *Southern Cross;* and Lyerly, *Methodism and the Southern Mind.* For a contrary reading, see Andrews, *Religion and the Revolution;* and Wigger, *Taking Heaven by Storm.*

more sharply drawn. Consider a 1789 journal account of Ezekiel Cooper, commenting on Annapolis:

> *Monday,* October 12. I was not a little sorry at beholding the preparations for the races which begin to-morrow in the fields. What pains the children of this world take to do wickedness! O Lord, have mercy on them! Since last year's races a number in this town have deserted Satan, are converted, and will not go this year. Glory to God for it.[41]

Conversion, commitment to the Methodist way, and adopting the life of holiness involved giving up the gay or genteel life. That can be seen in a Peninsula vignette that Cooper reported for the next year, 1790:

> *Tuesday,* August 10. I breakfasted with Mrs. Johnson, who told me her experience; how that she had formerly laughed, much at the Methodists and their conversion. One day being persuaded to come and hear, she unexpectedly was so cut to the heart that she could not refrain from crying through the street as she returned, though she kept it concealed as much as possible. From that time she could get no rest day or night. She visited Mrs. Rollings, a gay lady of her acquaintance, who, she thought, might cheer her up, and remove, by her flow of conversation, this distress. But, as God would have it, fell into conversation about religion. Mrs. Johnson said to Mrs. Rollins, "Why can't you and I be good?"
> Mrs. Rollings replied, "O we are as good as we can be."
> "That will not do," said Mrs. Johnson; "we must be better," and was struck with such a power that she fell on the floor in deep distress and prayers for mercy. Mr. Johnson was sent for, who was for having the doctor; but Mrs. Johnson said that the doctor could do her no good; she wanted the Methodist preacher sent for. He wanted to send for the Church parson, but she refused to have him. So I was sent for, at which time the Lord blessed her soul with his love, to which she has held fast ever since. She went and joined Society this afternoon.[42]

The key word in the above passage is *gay,* which stood for what Methodists stood against—dancing, racing, gambling, dueling, drinking, card playing, and the like. These seemingly innocent activities knit together into an elaborate fabric and ritual that, as events and gatherings, defined the genteel world. Methodists offered another way. They called it *holiness, perfection, sanctification.*

---

41. Phoebus, *Beams of Light,* 105. Cooper was (falsely) accused, a day or so later, of attempting to attend the races and dismissed the charge indignantly.
42. Ibid., 116-17.

Ambivalent Preoccupation with Slavery and Race

Nothing symbolized that other way better than antislavery, or per-haps we should say preoccupation with, but ambivalence over, slav-ery and race. Methodists—some at least—preached antislavery. On the Caroline circuit, Maryland, Asbury reported the Anglican minis-ter boldly preaching "against the freedom of the slaves." "Our broth-er Joseph Everett," said Asbury, "with no less zeal and boldness, cries aloud for liberty—emancipation."[43] Asbury himself boasted: "At Annamessex quarterly meeting I was at liberty on Rev. iii, 20. Again I preached on, 'Fear not, little flock,' &c.: most of our members in these parts have freed their slaves."[44] Asbury's phrasing indicates that *lib-erty* was a complex word. Chesapeake Methodists used it with some sense of its import in American Revolutionary politics; they used it frequently, as did Asbury here, to refer to the freedom they experi-enced (or did not experience—they complained as much when they lacked such freedom) in delivering the word; they used it also with reference to emancipation.

Ezekiel Cooper so noted in his journal for July 1790:

Wednesday, 7. I was told in the afternoon that the people in town were alarmed by our speaking up for freedom last Sunday night—the day of Independence. They fear it will hurt the Negroes; some are simple enough to fear an insurrection. If they fear, the ground of their fear must be their own injustice in keeping those poor creatures in slavery whom God made free. But, let them fear and be alarmed as they may, I must plead the cause of the innocent, and in so doing I have the word of God, and our own civil principles to uphold me. "Liberty is the theme." Our country and the Gospel, the principles of humanity and religion cry out, "Take off the yoke of oppression, and let the captives go free." I am ready to defend what I advanced last Sunday night from the pulpit, and I believe Brother Chalmers can readily answer to what he advanced. The justness of the subject is what gives the panic to those who wish to keep themselves quiet in the act of injustice.[45]

---

43. *JLFA* 1:582 (1 November 1788). On the importance of liberty see Fred Hood, "Community and Rhetoric of 'Freedom': Early American Methodist Worship," *Methodist History* 9 (Oct. 1970), 13-25.

44. *JLFA* 1:582 (7 November 1788).

45. Phoebus, *Beams of Light*, 108. See also the "Addenda" (pp. 312-28) for Cooper's antislav-ery activity and sentiments.

Cooper was outspoken against slavery while serving in Annapolis from 1789 to 1791, during which time antislavery legislation was being considered by the Maryland Assembly. He carried on a public debate through letters on the subject to the *Maryland Gazette*. Moved next to Alexandria, Cooper undertook a similar witness there, through the *Virginia Gazette*.[46] He later proposed to General Conference (1800) "that a committee be appointed to prepare an affectionate address to the Methodist Societies in the United States, stating the evils of the spirit and practice of slavery, and the necessity of doing away the evil as far as the laws of the respective States will allow."[47]

Boehm provides a similar report:

> I was glad to travel with my friend William Colbert. . . . We preached against slavery, and persuaded our brethren and those who were converted to liberate their slaves, and we were often successful. There was a revival both among the white and colored. Many slaves were made "free" by "the Son," and they enjoyed the liberty of the soul. We preached at Snow Hill. It was formerly a wretched place where the traffic in negroes was carried on. The Georgia traders in human flesh came there and bought slaves, and then took them south and sold them. Methodism made a mighty change here and destroyed this inhuman traffic. Snow Hill for years has been a prominent place for Methodism.[48]

Liberty in speaking, speaking about liberty—Methodists did use *liberty* variously. They also thought variously about race and slavery. But they did think about it, were troubled by it, knew that the gospel spoke in profound ways about slavery, and endeavored to discern God's will for all Americans—black and white. *Liberty* gave dramatic Chesapeake force to the central Wesleyan affirmation of free grace, freeing grace.

Biracial Society

White Methodists preached good news to the slaves and to freed blacks.[49] And soon blacks joined in declaring the good news—Black Harry being one of many. In consequence, Methodism elaborated a biracial society. Garrettson reported in 1783:

---

46. Ibid., 323-28.
47. Ibid., 328.
48. Wakeley, *Patriarch of One Hundred Years*, 68-69.
49. See Phillips, *Freedom's Port*, and Williams, *Slavery and Freedom in Delaware*.

Wednesday 8., And also as I returned from New Castle, I preached at Duck-Creek Crossroads with great freedom and hope good will be done. There is a small, but lively class of white and black. . . .

Sunday 19. I spoke with freedom to several hundreds. "All are yours and ye are Christ's and Christ is God's." I think a particular door was opened. A great discovery was made to me of the beauty of Holiness. The Christians, black and white, seemed to be going on joyfully to do the will of God.[50]

In an account later that year Garrettson noted:

Monday 10. I rode 15 miles and preached to about a hundred souls with great freedom. Half the number professed the love of God. By candle-light I met a company of blacks. I think in this place there are about 65 black people in society, 31 of which are free. I hope I never shall be reconciled to slavery.[51]

By at least 1800, segregation patterns had compromised that biraciality. Boehm reported: "We not only had separate classes for the colored people, but separate love-feasts; they were generally held in the morning previous to the love-feasts for the whites, and were seasons of great interest. Religion in its simplicity and power was exhibited by them."[52] As this report indicates, despite the emerging segregation, Methodism's biraciality spoke eloquently its gospel of universal atonement, God's love for all—the invitation to even the most wretched "to flee the wrath to come." *Biraciality dramatized atonement.*

New Roles and a New Place for Women

Chesapeake Methodists broke barriers on race. They did the same with women.[53] Methodism elaborated new roles and a new place for

---

50. Garrettson, *Methodist Pioneer*, 210-11 (January 1783).

51. Ibid., 232 (November 1783, in and around Kent).

52. Wakeley, *Patriarch of One Hundred Years*, 63-64.

53. See Diane Lobody, "'That Language Might Be Given Me': Women's Experience in Early Methodism," in *Perspectives*, 127-44; Jean Miller Schmidt, "Denominational History When Gender Is the Focus: Women in American Methodism" in *Reimagining Denominationalism*, ed. Robert Bruce Mullin and Russell E. Richey (New York: Oxford University Press, 1994), 203-21; *Spirituality and Social Responsibility: Vocational Vision of Women in the United Methodist Tradition*, ed. Rosemary Skinner Keller (Nashville: Abingdon Press, 1993); Susan Juster, "'In a Different Voice': Male and Female Narratives of Religious Conversion in Post–Revolutionary America," *American Quarterly* 41 (1989): 34-62; Juster, *Disorderly Women: Sexual Politics and Evangelicalism in Revolutionary New England* (Ithaca, N.Y.: Cornell University Press, 1994) and the volume Juster jointly edited with Lisa MacFarlane, *A Mighty Baptism: Race, Gender, and the Creation of American Protestantism* (Ithaca, N.Y.: Cornell University Press, 1996). The recent studies of early Methodism all devote major attention to the role of women: cf. Schneider, *Way of the Cross*; Heyrman, *Southern Cross*; Wigger, *Taking Heaven by Storm*; Lyerly, *Methodism and the Southern Mind*; and Andrews, *Religion and the Revolution.*

women. We have been slow to recognize this reality, in part because we have been and are so dependent upon the journals of the (male) itinerants for our accounts of early Methodism.[54] But even in the journals we encounter women on page after page, recognize the constant interaction of key women with the itinerants, note the very frequent funeral services thereof, and hear testimonies to their vital faith. When we read carefully, we discover that women led the movement. Consider this 1784 report by Freeborn Garrettson:

> *Saturday* 28—In the Morning I met the Class of young women. They have got a mother in Israel to be their leader. In the evening I met the Married Women. In this neighborhood there are many precious souls going on joyfully to do the will of their Father.[55]

Here again is the phrase employed by Ware and employed frequently to refer to women who exercised influence and leadership, "mother in Israel."

We get some sense of the force of that phrase in Boehm's recollection of his first circuit for 1800, Dorchester. In his account he gives considerable attention to the role of women, both in the longer story of Peninsula Methodism and in his own ministry. He credited "Miss Catharine, sister of Harry Ennalls . . . afterward Mrs. Bruff of Baltimore" with the "introduction of Methodism into Dorchester." After her conversion she influenced "her sister Mary, and her husband, the Hon. Richard Bassett," and also Henry Airey, Esq.[56]

These special women exercised leadership in their families, among women, and with the people. They also exercised considerable influence over the itinerants. This was particularly so for the women who routinely took them in. They were supporters, confidants, spiritual directors, counselors, confessors, "mothers," tutors, and more—as can be seen in the role Ennall's wife played for Boehm:

> Harry Ennalls's wife was one of the best of women. She was a Goldsbury, related to Governor Goldsbury. This was one of the great families of the Peninsula. They had no children, and always made the preachers very welcome, and considered the younger as their children. Mrs. Ennalls, who was a person of discernment, saw I was suffering

---

54. On this point see Marilyn Fardig Whiteley, "'I got my supper about eleven o'clock on Saturday night': Rereading the Sources of Methodist History," *Canadian Methodist History Society Papers* 13 (1999 and 2000).

55. Garrettson, *Methodist Pioneer*, 237 (February 1784, apparently in the Narrows area).

56. Wakeley, *Patriarch of One Hundred Years*, 57-58.

under deep depression of spirits. I was fearful I had mistaken my calling. Ingenuously she asked me a great many questions, till she drew from me the real state of my mind. When she found out that I was discouraged, and about to give up my work in despair and return home, she gave me such a reproof as I shall never forget. "My young brother," she said, "your eternal salvation may depend upon the course you are about to take. You may lose your soul by such an unwise, hasty step." Then she exhorted me in the most earnest and emphatic manner not to abandon my work, but to keep on. I resolved in the strength of my Master to try again, and though over threescore years have gone into eternity since "having obtained help from God, I continue unto this day." Well I remember that hospitable mansion; and the room in which we were, the attitude of the woman, her anxious countenance, her piercing eye, the tone of her voice, are all before me just as if it were yesterday. Her wise counsel has had an influence upon me all my days; it shaped my destiny for life. She has been in the grave for many years, and I remember her still with a heart overflowing with gratitude.[57]

After this visit Boehm went to the "widow of Squire Airey" a short distance away, who also entertained the itinerants: "In family prayer we had a gracious time. The Holy Ghost descended in copious effusions, and the widow was so baptized she shouted aloud for joy and was greatly strengthened and encouraged. I retired to my couch feeling that my soul was resting in God."[58]

Boehm enumerated key persons for other communities he served. For instance, he named persons in the class book for Cambridge including Dr. Edward White, his wife Mary Ann White, and three daughters Eliza, Sarah, and Mary. Women played key roles with the itinerants; they did so with women's classes; but did they also with the African classes? Boehm noted, for instance, that "two colored classes" met at Ennalls's.[59] Who took leadership there? Such dimensions of women's leadership may be difficult to recover. We do know that women served as exemplars, teachers, guides to family members, leaders in class (though not always given the formal responsibility as class leader), and hostesses to and ministers to ministers. Women's abilities were recognized. Thus did the Chesapeake give coloration to Arminianism—free will, free grace, and our human ability to respond to God's grace.

---

57. Ibid., 60-61.
58. Ibid., 61.
59. Ibid., 63.

A New Ethnicity

Methodism's new roles for women, its invitation to the outsider, its freedom in preaching to all varieties of people, its daring in crossing linguistic and racial boundaries, and its willingness to embrace the stranger, once redeemed, into new fellowship offered a radically new form of community to Americans. Methodism created, in itself, a new ethnicity, a new way of being people, a new structure for order. It was a voluntary ethnicity, an elective peoplehood, a structure for order Anglican-like and also aspiring to inclusion, but through "new birth" rather than ordinary birth. It was, in short, the *denominational* understanding of the church.[60] Peoplehood was not to be defined by country of origin (Ireland), or language (German), or race (African), but in an elective ethnicity: "All who would flee the wrath to come."

This new community is symbolized in Garrettson's appreciation of African American contribution to this new community: "This night my soul was transported with joy when meeting the black class, a company of humble, happy souls."[61] Here souls who were not accepted in the social order were nevertheless religiously accepted, incorporated by class into the denominational order. Class meetings were crucial. They were the base, the foundation, the single cell, the belonging unit out of which denomination was formed. Class created a new community; classes made individuals and groups of disparate homelands, languages, and race into a Methodist people; class evolved a new type of ethnicity; class made denomination possible.

Could Methodism's "discovery" of this new denominationalism have happened in another region? Where else were the preconditions: the religious pluralism, genuine toleration, an Anglican base, possibilities of antislavery, and a population receptive to aggressive Methodist pietism?

Territorial Conception of Purpose

In the Chesapeake, Methodism came face-to-face with the enormousness of the American landscape. In later years Methodists thought the Wesleyan principles of itinerancy and connection had been "provi-

60. For an elaboration of such an understanding of denominationalism see my essays "Denominations and Denominationalism: An American Morphology," in *Reimagining Denominationalism;* and "History as a Bearer of Denominational Identity."
61. Garrettson, *Methodist Pioneer,* 225 (19 June 1783).

dentially" fit for the American continent. That providential fit was hard won. Americans had to discover that Wesley's intentions to "reform the nation, particularly the church" could also "reform the continent." They made that discovery on the American landscape; they made it in trying to hold Methodism together; they made it in experimenting with structure that would express their unity of purpose. Asbury put it this way:

> I have thought, if we do wrong we rank among the vilest of the vile, as having been more favoured than any others. Many other Churches go upon the paths already trodden two or three hundred years. We formed our own Church, and claim the power of a reform every four years. We can make more extensive observations, because our preachers in six or seven years can go through the whole continent, and see the state of other Churches in all parts of this new world. We of the travelling ministers, who have nothing in mind but the gospel and the Church of God, may and ought to be very useful.[62]

Asbury led Methodists to think of their duty and purpose in territorial terms. He led them to "a day of solemn fasting and prayer for the Church, the conference, the continent, and for the world."[63]

Methodists did indeed struggle to embrace such new purposes. A good illustration of those struggles is Asbury's journal entry for the short-lived and ill-conceived "council" as an administrative structure:

> *Thursday, December 3.* Our council was seated. . . . All our business was done in love and unanimity. . . . During our sitting we had preaching every night; some few souls were stirred up, and others converted. The *prudence* of some had stilled the noisy ardour of our young people; and it was difficult to rekindle the fire. I collected about twenty-eight pounds for the poor suffering preachers in the West. We spent one day in speaking our own experiences, and giving an account of the progress and state of the work of god in our several districts; a spirit of union pervades the whole body, producing blessed effects and fruits.[64]

The experiment failed, but the spirit of union and the purpose—the sense of a mission to the territory, to the whole nation, to the continent—survived and prospered. It survived and prospered because

---

62. *JLFA* 2:155 (4 March 1798, in Virginia).
63. *JLFA* 2:342 (5 June 1802).
64. *JLFA* 1:614-15 (3 December 1789, Baltimore).

Methodists could connect their own experiences with the whole body and the world. This was no northern, no Puritan, impulse. Rather it was a distinctly Chesapeake corporate vision and moral order—"for the Church, the conference, the continent, and for the world."

Conclusion

Thus did the Chesapeake color American Methodism, imbedding Wesleyan principle in territorial practice. In nine regional facets, nine practices, American Methodism defined itself. Wesleyanism refracted itself in each facet. The Wesleyan commitment to catholicity was refracted in the Chesapeake's pluralism; the commitment to revival in their quarterly corporate drama; the commitment to evangelical Anglicanism in their voluntarism of the heart; the commitment to holiness in their social ethic, made concrete over against gentility; the commitment to liberty in their preoccupation with and ambivalence over race; the commitment to universal atonement in their biraciality; the commitment to class meetings in their ethnic community (denominationalism); the "Arminian" commitment to grace-empowered ability in their provision of new roles and a new place for women; and the commitment to itinerancy in their territorial conception of purpose. Each of these contextual factors, then, possessed intrinsically religious, even theological, hues. Through each facet, the Chesapeake gave Methodist distinctives cultural expression and praxis form. The Chesapeake made Wesleyan principle into American practice.

Why has the church—why have historians—not recognized the Chesapeake's refraction of Methodism, its refraction of Wesleyanism, the theologically expressiveness of social traits formed in the Upper South? Much of the blame lies with the historical commonplaces mentioned earlier—the Puritan bias in religious and even Methodist historiography, the easy division of Methodist experience into northern and southern, and the desire to construe Methodism as church, as fully national church, as soon after 1784 as possible.

A particularly powerful distortion derives from the construction of the Methodist story on a North-South axis. That North-South fixation has something to do with the contest over priority, between Strawbridge and Embury.[65] Contributory also has been the Fluvanna division, which from the beginning was named and has been

---

65. See Richey, *Early American Methodism*.

perceived as a North-South split (though almost the entire church that was split was Chesapeake). By imaging the Fluvanna division as North/South and thus construing fidelity to Wesley as northern, Methodist historiography built in a distortion. Subsequent splits in the church more clearly demanded a North-South telling of the story, particularly those involving the Republican Methodists, Methodist Protestants, and Methodist Episcopal Church, South. And with the terrific battles throughout the border states, before and after the war, the North-South division fixed itself as axial for the entire story. So the southern flavor to Methodism came increasingly to be stamped with its later Civil War content. The rich Chesapeake nuances were discounted, even lost.

The power and primacy of Baltimore, the importance of the border statements, of Middle America in the Methodist story—just the concentration of Methodists in a band that stretches from the Chesapeake west—ought to have pointed to the necessity of talking more about region. However, the border was the battle line between North and South. So the commonalities shared in border areas get less attention than the causes over which the battles raged, and in examining the causes we have tended to divert attention away from the conflicted middle to the points north and south where positions were held less ambiguously.

These contests were very real, and I do not mean to minimize their *subsequent* determining effect. But the focus should be on the middle where the battles were joined. And the midcentury sectional crisis should not be allowed to obscure the importance of the Chesapeake in the development of Methodism amid the ambiguities and tensions that would later polarize the country. Nor should the importance of the Baltimore area be rendered solely in terms of power and primacy of the Baltimore Conference. This was a B&O church,[66] a church profoundly affected by its origins in the Chesapeake, a church exported west and south and north from the Chesapeake, a church whose Chesapeake patterns gave American meaning to Wesley's gospel.

---

66. Its engine was not unimportant, but ultimately the cargo was what mattered.

CHAPTER 7

"To Extract Poison from the Blessings of God's Providence"
Producerist Respectability and Methodist Suspicions of Capitalist Change in the Early Republic[1]

William R. Sutton

The recent discovery of populist evangelicalism as a dynamic force in the creation of the American republic has been a fortuitous development.[2] Emerging from among the common folk of the "middling classes" and acting initially from the periphery of American society, populist evangelicals challenged the traditions of their Protestant inheritance. Insisting on the validity of emotional conversions and individualized interpretations of scripture, they flourished under the existential empowering of salvation. Reveling in the relaxation of ecclesiastical restrictions, they welcomed new congregational and political responsibilities. Questioning the continued validity of rigid social hierarchies and ethical boundaries, they willingly (though carefully) explored the potential of the emerging market economy. To be sure, many found themselves at times uncomfortable with the unprecedented opportunities securable in the early republic, especially when conditions threatened to degenerate into social anarchy on the one hand or when situations seemed to spawn a fresh set of

1. Many of the revisions to this paper are a result of further research on evangelical artisans and Washingtonian temperance, made possible by the fine people of the Pew Evangelical Scholars Program, to whom I wish to express my appreciation (especially to Michael Hamilton). I am also grateful to Nick Salvatore for his helpful comments on this research.

2. Nathan O. Hatch, *The Democratization of American Christianity* (New Haven: Yale University Press, 1989); Jon Butler, *Awash in a Sea of Faith: Christianizing the American People* (Cambridge, Mass.: Harvard University Press, 1990).

aristocrats on the other. Through it all, however, populist evangelicals used their experiences of the love, power, and righteousness of God to help construct the moral underpinnings of a novel American culture.

No group of populist evangelicals was more influential between the Revolution and the Civil War than the Methodists.[3] Early American Methodism replaced the circumscribed Calvinistic hope of election in the face of human inability with the Arminian assurance of immediate salvation, guaranteeing its adherents the rights of relative autonomy as well as charging them with the responsibilities of holy living. Methodist rejection of formalism and embrace of popular, emotional religion gave its adherents a vital sense of the presence of the Holy Spirit, whom they expected to lead them into new counter-cultural lifestyles. Methodist organization, with class meetings, love feasts, and local preaching, opened avenues of religious service for laypeople relatively unhampered by ecclesiastical oversight or doctrinal dogmatism. Yet Methodists were not antinomians; their disciplined structures and strict codes of behavior, reinforcing the Wesleyan tendency toward perfectionism and holiness while retaining the Calvinist emphasis on the state as a moral entity, directed Methodist energies into cultural respectability, political participation, and reform activism.[4] In short, post–Revolutionary Methodists embraced the secular options available in the liberal republican experiment every bit as much as they did individual salvation.[5]

---

3. Nathan O. Hatch, "The Puzzle of American Methodism," *Church History* 63 (June 1992): 175-89. For Methodist growth during this time period, see John H. Wigger, *Taking Heaven by Storm: Methodism and the Rise of Popular Christianity in America* (New York: Oxford University Press, 1998), 3-6, 60; Roger Finke and Rodney Stark, "How the Upstart Sects Won America: 1776–1850," *Journal for the Scientific Study of Religion* 28 (1989): 27-44; and Richard J. Carwardine, *Evangelicals and Politics in Antebellum America* (New Haven: Yale University Press, 1993), 43.

4. Donald Mathews, "Methodist Ideology," in Russell E. Richey and Kenneth E. Rowe, eds., *Rethinking Methodist History: A Bicentennial Historical Consultation* (Nashville: Kingswood Books, 1985), 95; Daniel Walker Howe, "The Evangelical Movement and Political Culture in the North During the Second Party System," *Journal of American History* 77 (1991): 1220, 1222; Carwardine, *Evangelicals and Politics*, 18, 114-16. Recent excellent works on early American Methodism include Wigger, *Taking Heaven by Storm*; A. Gregory Schneider, *The Way of the Cross Leads Home: The Domestication of American Methodism* (Bloomington: Indiana University Press, 1993); and Russell E. Richey, *Early American Methodism* (Bloomington: Indiana University Press, 1991).

5. Mark Noll has succinctly summarized this process: "It now seems clear that between the ratification of the Constitution and the election of William Henry Harrison the assumption of the nation's public philosophy evolved from a republicanism defined mostly by classical conceptions of self-giving service for the commonwealth to a mixed ideology combining an old stock of classically republican language with newer infusions of liberal concepts authorizing acquisition and self-assertion." Mark A. Noll, "Republicanism, Liberalism, and the Languages of Northern Protestant Theology in the Early American Republic," paper delivered at AHA meeting in New York, December 1990, 14. See also Lance Banning, "Jeffersonian Ideology

Socioeconomic aspects of liberal republicanism were, however, convoluted,[6] and Methodist negotiation of them contested. Encountering issues of race, gender, class, and power, Methodists eagerly and combatively entered into "the cultural ferment over the meaning of freedom" that characterized the era. Steeped as they were in the Protestant apprehension of the fallenness of human beings and their social structures, many Methodists remained cognizant of an inherent paradox related to increased freedom: that one person's opportunity could well depend on or eventuate in another's exploitation.[7] Thomas Stockton, editor of the Methodist periodical, the *Wesleyan Repository*, expressed the ambivalence of American liberty in an editorial written in 1821. "There is perhaps no subject so imperfectly understood as the *liberty* christians have to extract poison from the blessings of God's providence, and to gain perishing treasure at the expense of temporal and eternal good—at the cost of bodies and souls!" Stockton went on to assert that even though misery and death in the new system might well be inevitable, it was shameful that "the christian gets rich by being . . . in *fact* a profiting co-partner in ruining . . . immortal beings."[8]

The Potential Poison in Emergent Capitalism

The context of Stockton's remarks was the internal power struggle over lay representation within the Methodist episcopacy—a conflict over democracy that eventuated in the Methodist Protestant schism of 1828.[9] His comments, however, were equally pertinent to related cultural arenas where Methodists could "extract poison from the

Revisited: Liberal and Classical Ideas in the New American Republic," and Joyce Appleby, "Republicanism in Old and New Contexts," *William and Mary Quarterly*, 3d ser., 43 (1986): 3-34, esp. 23-25; Drew R. McCoy, *The Elusive Republic: Political Economy in Jeffersonian America* (Chapel Hill: University of North Carolina Press, 1980), 236-39; and James T. Kloppenberg, "The Virtues of Liberalism: Christianity, Republicanism, and Ethics in Early American Political Discourse," *Journal of American History* 74 (1987): 9-33.

6. Stephen J. Ross, "The Transformation of Republican Ideology," *Journal of the Early Republic* 10 (1990): 326-28.

7. Hatch, *Democratization*, 6. The most blatant example of this possibility, of course, was Southern slavery, an institution that had long caused some American Methodists great discomfort, and Methodists also continued to struggle with the implications of gospel liberty for believing women. See Donald Mathews, *Slavery and Methodism: A Chapter in American Morality, 1780–1845* (Princeton, N.J.: Princeton University Press, 1965), and Catherine A. Brekus, *Strangers and Pilgrims: Female Preaching in America, 1740–1845* (Chapel Hill: University of North Carolina Press, 1998).

8. *Wesleyan Repository and Religious Intelligencer* 1 (30 August 1821): 163.

9. For the story of the schism, see the relevant three chapters in the first volume of *HAM*.

blessings of God's providence." One of these was the incipient industrial capitalist system of production and exchange, presented as the key to the growth of the nation's economy. Capitalism presented entrepreneurs, investors, and consumers (outside the immediate productive nexus) with welcome chances, however risky, to enhance their situations. At the same time, many artisans appreciated modernizations that could free them from dangerous and tedious tasks, could make attractive consumer items more available to them, could expand their own markets, and could reward individual technological expertise or entrepreneurial effort.[10] But others greeted industrialization and capitalist transformation, if not with fear and loathing, at least with uncertainty. As technological advances bastardized and deskilled much of the mystery and uniqueness of their crafts, artisans' pride in craftmanship was destroyed. As master artisans became or lost out to capitalists, journeymen encountered new challenges to their traditional autonomy in the workplace. As competition replaced cooperation, workers bemoaned the shattering of personalized work relations based on mutual obligation. And as depersonalization and preoccupation with cheapness came to characterize market transactions, consumers forfeited their ability to control the implications of their purchasing power. With significant numbers of artisans experiencing all this change as damaging to their self-identities as well as demoralizing to their hopes for the future, resistance to capitalist innovation was not uncommon.[11]

Evangelical artisans shared in the general ambivalence toward capitalist transformation, and Methodists, so often a force in artisan communities,[12] were no exception. Capitalism, to be sure, proved particularly compatible to religious discipline, but it also raised questions of economic morality which, in the early nineteenth century, were not yet considered oxymoronic. Although some Methodists

---

10. Richard Stott, "Artisans and Capitalist Development," *Journal of the Early Republic* 16 (1996): 257-71; Jonathan A. Glickstein, *Concepts of Free Labor in Antebellum America* (New Haven: Yale University Press, 1991), 3-11.

11. The best summary of these processes and reactions is Bruce Laurie, *Artisans into Workers: Labor in Nineteenth Century America* (New York: Noonday Press, 1989). Representative and useful labor histories include Bruce Laurie, *Working People of Philadelphia, 1800–1850* (Philadelphia: Temple University Press, 1980); Sean Wilentz, *Chants Democratic: New York City and the Rise of the American Working Class* (New York: Oxford University Press, 1984); Charles G. Steffen, *The Mechanics of Baltimore: Workers and Politics in the Age of Revolution, 1763–1812* (Urbana: University of Illinois Press, 1984); Teresa Anne Murphy, *Ten Hours Labor: Religion, Reform, and Gender in Early New England* (Ithaca, N.Y.: Cornell University Press, 1992); and Ronald Schultz, *The Republic of Labor: Philadelphia Artisans and the Politics of Class, 1720–1830* (New York: Oxford University Press, 1993).

12. Terry D. Bilhartz, *Urban Religion and the Second Great Awakening: Church and Society in Early National Baltimore* (Rutherford, N.J.: Fairleigh Dickinson University Press, 1986), 19-27.

embraced revolutionary market opportunities without hesitation,[13] others remained suspicious of the accumulations of riches and possibilities for exploitation accompanying capitalism. To address their qualms about the morality of capitalism, Methodists joined their evangelical brethren in turning to two popular (and complementary) middling-class cultural constructions: producerism and respectability. Throughout the nineteenth century, producerism, as a traditional ethic governing artisan economics, remained quite critical of capitalist modernization, while respectability proved to be more flexible. Initially, however, the respectable ideal dovetailed with producerist scruples in areas of personal behavior, social mobility, and economic morality. Together, the two models provided standards by which common Americans could judge capitalist innovation and could work to make economic modernization moral.

The American middling classes of the early republic (yeomen, artisans, small shopkeepers, and other independent producers of no exalted status) were broadly inclusive, and not to be confused with the bourgeois middle class of later periods.[14] The concerns of respectability were equally broad, but in socioeconomic terms respectability championed the hard-working, purposeful achievements of nondependent commoners, within limits designed to reign in individual self-aggrandizement and the sanctification of greed.[15]

---

13. Richard J. Carwardine, "'Antinomians' and 'Arminians': Methodists and the Market Revolution," in Melvyn Stokes and Stephen Conway, eds., *The Market Revolution in America: Social, Political, and Religious Expressions, 1800–1880* (Charlottesville: University Press of Virginia, 1996), 282-307.

14. Bruce Laurie, "Spavined Ministers, Lying Toothpullers, and Buggering Priests: Third Partyism and the Search for Security in the Antebellum North," in Howard B. Rock, Paul A. Gilje, and Robert Asher, eds. *American Artisans: Crafting Social Identity, 1750–1850* (Baltimore: Johns Hopkins University Press, 1995), 98-100. For an excellent discussion of the long transition from the precapitalist middling classes to a bourgeois middle class, see Stuart Blumin, *The Emergence of the Middle Class: Social Experience in the American City, 1760–1900* (Cambridge: Cambridge University Press, 1990).

15. The notion of middling-class respectability as it was embraced by artisans and other workers enjoyed serious and nuanced treatments by British social and labor historians in the 1970s. See for example Thomas W. Laqueur, *Religion and Respectability: Sunday Schools and Working Class Culture, 1780–1850* (New Haven: Yale University Press, 1976); Brian Harrison, *Drink and the Victorians: The Temperance Question in England, 1815–1837* (London: Faber & Faber, 1971); and Trygve R. Tholfsen, *Working-Class Radicalism in Mid-Victorian England* (New York: Columbia University Press, 1977). But respectability and the possibility of middling-class uniqueness (distinct from understandings of bourgeois experience) have been largely ignored by American labor historians, whose predilection for Marxist explanations led them to emphasize protosocialist critiques over all other interpretive options. Producerist respectability, however, provides an alternative and appropriate avenue into artisan suspicions of capitalist change, distinct from the questionable preoccupation with socialist roots. As Peter Bailey has written, "It can be admitted that however disjunctive or calculative the practice of respectability among the working class, taken *in toto* it denotes a measure of compliance with bourgeois

And closely linked to respectability in the minds of common Americans was producerism, which defended the rights of industrious and temperate workers to the fruits of their labor and advocated opposition to market practices that would inevitably serve, in the popular idiom, to "grind the faces of the poor."[16] In the minds of many, producerist respectability promised to prevent the accumulation of excessive wealth and power, recognized as both dangerous to Protestant spirituality and anathema to political democracy. And whereas respectability and producerism demand further exploration, it is clear that common Americans often utilized this powerful combination as the means to make capitalism moral.

Challenge to a Capitalist Ethic in Producerist Respectability

As a synthesis of economics, religion, and culture, producerism combined the labor theory of value, traditional Protestant economic morality, and an aesthetic respecting the limitations of human endeavor. The labor theory of value equated work, as that which generated all wealth, with property, and concluded that those who actually produced goods deserved the first consideration in the distribution of profits. This perspective was reflected in the conventional craft system of masters and journeymen who mutually negotiated wage rates, helped set prices, and established work rules.[17] Traditional economic morality was more a sensibility than a system; its adherents rejected economic opportunism (benefitting or taking

norms that largely justifies its interpretation as a 'socially-soothing tendency.' But the recent analyses of respectability still underestimate the ambiguity of its operation in working-class life, and the extent to which it cloaked a form of deviancy or new style of counter-theatre." Peter Bailey, "'Will the Real Bill Banks Please Stand Up?' Towards a Role Analysis of Mid-Victorian Working-Class Respectability," *Journal of Social History* 12 (1979): 336-53, quote on p. 348. In fact, respectability was not quite even that subterranean.

16. Ronald Schultz, "The Small Producer Tradition and the Moral Origins of Artisan Radicalism in Philadelphia, 1720–1810," *Past and Present* 127 (May 1990): 84-108; Laurie, *Working People of Philadelphia*, 168-77; Tony A. Freyer, *Producers Versus Capitalists: Constitutional Conflict in Antebellum America* (Charlottesville: University Press of Virginia, 1994), 5-11, 39-43; Christopher Lasch, *The True and Only Heaven: Progress and Its Critics* (New York: W. W. Norton, 1991), 201-24, 265-70, 302-3, 486; and Victoria C. Hattam, *Labor Visions and State Power: The Origins of Business Unionism in the United States* (Princeton, N.J.: Princeton University Press, 1993), 17-18, 76-111, esp. 96-99.

17. Schultz, "The Small-Producer Tradition," 86-89; idem, *Republic of Labor*, 25; Gary B. Nash, "Also There at the Creation: Going Beyond Gordon S. Wood," *William and Mary Quarterly*, 3d ser., 44 (1987): 606-7; Laurie, *Working People of Philadelphia*, 75-79, 202-3; and Paul G. Faler, *Mechanics and Manufacturers in the Early Industrial Revolution* (Albany: State University of New York Press, 1981), 29-31, 43-44.

advantage of buyers' or workers' ignorance or unfortunate circumstances) and acknowledged the moral necessity of a just price ideal to guarantee that workers profit.[18] Finally, the moral economy of producerism was grounded in the notion of limited accumulation.[19] Its adherents believed that monopolies of wealth and power invariably oppressed the rest of the community, and sensed that unrestrained self-aggrandizement presented a blasphemous challenge to the prerogatives of God.

The intended result for the worker in the producerist tradition was to gain his "competence"—the ability to achieve meaningful skill levels and economic nondependence—an ideal that reflected in turn a sense of limited, reasonable advancement.[20] Producerism extended beyond workers, however, to describe appropriate behavior and proscribe antisocial activities for employers and consumers as well. Employers' responsibilities included recognizing worker privileges in the workplace, resisting the temptation to monopolize profits, and respecting the basic humanity of workers. Consumers were to accept the necessary reciprocity between the quality of worker's products and the prices they were to be paid, and were to resist making decisions based on mere market considerations. In both instances, because personal productive relations were seen as organically connected to community welfare, all would benefit from following the producerist ideal. This tradition, believed to be capable of making economics moral, resonated for many artisans and small proprietors, and as such was quite compatible to Methodist practice. But maintaining producerist ethics was not easy, as Methodist class leader and master tailor George Holtzman confirmed in an 1837 advertisement placed in a Baltimore newspaper. Praising the workmanship of his journeymen while acknowledging the necessity of meeting his competitors' prices, Holtzman made his appeal to the public for its patronage. In doing so, he demonstrated his producerist preoccupation with balancing acceptable profit for himself, affordable prices for his customers, and liveable wages for his workers.[21] This symmetry lay at the heart of producerist ethics.

18. William R. Sutton, *Journeymen for Jesus: Evangelical Artisans Confront Capitalism in Jacksonian Baltimore* (University Park: Pennsylvania University Press, 1998), 5-7, 31-35, 61-65; John E. Crowley, *This Sheba, Self: The Conceptualization of Economic Life in Eighteenth-Century America* (Baltimore: Johns Hopkins University Press, 1974), 50, 53.

19. Lasch, *True and Only Heaven*, 17, 22-24; Carwardine, *Evangelicals and Politics*, 56; Ross, "Transformation of Republican Ideology," 328; and Laurie, "Spavined Ministers," 98-100.

20. Schultz, *Republic of Labor*, 6-7. Christopher Lasch acclaims "the rich moral overtones" of the competence ideal in "Conservatism Against Itself," *First Things*, no. 2 (April 1990): 23.

21. Baltimore *Republican*, 17 April 1837.

The moral and economic scaffolding of producerism was buttressed by the cultural construction of middling-class respectability. The respectable were first and foremost concerned with character and self-control, and saw themselves as occupying the middle ground between the unrestrained excesses of the "rough," and the proto-aristocratic pretensions of the "fashionable" or "ambitious." According to this model of ideal types, the rough were competent and convivial yet capable of reacting to frustrated ambitions with brutality toward the non-privileged and each other; often ignorant but not stupid; irresponsible and impulsively opposed to excessive control (self- or externally imposed); given to rowdy entertainments and instant gratification; comfortable with transient social attachments; open to magical and charismatic spirituality without great regard for doctrinal niceties or behavioral constraints; and resigned to (or comfortable with) the status quo as long as there was still room in it for their self-expression.[22] The fashionable or genteel (distinguishable from hereditary, paternalistic elites) combined extravagant ambition with affectations of patrician refinement as representatives of the *nouveau riche*; as individualistic and restless as the rough, but intensely rational in their calculations and exploitative if necessary; forming social attachments primarily designed to further their own plans; driven to accumulate as much wealth and power as possible to rise in status; given to ostentatious display; sufficiently privileged to regard religious demands as personally superfluous but still socially beneficial in pacifying the rabble; and oblivious to or unmoved by the effects of their actions on those they proved willing to exploit.[23]

In between the rough and the fashionable were the respectable.[24] Sharing some of the ambitions of the fashionable while remaining

22. For a contemporary (and pejorative) description of the rough, see Timothy Dwight, *Travels in New-England and New-York* (New Haven: S. Converse, 1821–22), 2:458-60.

23. Richard L. Bushman, *The Refinement of America: Persons, Houses, Cities* (New York: Alfred A. Knopf, 1992). For contemporary descriptions of the fashionable, see Alan Taylor, *William Cooper's Town: Power and Persuasion on the Frontier of the Early American Republic* (New York: Random House, 1995), and Amy Bridges, "Becoming American: The Working Classes in the United States before the Civil War," in Ira Katznelson and Aristide R. Zolberg, eds., *Working-Class Formation: Nineteenth-Century Patterns in Western Europe and the United States* (Princeton, N.J.: Princeton University Press, 1986), 158-60.

24. For contemporary descriptions of respectable antipathy toward both the rough and the fashionable, see Charleston *Mercury*, 11 January 1843; Baltimore *Sun*, 25 June 1840, 8 March 1843; Portland (Maine) *Advertiser*, 27 May 1841, 24 June 1841; Savannah *Republican*, 28 July 1843; Charles Jewett, *Speeches, Poems, and Miscellaneous Writings, On Subjects Connected With Temperance and the Liquor Traffic* (Boston: J. P. Jewett, 1849), 189. These depictions, apparently assuming the nonrespectability of the rough, emphasize the antisocial aspects of the ambitious. The antipathy toward the ambitious is what modern historians usually fail to address.

suspicious of the latter's claims to superiority, the respectable were devoted to careful planning, deferred gratification, and upward mobility, but they operated within boundaries set by traditional pre-occupations with communal well-being. And asserting optimism toward the inherent value and possible elevation of the rough while remaining opposed to the latter's perceived irresponsibility, the respectable embraced familial obligations, operated under "reasonable" religious and ethical restraints, and advocated concern (including unsought and undesired expressions of benevolence) for the condition of others. Thus, the respectable were supposed to combine the unpretentiousness of the rough with the enterprise of the ambitious while maintaining a strict sense of limits and decorum in both their work and their amusements. These ideal types, of course, are merely descriptions to approximate human experience, and, in the real lives of individuals, they often overlapped or merged. Nevertheless, this was a paradigm that resonated with middling-class producers.[25]

The contest between the rough, the respectable, and the ambitious reflected genuine spiritual issues, especially for Methodists. The rough spirituality of primitive Methodism was well known, as Methodists encountered God in dreams, healings, prophetic utterances, and ecstatic visitations; to some extent such phenomena explain the affinity African Americans discovered for Methodist teaching.[26] For the rough, direct apprehension of God's love and care was foundational to their faith, and dependence on financial security, social position, or overly reasoned theology was seen as potentially dangerous, even heretical. As Methodist itinerant William Capers remembered, Methodists were well known "for being the most

25. The preceding paragraphs utilize insights and paradigms developed by Thomas Laqueur, Paul Faler, Bruce Laurie, Michael Kimmel, and Patricia Click. Laqueur, *Religion and Respectability*; Paul G. Faler, "Cultural Aspects of the Industrial Revolution: Lynn, Massachusetts, Shoemakers and Industrial Morality, 1826–1860," *Labor History* 15 (1974): 367-94; Laurie, *Working People of Philadelphia*; Michael Kimmel, *Manhood in America: A Cultural History* (New York: Free Press, 1996); Patricia C. Click, *The Spirit of the Times: Amusements in Nineteenth-Century Baltimore, Norfolk, and Richmond* (Charlottesville: University of Virginia Press, 1989).

26. John Wigger, "Taking Heaven by Storm: Enthusiasm and Early American Methodism, 1770–1820," *Journal of the Early Republic* 14 (1994): 167-94. For compatibilities between Methodist and African spirituality, see Harry V. Richardson, *Dark Salvation: The Story of Methodism as It Developed Among Blacks in America* (Garden City, N.Y.: Anchor Press, 1976); Albert Raboteau, *Slave Religion: The "Invisible Institution" in the Antebellum South* (New York: Oxford University Press, 1978); Mechal Sobel, *The World They Made Together: Black and White Values in Eighteenth-Century Virginia* (Princeton, N.J.: Princeton University Press, 1987); Margaret Washington Creel, *"A Peculiar People": Slave Religion and Community-Culture Among the Gullahs* (New York: New York University Press, 1988).

spiritual and least worldly," and "were regarded the most enthusiastic and least rational of all the sects of Christians."[27] Methodist discipline, however, often led to economic success and upward mobility, and not all congregants remained comfortable with the radical faith and the social opprobrium initially associated with American Methodism. Following the Enlightenment tendency to limit the prerogatives of God,[28] fashionable Methodists joined other privileged evangelicals in understanding God in increasingly rationalized terms. But respectable Methodists had to negotiate between these two poles, transferring their spiritual concerns into all areas of their lives.

In a time when notions of economic morality were still viable, then, the respectable rejected both the luxuries of the parasitic newly wealthy and the laziness of the indigent poor. Instead, they extolled the virtues of industry, frugality, temperance, and limited prosperity. And although respectable ideals could be accommodated to the market revolution, it was among these respectable middling-class producers that nineteenth-century suspicions of capitalism thrived. From post–Revolutionary Shays' Rebellion and Jacksonian trade unionism to the Gilded Age Knights of Labor, the turn-of-the-century Populist movement, and Debsian socialism, displaced farmers and artisans joined industrial workers to critique and resist rationalized and dependency-inducing capitalist economies.[29] But they found equally unpalatable capitalist reconstructions of middling-class respectability to privilege ambition and gentility, whereby mental work was celebrated over skilled manual labor, conspicuous consumption was elevated over effortful production, and restless striving for wealth was sanctified. At times intensely critical of wage labor and credit systems beyond their influence, morally outraged by the spread of aristocratic vices encouraged by the rise of the newly privileged, but also often ignoring the plight of genuine proletarians, especially immigrants and minorities (who were, almost by definition, considered "rough"),

27. Capers; quoted in Wigger, *Taking Heaven by Storm*, 73.

28. George M. Marsden, *The Evangelical Mind and the New School Presbyterian Experience* (New Haven: Yale University Press, 1970), 6.

29. Along with the previously mentioned literature on nineteenth-century trade unionism, see David P. Szatmary, *Shays' Rebellion: The Making of an Agrarian Insurrection* (Amherst: University of Massachusetts Press, 1980); Laurence Goodwyn, *Democratic Promise: The Populist Moment in America* (New York: Oxford University Press, 1976); and Nick Salvatore, *Eugene Debs: Citizen and Socialist* (Urbana: University of Illinois Press, 1982).

it was primarily respectable middling-class producers who sought to redeem American culture by imposing ethical stability onto the dislocations and uncertainties of capitalism.

Methodist Support of Producerist Respectability in the Early Republic

A bitter hatters' strike that broke out in Baltimore in July 1833 illustrates the connections between producerist anticapitalism and middling-class respectability within Baltimore's Methodist community. The strike, brought on in response to a combination formed by entrepreneurial masters to reduce unilaterally the mutually established wage agreement, inaugurated a wave of journeyman organizing and strike activity in Baltimore for the next four years. Early on, local newspapers published a strike manifesto written in part by hatter John H. W. Hawkins who was, by any account, an intriguing Jacksonian figure. A participant in Baltimore's successful defense against the British invasion of 1814 and an exuberant practitioner of the artisan recreational culture, Hawkins was also an ardent Methodist and had been active in the democratic reform movement that led to Methodist Protestantism. In the strike manifesto, Hawkins set forth a spirited defense of the journeymen, based on producerist arguments and presented in the language of respectability.

The hatters, Hawkins pointed out, had been largely operating under a consistent wage scale for eleven years, allowing the masters to thrive and the journeymen to get by. During this time, the journeymen had been content with their limited accumulations; "We have not taken any advantage from the *vast amount of wealth we have accumulated,* neither has it created for us any irregular desire." But now the masters' combination threatened to reduce wages by 25 percent, a change that would impoverish the journeymen and their families. Such a situation was unconscionable according to the producerist ethic of the artisans. "We hold the principle that every man should be rewarded according to the amount of labour by him performed; creating thereby stronger incentives to industry." Moreover, the decision by the overly ambitious violated the tenets of respectability by oppressing "nonrough" workers who deserved better. "But we are satisfied that many of our profession of industrious and temperate habits, have not been enabled to provide for their families a

233

respectable maintenance, many live in places that is neither conducive to health, nor the morals of their beloved offspring, and many at this time have not wherewith to support their families one month."[30] As a result, Hawkins and the hatters received an outburst of support from fellow artisans, a dozen sympathetic masters (including Methodist Protestant Jacob Boston and Methodist George Quail), and the public at large. The strike was soon concluded successfully for the journeymen.[31]

A catechism written for the Methodist Society in Baltimore in 1826 hinted at the biblical basis for Methodist support of producerism and middling-class respectability. Although the only information in the short catechetic answers were direct quotations from scripture, Methodists taking the catechism seriously could easily infer related prescriptions for economic morality. In lesson twenty, "Is Idleness forbidden," the catechism cited Genesis 3:19 and 2 Thessalonians 3:10 to affirm that neither the rich nor the poor had any excuse for not engaging in productive labor. The answers to lesson twenty-four addressed economic questions directly and made clear the basic outlines of traditional economic morality, citing the Levitical law and the Golden Rule to support the just price ideal and to suggest limited consumption for the godly.

Q. What is our duty in buying and selling with one another?
A. If thou sell aught unto thy neighbour, or buyest aught of thy neighbour's hand; ye shall not oppress one another. Lev. 25:14
Q. Have we any general rule to govern us in these things?
A. Yes; as ye would that men should do to you, do ye also to them likewise. Lk. 6:31
Q. Has St. Paul given us advice relative to the things of this world?
A. Yes, he saith, Godliness with contentment is great gain.
—For we brought nothing into this world, and it is certain we can carry nothing out. And having food and raiment, let us be therewith content. 1 Tim. 6:6-8

Finally, citing Matthew 5:42, Proverbs 19:17 and 21:13, Psalm 41:1-2, and 2 Corinthians 9:6-7, the catechism equated generous treatment of

---

30. Baltimore *Republican*, 30 June 1833.

31. Sutton, *Journeymen for Jesus*, 149-53, 235. In addition to the contributions of Hawkins, Boston, and Quail, there are indications that Jacob Rogers, Baltimore's largest hatting manufacturer and a leading Methodist layman, also purposefully shunned the masters' combination.

the poor with the assurance that God would deliver the "cheerful giver." In all, the catechism was a traditional statement granting no rationalization for liberal economics or fashionable mobility.[32]

Despite the propensity for producerism and middling-class respectability, neither Methodist traditions nor the Methodist catechism were capable by themselves of holding the line against the economic novelties of capitalism and the cultural alternatives to respectability. Therefore, certain Methodist writers, including William Stilwell in New York City and John Hersey in the Baltimore area, followed the lead of John Hawkins and other activist producers in critically assessing the effects of capitalist innovation within their communities. Stilwell's involvement reflected a thoroughgoing radicalism that advocated, within the denomination, lay representation and equal rights for women and African Americans, and defended the respectable limits of primitive Methodism. His most significant contribution, however, may well have come through his association with fellow Methodist radical Dr. James Covel and the New York Society for Promoting Communities, a group calling for evangelically oriented political solutions to capitalist dislocation.[33] John Hersey, on the other hand, labored for years in Maryland and Virginia independent from any organized radicalism. Throughout his writing and preaching career, Hersey pushed individual Christians to repent from the economic sins of holding slaves, violating just price restrictions, and taking advantage of workers' lack of power. He made a name for himself as a popular prophet of producerist respectability, opposing, in the process, the prerogatives of the powerful.[34] The contributions of Hawkins, Hersey, and Stilwell indicated the existence of broad-based if loosely articulated notions of producerist respectability approved by common Methodists.

---

32. *A Short Scriptural Catechism Intended for the Use of the Methodist Society* (Baltimore, 1826).

33. Material on William Stilwell can be found in Frederick E. Maser and George A. Singleton, "Further Branches of Methodism are Founded," in *HAM* 1:610-11, 625-29. For the brief historical mention of James Covel, see Samuel A. Seaman, *Annals of New York Methodism, Being A History of the Methodist Episcopal Church in the City of New York* (New York: Hunt & Eaton, 1892), 227; and William B. Sprague, *Annals of the American Pulpit* (New York: R. Carter & Brothers, 1859), 7:564.

34. John B. Boles, "John Hersey: Dissenting Theologian of Abolitionism, Perfectionism, and Millennialism," *Methodist History* 14 (July 1976): 215-34.

William Stilwell: Radical Defender
of Producerist Respectability

William Stilwell joined the Methodists (New York Conference) in 1814 and became a licensed itinerant, around the same time that James Covel was designated a local preacher. In 1819, then an ordained elder, Stilwell was appointed to serve two black Methodist congregations in New York City, Asbury and Zion. A year later Stilwell became embroiled in one of the periodic struggles within the MEC over issues of centralized power within the General Conference—a conflict that also epitomized the tension within Methodism between the rough primitivism of its origins and the increasingly fashionable orientation of some of its upwardly mobile leaders. John Street Church, of which William Stilwell was a member, was the oldest and most important Methodist church in New York; it was also renowned for its independent spirit. In 1820, the long-simmering issue of rebuilding John Street Church boiled over into conflict. On the one side were some of its trustees, most of the itinerants in the Conference, and those like Nathan Bangs who looked with favor upon the social attainments and ambitions of prosperous Methodists. On the other side were other trustees, regular members who regarded the opposition as representing the growing power of the Conference, and laypeople who opposed ostentation on the grounds of its nonrespectability. When the Bangs faction (and the Conference) prevailed and rebuilt the church with a carpeted altar and other modern "improvements," the conflict came to a head.[35] To be sure, ownership and control of the property upon which the church buildings were built were central issues, but even deeper beneath the turmoil lay fundamental questions about the meaning of Methodist respectability.

To this point, the conflict was internal, but when the New York Conference appealed to the state legislature (unsuccessfully, as it turned out) to support the move of the modernizers, a group of three to four hundred whites and some eight hundred blacks, under the leadership of William Stilwell, his iconoclastic Uncle Samuel, and

---

35. Seaman, *Annals of New York Methodism*, 215-29. For a discussion of Nathan Bangs's important reformulation of Methodist "respectability" toward "middle class propriety and urbane congeniality," see Hatch, *Democratization of American Christianity*, 201-5 (quote on p. 202); and Wigger, *Taking Heaven by Storm*, 189-90.

James Covel, protested vigorously.[36] "To seek for legislative aid to enforce the discipline of a church," wrote Samuel Stilwell, "is a step toward popery, that in this enlightened day we should suppose would hardly be submitted to, *except* by those who have lost the *spirit* of Christianity and of freemen." Complaining about the unethical nature of taking property from the hands of the people and granting it to a highly centralized and increasingly powerful bureaucracy, and decrying the lack of lay representation in the Conferences, the discontented faction immediately withdrew from the MEC. The African Americans, after asking Stilwell and Covel to officially ordain their elders on 17 July 1822, went on to form the still-existent African Methodist Episcopal Zion Church. The whites, led by the Stilwells and Covel, organized the short-lived but important Methodist Society in the City of New York, founded, in their words, "on Scripture and the equal rights of mankind."[37] The John Street dispute, in the end, featured an alliance between the rough and the respectable against the fashionable.

Stilwell's Methodist Society thrived in New York and surrounding environs in the 1820s, growing from three hundred to eight hundred members in the city and 2,000 *in toto* by 1825. Among its members (as a general missionary, deacon, and elder) was the quintessentially "rough" but respected revivalist, Lorenzo Dow.[38] In the words of one of its opponents (and later bishop), Joshua Soule, the Methodist Society was "disastrous . . . properly speaking, an ecclesiastical democracy, in the most extensive sense of the word."[39] Their General Rules reflected the progressive nature of the society, with women

---

36. Seaman, *Annals of New York Methodism*, 221, 226-27. Samuel Stilwell (author of a published rebuke of Thomas Paine entitled *A Guide to Reason; or, An Examination of Thomas Paine's "Age of Reason"*) was close to Silas Wood, a moderate candidate of the Working Man's Party in New York City in 1829. But Samuel rejected a political career for himself as he watched Alexander Hamilton succumb to the evils of ambition. Hamilton's death in the duel with Aaron Burr convinced Stilwell "that ambition might bring an honorable man into . . . a position that he must do wrong, or be disgraced." Subsequently, "contentment took the place of ambition in his mind and heart." Samuel Stilwell Doughty, *The Life of Samuel Stilwell, with Notices of Some of His Contemporaries* (New York: Brown & Wilson, 1877), 12, 22; Wilentz, *Chants Democratic*, 196-97.

37. Samuel Stilwell, "Rise and Progress of the Methodist Society, in the City of New York," *The Friendly Visitor* 1 (23 November 1825): 372; (1 November 1825): 348. The African American leaders, including Abraham Thompson, James Varick, Levin Smith, and Christopher Rush, continued to look to Stilwell for leadership even as they established their denominational autonomy. Like the white Methodist Society, both men and women in the AMEZ voted on all preaching appointments. David Henry Bradley, *A History of the AME Zion Church: Part 1, 1796–1872* (Nashville: Parthenon Press, 1956), 63, 71-79, 82, 95.

38. *Friendly Visitor* 1 (30 November 1825): 383 (7 December 1825): 390.

39. Horace M. Du Bose, *Life of Joshua Soule* (Nashville: MECS Publishing House, 1911), 161, cited in Bradley, *History of AME Zion Church*, 79.

being allowed to vote on all congregational matters and made solely responsible for disciplining wayward female Methodists. Retaining the inclusivity of the original Methodist invitation (that all were to be welcomed who expressed a *"desire to flee from the wrath to come, and to be saved from their sins"*), the Rules forbade certain capitalist innovations and fashionable attitudes; with "giving or taking things on unlawful interest," violating the Golden Rule, "borrowing or buying without a probability of paying," indulging in luxurious fashions, and "needless self-indulgence" all proscribed.[40]

The New York Society for Promoting Communities

In 1822 (the same year that they ordained the AMEZ elders), Stilwell and Covel joined Cornelius Blatchly, four other ministers, and twelve laymen to form the New York Society for Promoting Communities. Their manifesto, *An Essay on Common Wealths*, apparently written primarily by Blatchly, appeared shortly thereafter.[41] In this work, widely regarded as seminal in the American anticapitalist tradition, Blatchly, Stilwell, Covel, and the other members of the Society sketched out a biblical solution to the maldistribution of wealth exacerbated by both the traditions of feudalism and the innovations of market capitalism.[42] In doing so, the Society refused to accommodate scriptural norms to capitalist modernization and individualistic ambition; instead, they contrasted producerist ethics to various aspects of liberal economics, with the latter coming up short. Their goal was "to convince the pious of all denominations that their duty is to institute and establish in *every religious congregation*, a system of social, equal, and *inclusive* rights, interests, liberties, and privileges" to guarantee the economic justice of the kingdom of God.[43]

40. *Friendly Visitor* 1 (16 November 1825): 364-65; Seaman, *Annals of New York Methodism*, 229.

41. Five years earlier Blatchly had authored the strongly anticapitalist *Some Causes of Popular Poverty*, a work praised and reprinted by Methodist radical Thomas Branagan. Thomas Branagan, *The Beauties of Philanthropy, Extracted from the Writings of its Disciple* (New York: published by the author, 1839), 194.

42. For treatments of Blatchly's thought, see Wilentz, *Chants Democratic*, 158-62, 165-67; David Harris, *Socialist Origins in the United States* (Assen, the Netherlands: Van Gorcum & Company, 1966), 10-19; Arthur E. Bestor, *Backwoods Utopias: The Sectarian and Owenite Phases of Communitarian Socialism in America: 1663–1829* (Philadelphia: University of Pennsylvania Press, 1950), 97-100; and Walter E. Hugins, *Jacksonian Democracy and the Working Class: A Study of the New York Workingmen's Movement, 1829–1837* (Stanford, Calif.: Stanford University Press, 1960), 98.

43. Cornelius Blatchly, *An Essay on Common Wealths* (New York: New York Society for Promoting Communities, 1822), 3.

Their method was to rely upon the indwelling power of the Holy Spirit to convict individuals of the appropriateness of their critique and to organize godly communities accordingly.

Permeating the critique of the New York Society for Promoting Communities was the insistence that respectable self-denial was unalterably opposed to genteel ambition. As a corollary, the Society rejected the notion that communal welfare could best be maintained through the pursuit of self-interest and the accumulation of private property. Even as members of the Society promoted respectability as the spiritual antidote to the sin of self-aggrandizement, they located it in an economic and religious context by tying it to producerist ethics and the scriptural reminder that "the love of money is the root of all evil." In condemning emergent liberalism and the capitalist practices it rationalized, the Society refuted the claim that prosperity depended on "the stimulus of *selfish* and *exclusive* interest, profit and honour, to excite [people] to industry, science and enterprise." The Bible proscribed such "covetousness and avarice," which the Society promised to "demonstrate . . . are the inevitable consequences of *selfish* and *exclusive* systems of governing society," yet government protection of liberal economics promoted those sins. Moreover, property itself (the very foundation of Lockean liberal arguments) was "the *gift* of society" so that "the productions and wealth produced by society, should not be *individual, selfish,* and *exclusive property,* but *social* and *common* benefit and wealth." In contrast, the title page of *An Essay on Common Wealths* cited the communitarian example of the primitive church in Jerusalem as presented in Acts 2:44-45 ("And all that believed were together, and had all things common; And sold their possessions and goods, and parted them to all men, as every man had need.").[44]

---

44. Blatchly, *Common Wealths*, 6, 36, 25, 1. Rejecting the maxim, "That wealth should generate more wealth," Blatchly in another work suggested:

> "If wealth should produce opulence without the art, labour, or ingenuity of its proprietor, the opulent owner must necessarily obtain his increase from those who exercise art, labour, and ingenuity, and he may, without any exercise, study, genius, or industry, continually receive the products of other people's exertions; and he will necessarily accumulate property, and this will necessarily increase his income, till he or his posterity are plunged into luxury, excess, extravagance, and other abominable vices, that shall, like a whirlwind, scatter his golden feathers among others. . . . That money *may* be gotten by honest industry is certain and undeniable: but it is as certain and undeniable, that millions of industrious and frugal people toil from imbecile youth to decripid age, without being able to obtain riches."

Cornelius Blatchly, *Some Causes of Popular Poverty* (Philadelphia: Eastwick & Stacy, 1817), reprinted in Branagan, *Beauties of Philanthropy,* 197.

The problems of the overly ambitious were evident in the growing maldistribution of wealth and political privileging of the propertied few. Those criticized as proto-aristocrats used their easy access to government channels to foster policies promoting further accumulation, to the detriment of the common folk—especially those who actually provided the labor that generated wealth. The specific evils of these novel policies, most clearly manifested in the institution of slavery and long condemned by traditional economic morality, included "interest [which is elsewhere defined as 'usury'], rents, banks, tythes [i. e. to state churches], tolls, salaries, pensions, monopolies, land jobbing, stock jobbing, office hunting, party politics, slandering, peculation, private and public knaveries, &c." Moreover, these were the means whereby "the favoured have obtained wealth and power . . . which is very *oppressive* to the poorer part of mankind, who do not perceive how greatly they are thus trodden under foot by imposts, excise, and many kinds of taxation." In "disinterested and self-denying communities," where exclusive rights in property had been legally abolished, however, these "evils" could not exist.[45]

The immediate solution to this unfortunate situation, then, was to be found in redeemed attitudes and concomitant legislative changes, both of which, according to the Society's orthodox reading of scripture, were to be grounded in individual and collective self-denial. "Every sin," according to the Society, "is an act of intemperance: and a pure abstinence is nothing but a denial of self and taking up the power of God as that cross on which selfishness must be crucified, or destruction must overtake us here, and misery be our portion in eternity, awful eternity." But this doom was not merely personal; it had profound implications for American millennial expectations as well. "For as every man is evil who does not deny himself, take up the cross of Christ, and follow Jesus," asserted the Society, "so every government is wicked, which does not conduct all its civil polity in a complete system of *self-denial*. Without this, they must be under the dominion of satan and antichrist, and not under the government of the Lord and his Christ." The overriding principle of self-denial, moreover, though clearly compatible to producerism, even superseded its claim to moral preeminence. Maintaining the precepts of

---

45. Blatchly, *Common Wealths*, 39. Blatchly had made the same claim in *Some Causes*; the end result of liberal commercial practices was "*cruelly oppressive* to the *laborious*, and to *all* who are not bankers" because the "loss and gain between the bankers and the rest of the community is reciprocated inversely." Blatchly, *Some Causes*, 203.

traditional economic morality but challenging the labor theory of value, the Society even rejected the alleged "perfect right" of every individual "to the full fruits of his own honest ingenuity and labour," which "must equally belong to all" regardless of "the distinctions of fortune, of rank, or of talents."[46]

But if producerist rights were to be subordinate to the ideal of self-denial, producerism as an economic system was superior to emergent capitalism. This became clear in the scriptural solutions offered by the Society, based on the often cited Golden Rule, other Old and New Testament sources, and, most important, the Pentateuchal Jubilee. Citing Isaiah 9 and quoting 1 Corinthians 10:24 ("Let no man seek his *own*, but every man *another's* wealth."), the Society suggested encouraging self-denial through legislation.[47] To address the misuse of "the exclusive rights of fealties:—interests, rents and banks; monopolies, imposts miscalled *duties*, &c." by which "they grind the poor to powder," the Society proposed the rudiments of a system of progressive taxation. "The rich and poor," wrote Blatchly, "agreeable to Deut. xvi. 17.[*sic*] ought to pay in proportion to their income and wealth. It would put an end to litigation, imprisonment for debt, and debtor's jails; and to pensioners, office-hunters, war and a hireling ministry. Indeed what present *evils* of association would not cease to scourge us? *Evils*, by which men of opulence, office, learning and power now oppress the poor, weak, ignorant, servile and laborious parts of society; whose industry would, if society did them justice in her institutions and laws, produce them abundance."[48]

Even more radical, in the sense of cutting to the root of the inherent

---

46. Ibid., 4.

47. Blatchly, *Common Wealths*, 11, 6, 9.

48. Ibid., 27, 26. Thomas Branagan appealed to similar arguments when he advocated a ceiling on wealth accumulation:

"The only possible mode under heaven, of establishing human rights and happiness, and averting human wrongs, is the equalization of power, that is, of property; and this can be done by only one possible mode, viz: fixing by constitution a *maximum*, or limited amount, beyond which no one can own capital under any pretense. After this *maximum* is reached, the individual should have the full power of distributing the surplus, but if he neglects, the law will distribute for him, as, for example, in the case of wills. This, and this only, will wrest the oppressive sceptre from the grasp of monopoly and aristocracy. Auxiliaries, as industry, economy, sobriety, moral physiology, will of course be needed, but that they are auxiliaries only, and ineffectual without this measure, to ensure a competency to the mass of mankind, they have too ample and constant evidence."

In recognizing the fundamental notions that wealth begets more wealth and, in turn, more power, Branagan's producerism cut to the heart of the potential for excess and exploitation inherent in nascent American capitalism. Branagan, *Beauties of Philanthropy*, 109. He took his ideas on prorated property taxation directly from Blatchly. Ibid., 117.

inequities connected to the rise of capitalism, was the Society's sugges-tion of the political and economic viability of the Jewish Jubilee. This ancient ideal held that, on the fiftieth year, all property sold due to eco-nomic distress prior to the Jubilee year would be returned to the original owner (but not the profit accrued from its use during that time).[49] Such a system allowed for individual initiative and limited upward mobility based on industry and frugality, while at the same time, circumscribed the potential for accumulative abuses endemic to any accumulation of wealth and power. Noting that the feudal traditions of primogeniture and entail had been outlawed throughout the new republic in the inter-ests of creating a more just system of economic opportunity, the Society proposed an element of governmental intervention usually held suspect by American republicans in either political or ecclesiastical structures. To solve this problem, the Society promoted the ascension of "an evangeli-cal government" to enforce producerist morality.[50]

The Society's understanding of the proper place of human govern-ment in the divine economy had two important distinctions. In the first place, the understanding of a Manichean dualism between "the powers that be" and "the powers that ought to be" undermined and overruled the more conservative Pauline command (Romans 13:1) to obey all authority as from God; at the same time it made Christian orthodoxy more compatible to the prevailing republican sensibilities, which encouraged judging the legitimacy of all authority and chal-lenging those deemed illegitimate. Second, the notion that social sins were not simply a result of fallen human nature or individual sinful choices, nor a part of the divine design, suggested that, although the natural condition of present society was clearly under satanic influ-ence, it was still fully capable of temporal redemption.[51] The former

---

49. Blatchly, *Common Wealths*, 22-23. For an example of militant artisan use of the Jubilee arguments, see Robert Townsend's speech to the Journeymen Carpenter's Society of New York City in 1834. *National Trades' Union*, 17 January 1835. See also Peter Linebaugh, "Jubilating; Or, How the Atlantic Working Class used the Biblical Jubilee Against Capitalism, with Some Success," *Radical History Review* 50 (1991): 143-80.

50. Blatchly, *Common Wealths*, 14, 40. This is remarkably similar to Jonathan Edwards's nega-tive assessment of capitalist innovation many decades earlier. Mark Valeri, "The Economic Thought of Jonathan Edwards," *Church History* 60 (1991): 37-54.

51. Blatchly, *Common Wealths*, 12. As Blatchly explained elsewhere, "I really think, since God works by his saints and servants, that it is the duty of many of them to investigate the causes of the afflictions and sufferings of the poor and needy." Blatchly, *Some Causes*, 217. In addition, Blatchly rejected the increasingly popular liberal religious assumptions that contemporary pover-ty was due to the outworkings of the "providential" laws of nature: "And why ... must a poor, honest, and industrious man and his family suffer every way ... while the opulent overreaching drone, is blest from every quarter? Has God or man ordained this? If God, what kind of God is he? I have no hope on earth; and what, from such a God, can I hope for hereafter?" Ibid., 210.

understanding ruled out passive obedience in relation to prevailing power structures whereas the latter rejected a restricted definition of sin as merely the result of individual action. Society, led by churches, must take ethical duties as seriously as spiritual experience in order to gain the divine blessing necessary to realize the millennial potential of the United States.[52]

Such a scripturally grounded and thoroughgoing critique of capitalist practices was not unusual for Methodists and other populist evangelicals. And the Society's critique was not lost on other elements outside the evangelical mainstream. No less a personage than Thomas Jefferson commented favorably, if less than enthusiastically, on the copy of *An Essay on Common Wealths* that he received in 1822.[53] Equally important, the work was quite possibly a major source of inspiration for Thomas Skidmore's agrarianism, popular among New York workingmen throughout the Jacksonian years.[54] Despite Jefferson's guardedly encouraging reading of their manifesto and the popularity among New York's radical artisans of their ideas, however, official Methodism refused the Society's implicit invitation to be drawn into the debate. But that refusal did little to discourage the Methodist members of the Society, nor did it indicate the demise of producerist respectability among the Methodist rank and file.

John Hersey: Popular Prophet of Producerist Respectability

The economic critiques of Stilwell and Covel and their producer-oriented formulation of respectability was also evidenced in the work of John Hersey throughout the 1830s. The self-appointed bane of the

---

52. Blatchly, *Common Wealths*, 6.

53. Jefferson commented, in a return letter to Blatchly, that the "moral principles" of his work "merit entire approbation, its philanthropy especially, and its views on the equal rights of man." Jefferson went on to note that whereas such principles might well work in "various small societies," he did not "feel authorized to conclude . . . that an extended society . . . could be governed happily on the same principle." A. A. Lipscomb and A. E. Bergh, eds., *Writings of Thomas Jefferson* (Washington D.C.: Thomas Jefferson Memorial Association, 1903) 15:399. This letter was later released to various eastern newspapers, including the *Niles' Weekly Register* of Baltimore, where it appeared in October 1825. Reference to the correspondence between Jefferson and Blatchly appears in Bestor, *Backwoods Utopias*, 99.

54. Thomas Skidmore, *The Rights of Man to Property!* (New York: A. Ming Jr., 1829). It would appear that Skidmore's "thoroughly materialist, thoroughly democratic, 'agrarian' solution" of the General Division was, to a great degree, a secular restatement of Blatchly's Jubilee principles. Espousing a peaceful political revolution in which "the dispossessed" would electorally overthrow the federal government, Skidmore called for the redistribution of wealth and property, to be improved upon during an individual's lifetime, but reverting to the state for subsequent redistribution upon death. Wilentz, *Chants Democratic*, 186-87.

well born, Hersey remained within the MEC fold for his entire career, and his trenchant criticisms of creeping Methodist accommodation of fashionable practices earned him esteem, if not notoriety. In addition to doing work for the American Colonization Society, Hersey published between 1833 and 1841 a number of books dealing with practical Christian living, and he was the first Home Missionary to serve the poor of Baltimore. Hersey was an exceptionally dour individual; his idea of high humor was the parable of Lazarus and the rich man in the sixteenth chapter of Luke.[55] As a young man John Hersey had embarked on a commercial career that ended with disastrous results. Around 1819, deep in debt, disabused of his career choice, and determined to pursue spiritual repentance, Hersey found solace and empowerment in Methodism. Avoiding official itinerancy because he did not want to give the impression that he was avoiding debts, he eventually became a traveling local preacher in the Baltimore area in the early 1820s.[56]

Hersey made no bones about identifying with the common folk because he believed that such was the practice of Jesus. As a minister to the middling classes, he asserted that the "most honorable and independent employment on earth, is the cultivation of the ground; next to this stands *plain*, useful mechanism." Hersey's socioeconomic ethics were informed by his distaste for deference as well as his disgust with the rich, assuming in both cases that such status and accumulation had usually resulted from exploiting others.[57] Quoting from Exodus 22:21; Deuteronomy 24:14, 15; Psalms 9:9 and 72:4; Proverbs 22:22, 23; Isaiah 58:6; and James 5:5, Hersey reminded readers that *"Thou shalt not oppress a hired servant that is poor and needy"* because *"The Lord . . .* SHALL BREAK IN PIECES THE OPPRESSOR." Hersey

---

55. C. E. Weirich to John Hersey, personal correspondence, 28 February 1861, Fletcher Marine Papers, MSS 1016.3, Maryland Historical Society, Baltimore. For contemporaneous views of Hersey, see Fletcher E. Marine, *Sketch of Rev. John Hersey, Minister of the Gospel of the M. E. Church* (Baltimore: Hoffman & Co., 1879). Hersey's works included *Advice to Christian Parents* (Baltimore: Armstrong & Berry, 1839); *An Appeal to Christians, on the Subject of Slavery* (Baltimore: Armstrong & Plaskitt, 1833); *The Importance of Small Things; or, A Plain Course of Self-Examination to which is added, Signs of the Times* (Baltimore: Armstrong & Plaskitt, 1833); and *The Privilege of Those Born of God; or A Plain Rational View of the Nature and Extent of Sanctification* (Baltimore: Armstrong & Berry, 1841).

56. Marine, *Sketch of John Hersey*, 5-16, 25; Boles, "John Hersey," 215-16. As an example of Hersey's idiosyncrasies, he was alleged to have once reproved General Andrew Jackson for publicly exclaiming "By the eternal!" within Hersey's earshot. Reportedly, Jackson was sufficiently impressed with Hersey's well-known character to accept the reproof, and apologized. James E. Armstrong, *History of the Old Baltimore Conference from the Planting of Methodism in 1773 to the Division of the Conference in 1857* (Baltimore: King Brothers, 1907), 191-92.

57. Hersey, *Advice to Christian Parents*, 113, 83.

followed this warning with one suggesting that exploitation and injustice often occurred when the ambitious were set loose to amass fortunes. *"Go to now, ye rich men, weep and howl for your miseries that shall come upon you . . . Behold, the hire of the labourers which have reaped down your fields, which is of you kept back by fraud, crieth; and the cries of them that have reaped are entered into the ears of the Lord of Sabaoth."*[58]

Hersey never seemed to tire of rebuking the morally questionable practices of fashionable evangelicals. At the home of one, he declined a fancy meal prepared in his honor because he felt that it encouraged extravagance; at another, he refused to eat the bread offered him because he believed that it had been bought with money gained from liquor sales; and at a third he declined an invitation to dinner from a Methodist believed to be guilty of charging "usurious interest." He also warned against Bible, tract, Sunday school, and missionary societies because of their practice of elevating unregenerate elites to positions of leadership and honor. Similarly, he ridiculed the Sabbatarian movement's reliance on titled officers, sneering that "God's Word . . . is not sufficient authority" to keep the Sabbath holy, but "surely when such an assemblage of earthly dignitaries speak, all will hear and obey." For Hersey, such disdain extended to the grave; as requested, he was buried in a plain wooden box, and his eulogist memorialized him as one who "seemed . . . in the providence of God, to be a living rebuke to the worldliness of the churches, especially our own."[59]

Hersey's anticapitalism was not as thoroughgoing as Stilwell's, nor was he interested in political leveling. Like Stilwell, however, he favored the redistribution of unjustly amassed riches, although for Hersey such adjustments were to be achieved through persuasion, not through organizational or governmental pressures. For Hersey maldistribution of wealth reflected on the essential goodness of God and indicated an unwillingness on the part of Christians to take God's concerns for the poor seriously. "No *good father* would experience pleasure in seeing some of his children prosperous and happy, while others are pining in want and misery, and forgotten by their more fortunate brethren," Hersey wrote. "A good parent provides for the necessities of all his children; and were he to see one hoarding up those things which he had provided and designed for all, to the exclusion of others who were suffering, it would not be pleasing in

---

58. Hersey, *Appeal on Slavery*, 121-22.
59. Hersey, *Importance of Small Things*, 158, 189; Fletcher Marine Papers, MSS 1016.3, Maryland Historical Society, Baltimore; Marine, *Sketch of Hersey*, 134, 70.

his sight—nor could he say to such a one—well done my good and *merciful* child."[60]

Hersey's suspicions of capitalist innovation matched Stilwell's and represented the continued viability of the producerist ideal for many Methodists. His ringing endorsement of traditional economic morality in a section of his *Advice to Parents*, simply entitled "Justice," made this clear.

> Show them that a *desire* to get more for any article they may have to sell, than its real value, or to purchase any thing for less than its worth, discovers an unjust and dishonorable principle in the sight of God their heavenly Father. Suffer them never to higgle, nor use many words in their transactions one with another. Let them know that to ask any honourable man to take less than the price he asks for any article they may wish to purchase of him, should be considered a direct insult, and a dark reflection upon his character.[61]

In addition, Hersey equally distrusted commercial trickery and legal maneuverings as violations of economic morality, warning parents to guide their children away from law and commercial careers because of the temptations inherent in both.[62] Religious scruples, for Hersey, were always to take precedence over economic expediency.

Most significantly, Hersey's condemnation of modern commerce was matched by his advocacy for the labor theory of value. "If we withhold from others that which they are justly entitled to, and which belongs of right to them, we are as certainly *unjust* as if we had stolen or taken their property by force or fraud." Contemporary commercial practices were inherently unrighteous because the consumer was encouraged to purchase at the cheapest price possible, regardless of any concern for artisan profit. In an argument that mirrored those of the most ardent trade unionists, Hersey equated low wages and buying based on cheapest prices with stealing.[63] Such morality not only empowered artisans in the name of Christian justice, it also

---

60. Hersey, *Privilege of Those Born of God*, 106.

61. Hersey, *Advice to Parents*, 81, cited in Sutton, *Journeymen for Jesus*, 126.

62. Hersey, *Importance of Small Things*, 113. Hersey also cautioned his audience against dependence on credit and warned them to forbear accumulation. "*Don't save and then suffer it to accumulate on your hands,* or it will be like the excess of manna which the covetous Israelites gathered and laid up for future use; *it bred worms and stank.*" Ibid., 291.

63. Hersey, *Importance of Small Things*, 45, 276; idem, *Appeal on Slavery*, 63. For contrasting interpretations of Hersey's producerism, see Laurie, *Working People of Philadelphia*, 140; and William R. Sutton, "Tied to the Whipping Post: New Labor History and Evangelical Artisans in the Early Republic," *Labor History* 36 (1996): 251-81.

delineated the responsibilities of those outside direct production, and epitomized the breadth of the demands of producerist respectability.

Emerging Methodist Embourgeoisement

To summarize, then, the producerist respectability of Hawkins, Stilwell, Hersey, and others provided the foundations for Methodist artisans in the early republic to oppose economic exploitation and cultural embourgeoisement. As American culture developed, however, other Methodists joined the general social order in accepting capitalist innovations while ignoring producerist limitations, and embracing a more fashionable respectability while increasingly depriviliging the rough. A number of factors influenced this change. The simple fact of unprecedented opportunity and higher standards of living available to white Americans led many into substituting concern for how wealth was gained with concern for how portions of excess wealth were to be given away. According to John Wesley's oft-repeated doctrine of stewardship, "If those who *gain all they can*, and *save all they can*, will likewise *give all they can*, then the more they gain, the more they will grow in grace, and the more treasure they will lay up in heaven."[64] In addition, the demands of disestablishment made Methodists dependent on the largesse of contributors who were not likely to look favorably on criticisms of the genesis of their affluence.[65] At the same time, the heightened emotion and direct experience of the Holy Spirit—the foundation of primitive Methodist spirituality—fell into disfavor, as evangelical religion became more rational.[66] And the rough were further marginalized through the growing recognition, sensationalized by the popular press, of family

---

64. John Wesley, "Thoughts Upon Methodism," § 11, *The Bicentennial Edition of the Works of John Wesley*, ed. Frank Baker (35 vols. projected; Nashville: Abingdon Press, 1984), 9:530. This maxim was first given in Sermon 50, "The Use of Money," *Works* 2:266-80. See also Sermon 68, "The Wisdom of God's Counsels," § 16, *Works* 2:561; Sermon 87, "The Danger of Riches," § II.6, *Works* 3:237-8; and Sermon 122, "Causes of the Inefficacy of Christianity," § 9, *Works* 4:91. Much has been made of this maxim, but the context is usually ignored. Wesley offered this solution as a way for increasingly wealthy Methodists to escape what he referred to as "the nethermost hell."

65. *Mutual Rights and Christian Intelligencer* 2 (5 June 1830): 164; *Wesleyan Repository* 2 (July 1822): 90; *Mutual Rights* 1 (1825): 394; 2 (1826): 135, 276-77.

66. A contemporary article in the *Catholic Sentinel* described Methodism as "*irreligious, fanatic, and ignorant*" and "a living disgrace to the literature, liberality, and intellect of the age" because they had no "gentlemen of literary ability, of historical knowledge, or of expansive mind among them." *Methodist Protestant* 2 (22 July 1835): 55. This kind of residual prejudice was in fact one reason for some Methodists to overcompensate in the direction of fashionability.

turmoil caused by intemperate or undisciplined workers. Finally, pre-occupation with other issues of socioeconomic and cultural morality, especially slavery, drew off the reform energies of many, and would lead, by the 1840s, to the splintering of Methodism in a manner that presaged the fate of the nation. Even this development affected the reconstructions of respectability, as the vitriol earlier heaped on the overly ambitious in the North was, in a more narrow focus, now directed solely at aristocratic and exploitative southern planters. And while some Methodists turned their entire attention to the problem of slavery, others despaired of achieving perfection on this earth, concentrating instead on private and individualized religious experience and rejecting calls to achieve social justice through legislation.

The end result was a new approach to wealth and ambition. Methodist Protestant leader Nicholas Snethen, for instance, had earlier in his career favorably paraphrased John Wesley's warning: "Let all preaching-houses be built plain and decent; but not more expensively than is absolutely unavoidable. Otherwise the necessity of raising money will make rich men necessary to us. But if so, we must be dependent on them, yea, and governed by them. And then farewell to the Methodist discipline, if not doctrine too."[67] But elsewhere Snethen had reversed himself. "The old Methodist precautions against rich men . . . were only one eyed," he asserted. Instead, "we will neither preach nor write against money, but try to teach the people how to make it minister to their own liberty, while it feeds and clothes those who labour for them in the gospel." Snethen went on to recommend enlisting the aid of prosperous Methodists in checking any potential abuse of power from among the itinerants. And in praise of genteel refinement, he wrote, "As a people we must readily and speedily give up all our old peculiar Methodist prejudices. . . . Gentleness and courtesy have now become essentially parts of our religion. The old boast, viz. I am a plain spoken man, must no longer be indulged in."[68]

---

67. Wesley, "Large Minutes," Q. 63, *The Works of John Wesley*, 3rd ed., ed. Thomas Jackson (London: Wesleyan Methodist Book Room, 1872; reprint ed., Grand Rapids: Baker, 1979), 8:332. Snethen's version went, "The maxim once was; and if not a golden one, it was regarded as a true one, 'Let our houses be built plain; otherwise rich men will become necessary to us, and then farewell to Methodist discipline.'" Nicholas Snethen, *Essays on Lay Representation and Church Government* (Baltimore, 1835), xxv.

68. *Mutual Rights and Christian Intelligencer* 1 (Jan. 20, 1829), 38; *Methodist Protestant* (April 1, 1835), cited in D. S. Stephens, comp., *Defense of the Views of the Reformers*, (Indianapolis, 1884), no. 1, 22. Similarly, the proper response in opposing the avaricious, the ambitious, and the libertine, was to emulate their methods and attitudes in the service of the church. *Mutual Rights and Methodist Protestant* 1 (April 15, 1831), 115. The official Methodist Protestant *Discipline* also made this distinction, with the dress code calling for keeping clear "of the two extremes; antiquated singularity on the one hand, and fashionable foppishness on the other." *Constitution and Discipline of the Methodist Protestant Church* (Baltimore, 1830), 49.

Hawkins, Hersey, and Stilwell were clearly affected by such cultural shifts, but in many ways each remained true in his own way to the traditional ideals of producerism and respectability. John Hersey never left episcopal Methodism or abandoned his excoriation of the overly ambitious; relying on his ability to challenge individual economic sin through pointed preaching and austere example, Hersey held forth a producerist vision to which many were still drawn even as they failed to insist on its strictures as part of orthodox practice. In one sense, "Father Hersey," as he was popularly known, served as a Mother Teresa figure for Methodists increasingly infatuated with unrestricted economic practices and embourgeoisement. Embodying a more primitive (in fact, just barely respectable) lifestyle and advocating ethical positions difficult for increasingly comfortable Methodists to follow, Hersey became a well-respected yet marginalized crank—a moral surrogate for those who recognized the appropriateness of his prophetic denunciations but still lacked the will to follow his countercultural lead. In later years, antislavery became his passion, and although Hersey remained deeply committed to producerist morality until his death in 1862, his individualist ethics did not lend themselves to the kind of organized opposition to capitalism (or slavery) espoused by William Stilwell and the New York Society for Promoting Communities.

William Stilwell, for his part, pursued a slightly more convoluted path. His leadership of the Methodist Society in New York succeeded admirably throughout most of the 1820s, and in 1825 Stilwell began to publish a weekly religious paper, *The Friendly Visitor*, which reflected Methodist ambivalence toward issues of prosperity and respectability. In May 1825, for instance, Stilwell published a two-part article entitled "An Address to Master Mechanics, Whom it May Concern," concerning the problems of alcohol abuse on the job.[69] The anonymous author of this piece began by labeling the intemperate worker, in rough terminology, as neither "a fit husband, a good parent, nor a true friend." To supplant the tradition of on-the-job drinking to "animate" artisans, the author suggested that masters supply their journeymen with "a small luncheon twice a day" to guarantee a healthy, industrious work force.[70] After proposing the morality (not just the

---

69. This was a legitimate issue, as alcohol abuse levels reached record proportions in the 1820s. William J. Rorabaugh, *The Alcoholic Republic: An American Tradition* (New York: Oxford University Press, 1979), 233.

70. *Friendly Visitor* 1 (21 May 1825): 164-65.

expediency) of hiring those "who labour for those families, instead of those who spend all their earnings, for that which destroys both soul and body, and who never take any thing home to their families but poverty," the author asked, "Which has the greatest appearance of Tyranny, for one man to bend the minds of a hundred men to the welfare of their families and society, or for a hundred men to impoverish their families, by spending all their earnings for that which cannot benefit themselves or families?"[71] Whereas the author presented this argument as an archetypically respectable solution to a real problem, the trajectory of his reasoning would also prove amenable to capitalist control of workers.

In a similar turnaround, William Stilwell published a plea by the British Wesleyan Richard Reece for the efficacy of rented pews, one of the innovations that had driven him out of the John Street Church five years earlier. Although Reece admitted that the "fear of introducing Aristocracy into the Church" was "salutary," he claimed that making "the rich pay for their superior accommodations . . . enables us to build chapels for the benefit of the poor, where we could not otherwise raise them."[72] This new perspective freed the wealthy to maintain their evangelical standing if their profits promoted evangelical ends, and exhibited a willingness to suspend judgment regarding the accumulation of that wealth. The switch from espousing biblical solutions addressing maldistribution of wealth and the systemic causes of poverty at the points of production and exchange to enlisting the fruits of acquired wealth to assuage the pain of poverty was a significant harbinger of the future.

In other articles, however, Stilwell steadfastly maintained his espousal of producerism and rejection of genteel or ambitious innovation. In a perceptive article describing the changes in camp meetings, Stilwell decried the fact that it was now "fashionable" for Methodists to attend such gatherings, which had become essentially recreational rather than revivalistic.[73] In "The Sins of Trade," moreover, a pseudonymous author ("Crito") described a number of immoral commercial practices emerging in the nascent capitalist economy. Specifically rebuked were the "*dashing* tradesman" (whose obvious ambition and addiction to fashionable pretension would lead him to questionable credit procedures), the "*grasping* tradesman" (whose willingness to go to extremes to eliminate competition knew

---

71. *Friendly Visitor* 1 (28 May 1825): 173.
72. Ibid.
73. *Friendly Visitor* 1 (12 August 1825): 263.

no bound), and the *"grinding* tradesman" (whose commitment to personal success would necessitate oppressing his workers). And Crito concluded with a prophetic denunciation of subsequent capitalist development (and the undermining of producerist respectability) articulating the fear that such innovations might well "ruin all little tradesmen (who are often the most worthy) and reduce trade into the hands of a few overgrown monopolizers."[74]

After a year, *The Friendly Visitor* folded, with Stilwell explaining that his other ministerial duties simply demanded more time. Throughout the 1820s the Methodist Society continued to flourish, but by the end of the decade its critique of Methodist episcopacy and gentility was overshadowed by the turmoil that ended with the Methodist Protestant schism. By 1830 Stilwell's old ally, James Covel, had moved on to rapprochement with similar-minded reformers centered in Baltimore; when his efforts at reforming the Methodist polity through lay representation failed, Covel helped form the new Methodist Protestant Church. Covel then moved to Rochester where he led the Genesee Conference into immediate agitation to force abolition into the official discipline of the new denomination. Stilwell, for his part, pursued a model of creating an alternative independent congregation rather than attempting to reform the increasingly resistant MEC, and although he successfully led a vital Methodist congregation until his death in 1851, he soon disappeared from a position of wider influence.[75]

John Hawkins's subsequent career was the most intriguing. The success he and other journeymen hatters enjoyed in 1833 apparently did not last long, nor did the consolations of his faith. In the mid-1830s, Hawkins disappeared from both trade union and Methodist Protestant leadership, as he lapsed into increasingly acute alcohol abuse. In June 1841, after a particularly serious binge, Hawkins attended a meeting of the fledgling Washington Temperance Society, a group of respectable artisans who rejected both the contemporary alcohol-centered rough subculture of the workplace and the patronizing ministrations of elite temperance speakers.[76] Through the manly cama-

---

74. *Friendly Visitor* 1 (5 February 1825): 42-44.
75. Sutton, *Journeymen for Jesus*, 95, 106.
76. John Zug, *The Foundation, Progress, and Principles of the Washington Temperance Society of Baltimore* (Baltimore: J. D. Toy, 1842); Ian R. Tyrrell, *Sobering Up: From Temperance to Prohibition in Antebellum America, 1800–1860* (Westport, Conn.: Greenwood Press, 1979), 159-90; Milton A. Maxwell, "The Washington Movement," *Quarterly Journal of Studies on Alcohol* 11 (1950): 412-27; Jonathan Zimmerman, "Dethroning King Alcohol: The Washingtonians in Baltimore, 1840–45," *Maryland Historical Magazine* 87 (1992): 375-98.

raderie and boisterous empowerment of the Washingtonians, Hawkins returned to sobriety and Methodist Protestantism, seeing his Washingtonian-inspired rehabilitation as leading him back to evangelical-salvation.[77] The Washingtonian success was built on the testimony of ex-drunks at their revival-like meetings, and Hawkins proved to be one of their most effective speakers. Less than a year after his "conversion," temperance leaders in New York City called for Washingtonian missionaries, and the Baltimoreans sent Hawkins. The response was overwhelming, and a new occupation for the ex-hatter materialized. For the rest of his life (until his death in 1858), Hawkins crisscrossed the country as one of the preeminent temperance lecturers of the time. And although he never returned to his artisan work, his commitment to producerist respectability continued to guide his career. Forever sympathetic to the rough, he made it his goal to lift them, through total abstinence, into social respectability and economic stability. At the same time, he singled out "fashionable rum-sellers" for particular abuse, much to the amusement of his audiences.[78] Because they considered their individual ambition and pursuit of wealth to be more important than the welfare of the community, Hawkins held them responsible for the devastation visited upon drunks and their families. It was precisely the same argument he had directed toward the exploitative master hatters' combination back in 1833.

The Fate of Producerist Respectability in Later Methodism

A final question remains: What became of Methodist devotion to producerist respectability? The answer is, of course, multifaceted and deserves more attention than can be paid to it here. Although Methodism continued its assimilation to mainstream culture, subsequent schisms continued to center on these issues of respectability, with the Nazarene defection caused in part by perceived Methodist worldliness, and Holiness and pentecostal dissatisfaction generated to some extent by Methodist rejection of "rough" spirituality.

---

77. William G. Hawkins, *Life of John H. W. Hawkins* (Boston: J. P. Jewett & Co., 1859), 117. In March 1842, the Methodist Protestants of Malden, Massachusetts, officially ordained Hawkins. Ibid., 218.

78. Ibid., 71, 348. In a related (and well-received) denunciation of the fashionable, Hawkins singled out two young dandies leaving his speech early. "Ho, you gentlemanly wine-drinkers, you need not retire, for I shall say nothing to you this evening. My business lies wholly with the poor unfortunate drunkards. I wish first to save them, and when I have done with them, I will turn to you, and it will only be a continuance of my work, for as sure as you go on drinking your wine, by the time they are all reclaimed, you will assuredly be in their place and need the same charity." *Journal of the American Temperance Union* 7 (August 1843): 128.

Similarly, the counterhegemonic ideals of producerism persisted, as evidenced in significant Methodist participation in New England strikes against factory exploitation in the 1840s and 1850s; in National Labor Union and Knights of Labor trade unionism during the 1860s, 1870s, and 1880s; in the Populist movement of the 1890s; and in the Homestead and Pullman strikes in the same decade.[79] But the fact remains that such activities were not necessarily endorsed by official Methodism or even the majority of the rank and file.

These ambiguities of Methodist reaction to producerist respectability were made manifest in child-rearing decisions made by John Hawkins on behalf of his son, William George, and his son's subsequent career. Hawkins was insistent that his son receive an education to guarantee the latter's independence from the vagaries of artisan life, and the younger Hawkins graduated in due time from Wesleyan University. With his father's blessing, William became a clergyman (albeit a "low-church" Episcopalian) and had become active in various reform movements by the time the elder Hawkins died in 1858. Because John had never enjoyed a sufficiently level of prosperity to guarantee a comfortable situation for his widow (William's mother), William quickly put together a biography of his famous father, with proceeds to go to Mrs. Hawkins. Interestingly enough, in this lengthy biography William barely mentioned his father's participation in the Methodist Protestant upheaval, and omitted reference to his father's trade union activism altogether. But this is not to suggest that the younger Hawkins uncritically endorsed capitalist innovation or pursued a life of genteel complacency. Although there is little evidence related to the latter, William Hawkins was very active in the antebellum

---

79. Robert Craig, "The Underside of History: American Methodism, Capitalism, and Popular Struggle," *Methodist History* 24 (1989): 73-88; Jama Lazerow, *Religion and the Working Class in Antebellum America* (Washington, D.C.: Smithsonian Institution Press, 1995); idem, "Religion and Labor Reform in Antebellum America: The World of William Field Young," *American Quarterly* 38 (1986): 265-86; idem, "Religion and the New England Mill Girl," *New England Quarterly* 60 (1987): 429-53; idem, "Spokesmen for the Working Class: Protestant Clergy and the Labor Movement in Antebellum New England," *Journal of the Early Republic* 13 (1993): 323-54; Murphy, *Ten Hours Labor;* Ken Fones-Wolf, *Trade Union Gospel: Christianity and Labor in Industrial Philadelphia, 1865–1915* (Philadelphia: Temple University Press, 1989); Goodwyn, *Democratic Promise;* David P. Demarest Jr., *"The River Ran Red": Homestead, 1892* (Pittsburgh: University of Pittsburgh Press, 1992), 107-12, 121-22; and Nick Salvatore, *Eugene V. Debs: Citizen and Socialist* (Urbana: University of Illinois Press, 1982), 62-68, 151-52, 229-31, 236-40, 311-12. See also Mark Shantz, "Piety in Providence: The Class Dimensions of Religious Experience in Providence, Rhode Island, 1790–1860" (Emory University Ph.D. thesis, 1991) and Gregory Kaster, "'We will not be slaves to avarice': The American Labor Jeremiad, 1837–1877" (Boston University Ph.D. thesis, 1990).

abolitionist struggle as well as in post–Civil War efforts to aid ex-slaves, and, through this work, to incorporate the values of respectability into organized help for freedmen. Still, it seems clear that William Hawkins's notion of the respectable ideal was somewhat different from his father's.[80]

Yet another hatters' strike in Baltimore, this one in 1844, revealed more of the variabilities of producerist respectability. John Hawkins, of course, had long since embarked on his Washingtonian career, but the complaints of the hatters were essentially the same; they were being denied a liveable share of the profits their labor was generating, and concomitant downward mobility was threatening their respectable standing. And once again, the responses of various masters were made public. Commended for maintaining high wages was the Jacob Rogers firm. Rogers, a prominent Methodist, was recently deceased, and his sons were carrying on the tradition of resisting exploitative associations, as was evident in Rogers's apparent refusal to join the original combination in 1833. But the Rogers legacy was enigmatic; Jacob Rogers had been active in expelling Methodist Protestant dissidents in 1828 and had supported the unpopular building of the fashionable Charles Street Methodist Church. Equally puzzling was the stance of Methodist lay leader and master hatter, Charles Towson. In the 1830s, Towson had been president of the militant journeymen hatters union, yet now he was listed as unfriendly to the demands of his former compatriots.

But there was little ambiguity in the response of another master hatter, George Quail. Quail, too, was a Methodist lay leader and had been vocal in his support of the producerist arguments of the journeymen in 1833. Though not an alcoholic himself, Quail had become one of the leaders of the Baltimore Washingtonians in the 1840s in their drive to restore their fallen comrades to respectability. And in 1844 he remained in the vanguard of producerist respectability. Publicly praised for being nonexploitative by the striking journeymen, Quail justified their confidence by placing an ad during the strike in a local paper, identifying himself as a "No Combination" man, and introducing the note with the traditional slogan of artisan producers, "Live and Let Live." In the ad, Quail reiterated his determination to honor his commitments to both workers and customers by offering quality workmanship and by paying his journeymen

---

80. *Journal of the American Temperance Union* 22 (1858): 169; 23 (1859): 19, 48.

"highest wages." In his Washingtonian activity, in his pro-journey-men position eleven years earlier, and in this final statement, George Quail epitomized the tradition of producerist respectability that influenced Methodists to question the social and moral implications of capitalist transformation in the early republic.[81] And in these times of rampant corporate hegemony, a tradition capable of such prophetic challenge may well remain vital. As Christopher Lasch has asserted, the "producer ethic" of the respectable middling classes was often "anticapitalist but not socialist or social democratic, at once radical, even revolutionary, and deeply conservative; and it deserves a more attentive hearing, on its own terms, than it has usually received."[82]

81. Baltimore *Sun*, 10, 15 February, 2 March 1844. Quail's suspicion of unregulated ambition was also evident in his simultaneous Sabbatarian involvement. The only ambiguity in Quail's Methodist activity was his membership in the upscale Charles Street Methodist Church.

82. Lasch, *True and Only Heaven*, 205.

CHAPTER 8

The Methodist Invasion of Congregational New England

Richard D. Shiels

There is nothing more thrilling in American ecclesiastical annals than the study of the introduction of Methodism into New England.[1]
Samuel F. Upham, 1891

Few twentieth-century historians have shared Samuel Upham's sentiments. Studies of New England Congregationalism abound, but recent histories of New England Methodism are rare.[2] Rather than Methodist beginnings, it is the resuscitation of Congregationalism in the same decade in which Methodists came to New England that has drawn scholarly attention. However, these two developments are linked. Both are part of a much-studied development historians call

1. Samuel F. Upham, "History of the Methodist Episcopal Church in Bristol, Rhode Island" (1891), MSS in the New England Methodist Historical Society at the Boston University School of Theology.
2. Early American Methodism is a primary focus of several excellent books published within the past few years. These include Dee E. Andrews, *The Methodists and Revolutionary America, 1760–1820: The Shaping of an Evangelical Culture* (Princeton, N.J.: Princeton University Press, 2000) and John Wigger, *Taking Heaven by Storm: Methodism and the Rise of Popular Christianity in America* (New York: Oxford University Press, 1998). Christine Leigh Heyrman, *Southern Cross: The Beginnings of the Bible Belt* (Chapel Hill: University of North Carolina Press, 1997) and Nathan Hatch, *The Democratization of American Christianity* (New Haven: Yale University Press, 1989) both feature Methodism prominently. Thomas Umbell, "The Making of An American Denomination: Methodism in New England Religious Culture" (Johns Hopkins University Ph.D. dissertation, 1992), is the sole recent study of Methodism in New England. Umbell does not challenge the dominant interpretations of New England religion in this period.

the "Second Great Awakening." Moreover, when the Second Great Awakening had passed, Methodist churches were nearly as prominent as Congregational churches in New England.

New England Congregationalism

The resuscitation of Congregationalism has become a familiar chapter in histories of American religion. Congregationalism, of course, descended directly from New England Puritanism.[3] Most histories say that New England's churches declined in the late–seventeenth century, regained strength again in the Great Awakening of the mid–eighteenth century, and then declined again after the Great Awakening had passed. Indeed, New England religion is said to have reached its lowest point during the Revolution itself. However, revivals of religion breathed new life into Congregational churches in the last decade of the eighteenth century and the first three decades of the nineteenth century. These revivals constitute New England's Second Great Awakening.[4]

Occasionally historians have challenged this pattern. Jon Butler, for example, has argued that the Great Awakening is merely a historian's construct. Douglas Sweet has challenged the reality of religious decline in the decades of the American Revolution.[5] However, both literary and numerical evidence exist to refute Butler and Sweet, at least for New England Congregationalism.

The literary evidence is well known and well mined by historians. It includes Jonathan Edwards's "Faithful Narrative of the Surprising Work of God in Northampton," subsequent narratives published by Thomas Prince in the *Christian History*, scores of revival narratives and spiritual biographies in journals such as the *Connecticut*

---

3. The use of the term *Congregational* requires an explanation. The churches here referred to as "Congregational" were descended directly from New England Puritanism; most of them would affiliate with the Congregational denomination, which evolved in the early nineteenth century. In Connecticut and Massachusetts they were the "established" churches until 1818 and 1833, respectively. However, they were not uniformly referred to as "Congregational" in the late eighteenth or early nineteenth century. Billy Hibbard and Lorenzo Dow, early converts from this tradition to Methodism, called these churches "Presbyterian."

4. See, for example, Sydney E. Ahlstrom, *A Religious History of the American People* (New Haven: Yale University Press, 1972); Robert T. Handy, *A History of the Churches in the United States and Canada* (New York: Oxford University Press, 1976); Mark Noll, *A History of Christianity in the United States and Canada* (Grand Rapids: Eerdmans, 1992); and Peter Williams, *America's Religions: Traditions and Cultures* (New York: Macmillan, 1990).

5. Jon Butler, "Enthusiasm Described and Decried: The Great Awakening as Interpretive Fiction," *Journal of American History* 69 (1982): 305-25; Douglas Sweet, "Church Vitality and the American Revolution," *Church History* 45 (1976): 341-58.

Evangelical Magazine, the *Autobiography of Lyman Beecher,* and many other sources.[6] Documents like these reflect the perceptions and rhetoric of clergymen, and must be supplemented with other sources. Fortunately, in New England, significant numbers of Congregational church records remain. These corroborate the pattern.

Church records reveal membership trends. Figure 1 illustrates the admissions for Old South Church in Boston from 1730 to 1835.[7] Dramatic peaks on figure 1 suggest that Old South Church probably experienced revivals of religion in 1741, 1756, 1822, 1827, and 1831. All of these peaks except that in 1756 confirm the literary descriptions of New England's two Great Awakenings. Further, figure 1 reveals that admissions reached their nadir in 1776, remained very low through the end of the Revolutionary War, and did not increase dramatically until after 1810.

Figure 1. Annual Admissions to Old South Church,
Boston, 1730–1835

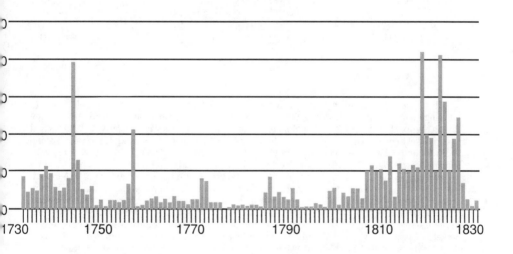

6. Jonathan Edwards, "Faithful Narrative" is in volume 4 of *The Works of Jonathan Edwards,* ed. C. C. Goen (New Haven: Yale University Press, 1972); *The Christian History or General Accounts of the Revival and Progress of the Propagation of Religion in Great Britain and America,* 2 vols. (Boston: Kneeland & Green, 1743–44); *The Connecticut Evangelical Magazine,* 15 vols. (Hartford: Hudson & Goodwin, 1801–1815); Barbara M. Cross, ed. *The Autobiography of Lyman Beecher,* 2 vols. (Cambridge, Mass.: Harvard University Press, 1961).

7. *The Confession of Faith and Form of Covenant of the Old South Church in Boston, Massachusetts* (Boston: Crocker & Brewster, 1855), 86–105. Admissions by transfer from other churches are omitted from figure 1; only persons who were joining a church for the first time in their lives are counted.

Old South was similar to many Congregational churches in that it experienced both Awakenings and an intervening period of declension. Figure 2 summarizes the pattern of admissions to ninety-seven Congregational churches in the same period.[8]

Figure 2. Mean Annual Admissions to Ninety-seven New England Congregational Churches, 1730–1835

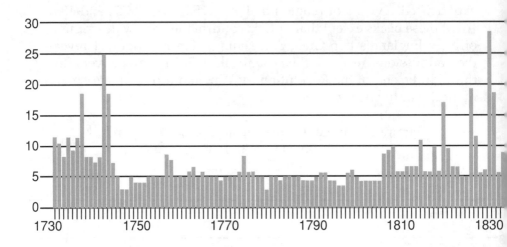

8. Forty-six church records were consulted from Connecticut. From Fairfield County: Huntington, New Canaan, Redding, Stamford, Trumbull, and Wilton. From Hartford County: New Britain, Avon, Granby, and Wethersfield. From Litchfield County: North Canaan, Cornwall Second, Kent, New Milford, Plymouth. From Middlesex County: East Haddam Second, Haddam, Hadlyme Second, Clinton. From New Haven County: Cheshire, Oxford, East Haven, Guilford, Meriden, New Haven, Fair Haven, White Haven, North Haven, Woodbridge. From New London County: Colchester, Colchester Second, Franklin, Goshen (Lebanon), Old Lyme, New London, Norwich, Preston, Stonington, East Stonington. From Tolland County: Bolton, Columbia, Somers, Vernon. From Windham County: Windham, Scotland, and Woodstock. Fifty-one church records were consulted from Massachusetts. From Barnstable County: West Barnstable, Falmouth. From Berkshire County: Great Barrington, Lee, Lenox, Stockbridge. From Bristol County: Attleborough Second, Berkeley, Easton. From Essex County: South Andover, Boxford Second, Danvers, North Haverhill, West Haverhill, Lynn, Marblehead, Methuen, Middleton, Rowley, South Salem. From Franklin County: Sunderland. From Hampden County: Springfield, Wilbraham. From Hampshire County: Belchertown, Ware. From Middlesex County: Cambridge, Framingham, Hopkinton, Lincoln, Newton, Newton Second, Reading, Stoneham, Tewksbury, Wilmington. In Norfolk County: Braintree, Foxborough, Medway Second, Millis, Randolph, Weymouth. In Plymouth County: Hanover, Plymouth. In Suffolk County: Brattle Square, Old South, West Boston. In Worcester County: Brookfield Third, Milford, Millbury, Sutton, West Brookfield. All of these churches were *Congregational* as the term is used here. Gaps occur in most of these records and some of these churches had not yet formed in 1730. For 1730, the sample is thirty-one churches, or 10.5 percent of the Congregational churches in these states. The sample is never less than forty churches after 1733.

An average of twenty-five new members (ten men, fifteen women) joined these churches in 1741, the peak year of the Great Awakening. An average of twenty-nine (ten men, nineteen women) joined in 1831, the culminating year of the Second Great Awakening. In between, admissions varied from year to year, but did not rise above an average of nine from 1743 to 1808. The low point was clearly 1776 to 1791, when admissions averaged four or five a year in each of these ninety-seven Congregational churches.

Together, literary evidence and church records suggest that New England's Congregational churches did in fact experience two periods of religious awakening separated by decades of declension. The resuscitation of Congregationalism began in the last decade of the eighteenth century. Edward Dorr Griffin, the Congregational pastor in Farmington, Connecticut, identified 1792 as the year in which "an unbroken series of revivals" began in New England.[9] The year 1798 was one in which revival fires lit up Litchfield and Hartford Counties in Connecticut.[10] Twelve percent of the ninety-seven churches surveyed for this study experienced a revival in 1792; 22 percent experienced revivals in 1798.[11] Early issues of the *Connecticut Evangelical Magazine* identified both of these years as "special seasons of grace" because revivals were widespread at these times among Congregational

It is fifty churches, 11.7 percent of all churches, in 1740; seventy-five, or 14.5 percent, in 1760. The sample is never less than fifty after 1740, or sixty after 1746, or seventy-five after 1760. Seventy-five churches represent 11.9 percent of all Congregational churches in these states in 1800, 10.3 percent in 1830. The number of Congregational churches in each decade in Massachusetts is found in Joseph S. Clark, *A Historical Sketch of the Congregational Churches of Massachusetts, from 1620 to 1858* (Boston: Congregational Board of Publications, 1858). The same information for Connecticut appears in *Contributions to the Ecclesiastical History of Connecticut* (New Haven: W. L. Kingsly, 1861) 1:341ff.

9. Edward Dorr Griffin, "A Letter to the Rev. Dr. William Sprague," *Lectures on Revivals of Religion*, ed. W. B. Sprague (New York: D. Appleton, 1833), 359.

10. See Bennet Tyler, *New England Revivals, as They Existed at the Close of the Eighteenth and Beginning of the Nineteenth Centuries. Compiled Principally from Narratives Published in the Connecticut Evangelical Magazine* (Boston: Massachusetts Sabbath School Society, 1846).

11. This sentence is based upon an arithmetic analysis of the church records cited. Identifying revivals by counting admissions requires methodical criteria. First, admissions by transfer must be eliminated; only persons joining the church for the first time can be counted. Second, differences in the size of the churches must be considered. Smaller churches than Old South Church experienced significant revivals but recorded fewer admissions. The *Religious Intelligencer*, a Congregational journal published in New Haven, referred to revivals in which as few as twelve persons were added to a church; see *Religious Intelligencer* 16 (1831): 30. It must be remembered that many revival "converts" had previously joined a church; hence, admissions understate the extent of a revival. I have divided the number of admissions in each church in each year by the mean number of admissions to that church in all years. A result of 1.0 identified an average year for the church in question. A result of 4.0 or higher was taken to be a revival if (a) twelve or more persons joined that church in that year; (b) admissions that year were greater than those in either of the two preceding or succeeding years; and (c) revival narratives confirmed that revivals were widespread in the area in that year.

churches. Subsequent "seasons of grace" appear in figure 2 and are confirmed in similar evangelical magazines: 1808–9, 1816, 1821, 1827, and 1831–32.[12] Hence, the Second Great Awakening spanned thirty-five to forty years. Nineteenth-century sources estimated that membership in Congregational churches climbed from 75,000 in 1800 to 140,000 in 1830, and to nearly 200,000 in 1850.[13]

Membership is but one measure of vitality, of course. Revivals of religion not only moved converts to join churches, but inspired both converts and members to deeper commitment and greater involvement. Journals such as the *Connecticut Evangelical Magazine,* the *Massachusetts Missionary Magazine,* the *Panoplist,* and many others were also founded very early in the nineteenth century. These journals renewed the efforts of Thomas Prince, who had published the *Christian History* at the time of the first Awakening. Nothing like them had appeared in New England in the intervening period of declension. Missionary societies, Bible societies, tract societies, Sunday school societies, and similar organizations were established under Congregational leadership in a quarter century starting in 1795. The "Benevolent Empire," well known to historians, was led by Congregationalists from New England as well as Presbyterians from other parts of the country. Both the journals and the vast array of evangelical societies stand as additional evidence of Congregational renewal.[14]

The scholarship on Congregational renewal is rich. David W. Kling, *A Field of Divine Wonders: The New Divinity and Village Revivals in Northwestern Connecticut, 1792–1822* (1993) is the latest book on Congregationalists in New England's Second Great Awakening.

12. Using the criteria described above, revivals can be identified in 26 percent of the churches studied in 1808, 32 percent in 1816, 26 percent in 1821, 43 percent in 1827, and 65 percent in 1831. These years are also identified in Charles Roy Keller, *The Second Great Awakening in Connecticut* (New Haven: Yale University Press, 1942) as years in which revivals were especially widespread; Keller's analysis is based upon revival narratives in evangelical journals.

13. Robert Baird, *The Christian Retrospect and Register: A Summary of the Scientific, Moral, and Religious Progress of the First Half of the 19th Century* (New York: M. W. Dodd, 1851), 220; Daniel Dorchester, *Christianity in the United States from the First Settlement* (New York: Phillips & Hunt, 1888), 373, 733, 349. These estimates are for the United States and not merely New England.

14. The *Connecticut Evangelical Magazine,* the *Massachusetts Missionary Magazine,* and the *Panoplist* began publication in 1801, 1803, and 1804 respectively. A sampling of these voluntary societies and the dates they were formed is as follows: the Connecticut Missionary Society, 1795; the American Board of Commissioners for Foreign Missions, 1810; the Domestic Missionary Society, 1816; the Connecticut Religious Tract Society, 1807; the Connecticut Bible Society, 1809; and the Connecticut Sabbath School Union, 1825. All of these were begun by New England Congregationalists. See Richard Shiels, "The Connecticut Clergy in the Second Great Awakening" (Ph.D. diss., Boston University, 1976), 418-24.

Earlier monographs include Sidney Mead's *Nathaniel William Taylor, Connecticut Liberal* and Charles Roy Keller's *The Second Great Awakening in Connecticut*, both published in 1942, as well as Stephen Berk's *Calvinism Versus Democracy: Timothy Dwight and the Origins of American Evangelical Orthodoxy* (1974).[15] None of these works give more than passing mention of the Methodists. Kling admits that Methodists may have been important elsewhere, but argues that they were not important in the counties he studies. Keller wrote that Congregationalists were "so dominant . . . that the story of the Second Great Awakening can be told largely in Congregational terms." So it has been told.[16]

These books disagree primarily over which Congregational clergy started the Second Great Awakening. Mead thought the movement began at Yale, under the preaching of Timothy Dwight. Mead's student, Stephen Berk, claimed that Dwight "contrived" the Second Great Awakening. Both are clearly wrong, since Dwight did not lead a revival until 1802. On the other hand, Keller gives credit to a school of Congregational clergy he labels "New Light." Kling is more precise than Keller. Kling argues that it was the third generation of "New Divinity" clergy (a particular kind of "New Light") who inspired the Second Great Awakening, at least in the two counties he has studied.[17]

Congregationalism was indeed resuscitated in the Second Great Awakening and yet, nationally, membership in Congregational churches fell behind membership in Methodist churches by 1840. The Methodist "upstarts" won, according to sociologists Roger Finke and Rodney Stark.[18] Within New England, historian Abel Stevens wrote in 1866, the Congregationalists remained the largest denomination and

---

15. David W. Kling, *A Field of Divine Wonders: The New Divinity and Village Revivals in Northwestern Connecticut, 1792–1822* (University Park: Pennsylvania State University Press, 1993); Sidney Mead, *Nathaniel William Taylor, Connecticut Liberal* (Chicago: University of Chicago, 1942); Keller, *The Second Great Awakening;* and Stephen Berk, *Calvinism versus Democracy: Timothy Dwight and the Origins of American Evangelical Orthodoxy* (Hamden, Conn.: Archon Books, 1974) See also Richard Birdsall, "The Second Great Awakening and the New England Social Order," *Church History* 39 (1970): 345-64, and Richard Shiels, "The Second Great Awakening in Connecticut: Critique of the Traditional Interpretation," *Church History* 49 (1980): 401-15.

16. Kling, *Field of Divine Wonders,* 233-36; Keller, *The Second Great Awakening,* 9. For an account that includes the Methodist contribution, see Richard Shiels "The Origins of the Second Great Awakening in New England: Goshen, Connecticut 1798–9," *Mid-America: An Historical Review* 78 (1996): 279-301.

17. Shiels, "Second Awakening in Connecticut"; Kling, *Field of Divine Wonders,* 16-43.

18. Finke and Stark, *The Churching of America, 1776–1990: Winners and Losers in Our Religious Economy* (New Brunswick, N.J.: Rutgers University Press, 1992): 54-108.

the Methodists were "the second religious denomination in numerical strength—and the first in progress, reporting about a hundred thousand members, nearly a thousand preachers, at least one academy for each of its conferences, a university, and a theological school."[19] Perhaps both came out winners in the Second Great Awakening. Upon closer scrutiny, the Methodists played a role in Congregational renewal even as they built churches of their own.

The Methodist Invasion

If there were any Methodist institutions in New England prior to 1789 they were a mere handful of isolated "classes" spread across the region.[20] American Methodism was still "largely a Southern phenomenon," as John Wigger has written.[21] A smattering of Methodist preachers, including Charles Wesley and Richard Boardman, had spoken in the region over the preceding decades. The most recent of these had been William Black of Nova Scotia, who passed through Boston and other New England cities on his way to and from the Christmas Conference in New York City in 1784. However, a concerted Methodist mission to New England began in June of 1789. In this month, three itinerant Methodists literally invaded. Freeborn Garrettson, who was stationed in New York at the time, traveled across Connecticut to Boston and back again. He was accompanied by Harry Hoosier, a black Methodist exhorter. Jesse Lee also crossed the New York–Connecticut border and canvassed Connecticut, Rhode Island, and Massachusetts. He preached his first New England sermon in Norwalk, Connecticut, in June. Lee's efforts marked something new, because the Conference had assigned him to work within New England for a period of eighteen months. It might seem strange that Methodists would send evangelists to Connecticut and Massachusetts, states with a Puritan heritage that were renowned for

---

19. Abel Stevens, *The Centenary of American Methodism: A Sketch of Its History, Theology, Practical System, and Success* (New York: Carlton & Porter, 1866), 103.

20. On his first tour of New England in 1789 Jesse Lee found "several instances of little bands of devout persons who had been in the habit of meeting periodically to pray and counsel each other respecting a higher Christian experience." Perhaps these were Methodists. See Abel Stevens, *Memorials of the Early Progress of Methodism in the Eastern States* (Boston: C. H. Peirce, 1852), 23. In the same year, Freeborn Garrettson found a Methodist society with three members meeting in Boston. See James M. Buckley, *A History of Methodism in the United States*, 2 vols. (New York: Christian Literature Co., 1897), 31.

21. Wigger, *Taking Heaven by Storm*, 5.

their churches and colleges—but Jesse Lee had heard that New England's Congregational churches were in a state of great decline.[22]

In each succeeding year additional Methodist preachers were assigned to the region. Like Jesse Lee, these men were itinerant. Often they traveled across New England in pairs. They organized small groups of followers in "classes" and, in time, churches or "societies." They created "circuits" for their itinerary such that they visited every class and society at regular intervals. They nurtured male converts in particular, moving these men up through the ranks of exhorter, local preacher, and circuit rider.[23]

Lee and his colleagues made something of a stir. Years later Nathan Bangs recalled "rumors . . . (in 1789) of a strange man who came to the state from the South and was traveling through its villages on horseback in a costume of Quaker like simplicity." Jesse Lee must have been unlike anyone the citizens of Norwalk had seen before. A massive man—more than three hundred pounds—he stood on the side of the road and shouted or sang to those who passed by.[24] Subsequent circuit riders were smaller in stature but they too were very different from the clergy New Englanders had known before, in both dress and demeanor. One of these, Billy Hibbard, recorded entering a town and hearing small boys proclaim, "He must be a Methodist preacher. See how he looks!" Unfortunately Hibbard did not record how he looked. Certainly he was not dressed in the powdered wig, breeches ending at the knee, knee buckles, white top boots, and silk stockings that were common among Congregational clergy. Whereas the established ministers dressed as members of the elite, Methodist itinerants dressed even more simply than common farmers. Bangs, Hibbard, and Lee were in fact common people lacking either the social stature or the formal education held by New England's Congregational ministers.[25]

22. Stevens, *Memorial of the Early Progress*, 1-25; James Mudge, *History of the New England Conference of the Methodist Episcopal Church 1796–1910* (Boston: New England Conference MEC, 1910): 30ff; Minton Thrift, *Memoir of the Reverend Jesse Lee with Extracts from his Journals* (New York: Bangs & Mason, 1823).

23. "Minutes of the New England Conference of the Methodist Episcopal Church from its beginning in New York in 1796." Typescript in the New England Methodist Historical Society, Boston University School of Theology. George Claude Baker, Jr., *An Introduction to the History of Early New England Methodism* (Durham, N.C.: Duke University Press, 1941), 131-37; Wigger, *Taking Heaven by Storm*, 31-36, 80-87.

24. On Jesse Lee's size, William P. Strickland, ed., *Autobiography of Dan Young, A New England Preacher of the Olden Times* (New York: Carlton & Porter, 1860), 16, 221.

25. Hibbard, *Memoirs*, 103. Abel Stevens, *Life and Times of Nathan Bangs* (New York: Carlton & Porter, 1863), 21-22.

In some areas these preachers drew large audiences. William Black is said to have drawn 1,500 hearers to services in Boston in 1784—so many that the floorboards splintered.[26] Jesse Lee recorded speaking to "as many as could fit in the courthouse" in New Haven in the summer of 1789. His audience included Yale president Ezra Stiles and Jonathan Edwards Jr.[27] Garrettson claimed that he and Harry Hoosier preached to one thousand people under the trees in Sharon, Connecticut, three hundred in Farmington, more than five hundred in Hartford, and more than one thousand in Boston.[28] The six New England states included fewer than five thousand Methodists by 1800, but many more had listened to the Methodist message and considered it. "Our members are few but our hearers are many," Francis Asbury wrote in his *Journal* in 1793, describing the Methodist mission in New England.[29]

Yet Methodist preachers were not generally well received. Many Congregational clergy spoke out against them or attacked their doctrine. Literally scores of anti-Methodist treatises were published over the next four decades.[30] In many New England towns, the Congregational clergy had the power to bar itinerant preachers from use of the meetinghouse—and often did so when the preacher was a Methodist. Often the civil authorities denied them use of the courthouse as well. Thomas Ware, one of Jesse Lee's successors, claimed that he never met a friendly Congregational clergyman; rather, he wrote, they were often "violent in their opposition to us and the rough manner in which I was usually treated by them rendered me unwilling to come in contact with them."[31]

Others in authority tried to thwart Methodist efforts as well. Husbands forbade their wives, and parents barred their adolescent children from attending Methodist meetings. Billy Hibbard recorded that "many young people that experienced religion were turned out

26. John Atkinson, *Centennial History of Methodism* (New York: Phillips & Hunt, 1884), 333.

27. Jesse Lee, *A Short History of the Methodists in the United States of America* (Baltimore, 1810; reprint, Rutland, Vt.: Academy Books, 1974), 145.

28. Freeborn Garrettson, *American Methodist Pioneer: The Life and Journals of the Rev. Freeborn Garrettson, 1752–1827,* ed. Robert Drew Simpson (Rutland, Vt.: Academy Books, 1984), 141-44, 268-71; Nathan Bangs, *Life of Freeborn Garrettson. Compiled from his Printed and Manuscript Journals and Other Authentic Documents* (New York: Emory & Waugh, 1829), 208-14.

29. Asbury is quoted in Stevens, *Memorials of the Introduction of Methodism* (Boston: C. H. Peirce, 1848), 177. Membership statistics are in Mudge, *History of the New England Conference,* 452-53.

30. See the bibliography of Baker, *Introduction to New England Methodism,* 94-103.

31. Thomas Ware, *Sketches of the Life and Travels of Rev. Thomas Ware* (New York: Mason & Lane, 1840), 212.

of doors by their parents. Some of them were whipped cruelly; two young women were so whipped by their father that the blood ran down from their backs to their feet, and he then turned them out of doors, and they walked fifteen miles to a Methodist society."[32]

Hibbard was himself one of the youth who had been converted in the 1790s by the preaching of a Methodist itinerant in Connecticut. Nathan Bangs, Dan Young, and Lorenzo Dow are other examples of teenagers converted by the Methodists in the 1790s. All four of them eventually left their families to become itinerant preachers; all four faced parental opposition. Bangs's parents were not church members themselves, but they forbade him to join the Methodist society. Young's mother pleaded with him to become a Presbyterian or a Baptist—anything but a Methodist. Dow's parents tried to dissuade him from preaching; Hibbard's father cut off his inheritance.[33]

Acts of violence against Methodist preachers and followers were not uncommon. In New Hampshire, a preacher named Rosebrook Crawford was "drawn on his back across the Connecticut River through the slush over the ice and bidden to go his way in Vermont."[34] In Bristol, Rhode Island, women who attended a Methodist meeting were followed home and pelted with stones. Crops were destroyed, livestock mutilated, and barns burned until two families left town.[35] In Seymour, Connecticut, opponents blocked the chimney of the house where Methodists were meeting and drove them out with smoke.[36] In New Haven, Methodists purchased a meetinghouse from the Sandemanians. A mob formed after midnight, entered the building, and attacked the pulpit with an ax. Methodists waiting in the dark clubbed the mob leaders and chased them from the building.[37] In Provincetown, when Methodists began to build a

---

32. Hibbard is quoted in Stevens, *Memorials of the Early Progress*, 79-81.

33. Billy Hibbard, *Memoirs of the Life and Travels of Billy Hibbard, Minister of the Gospel*, 2d ed. (New York: published for the author, 1843); Stevens, *Life of Nathan Bangs*; Strickland, ed., *Dan Young*; Charles Coleman Sellers, *Lorenzo Dow: The Bearer of the Word* (New York: Minton, Balely, 1928), and Lorenzo Dow, *History of the Cosmopolite or the Writings of Rev. Lorenzo Dow*, 8th ed. (Cincinnati: A. S. Robertson, 1850). Dow preached under Methodist auspices only briefly before being expelled from the Conference and launching a phenomenal career as an independent itinerant.

34. E. Farley Sharp, ed. *Laban Clark: Autobiography about His Early Life from 1778 to 1804* (Rutland, Vt.: Academy Books, 1987), 13.

35. Upham, "History of the Methodist Church in Bristol" (1891).

36. W. C. Sharpe, *Annals of the Methodist Episcopal Church of Seymour, Connecticut* (Seymour, Conn.: Record Print, 1885), 7.

37. George W. Woodruff, *History of Methodism in New Haven. A Discourse Delivered to the United Methodist Congregations of the City on Thanksgiving, November 24, 1859* (New Haven: J. H. Benham, 1859), 5-6.

chapel, a mob tore down the timbers and left an effigy of a circuit rider, tarred and feathered.[38]

Despite such hostility, or perhaps because of it, Methodists made converts. Progress was very slow at first. In Norwalk, where Jesse Lee first spoke, he eventually organized a class of three women. It was months before he organized another class. Still, the numbers who heard Methodist preaching and responded to it were much greater. As early as 1792 Methodist circuit riders were claiming to have led revivals. What they meant was not that they had organized camp meetings or protracted meetings—these would come after the turn of the century—rather what they meant was that large numbers of people in particular communities had responded to Methodist efforts by going through emotional experiences that Methodists and Congregationalists alike might recognize as conversion.[39]

Perhaps the most striking claim in Methodist histories is that Methodists sparked revivals that resulted in large numbers of converts joining Congregational churches. A related claim is that the Methodist example taught the Congregational clergy how to lead revivals in Congregational churches. Here are two ways in which Methodism contributed to the resuscitation of New England Congregationalism.

Abel Stevens, the premier nineteenth-century historian of Methodism, repeats both claims numerous times. For example:

> The fact is unquestionable that Methodism, with its numerous annual camp meetings, its perpetual revivals, its innumerable class meetings, prayer meetings, four day meetings, its emphatic mode of preaching, and its assiduous pastoral labors, **has aroused New England,** infecting or provoking its churches by its example. . . . While we have set an example to our predecessors, and provoked their zeal, it is a well known fact that a large proportion of our converts have been gathered into their churches, carrying with them, we trust, some of the spirit of our cause.[40]

Billy Hibbard was one of Stevens's sources. "I wanted to be a Congregationalist and be respectable," wrote Hibbard, who was converted by Methodist preaching. "But I wanted the love and serious-

---

38. Leroy Lee, *Life and Times of Reverend Jesse Lee* (Nashville: Southern Methodist Publishing House, 1860), 312. Abel Stevens tells the same story but places it in Boston. Stevens, *Memorials of the Introduction of Methodism*, 348.

39. Stevens, *Memorials of the Introduction of Methodism*, 149, 156, 356, 380, 412.

40. Ibid., 45.

ness of the Methodists." A few years later, while working as a Methodist circuit rider in New England, Hibbard wrote:

> Glory be to God, more than three hundred professed to be converted this year. [Unfortunately, it is unclear which year this was.] I know not of one instance where the revival of religion was through the instrumentality of any but the Methodists. Though many joined the Presbyterians and Baptists, they professed to be awakened and converted by attending the Methodist meeting; and there were so many joined them that it became a proverb, "The Methodists shake the bush, and the Presbyterians and Baptists catch the birds."[41]

Lorenzo Dow made the same claim. In the first ten months of his preaching, he says, "600 joined the Methodist society while as many turned to the Presbyterians and Baptists."[42]

Hibbard also claimed that the Congregational clergy copied Methodist techniques. He believed that Timothy Dwight himself had counseled the General Association of (Congregational) clergy to "preach as near like the Methodists as they could and not preach their own doctrines in their own town but to change with a minister of another town." Perhaps Hibbard was mistaken about Dwight. But Hibbard understood his own tradition. John Wesley stated that he had originally commissioned itinerant preachers in England to "provoke the regular ministers into jealousy" and spur them into action.[43]

Further, Samuel Goodrich, son of the Congregational pastor in Fairfield, Connecticut, lends some credence to the notion that Congregationalists followed the Methodist lead. In Fairfield, he wrote, the earliest Methodists caused quite a stir. Many wanted to attack their doctrine, others to run them out of town. His own father was too wise to adopt either course. He adopted evening meetings (which were common among Methodists), first at church and afterward at private houses.

> No doubt, also, he put more fervor into his Sabbath discourses. Deacons and laymen, gifted in speech, were called up to pray and exhort and tell experiences in the private meetings, which were now called conferences. A revival of religious spirit arose even among the

---

41. Hibbard, *Memoirs*, 60, 182-83.
42. Sellers, *Lorenzo Dow*, 49.
43. Hibbard, *Memoirs*, 302; Wesley is quoted in Russell Richey, "Itineracy in Early Methodism," in *Send Me?: The Itineracy in Crisis*, ed. Donald E. Messer (Nashville: Abingdon Press, 1991), 28.

orthodox. . . . And thus what seemed a mania, wrought regeneration; thus orthodoxy was in considerable degree Methodized and Methodism in due time became orthodoxed.[44]

Modern historians have simply overlooked the Methodist contribution to the Second Great Awakening in Connecticut. David Kling, author of the most recent study, credits a band of New Divinity Congregational clergy for inspiring the 1798 "season of grace." By his own account, the clergy he identifies were more like Methodists than most other Congregational clergy. They were less distinguished or wealthy than most other Congregational clergy, although it is true that they were college graduates. Further, they traveled around their counties preaching in pairs and they preached more evangelically than was the norm. However, Kling does not notice these similarities. He admits that Methodists might have provided the spark for religious revivals in some parts of New England, but insists that the Methodists stayed away from Hartford or Litchfield Counties (the counties he studies) in Connecticut until after the "village revivals" of 1798. Methodist records indicate that circuit riders were assigned to these areas every year after 1791 and that membership on that circuit rose to 429 a year later.[45]

The Methodist Alternative

Comparisons of the Congregational and Methodist efforts to compete for New England souls help explain both the controversy Methodism incited and its appeal for many converts. Three themes are important: the doctrines of the two churches; the nature of the community they represented; and the nature of their leadership.

In general, it is fair to say that the Congregationalists were Calvinists and the Methodists were Arminian. The particular doctrines that Billy Hibbard found most controversial as he traveled around New England were "good works, perfection, and falling from grace."[46] Historian Thomas Umbell reminds us that the Calvinist

---

44. Samuel Goodrich, *Recollections of a Lifetime, or Men and Things I Have Seen: In a Series of Familiar Letters to a Friend, Historical, Biographical, Anecdotal, and Descriptive* (New York: Miller, Orton & Mulligan, 1857), 1:216.

45. Kling, *Fields of Wonder*, 233-36. On Methodist activity in the area, see appendix A in Edgar F. Clark, *The Methodist Episcopal Churches of Norwich, Connecticut* (Norwich: n.p., 1867), and "Minutes of the New England Conference," 6.

46. Hibbard, *Memoirs*, 99.

struggle with the doctrines of good works (or justification by works) was older than New England—it was as old as Calvinism itself.[47] Puritans and their Congregational descendants struggled to resist believing some version of this doctrine for generations, and it may be that nearly every Calvinist harbored some Arminian doubts. No wonder, then, that an invasion by outsiders preaching Arminianism was threatening. No wonder that clergy in the Congregational churches refused to let them speak in the meetinghouses and published treatises against them.

Yet the Arminian doctrine of good works was what first attracted Billy Hibbard to the Methodists. For years he had doubted the doctrine of election and had longed for an alternative. He claimed to have received a revelation, several years before Jesse Lee first came to Connecticut, that God would send British preachers who would teach what he believed. He was not the only one to claim foreknowledge of this kind. A Connecticut woman told Freeborn Garrettson that she had dreamed of his visit seven years earlier and recognized him by the doctrine he taught.[48] These were both religious people who felt alienated from the Congregational churches, and there were others like them. In Lynn, Massachusetts, the first town in which significant numbers accepted the Methodist message, a Congregational critic observed that the people were Methodist before they ever heard Lee preach. Methodism took hold in Lynn, Parsons Cooke wrote, because it "took hold of the doctrines which lay in the hearts of all men here."[49]

Doctrine, however, is not the whole story. Methodism threatened communal institutions at the same time that it promised a new kind of community. For one thing, Methodists threatened the tax base of the local churches. Congregational churches were established, at least in Connecticut and Massachusetts: they received a portion of each household's taxes unless the head of the household formally applied to divert the money to a different church. In Lynn, Massachusetts, "upwards of seventy" persons who listened to Jesse Lee filed to stop paying taxes to the Congregational Church.[50] The possibility of similar action existed in many other towns.

---

47. Umbel, "Methodism in New England Religious Culture," 1-115.

48. Hibbard, *Memoirs*, 39-43.

49. Cooke is quoted in Paul G. Faler, *Mechanics and Manufacturers in the Early Industrial Revolution, Lynn, Massachusetts, 1780–1860* (Albany: SUNY Press, 1981), 46, 105.

50. Wade Crawford Barclay, *Early American Methodism, 1769–1844* (New York: Board of Missions & Church Extension of the Methodist Church, 1949), 1:135. Barclay reports that the number was somewhere between 70 and 108.

However, Methodism threatened more than the minister's salary or the citizen's tax bill. Methodism met with hostility in places where taxes were not an issue. The Methodist movement had inspired mobs in England from its inception in the 1730s. Attacks had been most common in the 1740s and were rare by the time Jesse Lee invaded Connecticut, but the parallels are instructive nonetheless. Historian John Walsh has argued that the British elite feared Methodism as a challenge to the social order, especially the authority of their class, whereas middle-class Englishmen feared Methodist itinerants as a challenge to local traditions and the institution of the family.[51] Much the same can be said about the Methodist reception in New England. In New England, Methodism threatened families and towns as well as churches.[52]

Methodism threatened the stability of some families. Often women went to hear the circuit rider without their husbands. For eighteen years after 1789 the Methodist class in Salsbury, Connecticut, was exclusively female. According to one Methodist historian, "it was not uncommon (in the 1790s) to see women riding twenty miles or more on horseback to attend a quarterly meeting" in Granville, Massachusetts.[53] Youth were also drawn to these meetings, which threatened both the unity of the family and the security of the parents. Young men often became circuit riders and left home. From a parent's point of view, no circuit rider amounted to anything. Few ever married and many died young. Circuit riders were unlikely to stay home to care for the family farm or aging parents.

Methodism threatened towns as well. The circuit rider was an outsider. Jesse Lee was a Virginian; Freeborn Garrettson was from Maryland; most of the circuit riders came from outside New England and many must have spoken with a southern accent.[54] The Methodist

51. Walsh, "Methodism and the Mob in the 18th Century," *Studies in Church History* 8 (1972): 213-28. See also David Hempton, *Methodism and Politics in British Society 1750–1850* (London: Hutchinson, 1984), 20-55.

52. John Wigger, who argues that Methodism became a popular religious movement after the American Revolution, notes violence against American Methodists in the 1770s. Wigger suggests that it was brought on by the Methodist refusal to endorse the fight for independence. Christine Heyrman, who argues that evangelicalism offended most white southerners, discounts the level of violence against Methodist preachers while delineating myriad ways in which early American Methodism threatened families, towns, and churches. Wigger, *Taking Heaven by Storm*, 57. Heyrman, *Southern Cross*, passim.

53. On Salsbury, see Daniel Curry, *Life Story of Rev. Davis Wasgatt Clark* (New York: Nelson & Phillips, 1874), 84. On Granville, "Items Concerning the Old Beach Church in Granville, Massachusetts, obtained by Rev. William Bridge at the Memorial Meetings, September, 1873," MSS at the New England Methodist Historical Society.

54. Russell Richey argues that "Methodism developed in the South and has had a Southern accent ever since" in *Early American Methodism* (Bloomington: Indiana University Press, 1991), chap. 4.

movement in its entirety was a rather recent British import. One rumor, which early Methodist histories say swept New England, was that the Methodist preachers were emissaries of the French government, which planned to subjugate New England as soon as the Methodists were sufficiently numerous. A corresponding rumor was that the British crown had commissioned six hundred Methodists to invade America and undermine the independence of the new republic by sowing dissension. According to this second rumor, there was a bounty paid by the British embassy to circuit riders: four dollars a head, or perhaps, a soul.[55]

This foreign faith offended New England natives in many ways. It was divisive, for one thing. Charles Giles wrote of "noisy reports" of "certain religionists who had intruded themselves into the state and were riding over parish lines, breaking up the repose of established societies." In Granville, Massachusetts, and in many towns the people divided over whether they would listen to the Congregational clergyman or the Methodist preacher.[56]

Whereas some formed mobs and tried to drive the Methodists from the community, others were drawn to Methodism because it offered a more attractive community. To some the dominant community, associated with the Congregational (and in some places, the Anglican) churches, seemed too worldly. This was a generation in which dancing masters and singing teachers itinerated through New England, and young adults gathered for parties and balls. Hibbard, Dan Young, Heman and Nathan Bangs, Elbert Osborn, Mary Tucker, and the daughter of Captain Butler were all New England youth who were put off by such frivolity. They waited in vain to hear dancing denounced from the pulpit. Nathan Bangs, an Anglican, was especially disappointed when his pastor organized balls in his home, drank liquor, and played cards. Mary Tucker was first convicted of sin at a ball, as she asked herself what penalty she would pay for that evening's entertainment.[57]

---

55. Strickland, *Dan Young*, 101; Hibbard, *Memoirs*, 65.

56. Charles Giles, *Pioneer: A Narrative of the Nativity, Experience, Travels, and Ministerial Labors of Rev. Charles Giles* (New York: Lane & Tippett, 1844), 56. On Granville, see "Items Concerning . . . Granville, Massachusetts."

57. Hibbard, *Memoirs*, 48, 59, 74; Strickland, *Dan Young*, 15-34; Stevens, *Nathan Bangs*, 20; Heman Bangs, *The Autobiography and Journal of Rev. Heman Bangs* (New York: N. Tibbals & Sons, 1874), 1-16; Elbert Osborn, *Passages in the Life and Ministry of Elbert Osborn, An Itinerant Minister of the Methodist Episcopal Church* (New York: published for the author, 1872), 13-16; Mary Orne Tucker, *Itinerant Preaching in the Early Days of Methodism. By a Pioneer Preacher's Wife* (Boston: B. B. Russell, 1872), 28-29. On the daughter of Captain Butler, see George Coles, *Heroines of Methodism* (New York: Carlton & Porter, 1857), 11.

Dancing was one component of what Methodists called "the gay life." Fancy clothing was another. Nearly the first thing Nathan Bangs did when he was converted was change his shirt and swear off fancy ruffles. Fanny Newell was first convicted when she realized that all her handkerchiefs were decorated with needlepoint! Conversion, which Methodists and Congregationalists agreed should follow conviction, did not come easily to Fanny Newell. At times she resisted the Methodist message—and when she did, she deliberately dressed in fancy clothes in order to demonstrate her allegiance to mainline society. Eventually, of course, she succumbed to Methodism and toned down her costume.[58]

Dancing and dress appear to have been particularly troublesome for these youth, but more than these two practices was at stake. The Congregational—and the Anglican—churches were an essential part of the social order in a society that they perceived to be corrupt. The Methodists called for Christians to come out of the world and be different: to believe something different from their neighbors, to live by a more stringent moral code, to renounce the gay life. In starting a new life, each entered into a new circle of friends. Here they found a new community. Becoming a Methodist meant joining a "class," a small group of like-minded people who met weekly and poured out their hearts to one another. By all accounts this was a fellowship that was both more intimate and more otherworldly than the Congregational churches. Behavior and dress were signs of allegiance to this new community.

Finally, leadership in the Congregational and Methodist communities was very different. The Congregational ministry was changing, but its members were still part of the elite. The vast majority were graduates of Harvard or Yale. Calls to serve Congregational churches were parallel to marriage contracts: in theory, at least, the relationship was settled for a lifetime. These "divines" expected deference and lived and dressed accordingly. They spoke with the authority of education and tradition, and presumed the support of the political authorities. The Methodist preacher, on the other hand, was likely to be a middle-class farm boy. His education consisted of reading his way through a pre-

---

58. Stevens, *Nathan Bangs*, 47; Fanny Newell, *Memoirs of Fanny Newell, Written by Herself*, 3d ed. (Springfield: G. & C. Merriam, 1833), 13-18. Dan Young tells the story of a young woman who was converted to Methodism against her parents' wishes. Her father won her back from Methodism by taking her to New York City and buying her expensive clothes. She died an early death and directed her dying words to her siblings: pointing to an expensive gown, she said, "This is the price of my soul." Strickland, *Dan Young*, 128-31.

scribed course of study as he traveled from place to place. He was itinerant and the ideal Methodist preacher was itinerant—unsettled—for a lifetime. By what authority did he speak? He claimed the authority of the Bible (which he could not read in Greek) and the spirit (he was likely to believe God spoke to him in dreams) and a foreign church.[59]

Striking differences can be visualized. In Andover, Massachusetts, the Reverend Doctor Samuel Phillips and his wife walked to the Congregational meetinghouse on Sunday, a manservant at his arm and a maidservant at hers. It was a procession. The men of Andover did not enter the meetinghouse until he arrived and all in attendance remained standing until the pastor mounted the pulpit.[60] In contrast to men like Phillips, most Methodist preachers must have appeared uneducated, uncouth, and poor. Perhaps Freeborn Garrettson appeared more respectable than most of the early Methodists. He visited Hartford in 1789, and a large crowd received him cordially. He too arrived with a black man walking next to him. However the people of Hartford turned abusive when he finished his address and Harry Hosier, his black companion, delivered an exhortation. Their roles were distinct: Garrettson preached and Harry exhorted, but Harry addressed the crowd nonetheless.[61]

Harry was a rare example of a black Methodist speaking before a New England audience in these years, but he is only one example of the gap between Methodist preachers and Congregational clergymen. Women and children were also encouraged to speak publicly. Enoch Mudge created a popular commotion when he burst upon the scene as the Methodist "child preacher."[62] Fanny Newell and Sally Thompson also served as itinerant exhorters. Fanny Newell did more than that. As much as any male, she believed herself called to preach. Indeed, she believed that Jesus had sent her back from the dead with a mission to preach, and even dreamed that the preacher who had brought her to Christ took off his cloak and placed it on her shoulders

59. Donald Scott, *From Office to Profession: The New England Ministry, 1750–1850* (Philadelphia: University of Pennsylvania, 1978).

60. Richard Shiels, "The Scope of the Second Great Awakening: Andover, Massachusetts, as a Case Study," *Journal of the Early Republic* 5 (1985): 226.

61. Bangs, *Life of Freeborn Garettson*, 203-14. Warren Thomas Smith, *Harry Hosier: Circuit Rider* (Nashville: The Upper Room, 1980).

62. Tucker, *Itinerant Preaching in the Early Days*, 28-29. It is likely that Mudge was fifteen at the time, not exactly a child but much younger than anyone addressing Congregational audiences; see Mudge, *History of the New England Conference*, 46. Wigger discusses other boy preachers in *Taking Heaven by Storm*, 52, 78.

as Elijah had done to Elisha. With no possibility of acceptance into the fraternity of Methodist preachers, Fanny married a circuit rider and rode with him far into the north woods of Maine. Far from the eyes of Methodist officials, Fanny did more than exhort; Fanny preached.[63]

Not surprisingly, many New Englanders dismissed the Methodist preachers out of hand. These upstarts seemed to have no right to speak, especially when they challenged the Congregational clergy and New England tradition. Even the young Billy Hibbard, converted by the Methodists and convinced that their gospel was true, could not bring himself to become a Methodist preacher for many months. How could he dare, he asked himself, with so little education, so little authority? In time, of course, he came to feel he had to preach. Soon he felt he had to attack the Congregational concepts of the ministry. With biting sarcasm, Hibbard and many of his colleagues made fun of the "man-made ministers" who, they implied, pursued their calling only for the power and prestige. Jesus chose fishermen like Peter and not college graduates, they were apt to say.[64]

Billy Hibbard, Enoch Mudge, Dan Young, and Lorenzo Dow would have never become Congregational ministers. Their families were simply unable to send them to college and no one in the family would have considered them as clerical prospects. Harry Hosier, Sally Thompson, and Fanny Newell would have never addressed Congregational audiences. They found opportunity as well as acceptance among the Methodists. Women, youth, even blacks might exhort; white males might enter a profession that was otherwise closed to them. The Methodists, it was said, were "turning the world upside down."[65] For some who had been nearer the bottom of society than the top, the experience was liberating.

---

63. Sally Thompson was encouraged to exhort and even preach by several male Methodist leaders, but was eventually disciplined for crossing the line from exhorting to preaching. See "Trial and Defense of Mrs. Sally Thompson, on a complaint of Insubordination to the Rules of the Methodist Episcopal Church, Evil Speaking and Immorality, Held Before a Select Committee of Said Church in Cherry Valley, June 10, 1830, To Which is Annexed An Exposition of Some Facts Relating to Her Former Movements and Encouragement in Said Society. Written by Herself" (West Troy, New York, 1837), Methodist Archives, Drew University. On Fanny Newell, see Newell, *Memoirs*, 64, 108-10, 137-69. Wigger explains the distinction between exhorting and preaching, and discusses other female exhorters in *Taking Heaven by Storm*, 29, 152-56.

64. Hibbard, *Memoirs*, 31-35; Goodrich, *Recollections of a Lifetime*, 1:196-97.

65. Stevens, *Memorials of the Introduction of Methodism*, 337.

Evangelicalism

Over time, as both groups changed, they became more alike. "Orthodoxy was in considerable degree Methodized," Samuel Goodrich wrote in retrospect, "and Methodism, in due time, became orthodoxed."[66] The generation of Congregationalists represented by Lyman Beecher, Nathaniel William Taylor, and Asahel Nettleton became more "evangelical" in preaching and approach. Beecher and many others ameliorated Calvinism by watering down the doctrine of election. Taylor, who taught theology at Yale, made the new approach academically respectable. Its adherents called it "the New Haven theology," while its critics claimed Beecher and Taylor were as Arminian as the Methodists. Nettleton, who sided with Taylor's critics, followed the Methodist lead in other ways. Calling himself a "Domestic Missionary," Nettleton never accepted a call to one community but took on a series of short-term assignments. Moving every few months from town to town, Nettleton also went to parties and balls in order to awaken the participants by attacking their behavior. In short, Nettleton invented a Congregational variant of itineracy and then sought adolescent souls by attacking the gay life.[67]

Beginning in the 1790s, Congregationalists also learned to organize their members into small groups. The Methodists had done this first, organizing classes, as we have seen. The Congregationalists organized their members into missionary societies, Bibles societies, tract societies, and the like. By 1810 most New England Congregational churches had several of these groups and the number would grow in succeeding decades. Hence, both Methodist and Congregational laity were encouraged to attend frequent midweek meetings in small groups in addition to the weekly worship services of the entire congregation. Most of those Congregationalists who attended these new societies, like most of the Methodists who attended classes, were women.[68]

The focus of the meeting, when Congregationalists met as a missionary, Bible, or tract society, was upon evangelizing the outside world. In contrast, the focus of a Methodist class meeting was the personal lives of its members. Nonetheless, it can be said that the func-

---

66. Goodrich, *Recollections of a Lifetime*, 1:216.

67. *Autobiography of Lyman Beecher*; Mead, *Nathaniel William Taylor*; Bennet Tyler, *Memoir of the Life and Character of Rev. Asahel Nettleton, D.D.* (Hartford: Robins & Smith, 1845).

68. Donald Mathews, "The Second Great Awakening as an Organizing Process, 1780–1830: An Hypothesis," *American Quarterly* 21 (1969): 22-43.

tion as well as the form of these "voluntary societies" borrowed from the Methodist example. The earliest of these groups, the Connecticut Missionary Society, for example, was established to send clergy to the inhabitants of frontier areas such as Ohio. In short, it was designed to accomplish what the Methodists had been doing all over the country. Subsequent societies were formed to supply missionaries with Bibles or tracts to distribute. Methodist circuit riders had been distributing similar literature for years. The Connecticut Moral Reform Society, established by Lyman Beecher at the end of the War of 1812, launched a Congregational counterpart to the Methodist attack upon the gay life: members of these societies swore to abstain from swearing, Sabbath breaking, and excessive alcohol. The Charitable Societies for the Education of Pious, Indigent Young Men, begun a few years later, raised money to enable young men of the working class to enter the ministry—something the Methodists had done first. Henceforth, both the Methodist and the Congregational ministry provided opportunities for lower-class men to advance in social status. Hence, Methodist Bishop Laban Clark could write that many of the benevolent societies "were first suggested to the minds of the benevolent by seeing the fruits of Methodism."[69]

Of course the Methodists changed too. One seemingly insignificant change indicates how the Methodist perception of themselves and their relationship to the world evolved. Samuel Goodrich wrote that Methodist women of the 1860s wore fancy bonnets just like Congregationalists. Newell Culver offered an explanation. The plain bonnet had once made Methodist women stand out, but then women within other churches began wearing very simple bonnets, too. In short, the Methodists had won the day and consequently had lost their sense of distinctiveness. When fashions changed and other evangelical women bought bonnets with fancy flowers, Methodist women did the same with little appreciation for the issue.[70] Goodrich and Newell were both talking about much more than bonnets, of course; they were talking about a Methodist style that stood at first in contrast to other styles Methodists associated with the gay life.

69. Laban Clark, *Semi-Centennial Sermon. Delivered before the New York East Conference* (New York: Lane & Scott, 1851), 20-21. The founding and function of the Congregational societies discussed here is discussed in Shiels, "Connecticut Clergy in the Second Great Awakening," 418-24.

70. Goodrich, *Recollections of a Lifetime,* 218. Newell Culver, *Methodism Forty Years Ago and Now: Embracing Many Interesting Reminiscences and Incidents* (New York: Nelson & Phillips, 1873), 63-64.

In matters of style Methodists became less distinctive because others followed their lead. In one other important measure, however—the character and preparation of the clergy—Methodism evolved toward the Congregational standard. Beginning with Enoch Mudge, generations of Methodist clergy arose who were born in New England, spoke with New England accents, and carried other New England traits. By 1810 it was increasingly common for them to be settled rather than itinerant and also to be married men with family responsibilities. After 1830 it became increasingly common for Methodist clergy to be educated.[71]

Wilbur Fisk and Stephen Olin are exemplars of the new Methodist ministry of midcentury. Both went to college. Both experienced a "new birth" after college and in both cases it happened in Methodist surroundings. Each came to believe himself called to the ministry, but even at this point neither was sure he was called to be a Methodist. Fisk considered the Anglican ministry; Olin considered theological seminary at Princeton or Yale. Eventually, each became one of the fathers of Wesleyan University, which opened its doors in 1831.[72] It was the third college in Connecticut, the first Methodist college in New England, and the first Methodist college to survive. The careers of Fisk and Olin, as well as the birth of Wesleyan, demonstrate what Samuel Goodrich described as Methodism being "orthodoxed." Laban Clark, who labored with Fisk and Olin to win financial support for Wesleyan in its first decade, spread the view that "any young man who thinks he is divinely called to preach the gospel can have no excuse for entering the ministry without a competent knowledge of English literature, Grammar, Rhetoric, Geography, and History." In another generation Boston University would begin to function as a Methodist theological seminary and its graduates would have parallel degrees to those of clergy in the Anglican, Unitarian, or Congregational churches.[73]

---

71. Mudge was the first native born New Englander to become a Methodist preacher. Born in Lynn, Massachusetts, in 1776, he was received into the New England Conference at its second session, in 1793. His biography can be found in Abel Stevens, *Sketches from the Study of a Superannuated Itinerant* (Boston: C. H. Peirce, 1851): 54-99. For other trends described in this paragraph, see Culver, *Methodism Forty Years Ago and Now*.

72. Joseph Holdich, *Life of Wilbur Fisk, D.D. First President of Wesleyan University* (New York: Harper & Bros., 1842) and Stephen Olin, *Life and Letters of Stephen Olin*, 2 vols. (New York: Harper & Bros., 1853), 1:1-91.

73. David Potts, *Wesleyan University, 1831–1910* (New Haven: Yale University Press, 1992), 1-22. Clark's words are from "The Importance of Education," an undated manuscript in the Laban Clark Papers, Wesleyan University; they are typical of many of the manuscripts in that collection. On Boston University, see Richard Morgan Cameron, *Boston University School of Theology 1839–1968* (Boston: Boston University School of Theology, 1968).

Over two or three generations, then, Methodists invaded Puritan New England, competed successfully with the descendants of Puritanism, and became quite like them. The Methodist invasion strengthened—literally resuscitated—Congregationalism, and changed it as well. Methodist preachers challenged the Congregational churches, empowered the women and the young and the uneducated, focused on the New Birth, and incited revivals. Further, when Methodist preachers attacked the gay life they attacked a set of mores increasingly accepted by northern Christians, even the descendants of the Puritans. By doing so they helped create the evangelical culture of the nineteenth century, which succeeded the Puritan culture of New England's colonial period.

CHAPTER 9

Consecrated Respectability: Phoebe Palmer and the Refinement of American Methodism

Kathryn T. Long

Before the construction in 1858 of the spired, all-marble St. Paul's Methodist Episcopal Church in New York City or the domestication of camp meetings through the appearance of cottages with ginger-bread trim, one visible symbol of the increasing social respectability of American Methodism was a weekly meeting that took place in the two second-floor parlors of a spacious home at 54 Rivington Street in New York City. A few blocks north of the Bowery and a short walk east from Broadway, Rivington Street was not one of the city's elite neighborhoods, even in the early 1840s; still, the home, its location, and design spoke of a solid, upper-middle-class gentility.

In addition to the parlors, the house contained an office, a dining room, nursery, and bedrooms sufficient not only for family members, but for numerous guests. Several servants helped maintain the whole and free its occupants for their many religious activities, including participation in one of Manhattan's largest Methodist churches, the thousand-member Allen Street congregation, located just around the corner.[1]

---

1. For a description of St. Paul's, see Jonathan Greenleaf, *A History of the Churches of All Denominations, in the City of New York* (New York, n.p., 1846), 70. Phoebe and Walter Palmer were members of the Allen Street Church until 1848 and returned in 1856; the description of the Palmer home is a composite, see especially Richard Wheatley, *The Life and Letters of Mrs. Phoebe Palmer* (1876; reprint of 1881 edition, New York: Garland Publishing Company, 1984), chaps. 1, 3, and 6.

For nearly three decades, from 1836 to 1865, the house on Rivington Street was the site of the "Tuesday Meeting for the Promotion of Holiness," directed for most of those years by Methodist teacher, author, and revivalist Phoebe Palmer. Anywhere from 50 to 150 people jammed the parlors and hallways of the Palmer home each week to sing, pray, enjoy the company of other Christians, and, most important, to seek holiness or entire sanctification. Such an experience of "perfect love" was a hallmark of Wesleyan spirituality and, to Phoebe Palmer, the essence of biblical Christianity.[2] Fanned by Palmer's zeal, the Tuesday meeting was the spark largely responsible for igniting a "holiness revival" among Methodists and other Protestants during the middle decades of the nineteenth century. As historians have increasingly recognized, Palmer's distinctive teachings laid the foundations for new patterns of religious experience—usually referred to as the "higher Christian life"—that became part of the fabric of modern evangelicalism during the post–Civil War era.[3]

Less attention has been given to the social and cultural dynamics that surrounded the early years of Palmer holiness, particularly the two decades prior to the Civil War. Yet Palmer and the movement she advanced flourished at a time when what has been described as the "refinement of America" was transforming religion for middle-class Protestants, particularly those along the eastern seaboard and in other urban centers. Richard Bushman has chronicled the tensions that arose as the "plain Christianity" of Methodists, Baptists, and others increasingly absorbed the values of vernacular gentility.[4] Such

2. Sanctification for Palmer was an experience after conversion that brought with it an awareness of being constantly saved or kept from all sin. See Phoebe Palmer, *Entire Devotion to God* (1845; reprint, Salem, Ohio: Schmul Publishing, n.d.), 9. There are numerous accounts of the Tuesday meeting, which was begun by Palmer's sister Sarah Lankford in 1836 as a women's prayer meeting; Phoebe Palmer assumed leadership in 1840, shortly after the meeting was opened to men and began to grow in popularity. The description in this paragraph reflects the ethos of the Palmer years. See Wheatley, *Life and Letters*, 238-57; Phoebe Palmer, *The Promise of the Father; or, A Neglected Specialty of the Last Days, Addressed to the Clergy and Laity of All Christian Communities* (Boston: Henry V. Degen, 1859), 226-40; and George Hughes, *Fragrant Memories of the Tuesday Meeting* (New York: Palmer & Hughes, 1886). For 1836 as the beginning of the Tuesday meeting, I follow Charles Edward White, *The Beauty of Holiness: Phoebe Palmer as Theologian, Revivalist, Feminist, and Humanitarian* (Grand Rapids: Zondervan, 1986), 259 n. 44.

3. Melvin Easterday Dieter, *The Holiness Revival of the Nineteenth Century* (Metuchen, N.J.: Scarecrow Press, 1980), 63; George M. Marsden, *Fundamentalism and American Culture: The Shaping of Twentieth-Century Evangelicalism, 1870–1925* (New York: Oxford University Press, 1980), 75.

4. Richard L. Bushman, *The Refinement of America: Persons, Houses, Cities* (New York: Random House, 1993), chap. 10. For surveys of Palmer scholarship, see Dale Simmons, "Phoebe Palmer—Enjoli Woman or Enigma? A Review of the Recent Scholarship on Phoebe Palmer," *Wesleyan/Holiness Studies Center Bulletin* 4, no. 2 (summer 1996): 1, 4; and Harold E. Raser, *Phoebe Palmer: Her Life and Thought* (Lewiston, N.Y.: Edwin Mellen Press, 1987), 1-19. Scholars such as

things as comfort, respectability, education, taste, and manners began to assume religious significance. During the years of the early republic, popular Protestantism offered egalitarian relationships based on religious experience and personal piety rather than on social graces or family status.[5] By the 1840s, that had begun to change. Little girls in one Methodist Sunday school, for example, not only learned about salvation, they also got a penny every time they wore their bonnets.[6]

Wearing bonnets and cultivating good manners seemed like innocuous, even praiseworthy, additions to Christianity, but as Bushman has argued, they were practices ultimately rooted in a competing cultural tradition—that of Renaissance civility, with its concern for "power, hierarchy, and worldly ambition."[7] Such a tradition measured human worth in terms of refinement and taste rather than Christian virtue. Not only did gentility threaten Christianity with such "worldly" temptations as dancing, fashionable dress, and "idle amusements," it also promoted a kind of secular sanctification where little girls who remembered their bonnets came to be viewed as better Christians than those who did not. Protestants of all denominations struggled as they sought to negotiate the rapidly changing boundaries between faith and worldliness. Methodists were particularly hard hit because they were the most upwardly mobile church body in the country. The spread of gentility coincided with Methodism's move from the cultural periphery to the center of American life.[8]

Timothy Smith and Melvin Dieter first called attention to Palmer as a significant figure in the history of nineteenth-century evangelicalism, and Palmer studies have become a small industry among historians of Methodism, but Palmer has shared in the general neglect of American Methodism among scholars concerned with the broader field of American religious history highlighted in Nathan Hatch, "The Puzzle of American Methodism," *Church History* 63 (1994): 175-89. The two biographies of Palmer, that by Raser, and *Beauty of Holiness* by White, provide helpful introductions and guides to Palmer's life and thought, although neither engages the broad social and cultural context of the decades prior to the Civil War. I am indebted to both books in preparing this article.

5. Works that describe this popular, egalitarian religion include Catherine A. Brekus, *Strangers & Pilgrims: Female Preaching in America, 1740–1845* (Chapel Hill: University of North Carolina Press, 1998), chaps. 3-6; Nathan O. Hatch, *The Democratization of American Christianity* (New Haven: Yale University Press, 1989); Donald G. Mathews, *Religion in the Old South* (Chicago: University of Chicago Press, 1977), chap. 1; Russell E. Richey, *Early American Methodism* (Bloomington: Indiana University Press, 1991); and John H. Wigger, *Taking Heaven by Storm: Methodism and the Rise of Popular Christianity in America* (New York: Oxford University Press, 1998).

6. John A. Roche, *The Life of Mrs. Sarah A. Lankford Palmer* (New York: George Hughes, 1898), 49.

7. Bushman, *Refinement of America*, 352.

8. Hatch, *Democratization*, 193-206, sketches this shift.

Most accounts of Methodist gentrification during the decades after 1840 have emphasized the church's accommodation to the cultural currents of the time.[9] Yet the popularity of Phoebe Palmer's holiness teaching suggests that many Methodists longed to create their own distinctive synthesis, balancing the religious zeal and populist vitality of the denomination's early years with the propriety and decorum of mainstream respectability. Palmer holiness offered a way to do just that. It was early Methodist rigor in a "parlor culture" setting—a call for entire devotion to God that was neither a capitulation to gentility nor a wholesale rejection of it. Although entire sanctification as presented by Phoebe Palmer contained within it the potential for social and religious subversion, Palmer herself and the movement she advanced stood at the center of urbane, cultured Methodism. The "way of holiness" was not so much a protest against the educational and social aspirations of Methodists and other middle- and upper-class evangelicals as it was a response to them. Perhaps more than any other figure in popular Protestantism during the twenty years prior to the Civil War, Phoebe Palmer sought to reconcile middle-class respectability with intense religious commitment.

Her approach represented an alternative to other more commonly recognized Protestant responses to gentility. In contrast to the tendency among many upwardly mobile Victorians to adapt to gentility by emphasizing the spiritual exceptionalism and influence of women, Palmer insisted that religious zeal and piety were mandates for all professed Christians, men and women alike.[10] She rejected the protest movements—the counterculture sanctificationists such as the Free Methodists—who denounced vernacular gentility outright as antithetical to genuine Christianity. She also criticized those at the other end of the spectrum, cultural accommodationists, including Harriet Beecher Stowe and her brother Henry Ward Beecher, who blended refinement and religion into a syncretized "gospel of gentility."[11] To Palmer, the protesters represented asceticism, and the accommoda-

---

9. Ibid. See also Bushman, *Refinement of America*, 346; and Roger Robins, "Vernacular American Landscape: Methodists, Camp Meetings, and Social Respectability," *Religion and American Culture* 4, no. 2 (summer 1994):165-91. Richey, *Early American Methodism*, xii, discusses the nineteenth century more broadly as a "loss of innocence, a kind of fall of Methodism."

10. Brekus, *Strangers & Pilgrims*, 292-94, traces this response among the Christian Connection, Freewill Baptists, Methodists, and African Methodists.

11. For the Free Methodists, see *HAM* 2:339-60. William G. McLoughlin, *The Meaning of Henry Ward Beecher: An Essay on The Shifting Values of Mid-Victorian America, 1840–1870* (New York: Alfred A. Knopf, 1970), chap. 6 and passim, traces Beecher's cultural accommodation.

tionists had surrendered to the world.[12] Instead, she offered her own hybrid of religious egalitarianism and social distinctions. Hers was a selective gentility, filled with ambivalence but promising perfection; respectability made subservient to a rigorous piety.

The sales of Palmer's popular religious books, the crowds who filled the Tuesday meeting each week, and Palmer's demand as a revivalist at the established Methodist camp meetings of the Northeast and Canada all suggest that her message struck a responsive chord. Ultimately, during the second half of the nineteenth century, the efforts of Palmer holiness to hold together the centripetal (respectable) and the centrifugal (radical) strains in Methodism could not be sustained. The 1840s and 1850s, however, were years of promise. Phoebe Palmer, supported by Walter and by Phoebe's sister, Sarah Lankford, preached classic Methodist simplicity in the midst of an urbane metropolis. Palmer had managed, it seemed, to separate herself from the world while still living firmly within it. Perhaps by following the way of holiness others could do the same.

The Social Setting: A Legacy of Respectability

The story of American Methodism during the first half of the nineteenth century is usually described as a "pilgrimage to respectability," the journey of an enthusiastic, popular movement that gradually cleaned up its act.[13] Phoebe Worrall Palmer, however, viewed respectability not as a pilgrimage, but as a legacy. It was an inheritance from the English Methodism of John Wesley that was a part of the atmosphere of the comfortable New York City home of Palmer's childhood. As a teenager, Henry Worrall, Phoebe's father and an English immigrant, had first heard the gospel message and had received a membership ticket to a Methodist class meeting from the aging John Wesley himself.[14] Growing up, Phoebe Worrall was steeped in stories of the "worthies" of English Methodism, and, throughout her life, she considered herself a spiritual and biological daughter of "Old England."[15] For Palmer, religious history proceeded

---

12. Wheatley, *Life and Letters,* 450-51.
13. Hatch, *Democratization,* 93; Robbins, "Vernacular American Landscape," 167; Roger Finke and Rodney Stark, *The Churching of America 1776–1990: Winners and Losers in our Religious Economy* (New Brunswick, N.J.: Rutgers University Press, 1992), chaps. 3 and 5.
14. Wheatley, *Life and Letters,* 13-14; Roche, *Life,* 17.
15. White, *Beauty of Holiness,* 4, 256, 257 n. 17; Phoebe Palmer, *Four Years in the Old World* (New York: Walter C. Palmer Jr., 1869), 16, chaps. 1 and 2, passim.

from the early church to John Wesley's Methodists to the faithful "Bible Christians" of the holiness movement. It was the idealized scenario of a religious movement that was predominantly urban—one that appealed to the masses but also attracted people of education, culture, and even wealth.[16] It fit Phoebe Palmer's own circumstances and bypassed the boisterous, circuit-rider, frontier Methodism of the early American republic.

This is not to say that American influences were absent from her life. Palmer was born into a context where vernacular gentility and revivalism existed, sometimes uneasily, side by side; a pattern that persisted throughout her lifetime. She came into the world about a year after her American-born mother, Dorothea, was converted during an 1806 revival at the Forsyth Street Church, the second Methodist congregation established in New York City. The revival broke out after organizers created an "altar," or designated space for penitents, at the front of the church; an early example of camp meeting techniques transplanted into an urban setting.[17]

Dorothea Worrall may have sealed her conversion in the emotional atmosphere of the Forsyth Street altar, but in the Worrall home dignity and order were the rule. Although information about Palmer's parents and childhood is scarce, the available details point to a family that by the early decades of the nineteenth century already had assumed the characteristics of upper-middle-class respectability. There were servants in the home on Manhattan's lower West Side, the house had a sitting room, and the Worralls occasionally entertained British diplomats. In a more subtle sign of social aspiration, each of the nine surviving Worrall children, except for Phoebe, was given a middle name.[18] All

---

16. See, for example, Palmer, *Four Years*, 34-36. Palmer viewed Suzanna Wesley as a type of Christ and certainly the prototype of the ideal Methodist; Darcy Lady Maxwell, a wealthy Scots supporter of the Methodist cause, was an "elect lady," whose "titled honours, wealth, loveliness of person, dignity of carriage" were all dedicated to the pursuit of holiness. Two other Methodist heroines favored by Palmer, Mary Bosanquet Fletcher and Hester Ann Rogers, had turned their backs on the worldliness of wealthy homes, but both obviously had come from refined backgrounds. See Palmer, *Promise of the Father*, 58-61; 101-6; Palmer, *Entire Devotion*, 29-31.

17. Samuel A. Seaman, *Annals of New York Methodism* (New York: Hunt & Eaton, 1892), 170-71; for the influence of Methodist practices on urban revivals, see Richard Carwardine, "The Second Great Awakening in the Urban Centers: An Examination of Methodism and the 'New Measures,'" *Journal of American History* 59 (1972): 327-40.

18. The Worralls attended the Duane Street Methodist Church, located on Duane between Hudson and Greenwich Streets, and probably lived within walking distance of the church; Wheatley, *Life and Letters*, 20; Greanleaf, *History*, 285; Raser, *Palmer*, 24-25. The children's names are listed in Roche, *Life*, 18, as Henry C., Caroline R., Sarah A., Phoebe, Noah M., Mary Jane, Wade B., Hannah A., and Isaac G. Although middle names are not given for all the children, Roche does mention Hannah A. as "Hannah Angelina," indicting the initials did stand for actual names. See also Bushman, *Refinement of America*, 296.

indications point to the accuracy of a nineteenth-century biographer's later assessment that Phoebe Palmer and her sister Sarah were "ladies by birth and education."[19]

Other urban Methodists had established themselves in a similar fashion and during the late 1820s and early 1830s the Worrall offspring found spouses who shared their religious faith and social status.[20] Phoebe married Walter C. Palmer, also a lifelong New Yorker and a college-educated physician; Sarah accepted the proposal of Thomas A. Lankford, an architect from Richmond, Virginia. During the 1830s, the Palmers purchased the house at 54 Rivington Street, which they shared with the Lankfords until Thomas and Sarah moved to Caldwell-on-the-Hudson in 1840.[21] The Palmer/Lankford families lived in "modest affluence" and were well connected socially. Phoebe later recalled that she and Walter began married life with "good ordinary prospects," although they moved in circles "often composed of persons of much larger means than themselves."[22] Well-to-do women made up part of the constituency of the two prayer groups that united under Sarah Lankford's leadership to form the first Tuesday Meeting in 1836. One group came from the nearby Allen Street congregation and the other from the uptown Mulberry Street Church, where the Lankfords were members. The Mulberry Street group clearly represented Methodism's wealthy echelon since theirs was one of only two of the denomination's churches in the city with rented pews—an elitist break from the usual practice of free seating.[23]

---

19. He referred to their education within home and church; there is no evidence either woman received a formal education. Roche, *Life*, 260. In this light, Palmer's recent biographer, Charles Edward White, *Beauty of Holiness*, 207, is somewhat misleading when he asserts, "Phoebe Palmer was no lady." White correctly emphasizes that Palmer did not live the life of the idle rich. But Palmer's actions and home life clearly reflected upper-middle-class respectability.

20. Roche, *Life*, 18. Hughes, *Fragrant Memories*, 28-29.

21. Walter Palmer was born in New Jersey, but his family moved to New York when he was three months old. He lived in the city for the rest of his life. George Hughes, *The Beloved Physician: Walter C. Palmer, M.D.* (New York: Palmer & Hughes, 1884), 18. Even after the Lankfords moved, Sarah Lankford spent several months each year in the city and continued to support her sister's holiness work. For the purchase of the Rivington Street house and information on the two couples sharing it, see Hughes, *Fragrant Memories*, 28-29; also Raser, *Palmer*, 43; and White, *Beauty of Holiness*, 7.

22. Palmer, *Faith and Its Effects*, 222-23. Although Palmer wrote in the third person of "a husband and wife," the context, in comparison with comments elsewhere, strongly suggests that the Palmers were the couple in question.

23. Roche, *Life*, 165-66. The Mulberry Street Church, also known as the Second Wesleyan Chapel or St. Paul's, was the predecessor of the marble St. Paul's Methodist Episcopal Church. Seaman, *Annals*, 321-24; Matthew Simpson, *Cyclopaedia of Methodism*, c.v. "New York City." Rented pews began to gain in popularity during the 1850s as urban Methodists increasingly sought money to finance elaborate church buildings. For a sketch of debates over the issue from the later free church perspective, see Leslie Ray Marston, *From Age to Age a Living Witness* (Winona Lake, Ind.: Light & Life Press, 1960), 128, 163-67.

Because of her family background and the cultural influences of the great metropolis, as a young woman Phoebe Palmer accepted the legitimacy of many aspects of vernacular gentility. She admitted in later correspondence that she "seemed to have inherited aristocratic feelings," which prior to her sanctification "unconsciously blended themselves with all her associations."[24] At the same time, however, as an earnest and active Methodist, the absorbing preoccupations of her life were religious. Since childhood, Palmer had been conscientious, even scrupulous, in her pursuit of salvation and later of the "heart purity" that characterized holiness.[25] There is no evidence that she experienced any tension between genteel refinement and godliness until after the tragic deaths, in infancy, of her first two children.

"Entire Consecration": A Separation from the Values of Gentility

In particular, Palmer's attempt to make sense of the death of her firstborn, Alexander, reflected concerns regarding gentility that would be elaborated and emphasized throughout her later holiness teaching. After the baby's birth, the new mother had spent hours embroidering an elaborate layette while she delayed presenting the infant for baptism. Palmer feared the potential consequences of the sacrament: that the baby, a frail child, might be taken from her if he were given up, "body, as well as soul, to God." She suspected that all the "little adornments" she had sewn were mute witnesses to her hesitancy, because, she reasoned, if the child belonged to God "Should I adorn him thus?" Alexander died before Palmer could overcome her reluctance. Her grief was intensified by the belief that the child had been "taken away," rather than freely offered to God.[26]

Two issues related to gentility surfaced in Palmer's interpretation of her son's death. The first, and more minor in this instance, concerned the actual frills on the baby clothes. They were outward signs that Palmer had not yet renounced the world and its hold on her child. Second, and more important, the energy she lavished on adornments was a diversionary tactic to avoid the central challenge of completely relinquishing the baby to God. This desire to hold something

---

24. Wheatley, *Life and Letters*, 86.
25. Palmer, *Way of Holiness*, 32.
26. Ibid., 254-55; Wheatley, *Life and Letters*, 26; Raser, *Palmer*, 38-39.

back signaled that God was not uppermost in Palmer's heart. These two elements—turning one's back on the world and surrendering all to God—comprised what Palmer later described as "entire consecration," the decisive first step on the way to sanctification. Both elements were critical aspects of Palmer's response to gentility after she experienced holiness in 1837 and began to write and teach on the subject a few years later.

The call to renunciation was clear cut. To Palmer, the biblical injunction, "Be not conformed to this world," affirmed traditional restrictions in the Methodist *Discipline* concerning fashionable dress, dancing, the theater, and frivolous conversation. Her three most popular books, *The Way of Holiness* (1843), *Entire Devotion to God* (1845), and *Faith and Its Effects* (1848), contain numerous cautionary tales emphasizing the danger of behaviors that represented any hint of spiritual indecision. Preoccupation with fashion, for example, was no trivial matter. There could be "no neutral ground" when it came to the boundaries between the church and the world; those who compromised risked severe chastisement from God, and perhaps their immortal souls.[27] Throughout her life, Palmer practiced what she preached. Her own clothing was plain, even severe, though obviously well cut. Engravings show her in a black dress with a simple collar, no jewelry, and a dark ribbon instead of a watch chain. Palmer and Sarah Lankford came to be known among their less pious New York acquaintances as "the drab sisters," an epithet that reflected the pressures of changing fashion mores.[28]

Although Palmer rejected everything associated with the trappings of "gay fashionable society," her attitude toward other aspects of refinement was more complex. Her emphasis on relinquishing or surrendering every aspect of life to God—the positive side of consecration—lay at the heart of her attempt to balance propriety and religious rigor. Wealth, education, even taste and manners, were compatible with holiness as long as they were dedicated to God. Palmer encouraged her followers to draw up a personal covenant or contract, signing over "body, soul, and spirit, time, talents, influence, family, and estate—all . . . for ever, and in the most unlimited sense," to God.[29]

27. Palmer, *Faith and Its Effects*, 197.
28. Roche, *Life*, 261. For various engravings of Palmer, see Wheatley, *Life and Letters;* Phoebe Palmer, *Incidental Illustrations of the Economy of Salvation* (Boston: Henry V. Degen, 1857); and Palmer, *Four Years in the Old World*.
29. Palmer, *Entire Devotion*, 73.

Palmer did not forget the lesson of Alexander's death. She had made her own covenant, and she applied the principle of consecration as literally as possible in her home. George Coles, a Methodist minister, conducted the prayer meeting that dedicated every room of the Rivington Street house for Christian use, a practice that was repeated in the two subsequent Palmer residences. Daily routines in the household also reflected Phoebe's and Walter's desire to be "wholly the Lord's." At mealtimes conversation centered around religious topics, and each person at the table, children included, recited a Bible verse at some point during the dinner hour.[30] If they were sacralized, then a comfortable home, good food, family, and friends could all be enjoyed with a clear conscience.

On a practical level, Palmer used three criteria for determining which aspects of gentility could safely be dedicated to God: conformity to biblical teaching, usefulness, and comfort. She affirmed good manners and aesthetic sensibilities because both, she believed, were sanctioned by the Bible. While rejecting worldly affectation, Palmer cautioned Christians against going to the opposite extreme and taking pride in boorishness. People who gloried in "unlovely habits, and manners uncouth," as evidence that they had mortified the flesh, were actually "sinning against . . . express Scriptural requirements."[31]

Usefulness also justified gentility. As Gregory Schneider has shown, the link between holiness and usefulness was deeply rooted in American Methodism, and Palmer used the two words, whether referring to persons or things, almost as synonyms. Usefulness meant doing the most possible good for God, particularly in terms of saving souls and promoting sanctification. She supported educational opportunities for unlettered but enthusiastic Methodist preachers because lack of preparation hindered their usefulness, even among the "common people." Spacious homes, including mansions, could be used for God if their owners had laid all "at the foot of the cross."[32] Although she rarely commented on church or denominational practices, Palmer approved of some architectural modifications to the early plain style of Methodist church construction, such as the addition of a steeple or bell. Again, the criteria was utilitarian: a church bell could be "useful in calling souls to salvation." The church build-

---

30. Wheatley, *Life and Letters,* 66, 150-52, 158-59, 162.
31. Palmer, *Way of Holiness,* 173-74.
32. Wheatley, *Life and Letters,* 235-36; *Guide to Holiness* 36 (1859): 97; A. Gregory Schneider, *The Way of the Cross Leads Home: The Domestication of American Methodism* (Bloomington: Indiana University Press, 1993), 56; also Raser, *Palmer,* 212.

ings themselves should be "scrupulously neat, properly commodious, and comfortable."[33] Palmer paid less specific attention to the idea of comfort; she simply assumed that comfort was useful to the work of God.

In her response to gentility, Palmer distinguished between spiritual egalitarianism and social differences. She insisted that holiness was open to all, and even more, was a biblical mandate for every genuine Christian. God did not distinguish between clergy or laity, rich or poor, women or men in bestowing the blessing. Palmer loved to speak of the "equalizing process," which took place at the Tuesday meetings, to obliterate distinctions of denomination or gender. However, this did not undermine the social order, nor did Palmer consider social distinctions inherently unchristian. She invoked the traditional Protestant concepts of providence and vocation to justify social distinctions. "The Lord generally calls us to be lights to those around us . . . in just the circle from which he has singled us out. . . . Thus with those of every grade in life."[34] Harking back to an earlier age, she emphasized the responsibility of the wealthy to care for the poor, both through acts of charity and through the work of evangelization.[35] Her social attitudes were not those of a dissenting Methodism, but of a *de facto* establishment. In contrast to the new patterns of social organization created by Methodists during the early republic, Palmer holiness provided a spirituality for people who already had a place in society.[36]

The key for the sanctified person was detachment from the things of this world in favor of love for God. For the upwardly mobile or prosperous Methodists who formed the bulk of the Palmer holiness constituency, this meant a spiritual rather than a literal separation. It was not the ascetic "way of the cross" embraced by the early itinerants. Instead, Phoebe Palmer and her followers sought to separate themselves from the *values* of gentility that conflicted with Christian ideals, in Palmer's words, "a coming out from the world in such a sense as not to be governed by its opinions."[37] Palmer's theology

---

33. *Guide to Holiness* 7 n.s. (March 1868): 122-23.

34. Ibid., 31 (May 1857): 137; Palmer, *Way of Holiness*, 172.

35. Palmer, *Faith and Its Effects*, 214.

36. Perhaps because of her identification with English social mores, Palmer's attitude reflected more of what has been described as the "deferential virtue of the early Christian republicanism of the Reformed" than was common among Methodists. However, her Methodist affinities are clear in that her concern for benevolence and the responsibility of the wealthy was linked much more closely to issues of personal sanctification than social stability or Christianization. See Schneider, *Way of the Cross*, 26.

37. Palmer, *Faith and Its Effects*, 192.

represented an attempt to sever gentility from its troubling cultural roots by sanctifying it. Holiness offered the possibility of wealth without selfishness, manners without condescension, education without pride, and comfort without complacency—in short, respectability purified from its worldly associations. This, coupled with Palmer's emphasis on sanctification as the *sine qua non* for a heroic, activistic Christian life, proved an attractive combination.[38]

The Appeal of Sanctified Gentility

The people who identified themselves with Palmer illustrated the appeal of her message. Nathan Bangs, one of the most influential figures in American Methodism during the half century prior to the Civil War and the personification of Methodism's move toward respectability, attended the Tuesday meeting from 1842 until his death in 1863. In some ways Bangs, a generation older than Phoebe Palmer, served as a father figure for the movement. Having known Palmer since her childhood, he supported her focus on sanctification and vouched for her rectitude and piety, even when he did not always agree with her theology. Together with Walter Palmer, Bangs shared the duties of opening the Tuesday meeting with Bible reading and prayer—providing a semblance of male leadership at a meeting actually directed by Phoebe Palmer, or, in her absence, Sarah Lankford. His presence helped give the private gathering an unofficial church imprimatur.[39]

In turn, the Tuesday meeting and the general character of Palmer holiness exemplified the style of Methodism Bangs had encouraged during his five decades of ministry in New York City—orderly, affluent, cultivated, and fervent. During the early years of the century, Bangs had lobbied for decorum in Methodist worship; a favorite Palmer maxim proclaimed "Order is heaven's first law."[40] Both

---

38. On occasion, early Methodism also sought to sanctify social hierarchy and wealth; however, by the 1840s and 1850s Methodists were having to cope with a substantial segment of the denomination, particularly in urban centers, who had achieved some level of affluence and vernacular gentility. See Schneider, *Way of the Cross*, 63. For Palmer activism, see Raser, *Palmer*, 162, 197-98, 211-18.

39. Bangs did criticize sharply some aspects of Palmer's theology, but overall their relationship was warm and deeply rooted. See, for example, Wheatley, *Life and Letters*, 70-71, where Palmer wrote of Bangs's fiftieth wedding anniversary. Abel Stevens, *Life and Times of Nathan Bangs* (New York: Carlton & Porter, 1863), 225, 350-53, 396-402, traces Bangs's relationship with Palmer and her holiness movement. On at least some occasions, as Stevens, *Life and Times*, 395, noted, Walter Palmer was Bangs's physician.

40. Palmer, *Faith and Its Effects*, 223. The picture of Bangs in this paragraph is based largely on Hatch, *Democratization*, 201-4.

believed that sanctification was essential to a vital Methodist piety, though Bangs came to emphasize the doctrine during the latter years of his life. He had experienced the blessing in 1801 as an earnest young convert, and returned to it almost as a way of coming full circle to reclaim a piety that would complete the respectability he had worked so hard to achieve.[41] Bangs represented the upward aspirations of second-generation Methodist leaders and their church. Palmer stood for the third generation. Confident in her social position, secure in an identity derived in part from English Methodism, she was living proof that Bangs and his colleagues were on the right track. As Nathan Hatch has pointed out, Bangs dreamed of Methodism "as a popular establishment, faithful to the movement's original fire but tempered with virtues of middle-class propriety and urbane congeniality."[42] The atmosphere of the Tuesday meeting and the overall character of the Palmer holiness movement showed that the dream could come true.

Another influential Methodist, Bishop Leonidas Hamline, and his wife, Melinda, were Phoebe Palmer's closest friends and supporters outside her immediate family. The son of a Connecticut school teacher, Hamline had considered the Presbyterian ministry, then studied law and married into a wealthy Ohio family prior to his conversion in 1828. Well known as a public speaker, young Hamline's identification with Methodism helped bring "influence and standing" to the denomination in Ohio. In the early 1830s, the new convert became a preacher on a western Virginia circuit, leaving his wife and the family mansion for months at a time. With a reputation, however, as a man of "refined tastes, classic culture, and rare pulpit eloquence," after a year Hamline was assigned to the growing city of Cincinnati, a place "more suitable" to his gifts.[43]

When he became a Methodist, Hamline turned his back on ostentatious wealth. He placed his financial affairs in trust, a practice he continued after his first wife's death in 1835. He and his second wife, Melinda, lived on the reduced but still very comfortable income of a thousand dollars a year.[44] Although Hamline displayed caution

---

41. Stevens, *Bangs*, 58-59.

42. Hatch, *Democratization*, 202.

43. F. G. Hibbard, *Biography of Rev. Leonidas L. Hamline* (Cincinnati: Hitchcock & Walden, 1880), 22, 47, 65.

44. Hamline gave away another one thousand dollars annually to Methodist causes; due to the appreciation of Chicago real estate, Hamline's estate was worth more than one hundred thousand dollars in the early 1850s. See ibid., 378-89.

regarding the lure of riches, he was enthusiastic about helping to bring culture to western Methodism. In 1836 he was appointed assistant editor of the newly established *Western Christian Advocate*, a regional weekly paper that would come to rival the New York City *Christian Advocate and Journal* in its circulation and influence.[45] In 1841 he became founding editor of the *Ladies' Repository*, Methodism's entry in the growing market of women's magazines. Through the pages of the *Repository*, Hamline advised readers on how to select "works of taste" in literature, as well as on strategies to prevent husbands from chewing tobacco in church.[46] Such tips, alongside more serious literary fare, attracted "ambitious and educated Methodist Christian women . . . [those] headed inexorably into the mainstream of middle-class sophistication."[47] In addition to his editorial work, Hamline maintained a grueling preaching schedule and sought to promote Methodist educational ventures in the West, helping, for example, to obtain property as a site for Ohio Wesleyan University.[48]

Hamline professed sanctification in 1842, and his wife a year later. Both were influenced by Phoebe Palmer in what proved to be the beginning of a lifelong friendship. The pair were frequent guests in the Palmer home, and Phoebe maintained a voluminous correspondence with both husband and wife. After Leonidas Hamline was ordained bishop in 1844, Phoebe prayed for him daily.[49] The Palmer and Hamline couples were soul mates in their commitment to the promotion of holiness, their intense religious activism, and their social backgrounds. In 1851, Melinda Hamline published the *Memoir of Mrs. Angeline B. Sears*, the biography of a young Cincinnati woman who renounced worldly privilege to become the wife of a Methodist minister. Mrs. Hamline had tutored Sears in the way of holiness, resulting in a triumphant deathbed experience of entire sanctification that, in turn, led to the conversion of family members and friends. The account communicated familiar themes of the attraction of Methodism to refined people, the power of the holiness message, and

---

45. James Penn Pilkington, *The Methodist Publishing House: A History from Its Beginnings to 1870*, 2 vols. (Nashville: Abingdon Press, 1968), 1:243, 247, 386.

46. *Ladies' Repository* 1 (February 1842): 34-47; and 2 (September 1842): 262-63.

47. Joanna Bowen Gillespie, "The Emerging Voice of the Methodist Woman: The *Ladies' Repository*, 1841–61," *Perspectives*, 262.

48. Hibbard, *Hamline*, 91.

49. Wheatley, *Life and Letters*, 98-99, and passim. During the mid-1840s and perhaps longer, Melinda Hamline and Palmer set a time each day when both would pray in order to be united in their efforts.

the evangelical concern for souls. It was the sort of book Palmer herself might have written.[50]

Phoebe Palmer's diary and letters, as well as subsequent histories, have documented the appeal of the holiness movement to other eminent Methodists. A virtual *who's who* of the northern church appeared at the Tuesday meeting or accepted Palmer hospitality.[51] When the Methodist General Conference convened in New York City, Palmer rarely missed opportunities to entertain church leaders, either as house guests or for dinner on a Tuesday. A diary note from 1849 recorded, "Bishops Hedding, Waugh, and Morris, in company with our dear Bishop Hamline and others, dined with us to-day. . . . At the meeting this afternoon we had a season of much interest."[52] Educators and editors also came within the Palmer orbit. Stephen Olin, Wilbur Fisk, and John Dempster, pioneers in Methodist higher education, all crossed the threshold of the Tuesday meeting. Accounts of the Palmers' social life portrayed a couple at ease with religious leaders in and outside of Methodism. On occasion they visited the Olin home near Wesleyan University or spent time in the country with the family of Bishop Edmund S. Janes. In the midst of a camp meeting tour in 1857, Palmer made a side trip from Boston to spend an hour and a half with Harriet Beecher Stowe. The following year she and Dr. Palmer made a similar stop in Providence, Rhode Island, to visit Baptist educator Francis Wayland.[53] Phoebe Palmer's friendship with and influence on Congregationalist philosopher Thomas C. Upham were also well known.

Palmer's social aplomb and spiritual acumen were reflected in an "editors' dinner" she organized in November 1855 for the heads of several Methodist publications, including family friend Thomas Bond of the *Christian Advocate and Journal*. The meal took place at the height of a controversy over certain aspects of her holiness doctrine, a dispute largely carried out in the pages of the same weekly papers. Palmer orchestrated the evening to express Christian love for her

---

50. See the discussion of Melinda Hamline, *Memoir of Mrs. Angeline B. Sears, with Extracts from Her Correspondence* (Cincinnati: Swormstedt & Poe, 1851) in Schneider, *Way of the Cross*, 182-86. Palmer did write two comparable books: *Mary; or, The Young Christian* (New York: Carlton & Porter, 1840) and *The Useful Disciple; or, a Narrative of Mrs. Mary Gardner* (Cincinnati: Swormstedt & Poe, 1853).

51. Wheatley, *Life and Letters*, 113-14, 162-64, 244-47; Hughes, *Fragrant Memories*, 149; also Dieter, *Holiness Revival*, 37; Thomas C. Oden, ed., *Phoebe Palmer: Selected Writings* (New York: Paulist Press, 1988), 11; White, *Way of Holiness*, xvi, 163.

52. Wheatley, *Life and Letters*, 162-63.

53. Ibid., 606-7, 336.

enemies and to present herself as a gracious hostess, hardly a menace to Methodist orthodoxy. She remarked, in a letter to the Hamlines, "Really, not only as a matter of religion, but of *taste* . . . it was one of the nicest things I ever did of that sort."[54]

The dignity of the Palmer parlors and dining room attracted people in the process of distancing themselves from the social shortcomings of Methodism's populist past. In addition, as the editorial dinner suggested, a certain sanctified graciousness helped reinforce the legitimacy of Palmer holiness in the eyes of powerful clergy. It served to mute the potential threat of what was essentially an extraecclesiastical enterprise spearheaded by a woman. The aura of respectability and culture surrounding the holiness cause enabled Palmer to mount a popular middle-class movement close to the centers of denominational power. Hers was a renewal rather than a protest effort, and she pursued it in part by seeking to persuade clergy of the rightness of her cause. During the 1850s, she seemed to be succeeding, a remarkable accomplishment in light of the backlash against women preachers—and by extension, women in leadership—that had characterized Methodism since the 1830s.[55] Criticisms by Methodist seminary professor Hiram Mattison and others were more an indication of Palmer's growing influence than a threat to the holiness cause.

The decade prior to the Civil War marked the most fruitful years of Palmer's North American ministry. Her books sold, the Tuesday meeting grew, she traveled widely as a revivalist to camp meetings in both the northeastern United States and in Canada. When home in New York City, she found time, at least in the early 1850s, to help establish the new Methodist city mission among the poor in the Five Points slum. At the same time, however, there were indications in Palmer's own life and the broader holiness effort that the worldly pull of gentility was not easily eradicated.[56]

At the heart of the difficulty was the continuing tension between the spiritual egalitarianism of the holiness message and the sensitivity of Palmer and other genteel Methodists to social distinctions. The

---

54. Ibid., 113, italics in the original. For a discussion of the controversy, provoked by Methodist seminary professor Hiram Mattison, see Raser, *Phoebe Palmer*, 65-67 and 267-77.

55. Brekus, *Strangers & Pilgrims*, 294-95; 337-38. Brekus laments Palmer's apparent inability to recognize the contributions of the popular women preachers of early American Methodism. However, Palmer's blindness in this area was not gender based. As noted earlier she distanced herself from all expressions of American "enthusiasm," represented by women or men.

56. For the 1850s, including Palmer's British trip, as the pinnacle of her career, see Raser, *Palmer*, 62-63.

shipboard experiences of the Palmer family en route to England in 1859 revealed in microcosm some of the dynamics behind her movement. The Palmers—Phoebe, Walter, and their son—had booked first-class passage. The cabins were commodious and the company congenial, but the journey became something of a trial because most of the other travelers passed the voyage drinking and playing cards or board games. To Phoebe Palmer's dismay, even the ministers in the group, none of whom were Methodists, joined in the games of dice or chess. The first Sunday out, however, the Palmer family discovered a more spiritually compatible atmosphere among the passengers in steerage. After an afternoon hymn sing on the lower deck, as one of her biographers has pointed out, Phoebe Palmer "congratulated herself that she had obeyed the scriptural admonition, 'Mind not high things, but condescend to men of low estate.'" Certainly Francis Asbury and others had cited the same instructions in justifying their mission to mobilize early Methodism in America as a popular movement. But whereas Asbury joined his preachers on their backcountry circuits, the Palmers returned to the upper deck once the service was over. Palmer idealized the poor as "heaven's nobility," but they were not the people with whom she regularly associated.[57]

At one level, Palmer intended the holiness movement to be for "the masses" in the broadest sense. Her extensive camp meeting ministry was aimed, in part, at extending her message to the grass roots. She wanted to write for a popular readership, and her goal was a return to the "primitive simplicity" of Wesleyan Methodism. Yet it still would be a movement run by the people in the first-class cabins. The time of the Tuesday meeting, from 2:30 to 4:00 in the afternoon, communicated clearly that this was not a gathering for the rank and file. That was also the message of a widely circulated story about the meeting. It told of a woman from Richmond, Virginia, who was staying at New York City's posh St. Nicholas Hotel, the city's premiere accommodation, when she visited the weekly gathering. Deeply moved by the proceedings, she returned to her room and continued to pray. According to the narrative, "purity of heart" was granted and "the St. Nicholas became the 'gate of heaven.'" The hotel, with its six hundred rooms, frescoed ceilings, grand staircase, and every possible "comfort, convenience, magnitude, and luxury," was a far cry from

---

57. Palmer, *Four Years in the Old World*, 17-23; White, *Beauty of Holiness*, 69.

the cabins or simple homes that had been the "gate to heaven" for earlier Methodists.[58]

The Free Methodist Challenge

Palmer's concern to accommodate wealth and holiness provided one of the sharpest contrasts between her movement and that of Benjamin Titus Roberts and the so-called "Nazarites," a holiness party of clergy and laity in western New York who formed the Free Methodist Church in 1860. In 1849, as a young minister, Roberts had experienced sanctification in a camp meeting south of Buffalo where Palmer spoke. The substance of his subsequent doctrinal teaching on the subject resembled Palmer's and both clearly stood in the Wesleyan tradition.[59] However, the unfolding of the Nazarite controversy demonstrated that the holiness revival kindled in the camp meetings and churches on the western edge of the "burned over district" was distant in geography and cultural context from that of the parlors at Rivington Street.

The dispute began as a quarrel between two groups of ministers— the Nazarites and the "Buffalo Regency"—in the Genesee Conference of New York Methodism. To the Nazarites, the liberal Regency faction represented all that was wrong with Methodism, as it had increasingly accommodated to genteel respectability. In the article that precipitated his eventual expulsion from the church, Roberts wrote that the Regency party, along with the denomination as a whole, suffered from the "intoxicating effect" of prosperity. Inebriated by elaborate architecture, rented pews, and professional church music, these "New-School Methodists," as Roberts called them, had traded revivals for fund-raising projects. They patronized "oyster suppers, fairs . . . festivals and lotteries" in order to build fancy churches. Methodism's mission, Roberts remonstrated, was not to appeal to

---

58. John A. Roche, "Mrs. Phoebe Palmer," *Ladies' Repository* 26 (February 1866): 69, seems to be the first account of the story. For a description of the hotel, which opened in 1854, see Charles Lockwood, *Manhattan Moves Uptown: An Illustrated History* (Boston: Houghton Mifflin, 1976), 151-52. For a sample of frontier dwellings seen as "heaven's gate," see Allen Wiley, "The Introduction and Progress of Methodism in Southeastern Indiana," *Indiana Magazine of History* 23 (1927), 175-76, 394, cited in Schneider, *Way of the Cross*, 97.

59. There is some dispute over the year of Roberts's sanctification. According to Roberts, it was 1849 at a camp meeting at Collins, New York. See Elias Bowen, *History of the Origin of the Free Methodist Church* (Rochester, N.Y.: B. T. Roberts, 1871), 346. The Palmers left no record of visiting Collins in 1849, although they did so in 1850 and 1851. See White, *Beauty of Holiness*, 41-42, 238, 266 n. 75.

"the proud and fashionable," but "to spread scripture holiness over these lands." It had fallen away from the "old paths."[60]

The Nazarite disaffection also tapped into rural/urban tensions and the perception that the urban-dominated Regency party had the ear, and the support, of church hierarchy. Antimasonry and antislavery played a role as well. Methodism had compromised not only in terms of individual piety, but also on issues of denominational, social, and political import.[61] Through church trials in 1858 and 1860, the Regency group proved that it did indeed control the ecclesiastical power in the district. Leaders from the Nazarites, including Roberts, were expelled from the church in 1860. Together with their lay supporters, they joined radical sanctificationists from the Midwest to form the Free Methodist Church, a church "delivered from secret societies, slavery, rented pews, outward ornaments, and . . . at liberty to have 'the freedom of the Spirit' in its worship."[62]

The apology mounted by the Free Methodists to justify their new church as a revival of "pure, primitive, Wesleyan Methodism" revealed holiness teachings in a sharply different context than that given them by Palmer. The Free Methodists appealed to a different past than Palmer did, and they viewed sanctification as the badge of a countercultural piety. First, although they cited Wesley as their ecclesiastical and theological authority, their history was American. Their primitive ideal was the original Methodist Episcopal Church of the early republic, a church of the poor, of plain people, where the "mighty impulses" of God's Spirit were expressed through "strong emotion" and preaching "in thunder tones."[63] Whereas Phoebe Palmer and many other urbanites were trying to overcome prejudice against Methodists as "ignorant fanatics," the Free Methodists gloried in their role as enthusiastic, persecuted outsiders.[64]

The American influence was also evident in the antiaristocratic bent of the new church—an egalitarianism that went well beyond the spiritual leveling Palmer advocated. The recalcitrant Nazarite clergy had been supported by "lay bands" of holiness adherents, and annual laymen's conventions between 1858 and 1860 provided grassroots

---

60. B. T. Roberts, "New-School Methodism," in Bowen, *Free Methodist Church*, 307-8, 310.

61. This summary based on *HAM* 2:342-43.

62. Ibid., 356.

63. Bowen, *Free Methodist Church*, 20, 230-31.

64. In the first book Palmer published, a biography for Sunday school readers, she described the mother of the subject of the book as a woman whose "prejudices had been strong against the Methodists. From her infancy she had been taught to look upon them as ignorant fanatics." See "First Book: Mary, or the Young Christian (1841)" in Oden, *Phoebe Palmer*, 149.

support for Roberts and other ministers in the face of official church discipline. In return, the Free Methodists gave laymen equal voice alongside clergy in church government, a privilege not enjoyed by the laity in mainstream Methodism. The church rejected "caste" systems that differentiated on the basis of race, ecclesiastical position, or wealth.[65]

The Free Methodists defined themselves in opposition to the genteel mainstream in other ways as well. They took the call to separation—to "come out" from the world—much more literally, particularly in reference to wealth, than did Palmer. To Phoebe Palmer the most important visible boundary between church and world lay in the realm of personal behavior; to the Free Methodists the line ran between rich and poor. Roberts insisted that Jesus "forbids his disciples to amass wealth," and that the church had a special mission to preach the gospel to the poor.[66] In theory, Roberts and Palmer were not far apart: Palmer idealized the poor and condemned the unwillingness of the rich to give to benevolent causes as "palpably wrong." She expressed reservations about those who professed sanctification "yet [did] not exhibit the fruits of holiness in relation to giving."[67] Roberts, for his part, accepted the possibility that wealth might, in some cases, be entirely consecrated to God.

However, the two were poles apart in emphasis and practice. Palmer stressed the potential of entire sanctification to unhinge the connection between wealth and spiritual decline. She highlighted examples in the Bible and Methodist history of sanctified affluence— Abraham, David, Joseph of Arimathea, the "elect lady" in the New Testament epistle of Second John, and her Methodist successor, Lady Maxwell. Palmer warned against "censoriousness" in condemning the rich, an attitude "not unfrequently indulged in by a class of persons who would unchristianize everything they cannot bring down to their own level."[68] In practice, she tended to view pietistic activism as sufficient evidence of detachment from the world. During their 1858 tour of Canada, Walter Palmer wrote from Prince Edward Island that the couple were staying at the mansion of "a Christian gentleman

65. Bowen, *Free Methodist Church*, 238.

66. Roberts, *Earnest Christian* (February 1865): 60-62, quoted in William C. Kostlevy, "Benjamin Titus Roberts and the 'Preferential Option for the Poor' in the Early Free Methodist Church," in Anthony L. Dunavant, ed., *Poverty and Ecclesiology: Nineteenth-Century Evangelicals in the Light of Liberation Theology* (Collegeville, Minn.: Liturgical Press, 1992), 59; see also Bowen, *Free Methodist Church*, 248-49.

67. Palmer, *Faith and Its Effects*, 214, 218.

68. Ibid., 216.

of wealth and influence," who roamed the congregation during Palmer meetings, "inviting sinners to Jesus." Phoebe expressed similar sentiments a year later about their hostess in London, "truly the elect lady . . . Her servants are all pious . . . The service of God was the Alpha and Omega of her hospitable mansion."[69]

For his part, Roberts viewed the link between riches and religious decline as axiomatic, with only rare exceptions. He believed that the few wealthy followers of Jesus literally relinquished their goods at the day of Pentecost. More than any other class in society, Roberts wrote, the wealthy were in "imminent danger of eternal damnation . . . If any of them are saved, it will be the exception, and not the rule." To Roberts, poor Christians, aware of their indebtedness to God, had greater potential to be useful and fervent for the gospel than did people of means.[70] Palmer inverted the equation; the rich could do more good because they had more to consecrate. In particular, Palmer admonished affluent women not to neglect religious work in favor of household duties, which they "should be paying another to do."[71]

The two movements—Palmer holiness and the Nazarite sanctificationists—reflected the adaptability of perfectionism, along with so many other aspects of American Methodism, to radically different social and cultural locations. On the one hand, sanctification could serve as an engine of populist protest; on the other, as a mediator of middle- and upper-class respectable religion. With only a few concessions, such as a commitment to education, the Free Methodists rejected the possibility that gentility in any form could be compatible with true Christianity. Palmer continued to demonstrate through the example of her own life and revivalistic successes that a rigorous, individualistic sanctification could be combined with urbane living. Paradoxically, through her British orientation, Palmer was quintessentially American in her ability to adapt popular Methodism to middle- and upper-class life.[72]

During the middle and late 1850s, while the strife escalated in the Genesee Conference, Palmer remained distant from the scene. Whether through their own initiative or because they were not invited, after 1851 the Palmers did not return to camp meetings in western New York and cut back on what had been an extensive upstate

---

69. Wheatley, *Life and Letters*, 340; *Guide to Holiness* 36 (1859): 97.

70. Roberts, *Earnest Christian* (February 1865): 60; also, January 1870, pp. 30-31; and March 1864, pp. 70-71, quoted in Kostlevy, "Benjamin Titus Roberts," 59.

71. Wheatley, *Life and Letters*, 597.

72. Hatch, *Democratization*, 208-9, and Hatch, "American Methodism," 188-89, point to this adaptability as a characteristic of American Methodism.

summer circuit. Instead, they focused their energies on meetings along the northern and western shore of Lake Ontario in Canada West, plus a few engagements in Massachusetts and Maine.[73] They then followed the winds of transatlantic revivalism to Great Britain, where they were when the Nazarites actually were expelled and the Free Methodist Church formed in 1860.

Palmer returned in 1864 to find a Methodism increasingly polarized over the subject of holiness. The radically different style of the Free Methodists existed as a tacit, if not explicit, condemnation of her own balancing act between gentility and sanctification. The new church also threatened her goal to promote holiness as a centrist reforming movement within Methodism by identifying it with schismatic fringe elements. Palmer excoriated the Free Methodists for their "factious and schismatic proceedings." She blamed them for undermining the effectiveness of all who professed holiness as a special emphasis of genuine Methodism. Her comments may have contained an edge of bitterness because not only B. T. Roberts, but also John Wesley Redfield, the Free Methodist leader in the Midwest, had professed sanctification in a camp meeting where Palmer had spoken. It seemed all too easy for disaffected individuals and groups to take the emphases Palmer herself had developed, and recast them into forms that destabilized her cause.[74]

The Perils of Accommodation

Palmer viewed the late 1860s as "perilous times" for the way of holiness, and not simply because of the Free Methodist defection. Other former friends were damaging the cause as well. In an 1869 letter to Melinda Hamline lamenting the damage of Free Methodism, Palmer also expressed alarm over the activities of Henry Ward Beecher and Harriet Beecher Stowe in "using their influence by way of aiding the kingdom of Satan."[75] Palmer's sense of betrayal was deep because both had been publicly identified as holiness sympathizers during the antebellum years. In 1845, Stowe had published

---

73. The few upstate engagements Palmer accepted after 1853 were in central New York, well east of the controversies. See the list of "Camp Meetings and Revival Services 1839–59" in White, *Beauty of Holiness*, 237–39. For the Palmers in Canada, see Peter George Bush, "James Caughey, Phoebe and Walter Palmer and the Methodist Revival Experience in Canada West, 1850–1858" (unpublished Masters thesis, Queen's University, Kingston, Ontario, Canada, 1985), especially the map following p. 111.

74. Wheatley, *Life and Letters*, 452; White, *Beauty of Holiness*, 100.

75. Wheatley, *Life and Letters*, 450.

"The Interior Life," a widely reprinted article setting aside the terminology of "sinless perfection" but advocating "higher spiritual attainments" as an expression of New Testament Christianity. During the
1850s her poems and an occasional essay appeared in the *Guide to
Christian Perfection* and the *Beauty of Holiness*, the two premiere publications of the movement. Reprints of articles by Henry Ward Beecher
also were featured; during 1857 his byline appeared in nearly every
issue of the *Beauty of Holiness*.[76]

Palmer had voiced concern about Stowe as early as 1857 because
the New Englander wrote religious fiction. To Palmer the idea of a
"pious novel" was an oxymoron that signaled "an unholy blending of
religious and irreligious practices."[77] Her choice of the word *blending*
pointed to the essence of her quarrel with the Beechers and their
response to the spread of vernacular gentility. They, along with many
others of the liberalizing New England evangelical elite, responded to
gentility by accepting a reciprocal relationship between piety, beauty,
and taste. Such things as art, fashion, architecture, and fiction could
be useful to Christianity to the extent that they refined people's taste,
and thus their spirituality and virtue. *Uncle Tom's Cabin*, as a sentimental novel, aimed in part to elevate readers' feelings until they
were "in harmony with the sympathies of Christ."[78]

Through the pages of *Norwood*, his own attempt at novel-writing,
Henry Ward Beecher wondered what would happen "if one were to
visit the poorhouse in each town and minister . . . to the taste and
sympathy of its inmates, with gifts of beauty."[79] A letter to the editor
of *Godey's Lady's Book*, a popular magazine that also propagated the
"gospel of gentility," reflected the allure of this intermingling to members of Palmer's holiness constituency. "Though many good people
condemn all 'fashion-plate' periodicals," wrote the subscriber, "I
think a well-conducted one, like the *Lady's Book*, is calculated to do
immense good, by presenting religious truths and the 'beauty of holiness' in company with good taste, refinement and genius."[80]

---

76. For "The Interior Life; or Primitive Christian Experience," an article apparently inspired
by Thomas C. Upham's first holiness book, *Principles of the Interior or Hidden Life* (1843), see the
New York Evangelist, 19 June 1845, reprinted in the *Guide to Christian Perfection* 8 (1845): 13-18. See
also the *Guide* 25 (January-July 1854): 58, 111, for other material by Stowe.

77. Wheatley, *Life and Letters*, 607.

78. Harriet Beecher Stowe, *Uncle Tom's Cabin* (1850–51; reprint, New York: Bantam, 1981), 442.
For an elaboration of the Protestant syncretism of religion and taste, see Bushman, *Refinement of
America*, 319-49.

79. Quoted in McLoughlin, *The Meaning of Henry Ward Beecher*, 131.

80. *Godey's Lady's Book* 35 (November 1847): 272.

An approach that so clearly identified refinement with Christianity blurred the boundaries between the two, and Palmer repudiated it with unusual vehemence, perhaps because it came so close to her own mix of refinement and holiness. She denounced *Uncle Tom's Cabin* as a "mongrel" work, an "admixture of truth and error." Evil consequences would come from such an amalgamation, an assessment confirmed when the book was adapted for the theater. "Who would ever have thought," Palmer lamented, "that the name of the author of an excellent tract on practical holiness, would one day be emblazoned in large letters on theatrical posters, by way of luring men to perdition." Henry Ward Beecher was little better, selling his name and ministerial influence to the "novel-mongers" for the reputed ten thousand dollars he was paid to write *Norwood*.[81] Palmer's critique pointed to the limits and ambiguities of her pragmatic approach to sanctified refinement. Wealth or church steeples might be justified for their usefulness in promoting the Christian message, but novels or plays, no matter how edifying, went beyond the pale.

Striving to Maintain the Synthesis

Within Methodism itself, events of the 1860s communicated a mixed message about the future of holiness teachings. Influential voices echoed the Palmer synthesis of rigor and respectability. As part of the centenary celebrations in 1866, John C. McClintock, future president of Drew University, stood in the pulpit of St. Paul's, the finest and most expensive Methodist church in New York City, to insist that the denomination must retain the "great central idea" of personal sanctification. "If we keep to that, the next century is ours."[82] Other occurrences, however, suggested that the "perils" represented by the Free Methodists and the gospel of gentility were tugging at the centrist position Palmer had crafted. In January 1864, Palmer admitted to her sister, Sarah, "how wearying to flesh and spirit" had been her efforts to call church members in Troy, New York, to the standards of entire consecration required for holiness. Although she ended the letter on a triumphant note, a local minister later reported that her success had been limited because "the age does not incline to the severe

---

81. *Guide to Holiness*, 7 n.s. (January 1868): 28-29.
82. *HAM* 2:611. Completed in 1857, St. Paul's cost an estimated $175,000. See Seaman, *Annals*, 325.

religion of . . . John Wesley." Prosperous church members sought a piety that made room for "lectures, skating parties, minstrels . . . and dancing parties."[83]

Only a few years later, the main body of Palmer sympathizers within Methodism took a subtle but significant step toward the periphery of the denomination with the organization of the National Camp Meeting Association for the Promotion of Holiness. Formed in the wake of a special holiness camp meeting at Vineland, New Jersey, in July 1867, the National Association boasted prominent urban pastors, such as John Inskip and Alfred Cookman, among its leaders. Nonetheless, the move to locate perfectionist renewal primarily in a camp meeting setting was a shift away from the urban parlor culture that had been at the heart of Palmer's ministry and that had maintained her movement close to the centers of denominational power. Of course, Phoebe Palmer herself had maintained an extensive and substantial presence on the camp meeting circuit. But the Tuesday meeting was the true locus of her influence, and she traveled to the peripheries from that center. As the National Association organized holiness camp meetings that extended farther afield each year from the eastern seaboard, it began to tap a grassroots constituency much broader than that represented by the affluent urbanites who filled the second floor of the Palmer home. The transition was a gradual one, and the official leadership of the National Association remained in the hands of the "disciplined Methodist mainstream," but the stage was set for the rise of populist "bands" who would once again reshape Palmer holiness along the radical lines of the Free Methodists. By the 1880s, strict "come-outer" churches such as the Church of God (Anderson, Indiana), the Church of God (Holiness), and the Holiness Church had begun to form, groups that looked askance at any compromise with gentility.[84]

The Palmer synthesis proved stubbornly persistent, however, as did the popularity of the Tuesday meeting. During the decade after

---

83. Wheatley, *Life and Letters*, 406; *Christian Advocate and Journal*, 28 January 1864, quoted in White, *Beauty of Holiness*, 101. Both White and Raser, *Palmer*, point to a lessoned responsiveness to Palmer's message among Methodists during the post–Civil War years.

84. Dieter, *Holiness Revival*, 106-7, 213, 239, and passim. Holiness revivalism and the rise of holiness denominations during the second half of the nineteenth century are a complex phenomenon, treated carefully by Dieter and other authors such as Timothy L. Smith, *Called unto Holiness: The Story of the Nazarenes, the Formative Years* (Kansas City: Nazarene Publishing Co., 1962). My point is simply that the choice of a camp meeting venue as the primary channel of holiness teaching, while not excluding middle-class Methodists, facilitated a resurgent, anti-genteel populism.

her return from England in 1864, even as age and ill health forced Palmer to relinquish a central role in the ongoing holiness cause, as many as three hundred people each week flocked to the meeting to seek or to bear witness to the reality of holiness. A need to accommodate the crowds helped justify moves in 1865 and 1870 to larger and more fashionable homes—changes also precipitated by the push of immigrants and tenements up Manhattan's lower East Side. Among the Tuesday visitors during these years were some who would adapt and promulgate Palmer holiness in broader evangelical circles as the respectable, activistic piety of the "higher Christian life." Presbyterian William E. Boardman already had published a book by that title in 1858. On at least some occasions after the Civil War he returned to the Palmer meeting. Hannah Whitall Smith, whose 1870 book, *The Christian's Secret of a Happy Life*, would become a higher-life classic, attended as well. Neither Boardman nor Smith professed sanctification as a direct result of Palmer's influence, and Boardman's work reflected Oberlin as well as Wesleyan emphases, but both were indebted to Palmer's teaching.[85] Their presence at the Tuesday meeting signaled the welcome a Palmer-style urbane sanctification would find in the independent world of northern evangelicalism. In a way somewhat analogous to Charles Finney's antebellum role as a mediator between the practices of popular religion and the middle class, Phoebe Palmer provided a pattern of piety that promised to bridge the gap between religious rigor and bourgeois respectability for late-Victorian Protestants and their descendants.[86]

Home during the final years of Palmer's life was a mansion at 316 East Fifteenth Street, on Stuyvesant Square. Once an exclusive enclave of luxury houses, by 1870 the area surrounding the square was too close to the tanneries and shanties along the East River for the comfort of the wealthy, who had migrated to the upper sections of Fifth Avenue. Still, with its expensive residences, Episcopal church, and the square as a park, the surroundings retained an aura of genteel opulence.[87] The walls of the ballroom-sized area where the Tuesday meeting met were crowded with pictures, plaques, and other

---

85. Hughes, *Beloved Physician*, 110, 121, mentions Boardman and Smith in the context of the postwar Tuesday meeting, although exact dates are not given; see also Dieter, *Holiness Revival*, 56, 57.

86. For Finney as a transitional figure, see Hatch, *Democratization*, 199.

87. M. Christine Boyer, *Manhattan Manners: Architecture and Style 1850–1900* (New York: Rizzoli, 1985), 12.

Christian bric-a-brac. Aware that the new mansion hardly represented Methodist simplicity, Palmer only consented to the move when she was assured it would "conduce to the glory of God." Her first biographer, Richard Wheatley, hastened to agree. A visit to the home while Palmer was still alive, he later wrote, would reveal "nothing but neatness, elegance, and order." "It is an ideal METHODIST home—for use and comfort—not at all for show." As her dwelling reflected the ideal Methodism of an increasingly affluent America, so Palmer holiness pointed the way to an ideal middle-class piety, a Christian life both respectable and dedicated "to the highest uses."[88]

88. Wheatley, *Life and Letters*, 150, 152. At some point, perhaps after Phoebe Palmer's death, a parlor organ was added to enhance the meeting. See Roche, *Life,* 112. An 1895 photograph of Sarah Lankford, who married Walter Palmer after Phoebe's death and lived in the Stuyvesant Square house, offers glimpses of the interior style. See Roche, *Life,* photograph between pp. 212, 213; also 209 for parlor decoration.

CHAPTER 10

Methodists, Politics, and the Coming of the American Civil War

Richard J. Carwardine

In 1868 Ulysses S. Grant remarked that there were three great parties in the United States: the Republican, the Democratic, and the Methodist Church. This was an understandable tribute given the active role of leading Methodists in his presidential campaign, but it was also a realistic judgment when set in the context of the denomination's growing political authority over the previous half century. As early as 1819 when, with a quarter of a million members, "the Methodists were becoming quite numerous in the country," the young exhorter Alfred Brunson noted that "politicians . . . from policy favoured us, though they might be skeptical as to religion," and gathered at county seats to listen to the preachers of a denomination whose "votes counted as fast at an election as any others." Ten years later, the newly elected Andrew Jackson stopped at Washington, Pennsylvania, en route from Tennessee to his presidential inauguration. When both Presbyterians and Methodists invited him to attend their services, Old Hickory sought to avoid the political embarrassment of seeming to favor his own church over the fastest growing religious movement in the country by attending both—the Presbyterians in the morning and the Methodists at night. In Indiana in the early 1840s the church's growing power led the Democrats to nominate for governor a known Methodist, while tarring their Whig opponents with the brush of sectarian bigotry. Nationally, as the combined membership of the MEC and MECS grew to over one and a half million by the mid-1850s, denominational leaders could be found complaining that the church was so strong that each political party was "eager to make her its tool." Thus Elijah H. Pilcher, the influential Michigan preacher, found himself in 1856 nominated simultaneously by state Democratic, Republican, and Abolition conventions.[1]

Such cases could be multiplied many times over. They indicate that during the early national and antebellum eras American Methodists had to confront the political consequences of their burgeoning numerical strength and increasing social influence. Though Methodism secured its early authority by its distance from, not association with, secular power, and appealed as a movement to those who were, as Donald Mathews has put it, "ill at ease with the way in which institutions and elites . . . affected their lives," clergy and laity had necessarily to fashion a place in America's experimental republican order and the world's first mass democracy.[2] Between the Revolution and the Civil War, Methodists sought to define their political responsibilities and a proper code of political engagement. Their contributions to the forms, functioning, and ideologies of party and electoral politics were substantial but by no means consistent or entirely self-conscious. Their political loyalties were complex, shifting, and shaped by more than simple denominationalism. Most dramatically, the internal stresses of Methodism, the largest religious

---

1. Walter B. Posey, *The Development of Methodism in the Old Southwest 1783–1824* (Tuscaloosa, Ala.: Weatherford Printing, 1933), 1; Donald G. Jones, *The Sectional Crisis and Northern Methodism: A Study in Piety, Political Ethics and Civil Religion* (Metuchen, N.J.: Scarecrow Press, 1979), 226-27; Alfred Brunson, *A Western Pioneer: or, Incidents in the Life and Times of Rev. Alfred Brunson, A.M., D.D., Embracing a Period of over Seventy Years*, 2 vols. (Cincinnati: Hitchcock & Walden, 1872), 1:217-18, 344-45; Robert D. Clark, *The Life of Matthew Simpson* (New York: Macmillan, 1956), 105-11; *CA*, 12 June 1856; James E. Pilcher, *Life and Labors of Elijah H. Pilcher* (New York: Hunt & Eaton, 1892), 115-16.

2. Donald G. Mathews, "Evangelical America—The Methodist Ideology," in *Rethinking Methodist History: A Bicentennial Historical Consultation*, ed. Russell E. Richey and Kenneth E. Rowe (Nashville: Kingswood Books, 1985), 91. The "alternative value-system" of early Methodists has long been a feature of the movement's historiography. Over the last twenty years or so, since Donald G. Mathews offered an analysis of the egalitarian elements of southern evangelicalism in the early republic in *Religion in the Old South* (Chicago: University of Chicago Press, 1977), the countercultural and antielitist thrust of early Methodism has been the subject of increasing scrutiny, most notably in William H. Williams, *The Garden of American Methodism: The Delmarva Peninsula 1769–1820* (Wilmington, Del.: Scholarly Resources, Inc., 1984); Nathan O. Hatch, *The Democratization of American Christianity* (New Haven: Yale University Press, 1989); Russell E. Richey, *Early American Methodism* (Bloomington: Indiana University Press, 1991); Christine Leigh Heyrman, *Southern Cross: The Beginnings of the Bible Belt* (New York: Alfred A. Knopf, 1997); John H. Wigger, *Taking Heaven by Storm: Methodism and the Rise of Popular Christianity in America* (New York: Oxford University Press, 1998); and Cynthia Lynn Lyerly, *Methodism and the Southern Mind 1770–1810* (New York: Oxford University Press, 1998).

force in the nation at midcentury, profoundly influenced the course of the Union as it tumbled toward the carnage of the Civil War. Consideration of each of these four themes will remind us of the salient truth that there were many different incarnations of Methodism across time and place, but it will also confirm the essence of Grant's verdict, that Methodists exerted a distinctive and potent influence over American political life in the nation's formative years.

Emerging Acceptance of Political Responsibility in Antebellum Methodism

Early American Methodists were, in general, unpolitical in outlook. Russell Richey describes the period between 1770 and 1810 as one of Edenic innocence for Methodists, whose radical egalitarianism and communalism marked them off from the corrupted secular order. Francis Asbury, echoed by his fellow itinerants, shunned temporal power: "What have we to do with it in this country?" he asked. "Our kingdom is not of this world." Richey argues persuasively that these Methodists, though often intensely patriotic and belonging to the first denomination to organize itself nationally, lacked a concept of the nation as a political entity; rather they saw America in spatial terms, as a continent to be converted. To a degree this was functional: Tory legacies within Methodism left political divisions, which full-hearted political engagement would expose. But it had more to do with early Methodists' understanding of being citizens not primarily of the secular state, but of "Zion," the church militant. In their response to the secular polity, early Methodists differed profoundly from those churches of the Reformed tradition—Presbyterian, Congregationalist, and Dutch Reformed—which had a strong sense of the political nation and of the need to fashion a new, post-Revolutionary relationship between church and state, and which were at ease with a "republican language" derived from the Declaration of Independence and the Federal Constitution. As Richey puts it, Methodists had access to Reformed "[n]otions of America as God's chosen people, of a covenant between God and the nation, of eternal purposes being worked out through the American experiment . . . of religion as requisite to national prosperity . . . of the millennium as an American affair," but significantly they made no use of these ideas in the earliest days.[3]

By the first and, more evidently, the second decade of the nineteenth century, however, these themes were becoming increasingly apparent in Methodism. The dissident minority of Republican Methodists under James O'Kelly had already, in the 1790s, fused Christian theology and the radical political ideology of the American Revolution, though with an Arminian and democratic outcome that distinguished it from the conservative republicanism of Reformed theologians more concerned with sustaining Calvinist civic order.[4] Historians have yet to chart the precise intellectual and geographical route by which the majority of Methodists moved to a Reformed understanding of Christian America, but it is clear that by the 1830s and 1840s the church's theologians, especially, but by no means exclusively, in the northern states, were comfortably speaking the language of Christian republicanism that their predecessors had largely eschewed. When, for example, the nation's clergy addressed the lessons of President William H. Harrison's unexpected death, the chorus of voices on the national fast day in 1841 included a number of Methodists whose analysis embraced the same elements found in the sermons of their Reformed brethren: Christianity as the source of the fundamental ideas and elements of republicanism and political freedom; America as the apotheosis of republican virtue and political freedom; the nation's unique consolidation of "the eternal with the temporal"; America as a model to the world; the vulnerability of republican freedom in the face of selfish individualism, public dishonesty, political corruption, and factional strife; and the harmful consequences of national sins for the country's destiny.[5]

The midcentury convergence of Methodist thought with Reformed public theology was just one expression of Methodists' journey away

---

3. Richey, *Early American Methodism*, xii-iii, xvii-iii, 33, 35-44, 102; Fred J. Hood, *Reformed America: The Middle and Southern States, 1783–1837* (Tuscaloosa: University of Alabama Press, 1980).

4. Richey, *Early American Methodism*, 40-41, 88-91.

5. Benjamin F. Tefft, *The Republican Influence of Christianity: A Discourse* (Bangor, Maine: n.p., 1841), 1-8. See also Daniel S. Doggett, *A Sermon on the Death of General William Henry Harrison, Late President of the United States, Delivered in the Chapel of Randolph Macon College, April 18, 1841* (Richmond, Va.: Christian Advocate, 1841); George Peck, *National Evils and Their Remedy: A Discourse Delivered on the Occasion of the National Fast, May 14, 1841* (New York: Lane & Sandford, 1841); WCA 24, 31 July, 7 August 1840, 24 September 1841 (Leonidas Hamline), 19, 26 February, 9 April 1841 (Rezin Sapp), 21 May 1841 (James B. Finley).

from Asbury's shunning of temporal power toward a fuller integration into the nation's political life, from an approach to political action, which George Marsden has labeled "pietist"—emphasizing the role of the Holy Spirit, holiness, freedom from law, a more private view of Christianity, and an essentially negative view of government and the state—to a "Calvinist" or Puritan vision of politics as a means of introducing God's kingdom.[6] The pietist, or quietist, outlook among some Methodists would remain a significant fact of antebellum life, their early unpolitical disposition reinforced by distaste for many of the features of the new mass democratic order that emerged into full maturity during the 1830s. In particular, the violent party battles of the so-called second- and third-party systems generated an antiparty reaction among those who believed that seemingly endless political contention promoted corrosive social and religious discord in a nation that was, as Chauncey Hobart put it, "really *one at heart.*" Methodist critics were repelled by low standards of public morality among those whom Calvin Fletcher called "bagatelle politicians": candidates and officeholders with an eye for the main chance, so often chosen not for their competence or sense of public responsibility, but for their "availability." Most debilitating of all was electioneering itself. Campaigns were widely understood to encourage bribery, drunkenness, outrageous slanders, deception, and sheer folly among candidates and the electorate; it was axiomatic among Methodists that religious revivals and vital piety flourished in inverse proportion to political excitement. Thus there continued to be ministers like Thomas B. Miller, who "had but little to say about politics [and] . . . always said they were a bad tick to bite," and Heman Bangs, who consciously shunned politics after becoming a minister. This attitude may help explain the high proportion of Methodists abstaining from politics in some areas in the Jacksonian period. And it certainly continued to shape the thinking even of those who energetically took part. The young Illinois itinerant, Leonard F. Smith, after the Republican campaign of 1860, worried that he had neglected eternal

---

6. George M. Marsden, *Fundamentalism and American Culture: The Shaping of Twentieth-Century Evangelicalism: 1870–1925* (New York: Oxford University Press, 1980), 7, 85-93, 252. Paul Kleppner, *The Third Electoral System, 1853–1892: Parties, Voters, and Political Cultures* (Chapel Hill: University of North Carolina Press, 1979), especially xix-xx, 185-97, distinguishes between *evangelical pietists,* who saw conversion as only part of a broader obligation to sanctify society, and *salvationist pietists,* who felt no responsibility to transform the wider culture. His categories correspond respectively to Marsden's *Calvinists* and *pietists,* which are less cumbersome and no less theologically nuanced.

313

considerations and "indulged in talking politics too freely, also in speaking of the faults of others rather than of their excellencies."[7]

The salient fact, however, was that Smith, whatever his subsequent anxieties, had enthusiastically participated in that campaign in a way that would have appeared quite alien to his late-eighteenth-century forebears. By 1860, Methodists had widely absorbed a "Calvinist" understanding of political responsibilities, viewing the state as a moral being and believing that Christians as active citizens had to take responsibility for ensuring that the highest standards of virtue flourished in civic life. James Watson rebuked those whose piety was "too etherial [sic] for the duties of citizenship." Thomas M. Eddy insisted that those who turned their back on politics demonstrated an apathy toward human progress. Charles Elliott called them "unchristian." They spoke for a denomination that, having shed its counter-cultural chrysalis, had been unable to resist the forces of a wider culture whose political enthusiasm was ubiquitous and where, as Samuel Patton explained, "there was scarcely any such thing as neutrality" in politics. Methodists joined other evangelicals in seeing that voluntary effort to achieve a godly society might founder on the rock of ungodly secular rule. Electing Christian rulers and effecting a Christian influence in passing and executing laws thus became part of Methodists' obligations.[8]

This would be pursued by a variety of means. It meant bringing men and women to Christ in sufficient numbers to ensure the religious orientation of the nation. It demanded earnest prayer for rulers. It also required regular use of the heaven-sent ballot box, a priceless privilege imbued with profound significance: though Christians were obliged to avoid personal denigration on the one hand and "man worship" on the other, they should understand, as Granville Moody

---

7. Chauncey Hobart, *Recollection of My Life: Fifty Years of Itinerancy in the Northwest* (Redwing, Minn.: Red Wing Printers, 1885), 202-3; Calvin Fletcher, *The Diary of Calvin Fletcher,* 6 vols., ed. Gayle Thornbrough, Dorothy L. Riker, and Paula Corpuz (Indianapolis: Indiana Historical Society, 1972–77) 3:80; Thomas B. Miller, *Original and Selected Thoughts on the Life and Times of Rev. Thomas Miller, and Rev. Thomas Warburton* (Bethlehem, Pa.: G. D. White, 1860), 17; Heman Bangs, *The Autobiography and Journal of Rev. Heman Bangs* (New York: N. Tibbals & Sons, 1872), 316; Leonard F. Smith, "Diary," 29 August, 17 November 1860 (Springfield, Ill.: Illinois State Historical Society); Harry L. Watson, *Jacksonian Politics and Community Conflict: The Emergence of the Second American Party System in Cumberland County, North Carolina* (Baton Rouge: Louisiana State University Press, 1981), 240-41, identifies a high proportion of political abstainers among the Methodists of that county.

8. *NWCA,* 12 November 1856; *WCA,* 6 January 1843; D. R. McAnally, *Life and Times of Rev. S. Patton, D.D., and Annals of the Holston Conference* (St. Louis: Methodist Book Depository, 1859), 239.

explained, that "the folded vote becomes a tongue of justice, a voice of order, a force of imperial law, securing rights, abolishing abuses, and erecting her institutions of truth and love." Even ministers, despite congregational and community pressures encouraging political neutrality, became active, even determined, voters. Wilson Spottswood rode out of Berwick, Pennsylvania, on election day in 1844 to fill an appointment and avoid the ballot; but, he recalled, after wrestling with his conscience and conquering his squeamishness about being seen to be a Democrat by Whig acquaintances, "I turned my horse's head, rode back to town, hitched my horse to a post, got a ticket, marched up to the polls, and exercised the sacred right of an American citizen, by casting my first vote." The pious Methodist had to consider his vote carefully, not automatically sustaining the party ticket, but following conscience and recognizing that at judgment day he would face uncomfortable interrogation over his election choices.[9]

But political engagement did not end at the ballot box. As more and more Methodists came to operate according to the conviction that, in John Inskip's words, "all political questions have a connection, more or less direct, with both morality and religion," the way was open to lobbying congressmen—circulating and signing petitions, attending political meetings to question candidates and officeholders, and even (in the case of preachers themselves) using their pulpits to address the public issues of the day. The ultimate imperative was to run for office. This was more commonly the course of laymen who perceived no tension between piety and public service: Ruliff S. Lawrence of New Jersey ran for the state legislature after his conversion in 1852, believing this was the most effective way of serving his God. But ministers also frequently stood for office, often successfully. Many had retired from the active ministry, but others managed to combine continuing religious responsibilities with their secular duties. It was said of Walter T. Colquitt, the Georgia judge and United States senator, for example, that he could make a stump speech, try a court case and plead another at the bar, christen a child, preach a sermon, and marry a couple "all before dinner."[10]

9. Granville Moody, *A Life's Retrospect: Autobiography of Rev. Granville Moody* (Cincinnati: Cranston & Stowe, 1890), 311; William G. Lewis, *Biography of Samuel Lewis, First Superintendent for Common Schools for the State of Ohio* (Cincinnati: Methodist Book Concern, 1857), 369; Wilson L. Spottswood, *Brief Annals* (Harrisburg, Pa.: Methodist Episcopal Book Room, 1888), 39.

10. William McDonald and John E. Searles, *The Life of Rev. John S. Inskip, President of the National Association for the Promotion of Holiness* (Boston: McDonald & Gill, 1885), 49; *WCA*, 25 June 1856; William H. Lawrence, *The Earnest Minister: A Record of the Life, Labors and Literary Remains of Rev. Ruliff S. Lawrence* (Philadelphia: A. Wallace, 1873), 29; *New York Evangelist*, 4 January 1844.

Methodist political activism reached its climax in the two decades before the Civil War as two developments converged. First, most Methodists in the first third of the century remained unconvinced that questions of public morality such as drink, sabbath breaking, and dueling were matters for political action as opposed to individual moral regeneration: they feared a return to Puritan "blue laws" and Reformed Protestants using religious legislation to reestablish a Calvinist imperium; but as moral suasion proved demonstrably insufficient, many came to reflect more sympathetically on the utility of legal action. When Luther Lee called for legal prohibition of the drink trade in the mid-1830s he recognized that he was one of an eccentric Methodist minority; but during the next fifteen years the denomination would experience a significant shift in opinion. "Enlighten the mind of the rum-seller?" scoffed Davis W. Clark in 1847. "You may as well attempt to reason with the midnight assassin, or the pirate on the high seas."[11] Second, the substantive issues that came to dominate the nation's public discourse in the immediate antebellum years were themselves an invitation to Methodist political engagement. As the central questions of political controversy in the early Jacksonian era— banking and economic development—yielded to those of Roman Catholic immigration, territorial expansion, the future of slavery, and the integrity of the Union, more and more Methodists ignored the warnings of their quietist brothers and sisters about political "meddling" and accepted Calvin Kingsley's dictum that evangelicals should "approve what is clearly right, and condemn what is clearly wrong, God's word being the standard, even though the thing condemned or approved may happen to have its political aspects."[12]

The Growing Political Influence of Methodism

When calculating the political influence of Methodism it is as well to estimate cautiously, even though the sheer number of church members and the yet larger population of adherents explain both the eager efforts of politicians to secure their active support and Methodist

---

11. *CA,* 5 June 1829; Luther Lee, *Autobiography* (New York: Phillips & Hunt, 1882), 233; Luther Lee, *A Sermon for the Times: Prohibitory Laws* (New York: Wesleyan Book Room, 1852); Davis W. Clark, *Evils and Remedies of Intemperance: An Address* (New York: William Osborn, 1847), 11, 13-15; Thomas A. Goodwin, *Seventy-Six Years Tussle with the Traffic; Being a Condensation of the Laws Relating to the Liquor Traffic in Indiana from 1807 to 1883* (Indianapolis: Carlon & Hollenbeck, 1883), 8-9.

12. McDonald and Searles, *Life of Inskip,* 49; *WCA,* 25 June 1856.

leaders' strong conviction of their church's unique position. As well as noting the negative influence of Methodist pietists who continued to disdain political activity, we need to keep in mind that Methodism, like other denominations, was composed disproportionately of women, who lacked the franchise and a position of political equality with men; and that Methodists, as will become clear, formed no political monolith, but cast their ballots for the full range of political parties, losing electoral leverage as a result. In fact, these qualifications are less crippling to the case for Methodists' political importance than they may seem. The pietist's apolitical stance had more than private significance and, despite itself, became a political fact in a democratic and sectionally polarizing society. Indeed, southern Methodists' claim to moral superiority for avoiding "meddling in politics" (a euphemism for "taking a stand against slavery") was, paradoxically, woven into an argument for their section's political superiority.

Nor should we assume women's entire exclusion from the male world of politics. From the early years of the century, evangelical women, working for benevolent causes and relief organizations, sought to influence local, state, and national governments. They engineered a torrent of petitions demanding action to criminalize seduction, regulate asylums and prisons, alter property laws, prevent Indian removal, restrict slavery, and prohibit liquor sales. They may have lacked the vote, but women did not lack visibility at election times, nor was their influence restricted to decorating the margins of the campaigns with their flag making and handkerchief waving. Some were known to stand outside the polls, handing out voting tickets for temperance candidates. Others, in the free states, attended Liberty, Free-Soil, and Republican rallies, and exerted themselves for antislavery candidates. The Methodist minister Wilson Spottswood alluded to two cases that implied a generic female political assertiveness: the wife and mother in a Pennsylvania Methodist family who, after James K. Polk's presidential victory in 1844, pointedly sought, as a "dyed-in-the-wool" Democrat, to redeem the pledge of her staunchly Whig Methodist minister that she should have his head "for a foot-ball" if Henry Clay lost the election; and his own wife, who shamed him out of his guilty participation in the clandestine midnight activities of "the dark-lanterned party," the Know-Nothings.[13]

---

13. Barbara Berg, *The Remembered Gate: Origins of American Feminism: The Woman and the City, 1800–1860* (New York: Oxford University Press, 1978), 167-68; Lori Ginzberg, *Women and the Work of Benevolence: Morality, Politics, and Class in the Nineteenth-Century United States* (New Haven: Yale University Press, 1990), 71-79; Spottswood, *Brief Annals*, 135-36.

Methodist ministers and leading laymen, even those who lacked education and wealth, did not lack moral authority over their gathered congregations, and whereas it was relatively rare for preachers to advocate openly support for a particular political party, they helped set an agenda for moral purpose in public affairs. Editors of the mass-circulation denominational newspapers had to be careful not to alienate readers by party endorsements or an ill-judged remark at election times, but this did not stop them from addressing moral issues—particularly temperance, Roman Catholicism, and slavery—with an immediate political significance. When Matthew Simpson took up the issue of the Fugitive Slave Law in the editorial columns of the *Western Christian Advocate* it caused "quite a fluttering among the 'smaller fry' politicians," and the paper circulated as widely as any political sheet in Indiana. Methodists successfully sought to gain access to political power at the different levels of government. They increasingly made their mark in the elections for congressional chaplains as Unitarians and Episcopalians lost influence: Henry Slicer was returned for a unique third term in 1853, while John Durbin, George Cookman, and William Milburn also enjoyed congressional respect. Methodists increasingly won political office, at first reflecting their local status, as in Ohio with Edward Tiffin's election as governor, but later suggesting a growing authority nationally, represented most notably by John McLean's appointment to the Supreme Court and James Harlan's election to the Senate. The Methodist elite also established close friendships with politicians. George F. Pierce, bishop of the MECS, was on excellent terms with Robert Toombs, Alexander Stephens, and Richard Johnson; Augustus B. Longstreet enjoyed a warm friendship with John C. Calhoun; John B. McFerrin's connection with James K. Polk as governor of Tennessee and later as president derived partly from his agency in converting two of Young Hickory's sisters at a Methodist revival.[14]

Methodists' political influence amounted to more than a simple accumulation of the contributions of "great men," significant though these were. At a more profound level, Methodists helped shape the

---

14. J. C. Chambers to M. Simpson (2 May 1850), J. L. Smith to M. Simpson (23 May 1850), W. Daily to M. Simpson (5 December 1850), M. Simpson Papers, Library of Congress; Lorenzo D. Johnson, *Chaplains of the General Government, with Objections to their Employment Considered* (New York: Sheldon, Blakeman, 1856), 63 and passim; George G. Smith, *The Life and Times of George Foster Pierce* (Sparta, Ga.: Hancock Publishing, 1888), 324; John D. Wade, *Augustus Baldwin Longstreet: A Study of the Culture of the South* (Athens: University of Georgia Press, 1969), 123-24; Oscar P. Fitzgerald, *John B. McFerrin: A Biography* (Nashville: MECS Publishing House, 1888), 91, 116, 168-69, 196-99, 243.

developing forms and language of politics in the early republic. The arrival of mass participatory politics and the simultaneous flowering of the Second Great Awakening were separate but not wholly independent events. Both derived their energy from ideologies that championed popular participation, individual enterprise, and equality of opportunity: universal white male suffrage in politics was parallelled in religion by the brushfire spread of Arminianism, principally through the agency of Methodism, at the expense of Calvinist exclusiveness. Moreover, in the generation after the War of 1812, politicians had to devise new organizing strategies by which they could mobilize mass support. The most immediate, indeed the only, models were those proffered by the evangelical churches: it was they that had made the Awakening the most impressive organizing process the nation had yet seen. The MEC, in particular, with its shrewd and productive balance of central control and local initiative, had drawn men and women with local loyalties into a movement that transcended the immediate community. Party organizers learned much from innovative Methodist preachers about reaching a mass audience, about persevering and dramatic effort, about rotating speakers to maintain and deepen interest, and about channeling mass enthusiasm and consolidating loyalties. It is doubtful if the extraordinary popular engagement in politics at this time—the greatest enthusiasm for politics the republic has ever seen—could have occurred had it not been for the integration of evangelicals and their organizational structures into the new order. To tap into the sources of revivalist excitement, party managers introduced political camp meetings, held over two, three, or four days. During August and September, the season of Methodist camp meetings, huge outdoor gatherings met on sites normally reserved for spiritual assemblies. Introductory prayer preceded sustained political "sermons." The fervent singing of political hymns to familiar tunes reminded listeners of Methodist revivals and the catchy melodies of religious folk music. Political managers invited ministers to offer prayer at party conventions (often held in churches, as the only appropriate buildings available). They spoke of their party as a political church and its activists as "missionaries," "presiding elders," "bishops," and "local preachers" who would "carry the glad tidings of our political salvation to every corner." Learning of Harrison's three-man campaign committee in 1840, one Whig reflected: "Where two or 'three' meet together in my name, there I am in the midst, and that to bless them."[15]

As this suggests, Methodism provided a model for the language as well as the form of political life. Though the perspectives of politicians were necessarily blinkered by the cold realities of the world, day-to-day realism and compromise gave way at election time to a more romantic, millennialist discourse. Campaigning politicians took advantage of the evangelical cast of mind, which saw the whole of history as a continuous conflict between God and Satan. The Methodist revivalist's sermon, with its polarized language of heaven and hell, good and evil, salvation and damnation, sin and grace, Christ and Antichrist, reinforced this framework of thought. This Manichaean perspective—a well-established element in the intellectual framework of the early republic and by no means limited to Methodists[16]—profoundly influenced the way in which evangelical Protestants interpreted politics. Candidates and platforms took on an ethical, even religious, significance. William Gannaway Brownlow, for example, commonly saw presidential elections in apocalyptic terms, as conflicts between "the cause of God and morality" and the devil's legions. This mentality allowed little scope for compromise, complexity, or consensus. As well as encouraging party propagandists to use antithesis and polarization to help induct the electorate into the ways of mass politics, the world of Methodist revivalism also led them to present the election campaign as the means of political redemption. The campaign, like the revival, would turn the community into the ways of righteousness through the multiplying of individual "conversions." Whigs sang lustily of "penitent Locofocos," apostates returning to the fold "like a prodigal son," and "political sinners" groaning on the "anxious seat." Interceding to protect a heckler at a New York meeting in 1856, a Methodist demanded, "Let him stay, he came to scoff, he may remain to pray." Presidential candidates were stewards of righteousness, agents of personal and national salvation: Whigs characterized Clay as "the *redeemer* of the

---

15. *Harrison Medal Minstrel: Comprising a Collection of the Most Popular and Patriotic Songs* (Philadelphia: Grigg & Elliott, 1840), 3, 21, 65; J. S. Littell, *The Clay Minstrel: or, National Songster*, 2nd ed. (Philadelphia: Greely & M'Elrath, 1844), 235-36; J. Campbell to W. B. Campbell (4 February 1840), quoted in T. B. Alexander, "Presidential Election of 1840 in Tennessee," *Tennessee Historical Quarterly* 1 (March 1942): 26-27; George Hickman, *The Life and Public Services of J. K. Polk* (Baltimore: N. Hickman, 1844), 5; *WCA*, 7 August 1840; *Jonesboro Whig*, 9 May 1840.

16. Ruth Bloch, *Visionary Republic: Millennial Themes in American Thought, 1756–1800* (Cambridge: Cambridge University Press, 1985), 56, 61, 63, 204-5 and passim.

country"; Brownlow called him a "Moses" who would help his people "gain the promised land!"[17]

Methodists' influence did not end with their role in shaping the language and forms, the style and institutions, of the nation's novel political order. The church made two further significant contributions to the substance of early national and antebellum politics. First, its members' party loyalties played a part in determining and redetermining the shifting political configurations of successive party systems from the Jeffersonian era to the immediate antebellum years. This was closely related, second, to Methodists' contributions, direct and indirect, to shaping the nation's agenda of issues for political action—in particular, the question of slavery—and to the process of sectional polarization.

Characteristic Methodist Political Loyalties

Ethnocultural historians, in emphasizing denominational loyalties and ethnic origins as primary determinants of nineteenth-century voting behavior, have prompted a number of objections about their methods and conclusions, principally from those who consider party alignments to have been based essentially on responses to the rapid socioeconomic changes wrought by the revolution in communications and the concomitant advance of a national market economy.[18] Those objections do not lack substance, yet it is useful to recall that the political managers of the early national era, recognizing the churches' power, consciously aimed to graft religion onto party loyalties. They were well aware that some of the most profound community conflicts and group loyalties of the early republic could be found between and within the different denominations. It was no accident that politicians wanted to be seen worshiping in churches

---

17. *New York Tribune*, 25 July 1856; *Jonesboro Whig*, 8 December 1847.

18. For ethnocultural approaches, see Lee Benson, *The Concept of Jacksonian Democracy: New York as a Test Case* (Princeton, N.J.: Princeton University Press, 1961), esp. 288-328; Ronald P. Formisano, *The Birth of Mass Political Parties: Michigan, 1827–1861* (Princeton, N.J.: Princeton University Press, 1971); Michael F. Holt, *Forging a Majority: The Formation of the Republican Party in Pittsburgh, 1848–1860* (New Haven: Yale University Press, 1969); Kleppner, *The Third Electoral System*. The classic economic interpretation is Arthur M. Schlesinger Jr., *The Age of Jackson* (Boston: Little, Brown & Co., 1945). Recent influential interpretations, based on the primary importance of a changing economy, include Watson, *Jacksonian Politics*; John Ashworth, *"Agrarians & Aristocrats": Party Political Ideology in the United States, 1837–1846* (London: Royal Historical Society, 1983); Charles Sellers, *The Market Revolution: Jacksonian America, 1815–1846* (New York: Oxford University Press, 1991).

themselves, played "recognition politics" by choosing candidates who were attached to particular denominations, and exploited issues that they believed would engage the attentions of evangelicals. Individual churches and the larger denomination provided networks of friendship and association whose political potential was well understood. When Trusten Polk, member of Centenary Methodist Church in St. Louis, ran successfully for governor of Missouri in 1856, he was staunchly supported by his close friend, fellow church member, and located Methodist preacher, John Hogan; when Hogan conducted a statewide canvass on his friend's behalf he was in a position to exploit all of his denominational as well as his political connections.[19]

In practice, few Protestant denominations maintained an essentially uniform partisan attachment: of the larger churches, only the Congregationalists presented something approaching a Federalist-Whig-Republican consistency across three party systems; Primitive Baptists remained loyally Democrat. Methodists certainly presented no uniform picture. "Lord, deliver us from Whiggery!" was the prayer of one preacher at a Tennessee campaign meeting. "God forbid!" came a brother's reply. Yet the lack of political consistency within Methodism does not mean that the relationship between church membership and party loyalty was wholly random. Although men and women did not generally join churches to advance a political cause, their view of the world expressed in their church fellowship had implications for their political outlook; whereas Methodist church leaders were careful not to link the institution with a particular political party, the concerns of Methodists *as Methodists* was one element among the several that shaped their partisanship.[20] It is possible to hazard some generalizations. We can confidently conclude that, during the first party system, Methodists were very largely drawn into the ranks of Jeffersonian Democracy. Under the succeeding party system, organized around the conflict between Jackson's Democracy and its evolving opposition, the majority of Methodists probably maintained a Democratic outlook, but a substantial body of

19. Sophia Hogan Boogher, *Recollections of John Hogan by His Daughter* (St. Louis: Mound City Press, 1927), 40-41.

20. *CA*, 4 November, 23 December 1840, 17 November 1841; William I. Fee, *Bringing the Sheaves: Gleanings from the Harvest Fields in Ohio, Kentucky and West Virginia* (Cincinnati: Cranston & Curts, 1896), 134-37; James D. Anthony, *Life and Times of Rev. J. D. Anthony: An Autobiography* (Atlanta: C. P. Byrd, 1896), 80-81; Richard H. Rivers, *The Life of Robert Paine, D.D., Bishop of the Methodist Episcopal Church, South* (Nashville: Southern Methodist Publishing House, 1916), 99.

the church rallied to Whiggery, including quite probably a majority of its ministers. The chipping away at Methodists' attachment to the Democracy continued through the early and mid-1850s as the second party system fragmented under the pressure of new parties—Free-Soilers, Know-Nothings, Prohibitionists, and Republicans—each of which attracted sizeable support from the denomination. Even so, some Whig Methodists in the South turned to the Democrats as the best sectional defense against Free-Soilism, and that party continued to enjoy substantial—probably the majority of—Methodist support, north and south, in the elections of 1860.

These are broad brush strokes, however, and they hide the multiplicity of experiences that can be observed locally. Paul Goodman has rightly stressed the importance of community context in explaining patterns of political attachment among New England churches; Harry Watson reflects similarly about Jacksonian politics in general. The advance of the market, the power of the new steam press, and improved transportation all had the power to erode provincialism, but "the intensely local character of American life and politics" remained a salient truth.[21] And among the most important of local influences on party attachment were the kaleidoscopic patterns of interdenominational conflict.

This is not the place to survey the whole range of sectarian rivalry in the early republic, and its implications for the ballot box. But it is clear that the pattern of Methodist voting was affected by the absence or presence of particular denominations and by changes in interchurch relationships over time. In New England in the 1790s and early 1800s the generally poisonous relationships between Methodists and the Calvinist standing order, which saw the new movement subject to fines, intimidation, violent attack, and other forms of persecution, understandably drove Methodists into the arms of Jeffersonian Republicans who beckoned with a language of religious toleration and pluralism. Even after disestablishment the bitterness continued, with the result that many New England Methodists found in Jacksonian Democracy a refuge from Congregationalist "bigotry." William Xavier Ninde recalled that in the 1850s Democratic politicians were still able to exploit residual tension between the two denominations in Connecticut: they "went in heart and soul to help the Methodists. It was a sort of 'you tickle me, and I'll tickle you' system, a kind of see-saw arrangement. When

21. Paul Goodman, "The Social Basis of New England Politics in Jacksonian America," *Journal of the Early Republic* 6 (spring 1986): 23-58; Watson, *Jacksonian Politics*, 23-24.

the Whigs and the Congregationalists went down, the Democrats and the Methodists went up and *vice versa.*"[22]

These conflicts appear to have carried over, for a period at least, in those areas outside New England where Congregationalists and Presbyterians of Yankee extraction were the dominant force, and where Methodists initially struggled for recognition, as in the Western Reserve of Ohio. Alfred Brunson, who had seen in Connecticut how Calvinist-Federalist persecution had made staunch Republicans of Methodists, encountered similar disdain from transplanted Yankee "Presbygationalists" when he began work as a licensed preacher in the Reserve after the War of 1812. The Methodist minority "were treated as intruders, and with much contempt": though all settlers united to subscribe to the building of schoolhouses on the understanding that they would be available to all denominations for worship, the informal "standing order" soon took them over at the expense of excluded Methodists in particular.[23]

Yet even when Methodists' (and, indeed, Baptists') fear of Presbygationalist power dominated their thinking, it did not necessarily drive them into the arms of the Democrats. In the late 1820s and early 1830s the operations of the interdenominational benevolent agencies that made up the "evangelical united front," which were dominated by Reformed churchmen of the Northeast, increasingly alienated Methodists and Baptists, including those who had lent their support to the Reform societies' operations. They were offended not just by a general sense of the presumption and arrogance of the Reformed leadership, but by Presbygationalist efforts to secure a charter of incorporation for the American Sunday School Union. That some leading Methodists, principally Nathan Bangs, saw this as an effort to reunite church and state was unsurprising given the Presbyterian Ezra Stiles Ely's simultaneous call for the creation of a Christian political party to support his favorite candidate, Andrew Jackson, a Presbyterian himself.[24] For some Methodists, Jackson's successful candidacy was the source of acute anxiety about Presbyterian ambitions. It partly explains evidence of considerable antipathy

22. George C. Baker, *An Introduction to the History of Early New England Methodism 1789–1839* (Durham, N.C.: Duke University Press, 1941), 41-49; Mary L. Ninde, *William Xavier Ninde: A Memorial* (New York: Eaton & Mains, 1902), 50-51.

23. Brunson, *Western Pioneer*, 1:35-43, 172-73.

24. Bangs, however, had his Methodist critics. Charles I. Foster *An Errand of Mercy: The Evangelical United Front 1790–1837* (Chapel Hill: University of North Carolina Press, 1960), 223-48.

toward Old Hickory among prominent Methodists. Alfred Brunson caustically recalled that when the president-elect attended his church in 1829, "I preached to him as I would to any other sinner."[25]

In some locations, away from the influence of New England Calvinism, aggressive rivalry between the two most successful Protestant denominations of the first half of the century, Methodists and Baptists, dominated the operations of the religious marketplace. Nathan Bangs described the conflict between the two movements in the West, in the early years of the century, as a "sort of warfare," and Peter Cartwright's reminiscences of his early career in Tennessee, Kentucky, and Ohio are seemingly little more than a succession of battles with evangelical rivals, of whom Baptists are the principal foe.[26] This antagonism persisted unrelentingly in some southern and western regions well beyond the heyday of the Second Great Awakening, on through to the Civil War. It achieved probably its most dramatic expression in the southern Appalachian highlands during the 1850s in the conflict between the partisans of two of Tennessee's finest polemicists—the Reverend James Robinson Graves, editor of the Nashville *Tennessee Baptist*, and the "fighting parson" of Knoxville, William Gannaway Brownlow. Graves's newspaper articles and tracts, which mixed vituperation, ridicule, theological argument over infant baptism, and a critique of Methodists' centralized and "autocratic" church government, were eventually (in 1856) consolidated in *The Great Iron Wheel: or, Republicanism Backward and Christianity Reversed*. Brownlow's venomous response, *The Great Iron Wheel Examined; or, Its False Spokes Extracted, and an Exhibition of Elder Graves, Its Builder*, appeared within the year, blending personal abuse with a sustained attack on Baptists' residual high Calvinist doctrine, their insistence on complete immersion of believers, and their unyielding sectarian exclusiveness. Whole communities were split by this chronic warfare, with clear political consequences. In one town the two religious groups had their own schools, stores, blacksmiths, taverns, and even ferries to cross the river. In politics, most of the Methodists were Whigs and most of the Baptists were Democrats.[27]

---

25. Brunson, *Western Pioneer*, 1:344-45.

26. Nathan Bangs, *A History of the Methodist Episcopal Church* (New York: Mason & Lane, 1838–41) 2:351; Peter Cartwright, *Autobiography of Peter Cartwright: The Backwoods Preacher*, ed. W. P. Strickland (New York: Methodist Book Concern, 1856), 64-72 and passim.

27. F. Richardson, *From Sunrise to Sunset: Reminiscence* (Bristol, Tenn.: King Printing, 1890), 107-8.

Such intense Protestant sectarianism, however, found it difficult to survive in urban and northeastern areas, which by midcentury had experienced a reshaping of their traditional religious topography: the huge influx of nonevangelical, principally Roman Catholic, immigrants in the 1840s and 1850s forced those evangelical Protestants in immediate proximity to adopt common strategies of response. The New York *Christian Advocate and Journal* spoke for many readers when it insisted in 1842 that "the times call for unity of spirit and effort among the evangelical churches." That unity demanded a common political front against a Catholic Church seemingly shameless in exploiting its own burgeoning power in the political, not just the ecclesiastical, arena. This understanding lay behind the conclusion of a western Methodist in 1841 that "the time is not likely far distant when the political parties will be, not Democratic and Whig, but Popish and Protestant." Given the consistently strong Democratic attachments of the overwhelming majority of Catholic voters through the whole of the period under review, it was understandable that the most deeply anti-Romanist of Methodists, as of other evangelical denominations, should be drawn to Whiggery; and that, when that party's leaders temporized in the face of immigrant voting power, evangelicals should flirt with new political organizations that promised to defend fragile republicanism against the Antichrist. Thus the Know-Nothing party of the early and mid-1850s benefited considerably from a substantial influx of Methodists, including ministers, who now happily rubbed shoulders with Congregationalists, Presbyterians, Baptists, and others who, in other contexts, remained political and religious rivals.[28]

The interdenominational rivalries that shaped political affiliations were not just rooted in differences of theology or religious practice, of course, but were often reinforced by conflict related to class and status, and to economic and social aspiration. It is a commonplace that early American Methodism comprised to a very large extent the poor, the powerless, and the socially despised, both black and white. Congregationalists, even where they did not function as the standing order, and Presbyterians were commonly the churches of the well-to-do and the sturdily independent. These Reformed critics of Methodism evinced a powerful social condescension toward what they regarded as a movement of the uneducated, the overexcited, and

---

28. *CA*, 14 December 1842; *WCA*, 18 November 1842; Richard J. Carwardine, *Evangelicals and Politics in Antebellum America* (New Haven: Yale University Press, 1993), 199-234.

the unwashed. Methodists looked benignly on Jeffersonian Republicanism because it offered a defense against the arrogance of Calvinist social power. But most Methodists were not social levelers or persisting communitarians or, despite the picture painted by Charles Sellers in his stirring study of Jacksonian America, wholly antagonistic to the social and economic opportunities presented by the burgeoning capitalist market. Over the first half of the nineteenth century, Methodists developed into a respected denomination that embraced men and women of social prominence and some wealth, able to mix on equal terms with fellow Protestants. Unsurprisingly, many Methodists—not least bankers and entrepreneurs like Calvin Fletcher and John Hogan—responded positively to the Whig party's doctrine of economic improvement, and its strong tendency to endorse the moral citizen's pursuit of self-control, self-discipline, and respectability. The Democrats' banking and currency policies of the 1830s and 1840s, together with their continuing tolerance toward dissenters from religious orthodoxy, led many Methodists to see them, in William Crane's words, as "the moral dregs, and scurf, and pollution of the land. Atheists, blasphemers, Sabbath-breakers, drunkards and brothel-haunters flocked to this party, because here . . . they were treated as nobility." A similar concern for "improvement"—in both its economic and moral sense—and antipathy to the social values of the Democrats later drew many northern Methodists into the Republican party. After attending a big Democratic meeting in 1860, Leonard F. Smith concluded that Lincoln faced a party "characterized by a noisy dirty ignorant rabble."[29]

The concerns of class and status were sometimes subsumed into the acerbities of ethnicity and regional chauvinism. Antipathy between the English and Scotch-Irish may have had some influence on Methodists' voting habits. The generally clear picture of Methodist support for the Jeffersonians grew murkier in Delaware, where the denomination drew considerably on former Anglicans of English stock, and where the Republicans were perceived as the Scotch-Irish Presbyterian party. Under the second party system Jackson may have held on more easily to Irish than to English Methodists. More clear-cut

---

29. Sellers, *Market Revolution,* 137-38, 157-61, 164-65, 178, 299-300; Fletcher, *Diary,* passim; Boogher, *Recollections of John Hogan,* 18; William W. Crane, *Autobiography and Miscellaneous Writings* (Syracuse, N.Y.: A. W. Hall, 1891), 84-85; L. F. Smith, "Diary," 9 October 1860; Richard J. Carwardine, "'Antinomians' and 'Arminians': Methodists and the Market Revolution" in *The Market Revolution in America: Social, Political and Religious Expressions, 1800–1880,* ed. Melvyn Stokes and Stephen Conway (Charlottesville: University Press of Virginia, 1996), 282-307.

was the cultural conflict in much of the lower north and upper south between Yankees and Southerners, each side invigorated with a sense of its own superiority. The New Englander Alfred Brunson found in Ohio's Western Reserve that southern-born Methodist preachers were openly contemptuous of Yankees, whom they regarded "as bordering upon the savage state," whereas Peter Cartwright's experience in the southern part of the same state brought him face-to-face with superior New Englanders whose learned ministers "were always criticising us poor backwoods preachers." Many of these southern-born settlers in the free states persisted in their dislike of the "meddling Yankee" and the parties that seemed best to represent their interventionist attitudes, the Whigs and the Republicans. Men like Cartwright remained Democrats up to the Civil War. "Old Father Gillham," a fellow Illinois Methodist, arrived there from South Carolina in 1821 and was still a staunch Democrat in 1860.[30]

Significant though sectarian rivalry, class, status, and ethnic chauvinism were as determinants of Methodist voting habits, it is important not to lose sight of the role played by particular issues of social policy in shaping party choice, especially those issues that had a direct bearing on the nation's religious and moral well-being. Methodists were not loyal to party through thick and thin. Like other evangelicals, they expected their political leaders to promote what they understood to be the nation's good and were ready to jettison a party label if betrayed. In the 1830s it is clear that Jackson's Indian policy, especially the removal of the Cherokee nation from Georgia, was an important element in the decade's political polarization and played its part in cementing the attachment of Methodists like William Winans, William Crane, and Alfred Brunson to the Whig party. Similarly, those Methodists most concerned about the state provision of free schools—Samuel Lewis in Ohio, David R. McAnally in North Carolina, Colin Dew James in Illinois, for instance—tended to gravitate toward that party, given its greater commitment to free public education as a means of securing a more disciplined population.[31] When, however, Methodists turned from moral suasion toward state

---

30. Williams, *Garden of American Methodism,* 174-75; Brunson, *Western Pioneer* 1:173; Cartwright, *Autobiography,* 98; L. F. Smith, "Diary," 3 September 1860.

31. Ray Holder, *William Winans: Methodist Leader in Antebellum Mississippi* (Jackson: University Press of Mississippi, 1977), 103-4; Crane, *Autobiography,* 79; Brunson, *Western Pioneer* 2:139 and passim; Lewis, *Biography of Samuel Lewis;* Edmund James, "Colin Dew James: A Pioneer Methodist Preacher of Early Illinois," *Journal of the Illinois State Historical Society* 9 (January 1917): 451.

intervention as the primary means for effecting an end to the liquor trade, they found both Whigs and Democrats too concerned about alienating voters, especially the newly arrived, to take a prohibitionist stand. Driven by conscience, many of them defected from the two main parties to support single-issue Maine Law and Prohibition parties in the early 1850s. Similarly anxious over Whigs' and Democrats' wobbles over defending the common school system, sustaining the King James Bible within it, and showing some steel toward Catholics, Methodists flocked in numbers to the American Party. Given the denomination's strength, it is no exaggeration to regard Methodists as the single most important agency in the creation and sustenance of a political force that tore apart the vulnerable fabric of the second party system.[32]

No single issue had greater power than slavery to shape Methodists' political responses. Northern Methodist anxieties over the implications of the annexation of Texas and the Mexican cession for the expansion of the peculiar institution drew some of their number into the Free-Soil Party, whose crusading stance and revivalist appeal to conscience generated such enthusiasm among its supporters that Matthew Simpson was led to conclude that a fundamental party realignment was not far off. Many more, uneasily mollified by the Compromise of 1850, would help fulfill that prediction between 1854 and 1856 when the storm of protest over the Kansas-Nebraska Act and subsequent events in Kansas and Washington led them, along with other Free-Soil and abolitionist Protestants, into the Know-Nothing and other anti-Nebraska fusion movements, which culminated in the primacy of the Republican party.

William E. Gienapp's detailed study of the origins of that party shows with great clarity the impressive political calculation and manipulation that went into its formation. To win national elections political parties needed managers, disciplined and professional politicians; coalition-building, essential to success, demanded a readiness to compromise and conciliate. Yet much of the Republicans' early energy and the party's continued impetus derived from the energies of zealous evangelicals, impelled by outrage, conscience, and obedience to a higher law. Many of these evangelicals had been

---

32. For an extended discussion of this theme, see Carwardine, *Evangelicals and Politics,* 199-234.

working for years to fuse religion and politics in an effective agency that would provide the route to the kingdom of God. That fusion, of sectional alienation and postmillennial aspiration, is clear in the diary of Benjamin Adams, a Methodist itinerant in New York, who on the weekend before polling day in 1856 officiated at a Methodist revival at Bridgeport: "The Lord came in power among the people and our souls rejoiced in the Lord. . . . May this work roll on in power and God's name be glorified among his people." Three days later he was pursuing a complementary means of advancing the kingdom: "Election. Today the battle is to be fought between right & wrong. I went to the polls and did my duty. . . . May God aid the right!" Fremont's defeat in that election seemed to Gilbert Haven a matter both for mourning and for rededication to Christ's work over the next four years; and when Lincoln triumphed in 1860, John Allen of Farmington, Maine, judged it the victory of "the Lord's side." Northern Methodists did not sweep en masse into this crusade, but enough of them stood as candidates, organized locally, raised funds, used their pulpits, and cast their votes—especially in New England and its diaspora (that is, western New York, the Western Reserve of Ohio, the Northern Tier of Pennsylvania, and the northern counties of the Midwestern states)—to understand why some contemporaries believed that the MEC, as "the largest and most influential denomination in the land," exerted "a most control[l]ing power in electing Mr. Lincoln" in 1860.[33] That judgment was no doubt an overstatement of Methodists' role, statistically speaking, in the election itself. When, however, we consider the part played by Methodists in the process of sectional alienation, itself inextricably connected with the Republicans' electoral successes, it encourages the conclusion that the denomination played a significantly more instrumental role than historians have generally recognized.

---

33. William E. Gienapp, *The Origins of the Republican Party 1852–1856* (New York: Oxford University Press, 1987), passim; B. Adams, "Diary," 1, 4 November 1856, Methodist Center, Drew University; Gilbert Haven, "The National Midnight," in Gilbert Haven, *National Sermons: Sermons, Speeches and Letters on Slavery and Its War* (Boston: Lee & Shepard, 1869), 120-21; Stephen Allen, *The Life of Rev. John Allen, Better Known as "Camp Meeting John"* (Boston: B. B. Russell, 1888), 41; William E. Gienapp, "Who Voted for Lincoln?" in *Abraham Lincoln and the American Political Tradition*, ed. John L. Thomas (Amherst: University of Massachusetts Press, 1986), 75; L. F. Smith, "Diary," 8, 29 August, 3, 10 September, 15 October 1860; *Chicago Tribune*, 25 May 1860; W. Hamilton to M. Simpson (23 February 1861), M. Simpson Papers, Methodist Center, Drew University. Cf. Charles Baumer Swaney, *Episcopal Methodism and Slavery: With Sidelights on Ecclesiastical Politics* (Boston: R. G. Badger, 1926), 283, which underestimates Methodist support for Lincoln in 1860.

Prefiguring the Division of the Nation

There is a sad irony in the fact that Methodism, a major instrument in the process of American national integration in the early republic, became a principal channel of sectional alienation during the middle years of the nineteenth century. When the MEC fractured after the General Conference voted to remove Bishop James O. Andrew for being married to a slaveowner, many believed that separation was in the nation's best interests. Southern radicals like William A. Smith regarded efforts to hold together abolitionist and pro-slavery Methodists within the same national organization as a source of continuing and dangerous tension for church and country. "The General Conference," he declared at the organizing convention of the MECS at Louisville in 1845, "had ceased to exert a conservative influence upon the political union": peaceable separation, by removing southerners from the influence of what Thomas Stringfield called the "reckless fanaticism" of abolitionist Methodists, was "highly important to the union of these states." Conservative evangelicals, on the other hand, north and south, took a far less sanguine view of schism. They believed in what Nathan Bangs called "Methodism's cohesive tendency," not least because of its system of itinerant exchange, which helped "do away with those prejudices which grow out of local circumstances and habits." Rupture would terminate this influence. It would also play into the hands of extremists. A slaveholding Methodist considered denominational unity the best guarantee that moderate northerners would assert their influence on behalf of southern interests, "but let division take place, and ... [t]he motives to induce moderation [will] no longer exist," and "the excitement of abolition will increase tenfold." Others feared that ecclesiastical rupture would embolden states-rights radicals inside and outside the churches. Indeed, there were those who speculated that Calhounites had deliberately engineered the Methodist schism as part of a grand design to undermine the American Union. One does not have to adopt their conspiracy theory to see the force of moderates' argument for circumspection. Hindsight allows us to see that voluntary separation opened the way to new sources of bitterness and sectional stereotyping, which seriously corroded Methodists' sense of belonging to a political and ecclesiastical Union based on common values.[34]

---

34. Fitzgerald, *McFerrin*, 186; *Pittsburgh Christian Advocate*, 30 April 1840; *CA*, 30 October 1844, 14 May 1845; T. Stringfield to his wife (4 June 1844), Stringfield Papers, Southern Historical Collection, University of North Carolina, Chapel Hill. For the schism in the MEC in 1844, and

The Plan of Separation, far from providing a basis for the harmonious coexistence of the two branches of a divided church, gave rise instead to a chronic and often ugly conflict that persisted in various guises on through to the Civil War. The Plan's authors were looking for a way of running a twelve-hundred-mile line through MEC border conferences, which embraced both nonslaveholding areas and parts of the slave states of Maryland, Virginia, Kentucky, Arkansas, and Missouri. They decreed that "societies, stations, and conferences" along the line between slave and free states, but not "interior charges," could take a binding vote on their allegiance, which the authorities of both the northern and southern churches would respect; the minority would refrain from forming their own societies. However, antislavery hardliners could see no moral case for limiting their activities in areas where they believed thousands of conscientious men and women would want to continue their membership of the unstained MEC and shun a "slavery church." The Plan also left much unclear. If, following a vote, the line separating churches were to be redrawn, was the society newly abutting the border also allowed a vote on allegiance? If the border took on the character of neutral common ground until loyalties were established, what was there to prevent a ceaseless and disruptive campaign of recruitment? This was exactly what vexed one slave-state critic of the proselytizing MECS: "They have declared the border a movable line, so that when they have procured the secession of a society, station, or circuit, from the Methodist E. Church, the next one north becomes a border, and so on, *ad infinitum*."[35]

The implementation of the Plan consequently generated enormous frustration and anger. Each side came to regard the other as "nullifiers" and predators. Cases of split congregations, irregular voting, political manipulation, and disregard for agreed procedures multiplied. Invective once reserved for the other section's radicals was directed at all the departed members. Southerners blamed Thomas Bond of the *Christian Advocate and Journal*, Charles Elliott of the *Western Christian Advocate*, and other free-state editors, for destroying

---

its implications for the Union and for sectional alienation, see Clarence C. Goen, *Broken Churches, Broken Nation: Denominational Schisms and the Coming of the Civil War* (Macon, Ga.: Mercer University Press, 1985); and Swaney, *Episcopal Methodism and Slavery*.

35. Arthur E. Jones, "The Years of Disagreement, 1844–61," in *HAM* 2:159-76; Fee, *Bringing the Sheaves*, 242-43; Henry Bascom et al., *Brief Appeal to Public Opinion, in a Series of Exceptions to the Course and Action of the Methodist Episcopal Church, from 1844 to 1848* (Louisville: J. Early, 1848), 93-106, 127-34; *CA*, 12 January, 24 May 1848.

trust and threatening social order. Their papers were regularly seized and even burned by magistrates at the post offices, their actions sustained by a combination of statute, grand-jury endorsement, and the demands of vigilance committees.[36]

In many cases anger and fear exploded into physical violence. MEC preachers in Missouri were seized and told to leave. Armed sympathizers of the MECS took over the church at Clarksburg, Maryland, camping in the church at night over several weeks to deny access by MEC loyalists. Probably the worst violence scarred communities in Virginia, especially in the Kanawha Valley and on the Eastern Shore. In Northampton and Accomac Counties social prestige and judicial power conspired with mobbism against the northern church. Valentine Gray, a preacher of the Philadelphia Conference, was forcibly ejected from the church and subsequently hounded from the county court when he turned up for redress. A jeering, missile-throwing mob at Guildford broke up the service of another MEC preacher, James Hargis, without any note of reproof from the *Richmond Christian Advocate* or the local magistracy.[37]

Higher courts offered some comfort to the southern church, as it sought to recover meeting places and secure what it considered its share of the property still controlled by the MEC. Litigation kept some premises closed to both parties. The bitter conflict over the status of the church at Maysville, Kentucky, was resolved by the state court in favor of the MECS in a judgment that delighted the South. By ruling that the southern church was not, as many northern Methodists contended, a secession from a continuing MEC, but rather one of two new churches created out of a now defunct institution, the court gave heart to the South in its attempts to secure a financial share of the two Methodist Book Concerns, in New York and Cincinnati. Not all northern Methodists were implacably opposed to the southern church's securing some part of what had once been considered common funds; not least, they conceded that superannuated preachers, their wives,

---

36. Freeborn Garrettson Hibbard, *Biography of Rev. Leonidas L. Hamline, D.D., Late One of the Bishops of the Methodist Episcopal Church* (Cincinnati: Hitchcock & Walden, 1880), 192-93, 216; *Knoxville Whig*, 22 July 1846; *CA*, 3 November 1847, 24 May 1848; *WCA*, 27 September, 25 October 1848, 9 October 1850; *Southern Christian Advocate* (Charleston, S.C.), 9 June 1848.

37. Lorenzo Waugh, *A Candid Statement of the Course Pursued by the Preachers of the Methodist Church South, in Trying to Establish Their New Organization in Missouri* (Cincinnati: Methodist Book Concern, 1848), 60-61; Waugh, *Autobiography*, 164-66; *Knoxville Whig*, 25 August 1849; Hibbard, *Hamline*, 211-15; J. Thompson to T. Bond (30 October 1846), P. Twiford to T. Bond (24 November 1846), T. E. Bond Papers, Dickinson College; *CA*, 5, 12 October; 11, 18, 25 November 1846; 20, 27 January; 3, 10, 24 February 1847.

and children had a just claim to the proceeds, regardless of section. But the failure of the northern annual conferences to ratify the Plan of Separation put constitutional doubts into the mind of the MEC General Conference of 1848, which called for legal arbitration. Incensed at what it considered evasion, the southern church brought suits against the MEC in the United States circuit courts in New York and Ohio. Judge Samuel Nelson's 1851 ruling in favor of the MECS in the New York case prompted cries of "southern aggression" from northern Methodists who explained the decision as the inevitable result of cotton influence and the "despotic spirit of slavery." The Cincinnati case went on appeal to the United States Supreme Court, which also ruled, under Roger B. Taney, in favor of the MECS. Nelson again wrote the opinion. The decision, described by Granville Moody as "astonishing, unparalleled, and unjust," elicited further Methodist denunciations of pro-slavery bias in the judiciary. Three years later antislavery forces would exploit the historic Dred Scott ruling to show that the Supreme Court was in the clutches of the slave power, but by then thousands of northern Methodists had already reached that unpalatable conclusion.[38]

The aftermath of the denominational schism thus led Methodists in each section to develop increasingly hostile mutual perceptions, with profound consequences for politics. Southerners increasingly identified all northern churchgoers with irreligious, fanatical abolitionism. They defended separation—constitutional and conservative—as the only option for orthodox believers seeking to defend true religion and the social order in the "war of subjection and extermination" facing the South. "We are compelled to repel invasion and assault," Henry Bascom insisted, "or be overthrown and trodden upon by the assailants." Northern Methodists' attack on slavery turned them into collaborators in a political scheme to deny southerners their constitutional rights. Addressing a southern camp meeting in 1847, William A. Smith aimed to show how the Free-Soil attack on southern political interests, as exemplified in the Wilmot Proviso, was a logical sequel to northern aggression in ecclesiastical affairs. Henry Bascom

38. *WCA*, 11 February; 17, 24, 31 March; 7, 28 April; 26 July 1848; 24 December 1851; *CA*, 19 July 1848, 21 March, 13 June 1850; *Southern Christian Advocate*, 28 March 1845; 2, 16 June 1848; 28 November 1851; 5, 19 November 1852; *Knoxville Whig*, 24 January, 6 April 1849, Bascom et al., *Brief Appeal*, 5; Hibbard, *Hamline*, 218-22; Edward H. Myers, *The Disruption of the Methodist Episcopal Church, 1844–46: Comprising a Thirty Years' History of the Relations of the Two Methodisms* (Nashville: A. H. Redford, 1875), 151; Jones, "Years of Disagreement," 177-81; Moody, *Life's Retrospect*, 227.

blamed the fracturing of Methodism on the work of "the great Northern Abolition and Antislavery party" in which "the politician, the demagogue, and the religionist all unite." Whereas southern Methodists upheld federal and church law, the MEC had become "a pander to political agitation."[39]

Northern Methodists also attached political significance to the traumas associated with separation. Southerners had seceded not to defend doctrine or polity, but "to continue and protect slavery." The MECS had become "a great politico-ecclesiastical party, for the defense and support of the peculiar political institution of the South." It had "practically nullified" the terms of separation by their aggression against the MEC in the border and by their resort to legal action. It had nailed its colors to the mast of the slave power by removing the antislavery section from the Methodist Discipline, by tolerating the denial of free speech in the border wars, and by preaching a gospel of ecclesiastical rebellion and secession that had implications for the stability of the political Union.[40]

During the climactic years of political polarization, following the passage of the Kansas-Nebraska Act, Methodists continued actively to participate in (as opposed to reactively respond to) the process of sectional alienation. The deterioration in relations between North and South from the mid-1850s was not solely a product of political conflict, narrowly defined. The poison of sectionalism seeped along ecclesiastical channels as well. Indeed, evangelicals' experiences, and especially those of Methodists, help explain how the issues raised nationally by slavery and the slave power took on meaning in local settings. Methodist and other denominational presses and preachers kept all these aggravations before the widest possible audience.

Not surprisingly, sectional warfare in churches reached unsurpassed levels of drama in Kansas and Missouri. From the outset missionaries from the free states, determined to win Kansas for liberty and Christ, faced a pro-slavery party just as committed to drive them away. "Law and order men" intercepted William Moore, a local preacher of the MEC, on his way to Kansas City, forced alcohol down his throat, and threatened to kill him. The presiding elder of the South

---

39. *CA*, 6 October 1847; Bascom et al., *Brief Appeal*, 10, 60, 165-69.

40. Waugh, *Candid Statement*, 70; Waugh, *Autobiography*, 149-71; *CA*, 5 January, 15 March, 24 May, 19 July 1848, 17 October 1850; Hibbard, *Hamline*, 205; Fee, *Bringing the Sheaves*, 239-40; *WCA*, 27 September 1848; John Stewart, *Highways and Hedges; or, Fifty Years of Western Methodism* (Cincinnati: Hitchcock & Walden, 1870), 260; Edward Thomson, *Life of Edward Thomson, Late Bishop of the Methodist Episcopal Church* (Cincinnati: Cranston & Stowe, 1885), 87-88.

Kansas mission district lost all his possessions, including his horses, to southern "outlaws."[41] Conflict spilled over into Missouri, where vigilance committees and their supporters broke up quarterly meetings of the Missouri Conference, blocked access to camp-meeting grounds, interrupted sermons, and drove preachers from the state. As free-state Methodists called ever more confidently for the exclusion of slaveholders from the MEC, and as Kansas grew bloodier, so the dangers to northern preachers increased. One young minister, C. H. Kelly, was ejected from his pulpit and forced to ride, thinly clad, through bitter December winds to Fort Madison, Iowa. He did not live long. In Rochester, Andrew County, pro-slaveryites set upon the Reverend William Sellers, filled his mouth and smothered his head with tar, then left him to fry in the sun, and shot Benjamin Holland, an elderly class leader. Blaming southern churchmen for creating the climate for these attacks, the *Central Christian Advocate* lamented: "There is an ecclesiastical as well as a political war raging, and we are shamelessly attacked and falsely represented as well by political demagogues and false-hearted slavery-defending preachers."[42]

At the same time, relations between the two branches of Methodism ulcerated in other parts of the border where the MEC maintained an active presence—in Arkansas, Kentucky, and Virginia. In parts of western Virginia, for instance, accusation, counterclaim, and paranoia raised public opinion to fever pitch through the mid-1850s. Charged by MECS leaders with incendiarism, infidelity, and treachery to the Constitution, Wesley Smith and other MEC preachers took their case to the people through press and pulpit. In West Milford circuit, Smith's four-hour public lecture filled the church to overflowing and halted the harvest and weekday business. He contemptuously dismissed pro-slavery ministers' efforts "to brand as abolitionists every non-slaveholder in the slave States who will not adopt the nullification doctrines of Drs [William A.] Smith and [Henry] Bascom." Ultras North and South sought the same end, he warned: a dissolution of the Union through dissolution of the churches. The result would be "a border war without a figure of speech—a war of bloodshed and carnage." He concluded: "If any future historian shall be called upon to write the history of the dissolution of the

41. *WCA*, 9 July, 17 September, 1 October 1856; L. B. Dennis to M. Simpson (22 January 1856), M. Simpson Papers, Library of Congress.
42. *WCA*, 2, 23 May; 25 July; 15, 22 (quoting *CCA*), 29 August; 5, 26 September; 10 October; 7 November 1855; *NWCA*, 25 May, 29 October 1856; *CA*, 10 July, 7 August 1856.

Union, he will trace it to the action of the southern Methodist preachers . . . [since 1844]. We hold them accountable before Heaven and earth for the exasperated state of feeling which exists at present between the North and South, and which is constantly increasing."[43]

Southern Methodists, for their part, perceived the MEC as an even greater threat to sectional harmony and found it difficult to remain calm when MEC border preachers described their church as "the most powerful and systematic organization on earth against slavery." The resolutions of various MEC annual conferences throughout 1858 and 1859, calling for resistance to slavery, prompted southern Methodists to assert their right to drive "abolition emissaries" out of their territory. After the volcanic rumblings at Harper's Ferry in October 1859 the operations of the MEC in the border South appeared all the more menacing. "It is a curious fact," ruminated William Brownlow, "that John Brown and his secret advisers selected a portion of Virginia lying within the bounds of the Baltimore Conference, as the most appropriate theatre of their operations." Here the MEC allowed blacks to testify against whites in church trials and refused to ordain slaveholders as local preachers. The church's influence was more dangerous to slavery than a dozen Harper's Ferry insurrections. Not only in western Virginia, but throughout the MEC's areas of operations in the slave states, vigilant southern Methodists took guard against its provocation and "sedition."[44] Their actions in one of these cases, and the subsequent northern reaction, provide probably the most graphic of all the indications of the destructive power of ecclesiastical alienation and its role in the politics of sectional polarization.

In the summer of 1860 a Texan mob seized and hanged the Reverend Anthony Bewley, an experienced MEC preacher of thirty years' standing and a member of his church's Arkansas Conference since its creation in 1852. Bewley, a southerner who had first served in Tennessee, had been involved in the feeble Texas Mission of the MEC for several years. Along with the handful of other preachers attempting to establish a presence in northeastern Texas, he had been regarded as a meddlesome abolitionist. When the Arkansas Conference, with impressive courage but little prudence, had

---

43. Wesley Smith, *A Defence of the Methodist Episcopal Church Against the Charges of Rev. S. Kelly and Others, of the M.E. Church, South* (Fairmont, Va.: n.p., 1855), 21, 42, 45, and passim.

44. *Richmond Christian Advocate*, 13 January 1859; *Southern Christian Advocate*, 11 February 1858, 16 June, 21 July, 11 August 1859; *Knoxville Whig*, 15 May 1858, 8 October 1859, 21 January, 18 February 1860.

convened under Bishop Edmund S. Janes at Timber Creek, near Bonham, Texas, in March 1859, a crowd of two hundred men armed with revolvers and bowie knives ("a committee of vigilance," in southern parlance) had forced the meeting's suspension and its later adjournment *sine die*. Apart from the region's German Free-Soilers, who shunned the MECS because of its positive approbation of slavery, few locally would have demurred from the description of the Arkansas Conference and of the Texas Mission in particular as "a screen behind which to hide emissaries known as abolitionists, and as dangerous to southern interests." Soon afterward the Texas District had been discontinued, but Bewley himself had retained a role as superintendent and missionary to Texas until he fled the state in fear of his life. There are conflicting and ambiguous accounts of what happened next, but it seems that, with a reward of one thousand dollars on his head, he was seized and held at Fayetteville, Arkansas, before being taken forcibly to Fort Worth, where he was subsequently hanged, "having been condemned by a jury of three hundred men."[45]

For northern Methodists the case confirmed all of their accumulated perceptions about their errant brothers' sad departure from the paths of righteousness. The murder was a "diabolical deed" of "Turkish cruelty" against a mild Christian of simple, modest character. Southern Methodists, to drive all traces of the MEC from the slave states, had evinced "the pure spirit of a mobocrat," by encouraging a rabble and then defending its appalling actions in their press and pulpit. They seemed blind to the inconsistency of their praising God "for the high privilege of worshiping him according to conscience" while simultaneously repressing republican freedoms. They had lost all capacity for rational judgment, failing to distinguish between radical abolitionists of the school of William Lloyd Garrison or George Barrell Cheever, and antislavery constitutionalists who cherished social order. "All who will not bow down to the idol, and acknowledge slavery to be right, and humane, and scriptural, are to be denounced as abolition tories and incendiaries," lamented the *Christian Advocate and Journal*.[46] The MECS had been annexed by an evil slave power.

---

45. Henry B. Ridgaway, *The Life of Edmund S. Janes, D.D., LL.D.* (New York: Phillips & Hunt, 1882), 224-29; *Central Christian Advocate* (St. Louis), 26 September, 10 October 1860; *CA*, 27 September, 22 November 1860.

46. *CA*, 30 August, 27 September 1860; *Central Christian Advocate*, 26 September 1860.

Apart from expressions of alarm in the columns of the *St. Louis Christian Advocate*, most southern Methodist spokesmen either vigorously sustained or resignedly acquiesced in the action against Bewley, dismissing the line between "abolitionism" and "antislavery" as a distinction without a difference. Their logic was clear. The MEC was committed to extirpating slavery, its position all the more assertive since the Buffalo General Conference of May 1860, controlled by "rampant Abolitionism," had altered the chapter on slavery to declare the institution "contrary to the laws of God and nature." The church had become the ecclesiastical arm of William Seward and the Black Republicans: Bewley and all agents of the MEC operating in the slave states were their "advance guard." According to the *New Orleans Christian Advocate*, conspiracy was the natural "fruit of the doctrine taught by the entire Northern Methodist press" of Thomson, Kingsley, Haven, and Elliott; "freedom of speech" was one thing, Methodist incendiarism another. For Texans, their minds full of John Brown and, through the summer of 1860, their state consumed by rumors of slave plots, arson, and rebellion, Bewley's death called for no apology. "There are cases in which Lynch law is expedient, necessary, just," explained the editor of the *Texas Christian Advocate*. Bewley had fallen "a victim to a reign of lawlessness, which he and other of his kind have for some time been laboring to inaugurate and promote in Texas." Having ignored several warnings to desist from his antislavery missionary work or be treated "as an aggressor," he had paid the predicted price. A North Carolinian editor was in no doubt that Bewley's "complicity with murderous abolition plots of insurrection and bloodshed was clearly proved," while William G. Brownlow, who remembered him from his Tennessee days as "rather a stubborn man," considered the vigilantes' work no more murderous "than the insurrection and burning of towns in Texas, under the direction of those associated with Mr. Bewley." If, as northerners insisted, he really was a pious man, then no harm had been done: "Hanging was 'a short cut' to the Kingdom of God."[47]

Bewley's case has scarcely received its historical due in discussions of the political crisis of 1860–61. It goes unremarked in Clarence Goen's thoughtful study of the fractured antebellum churches, and

---

47. *CA*, 10–31 May, 7–28 June, 5 July, 27 September 1860 (for *New Orleans Christian Advocate*); *Knoxville Whig*, 30 June, 29 September 1860; *Southern Christian Advocate*, 2 August 1860; *Texas Christian Advocate*, 31 May 1860, quoted in Wesley Norton, *Religious Newspapers in the Old Northwest to 1861: A History, Bibliography and Record of Opinion* (Athens: Ohio University Press, 1977), 122; *Texas Christian Advocate*, 13 Sept. 1860, quoted in *Central Christian Advocate*, 26 September 1860; *North Carolina Christian Advocate* (Raleigh), 6 November 1860.

receives only a single brief mention in Bucke's multivolume history of American Methodism.[48] Its neglect may have to do with the attention properly afforded the Harper's Ferry raid and John Brown's subsequent "martyrdom," and its occurring within the seemingly parochial world of Methodism. Yet the case did much to aggravate sectional tension at a critical time and in ways that John Brown had failed to do. Northern Methodists were certainly able to respond to Bewley's assassination with a unity of perception that they had failed to muster in Brown's case a year earlier. Whereas Brown's means seemed to many to have been bloody and dubious, Bewley's were constitutional and Christian: his was the genuine martyrdom of a "modest and peaceful" man, not the death of one whose prior career was stained by suggestions of horse-thievery and murder.[49] For southern Methodists, the case confirmed the dangers so fearfully exposed by Brown's raid, but showed the need for even greater vigilance to thwart more cunning assaults on slavery by supposedly Christian missionaries of recognized churches.

The timing of Bewley's death, during the course of a presidential election on which hung the future of the Union, ensured that its lessons were aired well beyond the confines of Methodism, in the political press of both sections. If southerners saw in Bewley's missionary operations the shape of a fiendish future under a Republican presidency, northern critics of the "pro-slavery" course of national politics treated his lynching as a test of the administration's commitment to defending Americans' fundamental constitutional rights. Among the most insistent of voices was that of Thomas Eddy, the outspoken editor of Chicago's *Northwestern Christian Advocate* and a barely camouflaged Republican. In an open letter to President Buchanan, he pointedly reflected that one million Methodists were asking "can an Administration be found which will protect the rights of conscience and the freedom of worship? . . . A few more such murders as that of Bewley, and the church will ask who will give us an Administration strong enough to uphold the rights dearest of all others? and for that man, be he whom he may, they will cast their united suffrage."[50] It

---

48. Goen, *Broken Churches, Broken Nation; HAM,* ed. Bucke et al. The Bewley affair is addressed in Wesley Norton, "The Methodist Episcopal Church and the Civil Disturbances in North Texas in 1859 and 1860," *Southwest Historical Quarterly* 68 (1965): 317-41. Donald J. Reynolds, "Reluctant Martyr: Anthony Bewley and the Texas Slave Insurrection Panic of 1860," *Southwestern Historical Quarterly* 97 (1993): 345-61, provides a more recent treatment, drawing on a wider range of sources.

49. *NWCA,* 13 September 1860.

50. *NWCA,* 13 September 1860.

was not long before Eddy's threat was repeated in the columns of the *Chicago Tribune* and other Republican organs across the North, to the acute discomfort of the Democratic press.[51] Such unabashed muscle flexing could leave no doubt that Methodists had reached their political majority.

Conclusion

Methodists who voted Republican in 1860 believed they were doing more than casting a ballot for a political party; when Lincoln won, their "flood of ecstasy," as Gilbert Haven expressed it, marked more than a party triumph.[52] Methodists joined with other Protestant evangelicals in a coalition driven not just by political calculation but by a burning sense of Christian duty and moral indignation, to realize a multiple vision: freedom for slaves, freedom from the terror unleashed on godly men like hapless Anthony Bewley, release for both black and white from the slave power's diabolical grip on both church and state, and a new direction for the Union. Of all Methodists, it was these triumphalist Republicans—nourished by a postmillennialist creed that celebrated conscience, obedience to a higher law, and a strong sense of social responsibility—who had traveled furthest from the outlook of their church's first apolitical generation by identifying the arrival of the kingdom of God with the success of a particular political party.

In rebuking their northern counterparts for this novel fusion of religion and politics, southern Methodists implicitly claimed the role of defenders of the primitive values of their church. Yet they too had drifted from the ground of their apolitical forebears, most pertinently and strikingly over slavery, where they moved from ambivalent hostility to ambivalent defense. Their leaders sustained that defense by maintaining a posture of political nonintervention, but in reality that stance was driven by a fundamental *political* need: the protection of the moral and socioeconomic basis of southern civilization. Moreover, southern Methodists could be as energetically engaged in partisan politics as any of their codenominationalists in the free states. And although they stopped short of Republican Methodists' linking of the inauguration of God's kingdom with the triumph of a party, they were ready enough to identify the interests of their section, and

---

51. See, for example, *Albany Evening Journal*, 19 September 1860.
52. Haven, *National Sermons*, 179.

subsequently the destiny of their Confederate nation, with the purposes of the Almighty. The experience of civil war would, of course, further transform American Methodists' understanding of their country's political mission at home and abroad, and their role in it. But already by 1861 the changes of fifty years had made them philosophically deaf to the language of Francis Asbury and in particular to his insistent prescription, "Our kingdom is not of this world."

Abbreviations

AME   The African Methodist Episcopal Church (1816–)

AMEZ   The African Methodist Episcopal Church Zion (1820–)

CA   *Christian Advocate*, New York (MEC)

CCA   *Central Christian Advocate* (MEC, African American edition)

HAM   *The History of American Methodism*, ed. Emory S. Bucke, 3 vols. (Nashville: Abingdon Press, 1964).

JLFA   *The Journal and Letters of Francis Asbury*, ed. Elmer T. Clark, 3 vols. (London: Epworth, and Nashville: Abingdon Press, 1958).

MC   The Methodist Church, USA (1939–1968)

MEC   The Methodist Episcopal Church (1784–1939)

MECS   The Methodist Episcopal Church, South (1844–1939)

Minutes MEC (1840)	*Minutes of the Annual Conferences of the Methodist Episcopal Church for the Years 1773–1828* (New York: T. Mason and G. Lane, 1840).
NWCA	*Northwestern Christian Advocate* (MEC)
Perspectives	*Perspectives on American Methodism*, ed. Russell E. Richey, Kenneth E. Rowe, and Jean Miller Schmidt (Nashville: Kingswood Books, 1993).
UMC	The United Methodist Church, USA (1968–)
WCA	*Western Christian Advocate* (MEC)

About the Authors

Catherine A. Brekus is Associate Professor of the History of Christianity at the University of Chicago Divinity School. She is the author of *Strangers and Pilgrims: Female Preaching in America, 1740–1845* (Chapel Hill: University of North Carolina Press, 1998).

Richard J. Carwardine is Fellow of the Royal Historical Society, and is Dean of the Faculty of Arts and Professor of History at the University of Sheffield, England. He is the author of *Transatlantic Revivalism: Popular Evangelicalism in Britain and America, 1790–1865* (Westport, Conn.: Greenwood Press, 1978) and *Evangelicals and Politics in Antebellum America* (New Haven: Yale University Press, 1993).

Will Gravely retired from the University of Denver's Religious Studies faculty in June 2000, where he had been Professor of American Religious History and Literature. His primary interests have been in the interaction of religion and race, as his essays on African American religion, United States Methodism, and lynching demonstrate. His book on white abolitionist and antiracist reformer Methodist Bishop Gilbert Haven was published by Abingdon Press in 1973.

Nathan O. Hatch is Professor of History and Provost at the University of Notre Dame. He is the author of *The Sacred Cause of*

Liberty: Republican Thought and the Millennium in Revolutionary New England (New Haven: Yale University Press, 1977) and *The Democratization of American Christianity* (New Haven: Yale University Press, 1989).

David Hempton is Fellow of the Royal Historical Society and is currently Professor of Church History at Boston University. He is the author of *Methodism and Politics in British Society 1750–1850* (Stanford, Calif.: Stanford University Press, 1984), *Religion and Political Culture in Britain and Ireland: From the Glorious Revolution to the Decline of Empire* (Cambridge: Cambridge University Press, 1996), *The Religion of the People: Methodism and Popular Religion c. 1750–1900* (London: Routledge, 1996), and coauthor with Myrtle Hill of *Evangelical Protestantism in Ulster Society 1740–1890* (London: Routledge, 1992). He is currently researching the rise of Methodism throughout the North Atlantic world and the religious culture of New England.

Kathryn T. Long is Associate Professor of History at Wheaton College. She is the author of *The Revival of 1857–58: Interpreting an American Religious Awakening* (New York: Oxford University Press, 1998). Her research interests include American evangelicalism, nineteenth-century American Protestantism, and the history of revivals.

Russell E. Richey is Dean and Professor of Church History at Candler School of Theology, Emory University. He is the author, coauthor, or coeditor of numerous books and articles, including *The Methodist Conference in America: A History* (Nashville: Kingswood Books, 1996), *The Methodists* (Westport, Conn.: Greenwood Press, 1996), *Connectionalism: Ecclesiology, Mission, and Identity* (Nashville: Abingdon Press, 1997), and *The Methodist Experience in America* (Nashville: Abingdon Press, 2000).

Richard D. Shiels is Associate Professor of History at the Ohio State University at Newark. He is the author of "The Scope of the Second Great Awakening: Andover, Massachusetts, as a Case Study," *Journal of the Early Republic* 5 (1985): 223-46, and "The Origins of the Second Great Awakening in New England: Goshen, Connecticut 1798–99," *Mid-America: An Historical Review* 78, no. 3 (fall 1996): 279-301.

William R. Sutton teaches at the University Laboratory High School, University of Illinois at Urbana-Champaign. He is the author of *Journeymen for Jesus: Evangelical Artisans Confront Capitalism in Jacksonian Baltimore* (University Park: Pennsylvania State University Press, 1998). He is currently researching the cultural and religious roots and manifestations of the artisan-led Washingtonian temperance movement of the 1840s.

John H. Wigger is Associate Professor of History at the University of Missouri, Columbia. He is the author of *Taking Heaven by Storm: Methodism and the Rise of Popular Christianity in America* (New York: Oxford University Press, 1998; Urbana and Chicago: University of Illinois Press, 2001), and is currently writing a biography of Francis Asbury.